A HISTORY OF THE CHURCH
THROUGH ITS BUILDINGS

Mosaic of Constantine and Justinian, south entrance of Hagia Sophia, Istanbul

A HISTORY OF
THE CHURCH
THROUGH ITS
BUILDINGS

ALLAN DOIG

OXFORD
UNIVERSITY PRESS

OXFORD
UNIVERSITY PRESS

Great Clarendon Street, Oxford, OX2 6DP,
United Kingdom

Oxford University Press is a department of the University of Oxford.
It furthers the University's objective of excellence in research, scholarship,
and education by publishing worldwide. Oxford is a registered trade mark of
Oxford University Press in the UK and in certain other countries

First Edition published in 2020

Impression: 2

Published in the United States of America by Oxford University Press
198 Madison Avenue, New York, NY 10016, United States of America

British Library Cataloguing in Publication Data
Data available

Library of Congress Control Number: 2020931169

ISBN 978–0–19–957536–7

Printed in Great Britain by
Bell & Bain Ltd., Glasgow

Acknowledgements

I am deeply indebted to so many people for help in the preparation of this book, especially considering all those who welcomed me and shared their knowledge and enthusiasm for the many wonderful churches that could not be included here, or made only cameo appearances. To all of them, and for their welcome and infectious enthusiasm, my deep and heartfelt thanks.

While preparing these chapters, I have been showered with help wherever I went. In Jerusalem, the late Fr Jerome Murphy-O'Connor provided a most convivial lunch as well as his immense erudition and valuable introductions. Fr Fergus Clarke and Fr Athanasius Thomac of the Franciscan community at the Holy Sepulchre provided unparalleled insight into the daily workings and limitations of the Status Quo. At the Haram, Dr Yusuf Natsheh, Director of the Department of Tourism and Archaeology, provided all that could be wished for in that holy place. In Rome, the late Most Revd Mons. Francesco Cardinal Marchisano, as Archpriest of the Papal Basilica of St Peter, and His Eminence Angelo Cardinal Comastri, as President of the Fabbrica di San Pietro, effected introductions and access, Dr Maria Cristina Carlo-Stella, Head of Office for the Fabbrica di San Pietro, shared her knowledge of the fabric, and Professor Paulo Liverani of the University of Florence shared his of the archaeology. His Eminence Gianfranco Cardinal Ravasi, President of the Pontificia Commissio de Bonis Culturalibus Ecclesiae and Vice-President, +P. Ab. Dom Michael John Zielinski, OSB, were extremely generous with their time. Fr Michael Dunleavy, OP, gave insight into the Basilica of San Clemente. At Hagia Sophia, I was welcomed by Defne Tekay Kucur and Sabriye Karahan Parlak of the Archaeological Department of the Museum. In Moscow, Olga Shashina of the Kremlin Museums opened the collections to me and commented on an early draft of the chapter on the Cathedral of the Dormition, and Dr Ekaterina Stanyukovich-Denisova, of St Petersburg State University, and her colleagues introduced me to the marvels of Novgorod and Vladimir. At Aachen Cathedral, Dombaumeister Helmut Mainz showed me the fabric in fine detail, and Professor Max Kerner and Isabel Blumenroth of the Department of History at RWTH Aachen placed it in historical perspective. Professor Benjamin Mouton, Architecte en chef and Inspecteur général des monuments historiques, offered his experience of the restoration of St-Denis. In Ewelme, Sally Fehr, Almsman of God's House, welcomed me into her house in the cloister, the Vicar, the Revd Dr Patrick Gilday, told me about the contemporary parish and Foundation, and Professor Vincent Gillespie cast an eye over an early draft of the chapter. In Cordoba, the Praecentor and Chapel Master Canon Antonio Francisco Murillo Turralbo received me warmly, and in Tarragona I visited the site of the martyrdom of Fructuosus with Dr Pablo Aparicio Durán. For the Crimean Memorial Church, I had the benefit of the work of Dr Geoffrey Tyack, the long experience of the incumbent, Fr Ian Sherwood, and the archival assistance of Emma Floyd and Jette Nielsen of the Paul Mellon Centre in London.

Besides these very specific contributions is the constant support given by colleagues, friends, and family. There are, of course, the librarians of the Bodleian, Weston, and Sackler libraries of the University of Oxford and James Fishwick of the College Library. Other colleagues at Lady Margaret Hall, Oxford, have given support throughout the project and the College itself has provided generous research grants, as has the University of Oxford from the John Fell Fund. Some of the Fellows of the College, including Dame Frances Lannon, Professors Anna Sapir Abulafia, Xon de Ros, Gillian Peele, Peter Hainsworth, and Vincent Gillespie, have read and commented on sections, making valuable suggestions and pointing out pitfalls. I would also like to thank my editorial team at Oxford University Press: Luciana O'Flaherty, who suggested I write this book, Matthew Cotton, Kizzy Taylor-Richelieu, Rosanna van den Bogaerde, Guy Jackson, and Hilary Walford. My two anonymous readers were immensely helpful with their comments, which greatly improved the final result, and Sir Diarmaid MacCulloch, Professor Richard Etlin, and Lord Williams all made invaluable suggestions and gave generous endorsements, for which I am extremely grateful. It has been a great pleasure to work with them all, and together they have made it a much better book. My sons, John, Jamie, and Nick, have been travelling companions and tolerant listeners. Finally, Liz Jones and Mark Potter have been regular travelling companions, readers, architectural commentators, and frequent hosts over the years of research and writing, and it is to them that I, with immense gratitude, dedicate this book.

For Mark and Liz

Contents

List of Plates

List of Figures

Introduction

Buildings are about people, the people who conceive, design, finance, and use them. Their stories become embedded in the very fabric itself, the bricks and mortar, and, as the fabric is changed through time in response to changing use, relationships, and beliefs, the architecture becomes the standing history of the passing waves of humanity. This process takes on particular significance in churches as places of worship and ceremony. The arrangement of the spaces places members of the community in relationship with one another for the performance of the rites and ceremonies of the Church. Moreover, architectural forms and building materials can be used to establish relationships with other buildings in other places and other times. Coordinated systems of signs, symbols, and images conjure beliefs, doctrine, and even extended narratives of the people and their faith.

As an example, the mosaic (see frontispiece) over the door to the entrance, or narthex, of the great church of Hagia Sophia in Istanbul (Constantinople), shows Emperor Constantine the Great to the right holding a model of the walls of Constantinople, which he founded as 'New Rome', the capital of a reunified empire, and to the left is Emperor Justinian I holding a model of Hagia Sophia itself, which he built on the ruins of the original built by Constantine. Together they offer these to the Virgin and Child, dedicating the church, the city, the empire, and the people to them.

Constantine had changed the course of history by his conversion, but what was the nature of his conversion? Was it the divine revelation he is said to have had in 312 at the Milvian Bridge before his victory over the 'tyrant' Maxentius, or was it a revelation of an altogether pragmatic kind about political as much as religious power? Whichever was the case, his friend and advisor Bishop Eusebius delivered him both through his development of a narrative theology of empire as a reflection of Christ's rule in the Kingdom of Heaven.

The pre-Constantinian Church met in existing buildings, mostly houses, borrowed for communal worship. Only when these buildings began to be altered for their changed use in ways that can be conclusively archaeologically identified is it possible to say that there is at least a proto-church building. The choice of building, and the nature of the alterations that were found to be necessary, together begin to flesh out the early story. Then suddenly with Constantine's 'vision' and consequent victory over Maxentius, great basilicas begin to appear. The victorious emperor completed the Basilica of Maxentius and Constantine, then in quick succession built a magnificent new one for the bishop of Rome at the Lateran, one for Peter, as Prince of the Apostles and founder of the Church in Rome, over what was believed to be his grave on the Vatican Hill, and one at the site revered as the place of the crucifixion and resurrection of Jesus.

The Church of the Holy Sepulchre (Chapter 1), in combination with other churches, shrines, and sites in the Holy Land, allows the pilgrim to relive biblical events and walk where Jesus himself walked. The death and resurrection of Jesus were key moments in the origins of the Church and the wellspring of its theology. The Holy Cave, which was the tomb of Christ, was itself buried under tons of rubble and had a pagan temple built over it. There is archaeological evidence that pilgrimage to the site began very early, despite its Christian significance being totally obliterated by the Roman pagan temple. When the temple was removed and the site excavated by order of Constantine, the tomb 'took on the appearance of a representation of the Saviour's return to life'.[1] It became 'the testimony', or witness to the truth, of the good news of the resurrection from death to new life. Constantine stipulated that the church that replaced the temple should be worthy of 'the world's most miraculous place'. When the basilica was built at the site, and as the pilgrimage grew, it would be a unifying touchstone for Christian belief, worship, and the celebration of the liturgy. Holy places are not only places of unity and healing; they can also be sources of conflict, and the Holy Sepulchre has more than once occasioned the clash of empires.

Christianity, according to strong tradition, was taken to the heart of the Roman Empire by St Peter and St Paul, who are both said to have died for their faith during the persecution under Emperor Nero. Peter was crucified upside down on the spine of the circus across the river from the capital on the edge of the Vatican Hill. Soon after defeating Maxentius and taking Rome, Constantine built the Lateran Basilica, the *Basilica Constantiniana*, as a thank offering to Christ for his victory. The nature of the Church was forever changed by the conversion of the emperor. In his project to consolidate and unify the empire, it is possible that Constantine thought that the Church, unified around its bishops, could contribute to that unity. In any case, the unity of the Church around the bishop of Rome, as the successor of Peter, Prince of the Apostles, would be enhanced by building another vast basilica focused on the apostle's grave on the Vatican Hill, despite the difficulty of the site. Claiming succession from Peter, the bishop of Rome also claimed the same authority bestowed by Christ when he said: 'you are Peter and on this rock will I build my Church' (Matt. 16:18). Ever since that claim was made, *St Peter's Basilica* (Chapter 2) has been the focus of Catholic unity and papal authority.

Building Constantinople as the 'New Rome' consolidated Constantine's power over both the eastern and western empire, and he built a grand basilica there as well. Constantine's confidant and historian, Bishop Eusebius of Caesarea, developed a theology in which the empire was a direct reflection of the Kingdom of Heaven and where the *Church of Hagia Sophia* (Chapter 3), the Wisdom of God, in particular was the bridge, as heaven on earth. That theological conception was shattered early in 532, when the basilica, the baths, and part of the Sacred Palace were destroyed in the Nika Riots, and

Emperor Justinian was very nearly deposed. To recover from such a devastating attack on the religious, symbolic, and ceremonial heart of the capital would require rebuilding on a scale, magnificence, and speed that would astonish, and make the destruction appear to have been God's providence. The result was everything Justinian could have hoped for, and in its materials, its coloured marbles from around the Mediterranean, the church gathered the geography of his empire symbolically into itself. In the fabric of this building, Church and empire were perfectly fused.

'New Rome' had interests through the Black Sea and beyond into Kievan Rus'. Its Grand Prince Vladimir converted in 988, along with all his people, and married the sister of the Byzantine emperor. The new church in Rus' came under the patriarch in Constantinople, and of course it took the same model, including a formally similar architecture, with Kiev and its churches, including its Cathedral of the Holy Wisdom, modelled on Constantinople. Its lineal descendant, the *Cathedral of the Dormition in Moscow's Kremlin* (Chapter 4), is the ultimate statement of the fusion of Church and State within the Russian national identity, with two thrones facing the iconostasis, one for the patriarch and the other the Monomakh Throne, which has carvings recording the gift of imperial honours from the Byzantine emperor to his grandson Vladimir, the tsar. The whole of the interior is peopled with images of angels, archangels, saints, and emperors, including Constantine and his mother, Helena. With these imperial, ecclesiastical, and architectural connections, it was not difficult at the fall of Constantinople in 1453 for the grand dukes, with their power base now in Moscow, to reconceive their city as the 'Third Rome'. The Russian Orthodox Church would be all-but extinguished under Stalin's regime, but since glasnost in the late 1980s there has been a resurgence, with old churches rebuilt and new ones established, all on the traditional model, reuniting Church and State within a renewed Russian identity.

In the eighth century, when the pope was under threat from the Lombards and also from his own curia, he was unable to depend on support from the eastern emperor, so he appealed to Charlemagne, king of the Franks, the most powerful leader in the west. Charlemagne's favourite palace was at Aachen, where he built the *Church of the Holy Mother of God* (Chapter 5). It was a 'Mirror of the Kingdom'. Significant parts of the building were of marble removed from the last emperor's palace in Ravenna or from Rome itself. His throne in the gallery was constructed of marble from the Church of the Holy Sepulchre in Jerusalem. It was a reliquary throne that also contained relics of St Stephen, protomartyr (Acts 6:5–7:60). The octagonal church was related in architectural form to San Vitale in Ravenna built during the reign of Emperor Justinian, who is portrayed in its mosaics, and to the palace chapel of SS Sergius and Bacchus, completed in 536 by Justinian in Constantinople. Charlemagne's church in Aachen was built between 794 and 799. In its form and symbolism, it was cultivating *Romanitas* (the quality of 'Roman-ness') and a Catholic realm in conformity with the Church in Rome. Under him, both the monasteries and the liturgy were reformed. Through education offered by the Church, that Roman practice (or at the very least an attitude of *Romanitas*) was gradually spread throughout the kingdom into the parishes. Charlemagne was crowned emperor on Christmas Day 800 in St Peter's Basilica, embodying his motto of RENOVATIO ROMANI IMPERII.

The Abbey of Saint-Denis (Chapter 6) was a basilical monastery providing services for the pilgrimage to the grave of the first bishop of Paris, St Denis, and his companions Rusticus and Eleutherius, who were all martyred during the persecution under the emperor Decius in the third century. With a burgeoning pilgrimage and under royal patronage, the abbey thrived. Charlemagne rebuilt its west end over the grave of his father, Pepin, the beginning of the royal line. At Saint-Denis, Pope Stephen had anointed Pepin king along with his sons Carloman and Charles, later to be Charlemagne. Pepin then obligingly defeated the Lombards, who were threatening Rome. Abbot Suger (Abbot of Saint-Denis 1122–51) put the abbey in good administrative and financial order after the rather loose hold of his predecessor, Abbot

Adam, and 'reformed' the abbey following the insistent promptings of Bernard of Clairvaux. Politically, Suger stiffened the resolve of King Louis VI to support the Church in the Investiture Controversy that split the Church and the politics of Europe from the late eleventh to the early twelfth century over the right of rulers to invest bishops with their insignia of office. Suger gave Louis the banner of the saint as a battle standard, and, when the threatened attack by the English king and the emperor never came, Louis fulfilled his vow to support the rebuilding of the abbey. The east end was completed in 1144, the first fully integrated Gothic choir. Suger appealed to the theological writings of Dionysius (Denis) the Areopagite, whom he associated with St Denis, despite the discrepancy in dates. When Louis went on the Second Crusade in 1145, preached by St Bernard, Suger served as regent of France, helping to unite France, and increased the power of the king. The glorious building served as a backdrop for royal cere-monial that enhanced the unity of the abbey, the Church, and the king.

In the middle of the fifteenth century in England, Alice Chaucer, Duchess of Suffolk and granddaughter of the poet, Geoffrey, founded *God's House* (Chapter 7) on the family estates in Ewelme in Oxfordshire. This foundation demonstrates how the Church reached into every aspect of medieval life, from cradle to grave, and beyond. There was a family chantry chapel in the rebuilt parish church, a cloister of alms-houses attached to its west end just down the hill, and a parish school just below that to the west. The almsmen were to work for their keep by praying for Alice and her family. The living were to be employed by the dead to see them through Purgatory to Paradise. Her tomb and the tomb of her parents were both emblazoned with coats of arms showing the family's connections with some of the grandest and most powerful names in the land. It was not simply name-dropping; it was a kind of display of where she fitted in the social order. Though the social structure seems clearly fixed by birth, it was in reality remark-ably unstable, with politics and power ebbing and flowing, so the look of permanence was belied by political realities. Christian religious reality was perhaps predictable, but there was great uncertainty about the tariff of prayer to see you through Purgatory to salvation. That prayer could leave the departed in Purgatory for a long time unless dedicated professionals were hired to organize and carry it out. The dual royal foundation of Eton College and King's College, Cambridge, began in a similar way to God's House at Ewelme, but soon was re-established for a grander, more outward-looking, educational purpose. Alice was also a benefactress of that broader educational purpose in her support for the building of the new Divinity School at Oxford. Chantry chapels and their clergy also contributed to the pastoral provision of the parishes, and the Church was involved in educational reforms, but the vast wealth tied up by the dead in employing the living was too much of a temptation to modern monarchs like Henry VIII, who had diplomacy to conduct and wars to fight.

After the conquest of Constantinople by the Ottoman Turks, Hagia Sophia, the Great Church, became the Great Mosque; after the *Reconquista*, the *Great Mosque of Cordoba* (Chapter 8) became the cathedral in 1236. That building had itself replaced the mid-sixth-century Cathedral of St Vincent, a Christian church that for a time seems to have been shared between the Christian community and the Muslim conquerors. The new mosque, begun in 785–6, was a magnificent architectural conception, reusing forms, details, architectural elements, and materials from what had gone before, and synthesizing it all into a fresh new style. It was a vast open forest of columns, directional aisles only subtly differentiated. Without extensive architectural changes beyond the provision of chapels after the *Reconquista*, it is difficult to imagine how the major liturgies of the Church would have been celebrated, but the building had to be retained and its worship replaced by Christian worship. In 1523, permission was given by Emperor Charles V to build a cathedral within the vast space. The result was the insertion of a late-Gothic/early Renaissance cathedral, laterally disrupting the seemingly endless and numinous space. The conflict displayed within the architecture continues to be played out in conflict between the religious communities.

Attacks on the authority of Rome and its bishop occurred in 410 with the sack of Rome by Alaric the Goth, in the eighth century with the Lombards threatening Rome, and in 1046 when Emperor Henry III charged Pope Gregory VI with corruption and deposed him. In 1076, Emperor Henry IV had Pope Gregory VII deposed over the Investiture Controversy. The pope excommunicated Henry, who laid siege to Rome for two years, Rome fell, and the end result was an anti-pope and a pope. Pope Clement V, who was French, abandoned Rome for Avignon in 1305, and, by the time Pope Martin V returned more than a century later, the fabric of Old St Peter's Basilica was found to be in such a poor state it had to be rebuilt. The papal basilica had to display the authority of St Peter's successor and the majesty and unity of the Church; Old St Peter's showed the age and the cracks of a creaking institution. A false start was made by Nicholas V in the middle of the fifteenth century; then, on 18 April 1506, Pope Julius II laid the foundation stone for what would finally develop into the present building, with contributions by some of the greatest artists ever to have lived, Bramante, Raphael, Sangallo the Younger, Michelangelo, Maderno, Fontana, and della Porta. The problem in building the new *Renaissance St Peter's* papal basilica (Chapter 9) was not artistic but financial. A lucrative deal struck with a German archbishop drew the protest of Martin Luther in his Ninety-Five Theses in 1517, and the building that was to proclaim the majesty and unity of the Church proved to be the spark in a lot of existing dry tinder to feed the flames of the Reformation.

The painted ceiling in the *Church of Sant' Ignazio in Rome* (Chapter 10) is an apotheosis of St Ignatius, founder of the Society of Jesus, the Jesuits, in 1540, and shows the evangelization of Europe, Africa, America, and Asia, by the Society. The Jesuits established schools everywhere, and this church is the chapel of the Collegio Romano, then the central educational establishment of the Society. It is a gorgeous preaching box with a very open east end, giving easy access to the sanctuary. Together, the church and its ceiling show the vigour of the Counter-Reformation (or Catholic Reformation) riposte to Protestant fury. There is a brief biblical text from the Gospel of Luke (12:49) on the ceiling: 'I came to cast fire upon the earth'—it was the fire of evangelization and conversion, and the narrative of the ceiling tells its story from Europe all the way to China. Despite its themes of light and fire, the narrative of the ceiling also reveals the dark side of this imperial venture, with some of the figures wearing what appear to be leg irons. Even within the triumphalist crescendo of an apotheosis, it is impossible to conceal the depth of human tragedy accompanying the advance of empire. The pope censured the treatment of slaves but was forced to soften his protest under imperial pressure. The Church's ministry to the victims was woeful, though more effective among indigenous populations in South America. The Jesuit 'way of proceeding' involved 'inculturation', visible in the hybrid detail of their architecture. This was both quite novel, and deeply offensive to many. In the Chinese context, the leaders of the Jesuit mission adopted the role and appearance of traditional Chinese scholars, translating both western sciences and the Christian message into Chinese and embedding them into a familiar cultural medium. The scientific achievements of the Jesuit Matteo Ricci in collaboration with the court official Xu Guangqui are still celebrated in China. Dominican and Franciscan missionaries objected to the policy of inculturation, and the Jesuits were censured for their acceptance of Confucian ceremonial rites.

In the eighteenth and nineteenth centuries, British missionary societies left an architectural record around the world. George Edmund Street was Diocesan Architect for the Diocese of Oxford from 1850, having worked as an assistant in George Gilbert Scott's office until just the year before. As Diocesan Architect, he restored a great number of its parish churches and built Cuddesdon Theological College near Oxford. In January 1857, he entered a competition to build the *Crimean Memorial Church* (Chapter 11) in Istanbul. Though he was placed second to William Burges in the competition, after many difficulties Burges was replaced by Street in 1863. Curiously, the Church of the Holy Sepulchre had been a proximal cause of the Crimean War, and in the wake of the war the British were a very powerful presence in Istanbul, but their presence was not marked by the dignity of a place of worship, as for other foreign communities.

Their presence was also marred by the behaviour of their sailors, who were constantly getting into trouble when at a loose end on Sundays, so three different interests came together to build the church: a national memorial was demanded by a people affected by war, the British ambassador to the Sublime Porte agreed an adequate British presence was needed as a projection of soft power, and the English chaplain, and his associate at the British hospital near the port, Florence Nightingale, saw the acute pastoral need for a place of worship. The Memorial Church was indeed eventually completed, but not until 1876. The second half of the nineteenth century saw the British Empire reach its greatest geographical extent, and English parish churches were built by missionary societies around the globe. It was an uncomfortable relationship, with most churches built in a hostile climate, either literally in places like Canada, or frequently in relation to the local population or indeed the colonial administration itself. The buildings themselves also have their stories to tell as 'standing history', when half the map of the world was pink, showing the British Empire. But communities and their pastoral needs change over time, a process that has left its mark on the fabric of the Memorial Church, as it has on these other far-flung exotic hybrids.

In the twentieth century, the world, and the Church, were racked by war. *Coventry* and its cathedral (Chapter 12), destroyed on the night of 14–15 November 1940, became so emblematic of the destruction and loss of life that the German word *Coventrieren* was coined. St Paul's Cathedral became the symbol of the survival of London, and the new cathedral at Coventry was to be the British 'Phoenix' rising from the flames. Both Church and nation were looking to this phoenix, but the renewed form of the one may not be the same as the renewed form of the other. Did the Church in particular have a clear vision for the future, or was it 'a Phoenix too soon'?

In this history of the Church in twelve buildings, the aim is to provide tangible connection to the lives of the people involved in some of the key moments and movements that shaped that history. Standing in the same place where they preached and taught, or in a space they built as a memorial, touching the stone they placed or that marks their final resting place, comes close to shared experience. It is the existential connection, the personal touch of a keepsake, or a relic. These are some of the places where the faces of the past may come more clearly into focus.

Figure 1. Demountable model of the Holy Sepulchre, Syrian Maple, made by Franciscan monks, probably seventeenth century, at least before 1710, when the upper stages of the tower were removed, Collection of the Hospital of St John of Jerusalem, London

I

'The World's Most Miraculous Place'

The Church of the Holy Sepulchre

*T*here is no better place to begin a history of the Church than at a site that many Christians believe to be the very place where key events of the biblical narrative actually took place. The Church of the Holy Sepulchre in Jerusalem is, according to Christian tradition, where Jesus was crucified, buried, and, crucially, rose again to new life. Relevant passages from the Jewish historian Josephus, from Bishop Eusebius, contemporary and biographer of Constantine, the pilgrim of Bordeaux, and the pilgrim Egeria (late fourth century) give a flavour of how contemporary Christians interpreted the sites of Jerusalem and its surroundings. The site of the Holy Sepulchre is as contentious as the events and their interpretation, as the long sequence of building, destruction, and rebuilding shows. The first building on the site obliterating what may already have been a place of Christian pilgrimage was a pagan temple to Capitoline Jupiter built in the mid-second century by Emperor Hadrian. That temple was finally removed, beginning in 326 CE, under Emperor Constantine the Great, and by 335 a great Christian basilica was ready to be consecrated. Only a few vestiges of that building survive. It was in its turn burnt by the Persians in 614, but soon rebuilt. When Omar wrested the territory from the Byzantines in 638, the basilica survived, but in 1009 its destruction was ordered by Caliph Hakim. In 1114, rebuilding began by the

victorious crusaders, who by the 1160s had completed the Romanesque church
that now stands where the original courtyard of the Constantinian basilica
used to be. The fabric of this ancient church is a palimpsest, with layers telling
the stories of different periods in the Church's history, but then almost all
ancient church buildings do that to some extent.

The Approach

The approach to the Church of the Holy Sepulchre reveals a surprisingly modest architectural arrangement. Coming down the long steps
from the west or up through the narrow gate from the soukh that had
been the old Roman *cardo* brings you to a low platform above a small
paved square opposite a narrow double-bayed church facade—an
unlikely entrance to the holiest site in the Christian world. This was
not always so, and there are still aspects of the present structure that
are impressive, even extravagant. This place, and all that happened
here, have been the triggers for events of wider, truly global, significance: it has been the object of almost two millennia of pilgrimage; it
was key in Constantine's creation of a Christian empire; the recapture
of this sacred site was the objective of the First Crusade and became
the heart of the Crusader Kingdom; it lit the fuse for the Crimean
War. It has been such a flashpoint for war that the Status Quo govern-
ing its daily life was enshrined in international law by the Treaty of
Berlin in 1878.[1] But many have questioned whether this precise spot
in the middle of the Old City of Jerusalem could really have been the
scene of the crucifixion and burial of Jesus, and there have been competing locations such as the 'Garden Tomb', or Gordon's Tomb.
Archaeological opinions vary, but there is broad agreement that the
events of the Passion brought Jesus to this place of execution and to
this sepulchre.[2] The rock of Golgotha, the Place of the Skull, is folded
into the chapels immediately on the right of the entrance to the
Church of the Holy Sepulchre, and the sepulchre itself is entirely clad

in the marble of what is known as the *aedicule* under the dome at the focus of the whole architectural complex.

According to Christian tradition, this is the location of what are considered to be the foundational events of the Christian religion, the Passion, crucifixion, entombment, and resurrection of Jesus. The belief that all this happened here is the reason why this site has for so long been the focus of Christian pilgrimage. The biblical narratives describing the events of the last week of Jesus' life, and the associated places, have created a sacred geography mapped onto the topography of Jerusalem (Plate 1). For almost two millennia, pilgrims have come to ponder the events of the last week of Jesus' life in real places bound as a holy geography centred around the sepulchre. It has always mattered that this be the very place, and the way it relates to other holy sites, Christian, Jewish, and Muslim, was crucial to the way its history unfolded. It is worth following the biblical narrative past the sites leading to the place that Emperor Constantine called 'the world's most miraculous place'.

Jesus' Final Journey

The year of Jesus' fateful arrival in Jerusalem for the Passover is thought to have been 30 CE.[3] The biblical account tells that he arrived not just with 'the twelve' but with 'the whole multitude of the disciples'. What brought Jesus from this triumphant entry into Jerusalem when he was hailed as 'the King that cometh in the name of the Lord', to Calvary, Golgotha, the Place of a Skull, and that most painful and ignominious of deaths, by crucifixion? The gospels relate that, during this triumphal entry, Jesus looked across the valley of the Kidron to the magnificent city, wept over it, and prophesied the destruction of both the city and its temple. The city at that date was the impressive result of rebuilding by the Hasmonean Dynasty in the late second century BCE, and, from the time of his crowning as King of the Jews in 37 BCE, Herod the Great had added huge building projects, including the Bethesda Pool, the Siloam Pool, the second wall, a marvellously engineered aqueduct, a lavish palace, and above all the recently finished magnificent new temple on a much extended platform. According to the Gospel of Luke, coming down the Mount of Olives to the east of the city, borne along by the crowd, Jesus prophesied:

> For the days shall come upon thee, when thine enemies shall cast up a bank about thee, and compass thee round, and keep thee in on every side, and shall dash thee to the ground, and thy children within thee; and they shall not leave in thee one stone upon another; because thou knewest not the time of thy visitation. (Luke 19:41–4)

In 70 CE, the temple was destroyed, and in this passage Luke is providing his theological reflection on that devastating event.

Herod the Great died in 4 BCE, and, when Jesus is said to have lamented over Jerusalem, it was Herod Antipas, his son, who ruled as tetrarch of Galilee. Jesus called him 'that fox'. But Jerusalem had clearly prospered under Rome, and local leaders of society had every reason to want to fall in with Roman authority.[4] The Jewish historian Flavius Josephus, writing in the years following the fall of Jerusalem and destruction of the temple, adds another perspective in *The Jewish War*. In what may be a later Christian interpolation, the text says of Jesus that

> there assembled unto him of ministers one hundred and fifty, and a multitude of the people. Now when they saw his power, that he accomplished whatsoever he would by word, and when they had made known to him their will, that he should enter into the city and cut down the Roman troops and Pilate and rule over us, he distained us not [or heeded us not].[5]

Quite apart from the commotion caused by this jubilant crowd at Jesus' entry into Jerusalem, the day cannot have been comfortable for those in authority, either in the temple or among the Roman garrison. Great festivals, like the approaching Jewish Passover, which brought upwards of two hundred thousand worshippers, and their animals for sacrifice, into Jerusalem, also brought a worrying potential for disorder.

The narrative does indeed describe a fracas in the temple precincts, with Jesus overturning the tables of the irate money-changers, spilling money everywhere, causing chaos, and disrupting the legitimate functioning of the place. The Romans, however, seem not to have reacted. In any case, Jesus continued teaching in the temple during the following days and had the effrontery to taunt its priests and officials, clearly referring to himself and his teaching; 'Have ye not read even this scripture; the stone which the builders rejected, the same was made the head of the corner.' It is interesting to observe that, in the quarry where he is believed to have met his end, his disciples would have cause to reflect on this saying concerning the 'stone which the builders rejected', both a reference to the psalms and a precise description of the rock of Golgotha.[6] This passage is cited in Matthew, Mark, Luke, and the Acts, which shows its importance in the context of the early Christian understanding of the arrest, trial and execution of Jesus.

Eventually, the gospels blame his challenge to authority and his betrayal by one of his own disciples, Judas Iscariot, for Jesus' arrest. When his barbed comments and stories were directed at them, the temple authorities tried to get their hands on him but were afraid of the reaction of the admiring crowds. The chief priests had a collaborator among the twelve, Judas Iscariot, who, for thirty pieces of silver, agreed to betray Jesus when he was away from his crowds of supporters (Luke 22:6). On the first day of unleavened bread, Jesus ate with his disciples in a specially prepared upper room in the city—a meal they were told never to forget, as they were charged by Jesus to continue to celebrate such a meal in remembrance of him. In response to this charge, a ritual re-enactment became, and remains, the central act of worship of all Christian communities, the Lord's Supper, Holy Communion, or Mass.

The gospels relate that, after the supper, they went a little way outside the walls back towards Bethany across the Kidron to a garden called Gethsemane at the foot of the Mount of Olives. At the appearance of Judas, who betrayed Jesus, identifying him with a kiss, swords were out, and in the clash the high priest's servant lost his ear; but Jesus stilled the fight and went quietly to his fate.

Jesus was taken first to the house of Caiaphas, the high priest, where the chief priests got him to confess that he was the Son of God, and so themselves became witnesses to this blasphemy. He was beaten and mocked. In the morning, he was bound and sent to Pontius Pilate at the Antonia Fortress, or possibly the Praetorium. Today, the site marked as the beginning of the Via Dolorosa is the Antonia Fortress at the north-west corner of the temple precincts, but it was just a large tower with a garrison and soldiers' quarters, not a palace. A trial was much more likely to have taken place on the Praetorium or raised platform of the citadel next door to the palace, at the north-western corner of the city walls, in which case the route to Golgotha, the Via Dolorosa, would have been very different, and shorter. The Stations of the Cross on the way to Golgotha today are observed by many Christians as a slow and contemplative exercise, whether here in Jerusalem or at marked points in procession around their own parish church. The precise sacred geography of Jerusalem has always mattered to the pilgrim, which is true for pilgrims of all three Abrahamic religions. For Christians, the holiest sites were those identified with the crucifixion and resurrection of Jesus, located by long religious tradition in the Church of the Holy Sepulchre.

Golgotha

In the return formed by the first and second walls on the north-west of the city was a worked-out hilltop quarry with a promontory approximately 10 (in places 13) metres above the floor of the workings. It had been a quarry since the iron age, from the ninth to eighth centuries BCE and in use until the first century BCE.[7] It is interesting to observe that the promontory literally was stone of the quarry that the builders had rejected, because there was a crack that ran down its red-veined whiteness. Today, that stone promontory is found just to the right, enclosed in chapels, on entering the Church of the Holy Sepulchre. It had the appearance of a skull, hence Golgotha, or, in its Latin derivation, Calvary. In 1988, it was archaeologically analysed when its marble covering was removed during excavations. The tradition maintains that it was on this rocky knoll that the grizzly procession stopped. They offered Jesus wine mingled with myrrh or gall, probably to numb the excruciating pain of what was about to happen. They crucified him with a *titulus* above his head: 'this is Jesus the King of the Jews.' The other two prisoners were crucified on either side of him. It would now take hours for them to die—only 'at the ninth hour' Jesus cried aloud and died. The Gospel of Mark then says that the veil of the temple was rent, the earth shook, and the rocks split.

Joseph of Arimathea (whose final tomb is said to be through the Jacobite chapel to the west of the sepulchre) then went to Pilate to ask that Jesus' body be released to him for burial, and, having determined that he was already dead, Pilate granted the request. Joseph clearly must have been a man of substance to gain direct access to Pilate himself. The biblical story recounts that, when the Sabbath was over, early on the first day of the week, those who came to anoint the body found not Jesus, but an angel, who declared that Jesus was risen from the dead. The gospels differ considerably in the details of the breathlessly excited narrative, but the core of each account is that angels call his followers to witness that the tomb where they had laid him was now empty. In what may well be an interpolation, the text of *The Jewish War*, by contrast, gives a very cool summary of the whole sequence of events:

> About this time [the uprising over Herod's building of the aqueduct] there lived Jesus, a wise man, if indeed one ought to call him a man...He was the Messiah [the so-called Christ]. When Pilate, upon hearing him accused by men of the highest standing amongst us, had condemned him to be crucified, those who had in the first place come to love him did not give up their affection for him. On the third day he appeared to them restored to life, for the prophets of God had

prophesied these and countless other marvellous things about him.
And the tribe of Christians, so called after him, has still to this day not
disappeared.[8]

So it was, and so it remains: the place was seen as the existential connection with the man, Jesus, and as evidence for the confirmation of
their faith.

Pilgrimage and Worship

To refer to pilgrimage at this early date may seem odd, but the Gospels
of Mark and Matthew, which were probably written between 65 and
100 CE, only a few decades later, insistently draw attention to the
physical place where they laid the body. This has the immediacy of
speech addressed directly by a narrator to a listener, perhaps even
during a liturgy or public performance.[9] Further, there is physical
evidence of pilgrimage before 135, when Hadrian had a temple of
Jupiter Capitolinus built on the site. A stone inscribed in Latin 'Lord
we have gone' with the drawing of a ship was found reused as part of
a foundation wall of Hadrian's temple, near the very spot recently
archaeologically proposed as the place of the crucifixion. The phrase
is connected with the Latin version of the pilgrim psalm 121 verse 1:
'Let us go into the house of the Lord.' The place of discovery, the
language and its peculiarities, and the subject of the drawing together
link the *graffito* to Christians coming from the western part of the
empire, probably from North Africa, Italy, Gaul, or Spain. So, by the
middle of the second century, it is very likely that there was already an
established pilgrim traffic coming from very considerable distances.
The drawing shows what appears to be a broken mast, so this may be
an early *ex voto*, offering thanks for deliverance on a perilous journey,
like the one experienced by Josephus himself on his way to Rome
(see Chapter 2).[10] There is no suggestion of building in this area
before Hadrian's temple in 135, but that does not preclude liturgical

use of the space around the tomb, just as today. The lower fill in the quarry would have aided this use, and it dates from as early as the first century CE.[11]

The first Christians continued to worship in the temple after the death of Jesus, and, when not in Jerusalem, they worshipped in synagogues. Both synagogues and the first distinctively Christian places of worship were most commonly conversions of domestic buildings in *insulae*, or mixed-use blocks, like the pair discovered in excavations at Capernaum between 1968 and 1991. Usually the community would outgrow occasional religious use of domestic space, and physical changes would be carried out on the structure in response to the pressure of its new religious use. In Capernaum, this process can be seen at work, both at the 'House of Peter' near the lake, and about 30 metres to the north at the synagogue.

Beneath the podium of the magnificent classical architecture of the late-fourth-century prayer hall of the synagogue are the remains of private houses under the side-aisles, and below its central nave is the pavement of the first-century synagogue. Mark tells us that, at the beginning of his public ministry, 'they went into Capernaum; and immediately on the Sabbath [Jesus] entered the synagogue and taught' (Mark 1:21).[12] A few verses later,

> immediately he left the synagogue, and entered the house of Simon [Peter] and Andrew, with James and John. Now Simon's mother-in-law lay sick with a fever, and immediately they told him of her. And he came and took her by the hand and lifted her up, and the fever left her; and she served them. (Mark 1.29–31)[13]

In the synagogue there are archaeological layers of Jewish worship, and the House of Peter likewise has layers of Christian worship.

The large room identified as the House of Peter in the *insula* stands out with a unique treatment in Capernaum. The lowest stone pavement in the courtyard had traces of a fire and late-Hellenistic potsherds, both dating it and indicating its domestic use. The stone pavement second from the bottom was from the first century CE. In the room itself there were also several layers with imbedded domestic remains, including cooking pots and so on dating from the second century BCE to the late first century CE. Above this were half a dozen layers of white plaster that had been kept very clean. There were no daily domestic items found in these levels, only small pieces of Herodian lamps from the second half of the first century CE. This appears to have been a Christian cultic centre, and services probably took place in this white room with the lamps, though questions remain. It was about 7 metres square, just adequate for worship, but the room was so sacred it was not itself enlarged for congregational use, unlike other similar domestic settings. It could, however, have been used within a service in the adjacent courtyards, in much the same way as the Cave of the Nativity is used today, with small processions entering the room at different points during the service. About a century later than the dating of those Herodian lamps, Justin Martyr wrote the earliest surviving description of the Christian eucharistic service, which harkens back to the supper of the gospel narrative in that upper room before the arrest of Jesus:

> We afterwards [that is after baptism and first eucharist] continually remind each other of these things. The wealthy among us help all those in need, and we always keep together. For everything we receive we praise the maker of all things through his Son Jesus Christ and the Holy Spirit. On the so-called Sunday everyone in town or countryside gathers together in one place, and the memoirs of the apostles or the writings of the prophets are read out, for as long as time permits. Next, when the reader has finished, the president in an address admonishes and exhorts us to imitate these good examples. Then we all stand up together and offer prayers; when we have finished praying, as I said before, bread, wine and water are brought out, and the president offers prayers of thanks, to the best of his ability; the people assent, saying Amen, and each person receives and shares in that over which thanks have been given, and a portion is taken by the deacons to those not present. The wealthy and willing each gives what he wants as each sees fit, and what is collected is deposited with the president. He helps orphans and widows, and those in need through sickness or any other reason, those in prison, foreigners staying with us; in a word, he takes care of everyone in distress.

On Sunday we make our common gathering since it is the day on which God changed darkness and matter and made the world, and on which Jesus Christ our Saviour rose from the dead.[14]

This celebration was clearly very closely associated with Jesus' resurrection, so it would be interesting to know what that meant for the associated site, the Holy Sepulchre. The House of Peter is only yards from the shore of Lake Galilee, so it would have been ideal as a place for baptism. A somewhat different form of worship celebrated in such places was also described by Tertullian, an early Christian apologist, at the end of the second century:

> We meet together as an assembly and congregation, that, offering up prayer to God as with united force, we may wrestle with him in our supplications...We assemble to read our sacred writings, if any peculiarity of the times makes either forewarning or reminiscence needful...Our feast explains itself by its name. The Greeks call it agapè, i.e. affection...The participants, before reclining, taste first of prayer to God. As much is eaten as satisfies the cravings of hunger; as much is drunk as benefits the chaste...After manual ablution, and the bringing in of lights, each is asked to stand forth and sing, as he can, a hymn to God, either one from the holy Scriptures, or one of his own composing,—a proof of the measure of our drinking. As the feast commenced with prayer, so with prayer it is closed.[15]

It sounds very informal, and the readings, songs, and prayers would clearly vary from service to service and from place to place, depending on what 'forewarning or reminiscence' was needed. The picture he paints is consistent with the detail from the gospels, Acts, and epistles, and interestingly he mentions the lights being brought in, consistent with the Herodian lamps in the white plaster layer at the House of Peter. There the walls were plastered too, and the summary archaeological report notes that they were covered with geometric designs and *graffiti* that were clearly Christian and dating from the early third to the early fifth centuries. The *graffiti* referred in various ways in different languages to Jesus, Peter, and the liturgy, so in the third century there were probably both a local congregation and also pilgrims.

One of those pilgrims in the early 380s was Egeria, who was a pilgrim to Jerusalem. She was a woman perhaps from Gaul or Spain who kept a remarkable journal in which she recorded that 'in Capernaum the house of the prince of the apostles [Peter] has been made into a church, with its original walls still standing. It is where the Lord healed the paralytic. There also is the synagogue where the Lord cured a man possessed by the devil.' Such a house being converted into a church was a common pattern at this period, and the Byzantines clearly believed that this was the House of Peter, since, in the second half of the fifth century, the church was transformed into an octagonal 'martyrium'.[16] The archaeological and literary evidence combined make the attribution as the House of Peter, at least of Egeria's pilgrimage, quite strong, despite lingering doubts.

If the House of Peter had been converted to a *domus-ecclesiae* and was the focus of liturgical celebration, possibly within a generation of the death of the Prince of the Apostles, then it would have been very strange if the tomb of Christ himself had not enjoyed the same focus, though there is no suggestion of architectural activity near the sepulchre. In any event, the identity of the place depended on the tradition of the community for almost two centuries while it was buried under Hadrian's Temple of Jupiter from 135 to its recovery under Constantine in 326. The height of the traditional rock of Calvary is so much higher than the rest that it may have protruded from the *temenos* or walled platform of Hadrian's temple and been topped by a statue of Venus, a particular abomination for Christians. This may have been a clear, if offensive, marker for the site.

The Destruction of Jerusalem and the Memory of the Christian Community

Without a strong succession after the death of Herod Agrippa, political chaos and exploitation ensued, inflaming resentment against Rome. There were other charismatic leaders of insurrections, including 'the

Egyptian who recently stirred up a revolt and led the four thousand men of the Assassins out into the wilderness' (Acts 21:38), whom the tribune thought Paul might be when he was arrested. 'All Jerusalem was in confusion', and a riot had started when Paul was accused of taking a gentile, or non-Jew, into the temple. Paul had been enormously successful in expanding Christianity, or 'the Way', among the gentiles, though he himself had been a deeply committed Jew who persecuted the Church before his own conversion. The core of the Christianity he preached was Christ crucified for the sin of the world and resurrected for its salvation, so it would not be surprising to find that early pilgrims to the Holy Sepulchre and Calvary were converts from that gentile mission come to see for themselves the 'place of witness'. Paul did not escape custody; as a Roman citizen he insisted on putting his case before Caesar in Rome, where Christian tradition maintains that he would encounter Peter before they were both put to death there in 64–5 CE.[17] Their shrines in Rome, especially Peter's on the Vatican Hill, would have immense importance for the history of the Church and the papacy (see Chapter 2).

The years from 66 to 70 CE saw the Jewish War, which was later chronicled by Josephus, who was himself a Jewish general for the early part of the war and later became so Roman as to take the emperor's name, Flavius Josephus. His writings clearly had a very particular bias. That notwithstanding, the course of the war and its devastating conclusion had more to do with politics in Rome than the threat in Judea.[18] Christians began to leave the doomed city of Jerusalem in 67, according to Eusebius (bishop of Caesarea and Christian historian under Constantine) in his *History of the Church from Christ to Constantine*. Nero had sent his general Titus Flavius Vespasianus to deal with the rebellion. It was eventually Vespasian's son Titus who crushed Jerusalem and destroyed the temple, as Jesus had prophesied according to the gospels. Josephus says: 'Caesar ordered the whole city and the Temple to be razed to the ground . . . All the rest of the wall encompassing the city [except around the citadel] was so completely levelled to the ground as to leave future visitors to the spot no ground for believing

that it had ever been inhabited.'[19] The booty from the city and the
temple treasure were taken to Rome in triumph, as recorded on the
Arch of Titus. The temple treasure was housed in the Temple of Peace,
but the veil of the temple went to the imperial palace.[20] The spoils
paid for the building of the Colosseum, where many Christians faced
martyrdom.[21] Jerusalem was a ruin, and the temple would never
be rebuilt.

Jerusalem remained a desolate ruin. Temple worship ceased definitively, and the synagogue became the focus of Jewish piety. Christians
had been a sect of Judaism, but now had every reason to separate
themselves, and they continued to worship in Jerusalem. When
Hadrian (Aelius Hadrianus) visited in 130 CE, the city was still a ruin,
'except for a few houses, and the little church of God. That was the
upper room, where the disciples entered when they returned from
the Mount of Olives after the Ascension of the Redeemer. It was built
there, namely on Sion.'[22]

There was another Jewish rebellion under Simon bar Kochba, who
dealt harshly with the Christians who would not accept that he was
the Messiah. Quoting the philosopher Justin Martyr, Eusebius says
that they were 'sentenced to terrible punishments if they did not deny
Jesus Christ and blaspheme him'.[23] Hadrian, in turn, was pitiless in his
devastation of the land and its people. This is an illustration of the
interpretation of Jerusalem that contemporary Christians would have
heard from the pulpit and that would have circulated among pilgrims.
The revolt had been crushed in 135, and Jews were then forbidden even
to approach Jerusalem. Looking back over two centuries, Eusebius
wrote with polemical zeal:

> From that time on, the entire race has been forbidden to set foot any-
> where in the neighbourhood of Jerusalem, under the terms and ordin-
> ances of a law of Hadrian... When in this way the city was closed to
> the Jewish race and suffered the total destruction of its former inhabit-
> ants, it was colonised by an alien race, and the Roman city which
> subsequently arose changed its name, so that now, in honour of the
> emperor then reigning, Aelius Hadrianus, it is known as Aelia.

Furthermore, as the church in the city was now composed of Gentiles, the first after the bishops of the Circumcision to be put in charge of the Christians there was Mark.[24]

Having renamed Judea as Palaestina, Hadrian laid out a new Roman city, Aelia Capitolina, to be named for Rome and his own family. The ghost of its shape is still visible; excavations at the Damascus Gate now reveal more clearly his Neapolis Gate (at the end of today's Nablus Road), where he reused huge Herodian stones. Inside the gate was an oval forum with a column at its centre, as seen in the sixth-century mosaic Madaba map. The two main roads forked from there, one running south-west (today's El Wad) towards the Antonia Fortress, the other (the *cardo*) due south (today's Suq Khan es-Zeit) to the temple of Capitoline Jupiter built on the old quarry, and the site of what would become the Church of the Holy Sepulchre. The quarry had to be completely filled, burying the sepulchre, but the rock of Golgotha itself may have protruded above the *temenos*, or sacred precinct, of the temple. A small section of the south-eastern *temenos* wall can still be seen.

Nor did interest in the holy sites abate after this architectural assault. During the reign of Antoninus, when Bishop Narcissus of Aelia was very old and too incapacitated to carry out his duties, Alexander, bishop in Cappadocia, travelled to Jerusalem 'in order to worship there and to examine the historic sites'.[25] Providentially, as a result of coming on pilgrimage to Jerusalem, he became its bishop and exercised authority there until his death in the persecution under the emperor Decius between 249 and 251. The contemporary Christian scholar and theologian Origen (*c.*185–*c.*254) went to Palaestina from Alexandria in 215. Origen settled in Caesarea in 231 and founded a school. It is in his writings, of which much is now lost, that ancient associations of the temple are seen to migrate to Golgotha. Christians made these stories their own, in the same way as they had made Jewish prophesies and scripture their own. Origen interpreted scripture on three levels, literal, moral, and allegorical, with a strong emphasis

on the last. It is in his writings, later repeated in 388 by St Jerome, who
had come to Jerusalem in about 385, that the grave of Adam is situated
at the foot of Golgotha.[26] With beautiful theological symmetry,
Origen made the blood of Jesus, the 'second Adam', flow down over
sinful Adam's bones. Like Bishop Alexander, Origen too perished as a
result of his injuries sustained during the Decian persecution.

Constantine and Christian Unity

The politics of empire, played out on a battlefield on the outskirts of
Rome, was to have an almost unimaginable impact on the history of
the Church; a reported vision of the cross, the instrument of Jesus'
brutal execution, would eventually lead to the unearthing of the
'Witness' to his resurrection. In 312 CE, following Constantine's vision
of the cross in a blaze of light over the sun with the command 'By this
conquer' at the Milvian Bridge outside Rome, he went on to victory
over the usurper Maxentius. An earlier account says that it was revealed
to him in a dream to 'put the sign of God on the soldiers' shields and
then engage in battle. He did as he was commanded and by means of
a slanted letter X with the top of its head bent round, he marked
Christ on their shields.'[27] This was made up of the first two Greek
letters of the divine name, *chi* and *rho*. He attributed his victory to the
risen Christ and converted to the new religion and immediately
began building the Lateran Basilica in Rome soon to be followed by
St Peter's Basilica on the Vatican Hill.[28]

His mother, the dowager empress Helena, may already have
been a Christian by this time, but in any case she came to play an
influential part in the practical effects in Jerusalem, at the very least, of
Constantine's conversion to Christianity. Whether he was converted
as a religious visionary or as an astute politician on a mission to reunify
the empire, the practical effects are indisputable. Licinius, ruler of the
Balkans, made a marriage alliance with Constantine and soon defeated
Maximinus, emperor in Asia Minor, who had failed to abide by the

agreement in the 'Edict' of Milan to stop the persecution of Christians and return their confiscated property. In the coming years, Licinius too returned to persecution and suffered defeats by Constantine in 316, and finally, in 324, Constantine was in full control of both east and west. Jerusalem and the Holy Places were now under his sole authority.

There was a simmering dispute within the Church over the date of the celebration of Easter. Then a more serious division arose over the nature of Christ (human or divine?) and this threatened to split the Church. With churchmen coming to blows and, very worryingly, insulting the image of the emperor, Constantine wrote to the disputants Arius and Alexander: 'My first concern was that the attitude towards the Divinity of all the Provinces should be united in a consistent view, and my second that I might restore and heal the body of the republic which lay severely wounded.'[29] The unity of the Church was clearly seen as essential to the unity of the empire.

Constantine warned the disputants to set their disagreements aside, but they persisted. In 325, all the bishops, including Bishop Macarius of Jerusalem, a suffragan or subordinate bishop, and Bishop Eusebius of Caesarea, his Metropolitan, were summoned to a general council at Nicaea to resolve the argument. Christians had been united during their persecution and fiercely loyal to their lord and one another. They were resourceful and well organized, so it was politically important for Constantine that the Church be a unifying force for the empire, which, in its vastness and diversity, was constantly threatening to fragment; he could not afford for his new religion to do the same. More than 250 bishops assembled from the whole world, from Spain to Persia, and the emperor himself entered the council dressed in purple and gold. Eusebius tells us that Constantine addressed them gently, as friends, and pressed them irresistibly towards unanimity. The council ended in the imperial palace to celebrate the twentieth year of the emperor's reign with a banquet, that 'might have been supposed . . . was an imaginary representation of the kingdom of Christ'.[30]

Building Unity

Constantine was determined to reverse the fortunes of the Church and wrote to Eusebius: 'Where therefore you yourself are in charge of churches, or know other bishops and presbyters or deacons to be locally in charge of them, remind them to attend to the church buildings, whether by restoring or enlarging the existing ones, or where necessary building new. You yourself and the others through you shall ask for the necessary supplies from the governors and the office of the Prefect, for these have been directed to cooperate wholeheartedly with what your holiness proposes.'[31] When the emperor made such a declaration, things happened quickly.

Following the Council of Nicaea and having resolved the argument over Easter, Constantine, no doubt at the urging of Bishop Macarius, decided to raise the dignity of Jerusalem by building a great shrine to the crucifixion and resurrection of Christ, saying that 'it is right that the world's most miraculous place should be worthily embellished'.[32] Pilgrimage to the major centres of St Peter's Basilica in Rome and the Holy Sepulchre in Jerusalem could play a major part in disseminating orthodox teaching and liturgical practice. It seems highly likely that building those huge shrines was an important part of Constantine's drive towards religious and political unity. Building a shrine to the crucifixion and resurrection of Jesus was within the policy that Constantine had declared to Eusebius to attend to church buildings, restoring the old and building new. Because the site for the shrine lay under the imperial Capitoline temple built in Aelia by Hadrian, it could only be by imperial command that it be removed. Eusebius thought it had been a deliberate policy to obliterate the tomb and desecrate the site. 'It was this very cave of the Saviour that some godless and wicked people had planned to make invisible to mankind, thinking in their stupidity that they could in this way hide the truth.'[33] He expressed disgust that there should be a sanctuary of Aphrodite there to obliterate the true sanctity of the place. On the contrary, resentment over such desecration may have played its part in keeping the memory alive in the Christian community.

Demolition work at the site started in 326. It was not until early 327 that Empress Helena arrived in Jerusalem on pilgrimage, and by that time the excavations for the foundations had probably reached bedrock, bringing what was then identified as the True Cross to light. She may have been in time for the discovery of the True Cross, but Eusebius does not mention her being there, and he would surely have preferred to see the credit go to her than to his more junior rival Macarius. It was only much later in the fourth century that Socrates Scholasticus (c.380–450) says she was 'directed by dreams' to find the sepulchre.[34] As Metropolitan Bishop of Caesarea, Eusebius was in overall authority, but the position of Aelia (Jerusalem), and Macarius as its local bishop, was being hugely enhanced, and the empress Helena, as a devout Christian and great influence on her son, was now on the scene. There must have been a degree of competitiveness between the two bishops. Eusebius was in a strong position as the recorder of events, but here he seems to be generous, at least as far as the accomplishments of his rival were concerned. Still, that did not prevent his giving all the honour for the success of the venture to the emperor's inspired foresight.

Constantine insisted on the enormous work of having the site cleared and having the polluted rubble, stones, timbers, and the pavement stained by pagan sacrifice all carted a long way away from the holy site. With a huge amount of well-cut stone already on site, a vast amount of work and time could be saved by reusing that *spolia*, in much the same way as he was using *spolia* in the building of St Peter's Basilica in Rome, but Eusebius implies that it had been disallowed by the emperor for the Church of the Resurrection. Archaeological remains show that, if it was indeed commanded by Constantine, then it was not strictly followed. In the archaeological excavations east of the Holy Sepulchre, you can still see Herodian cut stones reused in part of the *temenos* wall around Hadrian's temple, which had been incorporated in the wall of the atrium in front of Constantine's basilica.

That wall still continues towards the north and is seen again in the back of the shop beside the stairs off the Suq Khan es-Zeit up to the roof of the Church of the Holy Sepulchre. The main gate into the atrium was here. The present Suq follows the line of the Roman *cardo*, or main columned thoroughfare, all very clearly illustrated on the sixth-century Byzantine Madaba map. There is also the puzzling example of the pair of columns on the north-east of the Rotunda, which have been identified as having originally been a single monumental column, originally 7.15 metres high. It is from a first- to third-century Roman building, so it could well have been from the Hadrianic temple.[35]

> As stage by stage the underground site was exposed, at last against all expectation the revered and all-hallowed Testimony [*martyrion*] of the Saviour's resurrection was itself revealed, and the cave, the holy of holies, took on the appearance of a representation of the Saviour's return to life. Thus after its descent into darkness it came forth again to the light, and it enabled those who came as visitors to see plainly the story of the wonders wrought there, testifying by facts louder than any voice to the resurrection of the Saviour.[36]

The Witness

Eusebius was explicit that the tomb, emerging once more from the darkness of burial, itself was seen as an icon of the resurrection of Jesus. He presents it as the *martyrion*, the testimony, the witness, the proof of the resurrection. This implies that pilgrims had already been visiting the site, whether anything could be seen or not. Some believe that pilgrims would climb into the foundations of the Capitoline temple to worship as near as possible to the site of the Passion.[37] Now it had achieved the status of the new Holy of Holies, accepted as standing proof of the resurrection.

Constantine wrote to Macarius that he wanted beautiful buildings to be built there at the sacred site where the 'pledge of the Saviour's passion' was brought to light.[38] That 'pledge' was the tomb, or possibly the cross.[39] By Constantine's command, the basilica was to be the most beautiful anywhere: Macarius was 'to make such order and provision of what is needed that not only a basilica superior to those in all other places, but the other arrangements also, may be such that all the excellences of every city are surpassed by this foundation'. The governor, Dracillianus, would provide all that was needed.

> As to the columns or marble, you should after a survey yourself write promptly to us about what you may consider to be of most value and use, so that whatever quantity and kind of materials we may learn from your letter to be needful may be competently supplied from all sources. It is right that the world's most miraculous place should be worthily embellished. As to the vault of the basilica, whether you decide that it be coffered or in another style of construction I would wish to learn from you. If it were to be coffered, it might also be decorated with gold. In short, in order that your Holiness may make known with all speed to the aforementioned magistrates how many labourers and craftsmen and what other expenditures are required, take care to refer immediately also to me not only the matters of the marble and pillars, but also the lacunary panels, should you judge that best.[40]

Between Calvary and the *cardo*, the magnificent basilica rose with its entrance at the east end from an atrium off the *cardo*. Its interior was lined with sheets of varied marble (*revetment*), and the exterior was of finely cut stone polished like marble. On the exterior, the roof was of lead, and inside it was coffered and gilded. It had double colonnaded aisles in two storeys with gilded capitals. At the west end was a dome (*hemisphairon*) supported by twelve giant order columns, representing the twelve apostles, topped by silver capitals presented by Constantine. This dome may have acted as a great canopy over the relic of the True Cross or the place of its discovery. On the other hand, some identify this *hemisphairon* with the aedicule in the Anastasis, or Church of the Resurrection. Such an interpretation of Eusebius' description would be consistent with the appearance of domes in both the Madaba map (sixth century) and the apse mosaic (Plate 2) installed at Santa Pudenziana in Rome very late in the fourth century.[41] Gold, silver, and precious stones were a physical expression of the spiritual importance of the site.

The rock of Golgotha is on the right of the present entrance to the Church of the Holy Sepulchre, and the sepulchre itself is under the present dome at the focus of the whole architectural complex as it now exists. The Constantinian building took shape with the axial focus on the tomb 'full of agelong memory', which was sumptuously decorated 'with superb columns and full ornamentation, brightening the solemn cave with all kinds of artwork'.[42] At this early period, the area containing the tomb was probably open to the sky, and to the east let onto a paved courtyard with colonnades on three sides and the rock of Calvary in the south-west corner.

It is this architectural complex that Eusebius refers to, saying:

> New Jerusalem was built at the very testimony to the Saviour, facing the famous Jerusalem of old, which after the bloody murder of the Lord had been overthrown in utter devastation...Opposite this then the Emperor erected the victory of the Saviour over death with rich and abundant munificence, this being perhaps that fresh new Jerusalem proclaimed in prophetic oracles.[43]

Work on the architectural complex around the Holy Sepulchre proceeded quickly. They had started in 326, and there is an eyewitness account by an anonymous pilgrim from Bordeaux in 333. The date can be precisely fixed because he mentions the names of the Consuls for that year. He travelled via Rome, Milan, and Constantinople, founded only three years before. It was less than a decade since Constantine's conquest of the East and already a Christian sacred geography was redefining the Empire. In a matter of two decades, Constantine was creating a different world; in 312, he had conquered under the sign of the Cross and demanded a halt to the persecution of Christians throughout the empire. In 330, he had moved to a new Christian imperial capital named for himself, Constantinople. He ruled supreme in an empire now becoming united under the sway of the Church. But once the Church was free to expound the Kingdom of God and the fullness of a universal Christian theology within the universal Empire, theological disputes were exposed which were as dangerous to Constantine's project of unification as the political disputes threatening the Empire. Under Constantine's direction, the Council of Nicaea in 325 had resulted in remarkable agreement, the Nicene Creed, but the disputes were by no means wholly resolved.

Constantine's Jerusalem

In 333, this is what the Pilgrim of Bordeaux described walking north up the *cardo*:

> as you leave there and pass through the wall of Sion [where there are still remains just by Jewish Quarter Road and Plugat HaKotel[44]] towards the Gate of Neapolis [Nablus gate, now the Damascus Gate]...on your left is the hillock Golgotha where the Lord was crucified, and about a stone's throw from it the vault where they laid his body, and he rose again on the third day. By order of the Emperor Constantine there has now been built there a 'basilica'—I mean 'a place for the Lord'—which has beside it cisterns of remarkable beauty, and beside them a baptistery, where children are baptised.[45]

Two years later, in 335, Constantine planned to celebrate the consecration of the Church of the Holy Sepulchre, but dissension in the wider Church intervened. With further disputes within the Church in Egypt, he summoned the bishops of the eastern Church to convene a synod at Tyre to resolve them and then to proceed to Jerusalem for the consecration of the building. In the event, they were ordered not to delay in Tyre and to proceed directly to Jerusalem, where they assembled under the emperor's personal representative, who received them with splendid feasts. They performed rites and preached and gave addresses praising the emperor for this great building, which was further embellished with imperial dedications. Eusebius himself gave orations, laying out Constantine's ideas in one panegyric delivered at the dedication of the architectural complex, including the Rotunda of the Holy Sepulchre, on 13 September 335,[46] and in another he applied the writings of the prophets to these dedicatory rites and the significance of that church.

The whole of the emperor's career had been contingent on his claimed vision of the cross-shaped trophy in the sky as the promise of victory. This building was the celebration of the holy site that yielded up the 'pledge' or very testimony itself. Eusebius described the cross as 'a token of immortality, and was an abiding trophy of the victory over death'.[47] The crucifixion and resurrection are inseparable in this symbolism, with both cross and tomb as fully adequate embodiments. On 25 July 336, Constantine's thirtieth jubilee, Eusebius repeated his panegyric before the emperor himself in the palace in Constantinople.[48] The Holy Sepulchre was clearly central to his reign, and evidently the emperor was delighted with the theological account of the building, the tomb, and the offerings he had made, possibly including a jewelled cross set up on the rock of Calvary, as seen in the apse mosaic of Santa Pudenziana (Plate 2) at the end of the fourth century. In that mosaic, with Christ enthroned on Golgotha surrounded by the apostles in the courtyard of Constantine's buildings, earthly and heavenly Jerusalem are presented as one and the same.

The history of this site and its buildings has long been intended to bring the pilgrim into the presence of the key biblical events that are the cornerstone of the Christian religion, the death and resurrection of Jesus. Over the course of the two millennia since that time, the site has been desecrated and buried, perhaps accessed in a clandestine way for worship by pilgrims from the far shores of the Mediterranean, then itself resurrected and revered as the 'witness' to those foundational events.

The way the site itself has been conceived and presented, its access denied or controlled, its architecture gleaming and gilded or ruined and rebuilt, all reveals how its history, traditions, worship, and theology have from the beginning been refined in the crucible of imperial politics. Only a few fragments, including the foundations of the main part of the present building, remain of the great basilica of Constantine, the worthy embellishment of 'the world's most miraculous place'.[49]

The basilica was torched by the Persians in 614 but reconstructed by Patriarch Modestus. In 638, the Byzantines capitulated to Omar, and Jerusalem came under Muslim rule, but the basilica came through unscathed. In 1009, however, the Fatamid Caliph Hakim ordered its systematic destruction, even chipping away at the rock of the sepulchre itself. The whole site was again buried in the rubble of the destruction. Yet the pilgrimage continued, and from 1012 the offerings began the restoration of the Rotunda and the courtyard; but even the offerings of the Byzantine emperor were not sufficient to restore the basilica itself, which was never to rise again. What is seen today is largely the result of Crusader modifications after their capture of the city in 1099. Their work began in 1114, and the Romanesque church on what had been the courtyard was completed in the 1160s, followed by the bell tower about 1170.

This vestige of the crusader Kingdom of Jerusalem of today is a palimpsest of more than a millennium, now frozen in time by the Status Quo. The overlayering of fragments reveals both the depth of meanings invested in the site and also the violence that marked the religion from the crucifixion of Jesus, through the destruction of the city by the Romans in 70 CE, and the sequential levellings of the site by Hadrian and later by Hakim, not to mention the terrible destruction of so much of the rest of the city by the Crusaders.

What is meted out to buildings is meted out to those for whom they stand. Buildings are the index of community, telling us of their history, of course, but also their organization, aspiration, beliefs, religion, worship—their life from generation to generation. The pilgrim sets out to stand in the very place, to follow the same path, to stand within the story and be part of that story. The Church of the Holy Sepulchre connects us physically with the events that were the birth pangs of the Church.

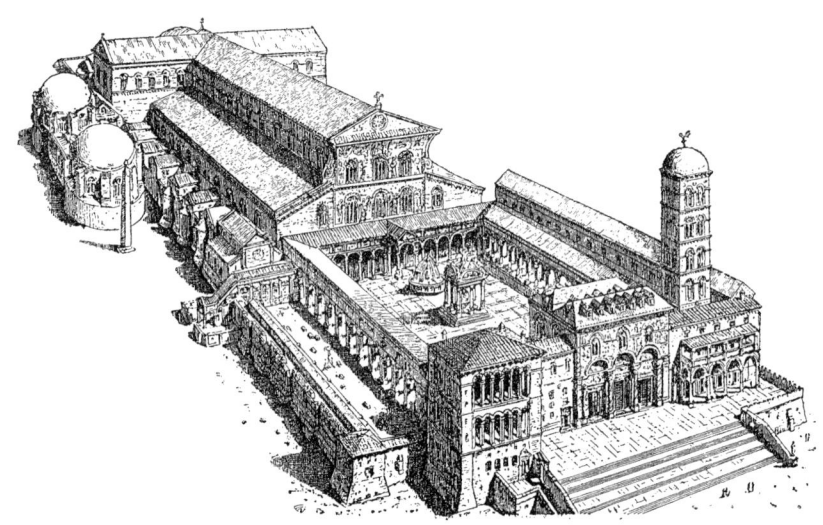

Figure 2. Reconstruction of Old St Peter's Basilica

2

Christianity at the Heart of the Roman Empire

Old St Peter's Basilica on the Vatican Hill

*T*he growth and consolidation of the Church in the first three centuries of its history happened in surprising ways. St Paul, 'Apostle to the Gentiles', was arrested in about 55 CE and brought to Rome to be tried before the emperor. According to Christian tradition, both he and Peter, 'Prince of the Apostles', were executed in Rome in about 64 CE during the persecution of Christians by Nero.[1] As apostles and martyrs, Peter and Paul had immense prestige in the Church, Peter being called the 'rock' on which the Church was founded. Their presence, alive and dead, shifted the centre of Church authority to Rome at the heart of the empire. From at least the time of Pope Stephen I in the middle of the third century, the pope claimed to inherit the authority of Peter within the Church. Pilgrims were drawn to his place of burial to be near the saint when praying for his intercession, so there was a growing pilgrimage to the supposed place of his burial on the Vatican Hill, and soon after Constantine had secured supremacy over the western empire through his victory at the Milvian Bridge in 312 CE, he began building a huge basilica for the Christians. The building was focused on Peter's funerary monument. We are separated from the apostle by almost two millennia, but, even during the 1940s, Pope Pius XII and the dictator Mussolini vied to enhance their own authority through archaeology, Mussolini by creating a Roman imperial processional

route from the Colosseum through the forum, and Pius by excavating the
funerary monument to find the 'bones of the fisherman'. Archaeology matters,
and places matter as existential connections to people and events of the past, so
this chapter begins with the approach to St Peter's in the Vatican.

The Approach

Walking westwards along the bank of the Tiber from the Ponte
Umberto past Castel Sant'Angelo gives a view through the Via della
Conciliazione, providing a long vista of St Peter's Basilica. The building is simply sublime. This long approach gives the visitor time to
reflect on its great beauty and the statement it makes about the
Roman Catholic Church and its unity, but this extended axial view
has been possible only since the 1930s. The decision was taken in 1935
to remove the buildings of the *Borgo* to clear the approach to St Peter's.
It followed Italy's invasion of Ethiopia. The long open link turning
from St Peter's in the Vatican via the Ponte Vittorio Emanuele II to

Figure 3. Distant view of St Peter's Basilica up the Via della Conciliazione

Rome across the Tiber was begun by Mussolini himself, who landed the first blow with a pickaxe during the celebration of the fourteenth anniversary of the 28 October Fascist March on Rome. *Il Duce* was hailed as 'Founder of the Empire and Fascist Italy'.[2] As the name of the street makes clear, this broad avenue was a monument to the reconciliation between the papacy and the Kingdom of Italy. In 1870, the recently united kingdom annexed Rome and the swathe of land across the ankle of the boot of Italy that had constituted the Papal States since Pepin and his son Charlemagne had created them in the eighth century. The dispute between the two states raged until 1929 and the signing of the Lateran Pacts by the Secretary of State to Pius XI, and Mussolini on behalf of King Victor Emanuel III.

The Via della Conciliazione has always been deeply controversial for both political and artistic reasons. Until its creation, the approach to St Peter's was through the narrow streets of the *Borgo*. There had been many designs for the handling of this most important approach, but controversy and expense had imposed a stalemate that was most satisfactory. Squeezing through the constricted streets of the *Borgo* before suddenly emerging into the sweeping embrace of Bernini's

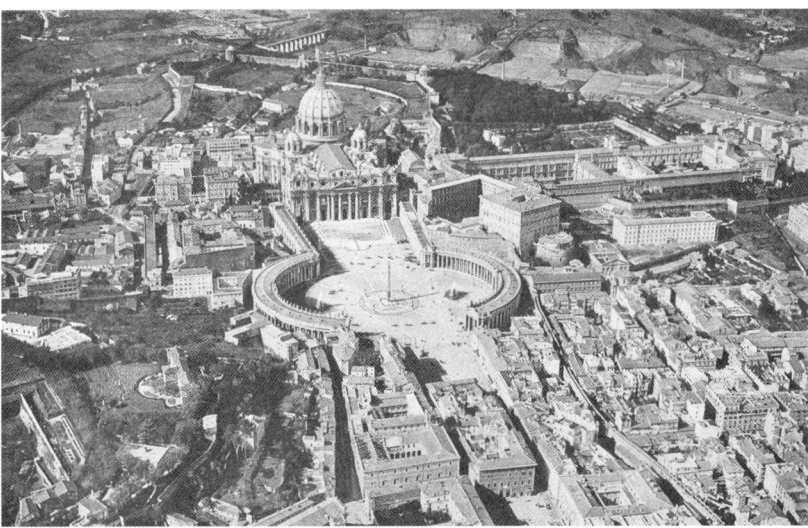

Figure 4. View of the *Borgo* and St Peter's, *c.*1900

colonnade provided a contrast that gave full effect to the sublime scale of St Peter's and its square, which is heart-stoppingly beautiful.

Mounting the great flight of steps of the basilica then sets the heart racing. The gigantic-order columns of the portico force the visitor to reassess the scale and the entrance in humility. The cavernous space retains a kind of abstract silence, despite the milling, though respectful, noise from the crowds. Down the long axis, at the crossing, are the four huge piers that support the great dome (Plate 3), bound at its base by an encircling inscription in Latin from the Gospel of St Matthew: 'You are Peter, and upon this Rock shall I build my Church...I will give you the keys of the kingdom of heaven.' The dome is the world's grandest canopy, sheltering another canopy of bronze by Bernini with twisted columns. Beneath that is the high altar and below that the *confessio*, giving access to what is believed to be the grave of the Prince of the Apostles. Very often it is the secret spaces, buried deep within the architecture, that are the real power-houses. That is certainly true here, where two levels below the nave it is possible to follow the same axial route, but as it was two thousand years ago. First it is necessary to establish the historical context.

From Jerusalem to Rome

In the first century, Rome was the *caput mundi*, the centre of the world, and what happened within, and even near, its walls on the edge of the Vatican Hill would reverberate throughout the world and down the ages. From the arrival of St Paul and the other apostolic founder of the Church of Rome, St Peter, the histories of Christianity, the city of Rome, and the world would be inextricably bound together in this emblematic city. Legal disputes and trials, and not only for the most serious charges, could be brought from distant provinces before the emperor himself in Rome. This is what happened to St Paul, who was falsely accused of bringing a gentile, that is to say, a non-Jew, into the temple of Jerusalem and so polluting it. A riot ensued.

This situation had arisen because of Paul's known missionary work with gentiles at a time when Christianity, under the leadership of the apostle Peter, was effectively still a Jewish sect. During the disturbance (Acts 21.27 ff.), Paul was arrested and bound in chains; ordinarily he could have expected a pretty summary and brutal result, but, as a Roman citizen, he had a right to be tried before the emperor in Rome. First, he came before the retiring local governor, Felix. Soon after that, he came before the new governor, Festus, who arrived in 55 or 56 CE. At that point, Paul chose to be tried at Rome (Acts 25.11–12). Crossing the sea of Adria, the ship carrying Paul ran aground and was wrecked (Acts 27.41), but all on board reached the shore of Malta (Acts 28.1). Three months later, another ship took him to Puteoli, the principal port serving Rome, from where he travelled along the Via Appia to Rome itself (Acts 21.11–16).

With justice for Roman citizens focused on the emperor in Rome, Paul's story was not uncommon, and the Jewish historian Josephus records his own very similar experience in about 61 CE:

> At the time when Felix was procurator of Judaea [before 55 CE], certain priests of my acquaintance, very excellent men, were on a slight and trifling charge sent by him in bonds to Rome to render an account to Caesar [Emperor Nero]. I was anxious to discover some means of delivering these men…I reached Rome after being in great jeopardy at sea. For our ship foundered in the midst of the sea of Adria, and our company of some six hundred souls had to swim all that night. About daybreak, through God's good providence, we sighted a ship of Cyrene, and I and certain others, about eighty in all, outstripped the others and were taken on board. Landing safely at Dicaearchia, which the Italians call Puteoli, I formed a friendship with Aliturus, an actor who was a special favourite of Nero and of Jewish origin. Through him I was introduced to Poppaea, Caesar's consort, and took the earliest opportunity of soliciting her aid to secure the liberation of the priests. Having, besides this favour, received large gifts from Poppaea, I returned to my own country. There I found revolutionary movements already on foot.[3]

Josephus eventually left Rome in 65–6, just after the persecution of Christians by Nero, in which both Peter and Paul are believed to have perished. The revolutionary movements mentioned by Josephus were

to be the initial developments leading to the Jewish War that eventually resulted in the destruction of the temple of Jerusalem in 70 CE.

In Rome, Paul had essentially been put under house arrest, 'preaching the kingdom of God and teaching about the Lord Jesus Christ
quite openly and unhindered'—the words with which Luke ends the
Acts. He closes the narrative at this point in order to show the completion of God's providential delivery from Jerusalem of the good
news of salvation open to all, first to Rome at the heart of empire and
from there, within decades, throughout the Roman world.

At that time, Rome was the very image of universal worldly power.
When the emperors ceased to reside in Rome in the early fourth
century, it was to begin to reconceive itself as the seat of universal
spiritual power, the city of the holy Catholic Church, the City of
God. That would be put within a very particular perspective after the
sack of Rome by Alaric in 410, when Augustine maintained that the
Roman Catholic Church is itself the 'City of God'.

The Site of St Peter's Basilica

The Acts of the Apostles does not follow Peter as far as Rome; in fact,
the first written source firmly connecting Peter with the foundation
of the Church in Rome is Irenaeus' book *Against Heresies*, written
during the time Eleutherius was bishop of Rome from about 175 to
189 CE. Irenaeus gave pride of place among all churches to Rome,
because of its dual foundation by these two great apostles:

> The church that is greatest, most ancient, and known to all, founded
> and set up by the two most glorious apostles Peter and Paul at Rome,
> while showing that the tradition and the faith it proclaims to men
> comes down through the succession of bishops even to us...it is neces-
> sary for every church—that is, the believers from everywhere—to
> agree with this church, in which the tradition from the apostles has
> always been preserved.[4]

The tradition was strong, as was the authority it bestowed, and at the
point when Irenaeus was writing, in the third quarter of the second

century, it was roughly three generations long. So the grandparents of those in authority at the time could themselves have been eyewitnesses of the martyrdom and burial of the apostles Peter and Paul in Rome.

Perhaps as early as the end of the first century CE, until just before Irenaeus was writing, there would have been two attractions to draw people westward out of the city of Rome across the Neronian Bridge over the Tiber, and towards the Vatican Hill. Large crowds would be on their way to games in the Circus of Nero, but a smaller persistent group would bear right along the northern side of the circus, up the hill to a spot honoured as the memorial of the apostle Peter. Tradition maintains that he was martyred on the spine of the circus near the obelisk. He was crucified upside down, probably in 64 CE during the Neronian Persecution.

The *tropaion*, or small architectural memorial trophy, on the hill above the circus is very ancient. Since there is supporting archaeological evidence to suggest that it may well be the grave of Peter himself, it may mark the earliest known burial in the vicinity, though a burial tomb nearby is datable to just a few years later.[5] Another monument of a similar date on the Via Ostiense marked the shrine of St Paul. Both are documented by Bishop Eusebius (historian to Constantine the Great) to at least as far back as the year 200. He quotes from a now-lost dialogue of that date by a churchman called Gaius as saying: 'I can point out the monuments of the victorious apostles. If you will go as far as the Vatican or the Ostian Way, you will find the monuments of those who founded this church.'[6] Archaeology and documentary history have contributed to this picture, but archaeologists, historians, and churches themselves give different weight, and even different dates, to different aspects of the evidence, or they interpret the same evidence differently to make the resulting history coherent within their own wider perspectives.

'On this rock I will build my church'

Peter was an apostolic founder of the Christian community of Rome, a companion of Jesus, and a martyr, so the sites of his death and his nearby last resting place just outside the capital of the empire were of immense importance. Moreover, according to the biblical narrative, Peter had been given the keys to the kingdom by Jesus himself, which gave him a distinct precedence over Paul. The Gospel of Matthew tells of Jesus asking his disciples:

> 'Who do men say that the Son of Man is?' And they said, 'Some say John the Baptist, others say Elijah, and others Jeremiah or one of the prophets.' He said to them, 'But who do you say that I am?' Simon Peter replied, 'You are the Christ, the Son of the living God.' And Jesus answered him, 'Blessed are you, Simon Bar-Jona! For flesh and blood has not revealed this to you, but my Father who is in heaven. And I tell you, you are Peter, and on this rock I will build my church, and the powers of death shall not prevail against it. I will give you the keys of the kingdom of heaven, and whatever you bind on earth shall be bound in heaven, and whatever you loose on earth shall be loosed in heaven.' (Matt. 16:13–20)

As a result of this saying of Jesus, images of Peter are usually identified by a pair of keys he holds. It is by no means obvious exactly what Matthew meant by this, but as early as the middle of the third century, Stephen, the then bishop of Rome, made the first recorded appeal to this text in claiming precedence and authority as Peter's direct successor. The biblical text was extremely useful to Stephen in combination with Irenaeus' text from half a century earlier to settle doctrinal disputes and fight against current heresies. That had been a very painful time, because Stephen was in dispute with St Cyprian of Carthage about the validity of sacraments administered by heretical bishops. Cyprian himself referred specifically to these words of Jesus in his correspondence with Rome, but he left the thrust ambiguous, saying: 'Certainly, the other Apostles also were what Peter was, endued with an equal fellowship both of honour and power; but a commencement is made from unity, that the Church may be set before us as one.'[7] Cyprian received a supportive letter from St Firmilian, Bishop of Caesarea in Cappadocia, who wrote:

> And herein I am justly indignant at such open and manifest folly in Stephen, that he who so boasts of the seat of his episcopate, and contends that he holds the succession from Peter, on whom the

foundations of the Church were laid, introduces many other *rocks*, and *builds* anew many Churches, in that by his authority he maintains baptism among them.[8]

Ironically, he was not so much denying Stephen's authority as complaining that Stephen was using that authority to maintain the validity of baptism administered by heretical bishops who themselves were denying that authority.

Meanwhile, at precisely this date in the middle of the third century, in the frontier trading post of Dura Europos above the River Euphrates, a house church was clearly a thriving little Christian community in a garrison town, despite persecution elsewhere in the Empire. It was a cosmopolitan place, with a whole range of places of worship, including a military temple, temples of Zeus Theos, Zeus Megistos, Artemis, a Temple of Bel, a Mithraeum (very popular with the military), a Temple of Adonis, a synagogue, and this Christian church converted from a typical, large courtyard house near the city wall, with its entrance discretely screening the interior. Archaeological evidence indicates that the house was probably converted about 232 CE.[9] In preparation for an assault by the Sassanids, the walls were strengthened by heaping earth and rubble against them, burying the church. Despite these precautions, the walls were mined, and one of the tunnels collapsed, burying a soldier who had just been paid, and the latest of the coins was dated 256. Because the church had been buried, it was well preserved in the dry desert sand, and it therefore gives a remarkable glimpse of the life of a Christian community on the edge of empire. They clearly continued to worship during the persecution under Emperor Decius, when Origen perished in Palestine, and, contemporary with the fall of Dura, when in 257 St Cyprian was martyred in Carthage in the Valerian persecution. In one of his letters, Cyprian relates that there were many Romans of high rank, including members of the imperial household, who were Christians, and that Emperor Valerian was determined to root them out.[10] By this time, the Church was well rooted at the heart of empire, roots that went back almost two centuries to Peter himself.

The Vatican Necropolis and Peter's Memorial:
The Uses, and Abuses, of History

The circus next to the Vatican Hill had been built in the second quarter of the first century. It seems to have fallen out of use round about a century later, since by that time a tomb had been built against the obelisk in the centre of the circus. Under Roman law, the dead had to be buried outside the city, and a city of the dead, a *necropolis*, had overtaken the games. The cemetery developed parallel to the road and the northern wall of the circus, and, as a result of extensive archaeological excavations under the nave just off the main axis of St Peter's Basilica (Plate 4), you can again walk up the hill along a subsidiary track between two rows of tombs, all facing south towards the circus and its obelisk (which much later, in 1586, was moved to the centre of St Peter's Square by Domenico Fontana). The tombs are mostly large and rather impressive structures, many of them beautifully decorated, so they were clearly owned by families of some social standing and with considerable resources.

By the late fourth century, pilgrims walking up the hill passed the particularly large tomb of the Caetenni and Tullii; the front has terracotta decoration, and the interior is impressive with its red and white architectural plasterwork and fine mosaic floor. Next door but one up the hill is the even larger tomb of the Valerii, dating from about 160 CE. Beginning then, and for generations to come, the owners filled its niches with memorial sculptures of members of their family, the gods, and philosophers.

Just beyond another couple of chambers on the way up the path is a tomb of very special interest, the second-century tomb of the Julii. The mosaic decoration of the vault and in the arches was probably added about a century after it was built—perhaps when the family converted to Christianity. Though the images like the *Sol Invictus* that dominates the middle of the vault are drawn from the pagan tradition, from the decoration of the arches showing a fisherman, a shepherd carrying a sheep, and Jonah and the whale all within a trailing vine, this is clearly a

Christian tomb. Moreover, the funeral practice in this tomb also changed from cremation to burial, reflecting Christian practice.[11] The *Sol Invictus* has been transformed with shining rays in the form of a cross round his head into Christ the Sun of Righteousness, recalling the ascension of Elijah in a chariot. It also nicely reminds the visitor of the by then abandoned circus down the hill behind. The fisherman points to the call of Peter and his brother Andrew, who were fishermen called by Jesus to be fishers of men (Mark 1:16–17). The Good Shepherd is, for a mourner, a comforting image of the care of Christ for the Christian soul. Jonah, who was swallowed by the whale and vomited up safely after three days, was a symbol of hope in the resurrection. The Bacchanalian vine has become Christ the True Vine embracing all.[12]

Many of these tombs, though not this rather small Christian tomb itself, had internal stairs giving access to roof terraces. There the *refrigeria*, or family funeral banquets or picnics with the dead, would be celebrated by both pagans and Christians. From the top of the Christian tomb of the Julii, it would have been possible to see over the terraces of the next two tombs to the top of Peter's memorial in a small open courtyard just further up the hill.

This line of tombs and Peter's memorial were not excavated until 1940. The beginning of the Second World War was not an easy time to pursue archaeology, though Mussolini did a huge amount of hasty 'archaeology' in the 1920s and 1930s, stripping away both housing and accumulated historic layers of Christian Rome to expose the magnificence of imperial Rome. Like Charlemagne, Mussolini was engaged in a *Renovatio Romani Imperii*, a 'revival of the Roman Empire'. In 1938, he associated himself with Augustus, celebrating his bimillennium and restoring his *Ara Pacis*, ironically the 'Altar of Peace', which he moved to a new site beside the Tiber.

The *Biblical Archaeologist*, published by the American Schools of Oriental Research, wrote very positively in its lead article in September 1939:

> Because of the interest of Il Duce and the Fascists in the imperialism of early Rome from Augustus to Trajan, Italian preoccupation with

classical Roman archaeology is most intense just at present. The Bimillennium Augustanum, which culminated on the 23rd of September 1938, brought a sharp focusing of this concern on the culture of the Golden Age of Augustus, in the midst of which Jesus of Nazareth was born.[13]

With hindsight, it is more to the point that Mussolini also created a historic stage-set for fascist parades, including the one to welcome Hitler to Rome in that year: 'One of the most grandiose and permanently impressive archaeological accomplishments of the Mussolini regime in Rome has been the opening up of the long line of ancient imperial fora in a great parkway extending from the Colosseum to Trajan's column.'[14] It was clearly an impressive historic stage-set, but Mussolini's archaeological work was hugely destructive and ill-recorded, considering the many historic layers that were stripped away.

As can clearly be seen with Mussolini, our perspective on history has an immense impact on our creation of the present, particularly when it comes to questions of legitimate authority.

Archaeology, Authority, and the Bones of the Fisherman

It may be that the gesture of Pope Pius XII, to search for the grave and bones of the Fisherman himself as the source of his own authority, was intended as a riposte to Mussolini's highjack of history across the Tiber. In his first encyclical *Summi Pontificatus*, 'On the Unity of Human Society', of 20 October 1939, the new pope refers frequently to the authority of the Chair of Peter, and more directly to the biblical source of his own authority as the apostle's successor: 'On this Corner Stone the Church is built, and hence against her the adversary can never prevail: "The gates of hell shall not prevail" (Saint Matthew xvi.18), nor can they ever weaken her!'[15] Finding the bones of Peter would place a historical seal next to the biblical seal on the charter of that authority. The excavations were carried out by distinguished archaeologists of impeccable reputation,[16] but, when so much is at stake, controversy follows in like measure, and the results of the excavations that began the following year continue to be disputed now.

The excavation below St Peter's was a slow process, altogether different from Mussolini's digging. The pope wanted neither interruption to the life of the basilica, nor publicity, which presented its own particular problems for the archaeologists. The site is difficult; access is limited and always awkward. To cap it all, the fabric into which they were probing is not just venerable but sacred. Even the most responsible archaeology can be destructive, and that had to be severely limited in this context. The result is that evidence would always remain incomplete and contestable. Enough evidence had emerged for Pius XII to announce the discovery of the tomb of St Peter in his Christmas message of 23 December 1950. In 1951, the magnificent archaeological report presented all the evidence and argued convincingly that the *tropaion* referred to by Gaius, and the tomb of Peter, had been discovered.

At a papal audience on 26 June 1968, after tests had been carried out on bones that had been set aside in a storeroom, Pope Paul VI announced that the relics of St Peter had been found:

> We have every reason to believe that we have found a few of the most holy mortal remains of the Prince of the Apostles, Simon, son of Jonah, the fisherman Christ called Peter, him who was chosen by Christ as the foundation of the Church, to whom the Lord entrusted the keys of his kingdom, with the mission to shepherd and reunite his flock.

Not surprisingly, not everyone was convinced, not even all of the archaeologists who had been involved in the excavations.[17] The pope must also have realized that this would not be the end of the matter, because he indicated that the discussion and debate would continue.

Access to the area traditionally identified as the tomb of Peter was from the chapel below the sanctuary behind the high altar and from the *confessio* below it on the other side. Exploration would have to begin from the side of the chapel, and, if work had to be done within the *confessio*, it would have to be done at night. Beginning behind the target site of the traditional location of Peter's tomb, work began in the chapel, the *Capella Clementina*.

Carefully breaking through its Renaissance wall, the archaeologists found another marble and imperial porphyry panelled wall clearly from the time of the Emperor Constantine.[18] They were able to remove part of the panelling to inspect the upper part of the monument, but this was obviously too important a find to disturb further, so they broke through to its left and right. It became evident that Constantine's stone panels encased an older structure that became known as the 'Red Wall'. The forensic detective work continued. Removing more of the Renaissance wall exposed spaces where bits of the Constantinian paving were still in place. Marks on the paving were interpreted as the feet of columns with fixed barriers between them. The remains, the surviving columns reused by Bernini in the piers of the present dome, and a detailed image of the monument carved on an ivory panel of the Pola Casket (now in the Archaeological Museum, Venice), allow reconstruction with a degree of confidence of the Constantinian Memoria and its setting. But what the churchman Gaius might have seen at the end of the second century is less certain. Some also question whether it was at that time the grave of Peter.[19]

In their reconstruction of the original memoria, the excavators proposed that it had been a raised pavement with a disengaged column at either corner framing the niche on the side of the 'Red Wall' towards the *confessio*. They showed the columns supporting a stone entablature with a pedimented frame to the top of the niche. Critics respond that the sparse evidence does not support that degree of detail. Below this was a cavity where the tomb of Peter had traditionally been located. In it were found a few bits of bone, none of them appropriate remains for a first-century man. On the floor were 1,418 coins—one extremely worn example from the time of Augustus, the others dating from 268 CE at the earliest. There was also a sixth- to seventh-century *ex voto* plaque showing two eyes with a cross between, presumably a thank offering for the cure of an eye complaint. Offerings appear to have started only about 270, so what had happened then?[20]

Other Possible Sites for the Tomb of Peter

As so often with archaeology and history, the evidence is made up of fragmentary physical remains and texts (in this case including graffiti) that can be dated and interpreted with more, or less, confidence. All of that has to be fitted into what is already known and believed to be true. So naturally interpretations vary widely. This is not the place to rehearse every scrap of technical evidence, but, in brief, the main problem is that there are two candidates for the burial place of St Peter, this one on the Vatican Hill, and below the Basilica of the Apostles, now called San Sebastiano, on the Via Appia.

There is an entry in the *Liber Pontificalis* that records of Pope Cornelius, who was bishop of Rome between 251 and 253, that:

> In his time, at the request of a certain matron Lucina, he took up the bodies of the holy apostles Peter and Paul from the catacombs by night; first of all the blessed Lucina took the body of St Paul and put it on her estate on the Via Ostiensis close to the place where he was beheaded; the blessed Bishop Cornelius took the body of St Peter and put it near the place where he was crucified, among the bodies of the holy bishops at the temple of Apollo on the Mons Aureus, in the Vatican of the Palace of Nero on the 29th of June.[21]

There are graffiti both on the Vatican monument, interpreted to read *Petros en[i]*, 'Peter is within' (on the wall that has a marble-lined niche), and at San Sebastiano (on the *triclia* or small pavilion used for *refrigeria*), which repeatedly offer prayers to Peter and Paul. At the Vatican there is a memorial, at San Sebastiano there is none. There are texts that can be used to support both as burial places of the apostles, and those concerning San Sebastiano include the movement of remains between sites. At the Vatican there are bones, discovered in a storeroom following an anecdote by a workman—but scientific analysis confirms that they are of a robust first-century male whose ankles and feet are missing—interpreted as having been hacked off when he was removed quickly from the cross.

Conclusions concerning the original burial place of Peter vary. One of the original excavators, Kirschbaum, believed that the memorial marked the original grave, though the other, Ferrua, was never convinced they had found the bones of Peter; other scholars believed that the memorial honoured the place of his martyrdom and that his bones were brought from San Sebastiano to the Vatican later; still others believed that Christians had two different traditions; and, finally, some believed that the bodies had been taken to San Sebastiano for a period, then back to their original graves. The most recent hypothesis is that the bodies of Peter and Paul were buried in San Sebastiano (remembering the original name was the *Basilica Apostolorum*), and that in 251 Pope Cornelius moved the bodies, as the *Liber Pontificalis* says, to the Vatican and the Via Ostiensis.

> The tradition of the victory won in martyrdom by Peter at the Vatican and Paul by the Ostian Highway, reflected the boast of Gaius some half century before, was strong enough to give a pope, in a moment of crisis, the inspiration of rallying Christian sentiment around the field of martyrdom of the two apostolic saints.[22]

This was the time of the Valerian persecution, and the remains could be more safely visited in pagan cemeteries. The argument points out that the coins in the small chamber of Peter's memorial in the Vatican excavations began to be deposited as offerings about this same time. It also maintains that some relics of the apostles remained at San Sebastiano, which would explain the continuation of the cult there.

The arguments point to two main possibilities: first that the remains were taken for a period to San Sebastiano and united there before being returned to their original burial places; or, secondly, that another cult grew up at San Sebastiano around a sanctuary containing 'contact relics' such as cloths left in contact with the apostles' tombs and then brought to San Sebastiano.[23] This latter explanation is less satisfying than the former, but it proceeds from the assumption that the original and continuously occupied tomb had been securely established at Peter's memorial in the Vatican. The currently favoured position accepts the reconstruction of the memorial and assumes that Peter's body was originally buried in the earth at its base. The archaeology is consistent with the tradition that was itself strong enough for the

Emperor Constantine to feel constrained to overcome the considerable difficulties of the Vatican site to build a great basilica focused on the memorial that marked Peter's grave. The currently favoured position is that Peter's body was later removed as disarticulated bones and walled up in the marble-lined niche in the graffiti wall bearing the words 'Peter is within'. This places little weight on the passage about Pope Cornelius in the *Liber Pontificalis*, which is, after all, unreliable in parts, especially concerning the early bishops. So, details of the reconstructed monument may be in dispute, but the weight of evidence indicates that this is the original tomb of Peter.

The Building

The terraces on top of the tombs on the Vatican Hill, where pre-Constantinian mourners would have gathered to participate in their *refrigeria* or memorial picnics, are at the level of the original pavement of the great basilica built by Constantine in honour of Peter. In the basilica itself, those banquets would continue to be held at least until 396 CE, when Pammachius filled the vast nave with guests at the funeral banquet for his wife Paula.[24] The basilica was built primarily as a memorial, both to Peter and to those who wanted to be buried near him to benefit from his great sanctity. Constantine had commissioned the building of the Lateran Basilica for the Bishop of Rome, possibly within weeks of his victory over Maxentius. St Peter's Basilica was begun a few years later, usually dated to 319 in the time of Pope Sylvester I. When the apse was demolished in 1592, brickstamps with Constantine's name were found, so that part at least must have been built prior to 337, the death of Constantine.[25]

The site surrounding the memorial of Peter and extending eastwards was an exceptionally difficult place to build a vast basilica, because it would have covered a large cemetery. There were laws forbidding the desecration of tombs, and here it was necessary to destroy some, and fill in a very large number of others, in order to create a vast platform to provide a new floor level at the height of the roof terraces. This left the porphyry and marble-clad memorial 2.34 metres above the patterned marble floor and just forward of the apse. The memorial, encased in white marble banded with porphyry, was sheltered under a baldacchino with a twisted column at each corner, supporting an entablature with ribs forming an open crown. There were columns left and right, creating a screen just within the apse. There was no fixed altar, and a moveable wooden table was probably used.

The basilica that rose to shelter the sacred monument was only the second basilica to have been built for a strictly religious purpose, the first being the Lateran, or *Basilica Constantiniana*. Before that, basilicas were used as law courts or public markets, where bargains were struck before an image of the emperor. As Christianity was integrated into the imperial system by Constantine, it would have made sense to use this building type for Christian gatherings, where the ceremonial was beginning to borrow from that used in the imperial court.[26] St Peter's Basilica was approached axially from the east up a long series of steps through a portico into a colonnaded courtyard with a central fountain in the form of a pinecone under a bronze baldacchino. Colonnades along the sides were built during the late fifth century, and in the early sixth century it was fully enclosed.

A number of entrances gave access to the nave and double aisles of the huge interior, measuring about 391 × 208 Roman feet. A high clerestory lit the nave. A very good impression of the interior is given in frescoes by Domenico Tasseli in the side chapels of the crypt. Before Old St Peter's was completely demolished, drawings were also made by Bramante, Peruzzi, Sangallo, and van Heemskerck. The nave and aisles ended in a large transept, creating the first cross-shaped plan, with St Peter's monument on axis on the chord of the apse. There is some evidence that the transept was built first, with the nave and perhaps the second aisle added later. With no fixed altar, the liturgical function was subordinate to the memorial one. It was a pilgrimage church from the beginning, its vast size anticipating the enormous crowds. It was the premier pilgrimage site of the west, with the added attraction of St Paul and all the many other saints and martyrs in nearby Rome.[27]

After 324, when Constantine defeated Licinius, emperor of the east, at Chrysopolis opposite Byzantium at the entrance to the Bosphoros, Constantine gave rich endowments to St Peter's in the form of extensive lands in the eastern empire. That ensured there would be resources to continue to embellish the structure. It would appear that the basilica was substantially complete by 329 or 330, when Constantine's mother, the Augusta Helena, died, because the *Liber Pontificalis* records their gift of a large gold cross weighing 150 pounds. By 400, there was a coffered ceiling and mosaics above the shrine, and by the middle of the fifth century there was a mosaic on the main facade of the Lamb of God, worshipped by the four and twenty elders.

Constantine's Conversion and the Politics of Empire

Constantine had already built the enormous and magnificent *Basilica Constantiniana* at the Lateran for the Christians, who were still being persecuted in the Eastern Empire, sometime between 312 or 313 and 318, so there is a serious question as to why he would build a second huge imperial basilica for this newly favoured religion, and why just to honour Peter rather than Peter and Paul, or even just Paul, where St Paul Outside the Walls now stands. The *Liber Pontificalis* claims that he did build 'a basilica to St Paul at the suggestion of Bishop Sylvester', but some consider the entry to be unreliable and think it may have referred to Constantine II, his son.[28] The answer might be found in the reason for the conversion of Constantine—however complete that conversion might have been. Bishop Eusebius, Constantine's friend and historian, described Constantine's vision:

> If someone else had reported it, it would perhaps not be easy to accept; but since the victorious Emperor himself told the story to the present writer a long while after, when I was privileged with his acquaintance

and company, and confirmed it with oaths, who could hesitate to believe the [emperor's own] account, especially when the time which followed provided evidence for the truth of what he said? About the time of the midday sun, when the day was just turning, he said he saw with his own eyes, up in the sky and resting over the sun, a cross-shaped trophy formed from light, and a text attached to it which said, 'By this conquer'. Amazement at the spectacle seized both him and the whole company of soldiers which was then accompanying him on a campaign he was conducting somewhere, and witnessed the miracle.

He was, he said, wondering to himself what the manifestation might mean; then while he meditated, and thought long and hard, night overtook him, Thereupon, as he slept, the Christ of God appeared to him with the sign which had appeared in the sky, and urged him to make a copy of the sign which had appeared in the sky, and use this as protection against the attacks of the enemy.[29]

'Who could hesitate to believe?', asks Eusebius, giving away that some probably did. We tend to hesitate too, but the sign in the sky has been explained by one commentator as a natural phenomenon that under the right atmospheric conditions would have appeared just about over Peter's memorial on the Vatican Hill from the direction of the Milvian Bridge.[30] The more cynical might say that divine intervention leading to a military victory would put Constantine in a very strong position for the future. Most importantly, it would bring the Christians, who had been extremely resistant to forced allegiance (which had to be shown by sacrificing to the emperor), instantly into the imperial fold and provide a focus for pilgrimage.

Christians were a large and growing constituency, with tens of thousands at the least and some say hundreds of thousands in Rome alone.[31] They were well organized and incredibly loyal to their leaders and their God. As a force for good (that is to say, the good of the empire and the emperor), they could be a force for unity in an empire threatened with fragmentation. At the same time, Constantine could not afford to alienate the almost wholly pagan aristocracy of Rome, and, on the Arch of Constantine erected by 315 for him by the senate next to the Colosseum, he is shown very much within the mould of his imperial predecessors, with his own features recut on marble panels that had originally shown Hadrian carrying out the expected duties of the imperial office, including sacrifice. There is no Christian imagery, nor any reference to the miraculous sign, on the triumphal arch. The only possible connection is above the panel showing his victory at the Milvian Bridge on the side next to the Colosseum. There is a roundel showing *Sol Invictus*, but in this context it remains deeply ambiguous at best. He would retain this symbol on his coinage until 320–1, and the consecration coin struck after his death shows him as a charioteer (similar to the *Sol Invictus*), with a divine hand reaching down to him from above. Whose divine hand was that? Both pagans and Christians could interpret it within their own traditions, which allowed a unity of purpose in honouring the emperor. In death he was given the traditional title *divus*, but then so were later Christian Byzantine emperors.

If the importance of unity under the emperor played a part in his conversion, then competing Christianities could not be allowed to fragment the Church community, which was beset by heresies. Pilgrimage would help establish a centralized orthodoxy and weaken local competing Christianities. Furthermore, for a century and a half at least since the time of Stephen I, the bishops of Rome had maintained that their authority and primacy stemmed from Peter. That being the case, Sylvester might well have convinced Constantine that a basilica dedicated to Peter and focused on the grave of the martyred Prince of the Apostles would enhance the unity to be found in the bishop of Rome as his successor. In the event, Constantine would foster the orthodoxy and unity of the Church by presiding over its councils and settling its disputes (see Chapter 1, 'Constantine and Christian Unity'), while at the same time retaining his distance by putting off baptism until shortly before his death.

Whatever the motivation, Constantine showed his favour on a magnificent scale, both in the privileges granted to the bishops and clergy and in the lavish buildings to house their ceremonies and memorials. St Peter's Basilica was of a magnificence and on a scale to enhance the prestige and authority of the bishops of Rome. It was approached up long steps and across a garden called 'paradise' past the large bronze pinecone fountain, still to be found in the Vatican museums on the steps of the Belvedere niche. The facade was covered with mosaic above doors opening into a tall nave with double aisles on either side. The nave was almost as long as the present one, and in the distance in a transverse hall just in front of the apse was the marble and imperial porphyry memorial of Peter under a baldacchino. There were gold and silver furnishings, coffered ceilings, and glittering mosaics. All this was an indication of the prestige of Peter—and of the bishop of Rome, who had also been granted imperial honours, including being greeted by genuflection.

The Chair of Peter and *Romanitas*

Rome was still the *caput mundi*, and the senate still met to ratify laws, but by this time more as an exercise of privilege than of power. Rome was the heart of empire, rather than its capital. The *de facto* capital was wherever the emperor was resident. The defeated Maxentius was the last emperor to be permanently resident in Rome. In 324, Constantine marked out the walls of what was to become a new capital, and in 330 named it Constantinople, the 'Second Rome'. In 366, at the death of Pope Liberius, who had been in exile, the Roman Church was beset by factionalism. During Liberius' exile, the Arian emperor Constantius had named Felix to administer in his stead, but he failed to gain the papacy for himself on Liberius' death. Two rival factions met to elect the next pope, and the first anti-pope: one faction elected the deacon Ursinus, the other the deacon Damasus, who was better connected. In the ensuing struggle, well over a hundred were killed. Having secured the succession, Damasus built churches for Roman martyrs. He composed verse inscriptions in their honour and to commemorate the peace and unity of the Roman Church. Both were desperately needed. One of these inscriptions was in St Peter's baptistery built by Damasus (366–85) near the font: 'One chair of Peter, one baptismal washing'. The implication is that, just as baptism is what makes a Christian, so the recognition of the authority of the pope is another defining characteristic.

The Basilica of St Paul Outside the Walls was completed by Damasus, perhaps recalling Irenaeus' appeal to the foundation of the Roman Church by both Peter and Paul, or perhaps just as a belt and braces approach to authority.[32] As far as the bishop of Rome was concerned, the absence of the emperor over the coming century meant that he was free to consolidate his position. By the time the pagan cults had been suppressed in 391 (after which hitherto staunchly pagan senators were rather quick to convert),[33] the pope increasingly gained secular as well as spiritual authority in the city and its neighbouring territories. His power base, the seat of his authority, was not his cathedral in the Lateran, but St Peter's Basilica on the Vatican Hill.

As the inheritor of Peter, Prince of the Apostles, the bishop of Rome was the focus of unity and orthodoxy. This gave the Church remarkable resilience during times of persecution, when those who refused to pour libations to the emperor as a god were guilty of treason and subject to execution. That unity, the loyalty of Christians to their bishops, and resilience were much needed by the empire, which was stretched across a vast geography and liable to fragmentation because of its huge diversity. This capacity for unity, loyalty, and resilience alone would have been attractive to Constantine, quite apart from any vision he might have had, or promptings from his mother, Helena, who may already have converted by the time of Constantine's victory at the Milvian Bridge. Even in the middle of the third century, Pope Stephen I appealed to his status as Peter's successor to establish his primacy, which was grudgingly recognized. When Constantine built St Peter's as a second great basilica for the heir of Peter, and gave the Bishop of Rome imperial honours, it began to look as though he was recognizing and enhancing that authority in order to integrate it into his own imperial project. It did indeed revitalize the empire, at least for another century, but it changed the nature of the Church forever.

Figure 5. Distant view of Hagia Sophia, Istanbul

3

New Rome and the Horizons of Empire

Hagia Sophia in Istanbul

*T*he capital of the Roman Empire moved to Byzantium in 324 CE and *was named Constantinople after its founder, Constantine the Great. He dedicated the city on 11 May 330. By the accession of Justinian I in 527, the western half of the empire had been lost, and he began to restore former territories in North Africa, Spain, Dalmatia, and Italy, including Rome itself. Belisarius was his chief general in these victories. In early 532, however, when Belisarius was back in Constantinople from successful campaigning against Persia, riot and arson came within a hair's breadth of toppling Justinian. The resolve of Empress Theodora and the military skill of Belisarius saved the day, but the fire destroyed the original Hagia Sophia (the Church of the Holy Wisdom of God), the Great Church built by Constantine and finished by his son Constantius in 360. It was a very real question in Byzantine theology and imperial polity whether God had deserted Justinian. The charred ruins of Hagia Sophia posed the question, and Justinian needed to reply quickly and definitively with the greatest church the world had ever seen, one that would embody both the earthly and heavenly kingdoms and provide a setting for the integration of imperial and sacred ceremonial, a ceremonial that would embody that imperial theology for almost another thousand years.*

The Approach

Flying into Istanbul is a stunning experience, especially when the plane is placed in a holding pattern encircling the city, with the Hagia Sophia lit up on its promontory above the sea. Then the tram ride in from Ataturk Airport closely follows the ceremonial route of the emperor, from the former site of the Hebdomon military ground near the airport, via the Golden Gate, past the *fora* and on to the *milion*, the marker from which all distances in the Byzantine empire were measured. The *milion* stands at the north-west corner of the huge Sultan Ahmet Square, with Hagia Sophia to the north on the left, the open space of the former Augustaion to the east, and the dual carriageway to the south on the right, occupying the site of the racetrack of the Hippodrome, while the open space stretching towards the Blue Mosque was once covered by the vast Sacred Palace.

Hagia Sophia, the Sacred Palace, and the Hippodrome together formed a model of the Byzantine Empire. They configure the complex interrelationships of religion, politics, and populace. Their physical relationships, borders, intersections, boundaries, restricted spaces, and processional pathways define, separate, and link functional spaces, giving rise to the metonymy of architectural elements in relation to social, political, and religious elements. This symbolic linking is enacted in the ceremonial use of the spaces and is articulated in ceremonial texts. The Byzantine example finds its focus in Hagia Sophia, built between 532 and 537 CE, and how it gathered into itself the borders and geographical horizons of empire that are physically present in the colourful decorative geology of its stonework. The heart of Byzantium embodied imperial theology, politics, and power relationships. The ceremonial texts that will guide the exploration of this matrix of meaning include ancient writings in the formal genres of panegyric (acclamation), ekphrasis (detailed description of works of art as a literary device), and the antiquarian record of the *De Cerimoniis* of the Byzantine Emperor Constantine VII

Porphyrogenitus (913–59). All this is at work in the dramatic destruction by fire, and restoration by the Emperor Justinian, of the heart of Constantinople.

Riot and Revolt in Constantinople

Towards the end of 531, Emperor Justinian summoned his general Belisarius back to Constantinople from the defence of the eastern frontier in the war against Persia. As a fragile peace was being brokered, an unexpected, but far greater, threat struck at the heart of Byzantium. The Blue and Green 'factions' were supporters of the opposing sides in the games in the circus or Hippodrome. Football hooligans can be pretty unruly, but the Greens and the Blues frequently resorted to murder, assassination, and arson, and they permeated every aspect of society, including politics and religion. There were important credal differences between them, which at the time were matters of everyday debate on the streets. Greens were, on the whole, Monophysite (believing that Christ was divine only), while the Blues were Orthodox (Christ was both human and divine). Justinian, like his uncle the emperor Justin, was a Blue and Orthodox, though Empress Theodora was from a Monophysite background.[1] The antagonism of the factions frequently bubbled into public disorder and even riot. Usually it was easily suppressed, and the fires quickly brought under control, but, as the year 532 opened, some rioters were being led away to execution, and an unexpected alliance between the factions released the captives and emptied the prisons, and riot became rebellion against a corrupt administration. Officials were indiscriminately murdered, and fires ripped through the city, where all but the monumental buildings were closely packed wooden structures. The public baths, part of the Sacred Palace itself, and Constantine's Great Church, Hagia Sophia, the Church of the Holy Wisdom, were swept away in the conflagration, and the Hippodrome, including the *kathisma* (or imperial box), which was effectively part of

the palace, was occupied by the mob. The watchword of the insur-
rectionists was *Nika*, 'Conquer'.

These monuments at the heart of the capital were a diagram of the
empire, within which the complex interrelationships of religion,
politics, and the populace were negotiated through ceremonial
encounters. In a highly structured society where every formal gesture
was laden with meaning, such a violent assault on, and ultimate
destruction of, this physical matrix of meaning was a devastating blow
to the stability of the empire. On the basis of the theology of empire,
set out by Bishop Eusebius, friend and counsellor of Constantine the
Great, it was all too easy to conclude that God had abandoned
Justinian. If imperial power could not be seen to function, could the
limes, the boundaries, the horizons of empire, hold? Or would they
simply implode?

Holed up in the palace, Justinian dismissed the worst and most senior
officials, John of Cappadocia and Tribunianus of Pamphylia, but the
insurrection continued unabated. Justinian suspected danger from two
nephews of the late emperor Anastasius and sent them away from the
palace. In the event, they were seized by the crowd, and one of them,
Hypatius, was taken to the Forum of Constantine and proclaimed
emperor in a makeshift ceremony. Justinian and his loyal officials were
discussing means of flight when Empress Theodora dismissed such
talk, saying:

> the present time, above all others, is inopportune for flight, even though
> it bring safety. For while it is impossible for a man who has seen the
> light not also to die, for one who has been an emperor it is unendurable
> to be a fugitive. May I never be separated from this purple, and may I
> not live that day on which those who meet me shall not address me as
> mistress. If, now, it is your wish to save yourself, O Emperor, there is no
> difficulty. For we have much money, and there is the sea, here the boats.
> However consider whether it will not come about after you have been
> saved that you would gladly exchange that safety for death. For as for
> myself, I approve an ancient saying that royalty is a good burial-shroud.[2]

With these words, she turned what seemed an unstoppable tide.
Justinian and his loyal retinue were galvanized into action. General

Belisarius, back from engagement in war with the Persians, had with him a following of soldiers seasoned in the recent campaign. Belisarius moved against Hypatius, who by this time was installed in the *kathisma*, or imperial box (in the middle of the eastern side of the Hippodrome), attached to the palace, and the stadium was filled with a huge milling crowd. Belisarius and his soldiers rushed the disordered crowd, and they fled in the direction of another detail of soldiers pouring in from an entrance that the contemporary historian Procopius called 'the Gate of Death'. Procopius recorded these events, claiming that more than 30,000 died that day. Hypatius was taken and executed the following day. Theodora had saved Justinian's throne, though the heart of Byzantium was now a smouldering ruin, including the original Church of the Holy Wisdom built by Constantine.

That very building, the Great Church, had been begun as part of Constantine's foundation of his new capital, Constantinople. As Justinian's official historian, Procopius was eager to establish that the first Hagia Sophia was not completed until 360 by Constantine's son Constantius,

> more or less 34 years after its foundations had been laid by Constantine, the Victorious Augustus. This dedication was carried out...the 16th day before the Kalends of March [14 February]...At the dedication, the Emperor Constantius Augustus presented many offerings, namely vessels of gold and silver of great size and many covers for the holy altar woven with gold and precious stones, and furthermore, various golden curtains [*amphithura*] for the doors of the church and other of gold cloth for the outer doorways.[3]

This church was to be the cathedral of a bishop second only in authority to the pope himself. The form of the original building was probably very like Constantine's other great basilicas at Jerusalem (the Great Church or Church of the Holy Sepulchre) and Rome (St Peter's and the *Basilica Constantiniana* in the Lateran)—that is to say, it was another double-aisled basilica preceded by a large atrium. The only part of this whole complex in Constantinople to survive the conflagration was Constantine's *skeuophylakion*, that is to say the *diaconicon* or sacristy where they kept the treasures, including some given by Constantius at the dedication.

It was to this first church that the 'golden-tongued' St John Chrysostom was brought under protest in 398 to be made bishop of Constantinople. A famous preacher, he would hold forth for as long as two hours from a throne he had placed in the middle of the church on the ambo. Presumably this was to make himself heard better over the continuing murmur of the milling crowd. With the connivance of the hostile empress Eudoxia, Chrysostom was deposed in 404, and Hagia Sophia was badly damaged by a fire that started near the ambo during the resulting riot. Hagia Irene, the Church of the Holy Peace, only a few hundred yards away, took over the cathedral's function until 415, when Hagia Sophia, restored by Theodosius II, was rededicated on 10 October.

The Ceremonial Core and its Elements

After the complete destruction in the Nika Riots, it was blindingly obvious that the monumental elements of the ceremonial core of the imperial city had to be rebuilt. This core was still a direct expression of the theology of empire, as established by Eusebius, and not yet (as it would be by the time of Constantine VII Porphyrogenitus and his *Book of Ceremonies*) a dusty set of props for keeping up appearances. Still, as Constantine VII maintained, 'the harmonious working of the imperial order at court [was] an index of the empire's general health'.[4]

The rebuilding of the ceremonial core, including Hagia Sophia, was described by Procopius in his volume on *The Buildings*. He had been appointed advisor to the youthful general Belisarius when he was made commander in the east, and, as his advisor, Procopius wrote an eye-witness history of changing frontiers of the empire in his books on *The Wars*. Books I–VII were complete by 550, and book VIII not long after. The defence of the boundaries, or *limes*, was one important imperial function. Other closely related imperial expressions were religious harmony, the rule of law, and building. Not long after the completion of those books (perhaps in 554–5 or 559–60[5]), he produced the volume on *The Buildings*. It was a sustained panegyric, or paean of praise, perhaps commissioned by Justinian himself.

In the opening chapter, Procopius ticks off each of these imperial achievements, referring to the expulsion of barbarians from the empire, the addition of states and their transformation, the defence of orthodoxy, the Justinianic code of law, and the prosperity of the state, ending: 'Furthermore, he strengthened the Roman domain, which everywhere lay exposed to the barbarians, by a multitude of soldiers, and by constructing strongholds he built a wall along all its remote frontiers.'[6] Much of the volume is concerned with these fortifications along the boundaries of the empire, but he begins at its heart with the rebuilding of Hagia Sophia.

As rebuilt by Justinian, the public square giving access to the main entrances of Hagia Sophia, the Senate House, and the Chalkê Gate of the Sacred Palace was called the Augustaion. At its centre at the west end near the *milion* was a great column on a large square base and supporting an equestrian statue of Justinian. Initially, it seems odd that it had its back to the city, facing east. Procopius explained:

> The Emperor...is habited like Achilles...And he looks towards the rising sun, directing his course, I suppose, against the Persians. And in his left hand he holds a globe, by which the sculptor signifies that the whole earth and sea are subject to him, yet he has neither sword nor spear nor any other weapon, but a cross stands upon the globe which he carries, the emblem by which alone he has obtained both his Empire and his victory in war. And stretching forth his right hand toward the rising sun and spreading out his fingers, he commands the barbarians in that quarter to remain at home and to advance no further.[7]

Like the pinprick at the centre of a circle made by a pair of compasses, this figure of the emperor defines and maintains the horizons of empire under the sign of the cross.

Opposite the statue on the south-east corner of the Augustaion was the Senate House, which was also rebuilt by Justinian. On the south of the square was the Chalkê, or Bronze Gate, of the Great Palace, the section destroyed in the riots. Though Procopius does not describe the rest of the complex, saying that 'you know the lion, as they say, by its claw',[8] he does describe the gate's architectural form and dwells on the imagery of its ceiling:

> So, this entrance, which they call Chalkê, is of the following sort ... And the whole ceiling boasts of its pictures, not having been affixed with wax melted and applied to the surface, but set with tiny cubes of stone beautifully coloured in all hues, which represent human figures and all other kinds of subjects. The subjects of these pictures I will now describe. On either side is war and battle, and many cities are being captured, some in Italy, some in Libya; and the Emperor Justinian is winning victories through his General Belisarius, and the General is returning to the Emperor, and his whole army is intact, and he gives him spoils, both kings and kingdoms and all things that are most prized among men. In the centre stand the Emperor and the Empress Theodora, both seeming to rejoice and to celebrate victories over the King of the Vandals and the King of the Goths, who approach them as prisoners of war to be led into bondage. Around them stands the Roman Senate, all in festal mood. This spirit is expressed by the cubes of the mosaic, which by their colours depict exultation on their very countenances. So they rejoice and smile as they bestow on the Emperor honours equal to those of God, because of the magnitude of his achievements.[9]

The subject of the mosaics is again about the horizons of empire, and their positioning at this key transitional space between Hagia Sophia, the public square, and the Sacred Palace reveals the importance of events on the *limes* to the state of the centre of empire—so important in fact that Justinian was given 'honours equal to those of God'. Of course, all this monumental art has been lost, but the quality must have been equal to, or surpassed in their unusual emotional vitality, the contemporary and rather hieratic portraits of Justinian and Theodora in San Vitale, or contemporary work excavated between 1935 and 1954 deep in the palace behind where the Blue Mosque now stands.

The Great Church: Hagia Sophia

On the opposite side of the public square from this great Bronze Gate was Hagia Sophia. Before the Nika Riot, the church building previously standing there had been the work of Constantine the Great, as repaired by Theodosius II between 404 and 415 after another fire resulting from another riot. Since more than a decade had been needed just to repair the Great Church then, things must have looked very bleak indeed now that both Hagia Sophia and Hagia Irene had been utterly destroyed along with much of the centre of the city. Justinian had turned this near-fatal disaster into triumph, and, as Procopius said, the new buildings became standing evidence of a reign that made even the glories of Cyrus the Great look like 'a sort of child's play'.[10] Procopius said that he had embarked on his book on the buildings of Justinian because otherwise posterity would not believe that all were the work of one man. The greatest building of all was described first:

> Some men of the common herd, all the rubbish of the city, once rose up against the Emperor Justinian in Byzantium, when they brought about the rising called the Nika Insurrection, which has been described by me in detail and without any concealment in the Books on the Wars. And by way of shewing that it was not against the Emperor alone that they had taken up arms, but no less than against God himself, unholy wretches that they were, they had the hardihood to fire the Church of the Christians, which the people of Byzantium call 'Sophia', an epithet that they have most appropriately invented for God, by which they call His temple; and God permitted them to accomplish this impiety, foreseeing what an object of beauty this shrine was destined to be transformed. So the whole church at that time lay a charred mass of ruins. But the Emperor Justinian built not long afterwards a church so finely shaped that if anyone had enquired of the Christians before the burning if it would be their wish that the church should be destroyed and one like this should take its place, shewing them some sort of model of the building we now see, it seems to me that they would have prayed that they might see their church destroyed forthwith, in order that the building might be converted into its present form.[11]

Justinian is portrayed in this text, and around four centuries later, in the tenth or possibly early eleventh century (the dating is controversial), in a mosaic in the tympanum above the vestibule to the narthex of Hagia Sophia, as at least the equal of Constantine (see frontispiece). In the centre is the Virgin enthroned with the Holy Child on her lap, with Constantine on her left offering the city he had founded, and in the position of precedence on her right hand is Justinian, offering a model of the magnificent church beyond the portal. Justinian had demonstrated his military power in dealing with the revolt, but he had to demonstrate continuing divine favour in order to maintain his authority and legitimacy as emperor. He had to rebuild the Hagia Sophia as the icon of empire and leave no one, neither his contemporaries nor generations to come, in doubt that he, Justinian, was the equal of Theodosius and of Constantine the Great himself. This later mosaic above the entrance to the narthex is proof that he succeeded.

Justinian was able to command the greatest craftsmen and the very best materials from every region of the empire. The work was overseen by Anthemius of Tralles and Isidore of Miletus, two great master builders. The greatest building in the world would be in every sense the embodiment of empire and of the legitimacy of Justinian's power. The speed with which he re-established his imperial power was clearly reflected by the speed of construction. The materials were evidence of his immense wealth and the geographical extent of his sway. The speed of construction was due to his driving force. The astonishing innovation of the design and the sublime scale of the Great Church could be accomplished only with divine support. The greatest building in the world could be realized only by the greatest man in the world; who could resist his will? That is certainly the message of Procopius' presentation of the building. This section of *The Buildings* rises from panegyric to full ekphrasis.

Procopius recounted how it was not just immense financial resources that Justinian provided, but Justinian's own intellectual and spiritual powers. He relates how the master builders themselves, when at a loss how to solve the most difficult engineering problems or avert impending disaster, would turn to the emperor 'and straightway the Emperor, impelled by I know not what, but I suppose by God (for he is not a master-builder)' would command a course of action that would save the situation. 'And if this story were without witness, I am well aware that it would have seemed a piece of flattery and altogether incredible; but since there are available many witnesses of what then took place, we need not hesitate . . .'[12] The very engineering miracles that allowed the structure to stand, were presented as testimony to the greatness of Justinian.

Ceremonial Choreography and the Magnificence of Staging

This divine favour was about power, but more importantly it was about imperial legitimacy. The legitimacy of a Byzantine emperor was not entirely by family inheritance, since the throne was not the possession of a single family by right, even though it tended to pass to someone 'born in the purple'. This degree of uncertainty in the succession made the transition of power an exceedingly dangerous moment, and the ceremonial surrounding imperial accession enacts both the assumption of military power and the bestowal of legitimate temporal sway by divine blessing.

In *The Book of Ceremonies*, an ancient rite is described from the middle of the century before Justinian's reign for the accession of Leo I, proclaimed emperor by the army in 457. It started at the military parade ground, the Hebdomon, outside the Theodosian walls of Constantinople at the seventh milestone. The *labara*, or military standards with Christ's monogram, lay on the ground as a sign of the dejection of the empire without an emperor, and all those present prayed for God's approval of the army's choice. Divine election was the foundation of imperial legitimacy. Army commanders then placed a circlet on Leo's head and another in his right hand, and the standards were raised with a shout of triumph—the prayer that followed included the words 'God has given you, may God protect you!'[13] At this, the man became an embodiment of empire. He was then screened from sight by military shields while being vested with the imperial cloak, a diadem, a lance, and a shield. When he was revealed again, the people prostrated themselves and acclaimed him. The clergy departed to await him in Hagia Sophia, restored a few decades before by Theodosius II in 415. The emperor retired to the Church of the Hebdomon, where there was a head-reliquary of St John the Baptist, the forerunner of Christ, and placed his crown and offerings on the altar as a sign of his dedication of his reign to God, who had granted sovereignty to him.[14] The emperor then rode to another sanctuary of John the Baptist, most likely near the Golden Gate of Constantinople, where his crown was again dedicated at the altar.

The procession then took the new sovereign through to the Constantinian walls, where he was met by the Keeper of the Palace and a cross. He was clothed in purple, and, mounted on a chariot, he was preceded by the cross through the gate to the Forum of Constantine. There he was met by the prefect of the city and the Senate before continuing to the Augustaion, or imperial square between the palace and Hagia Sophia. He performed the liturgy of entry to Hagia Sophia (Plate 5), removing his crown just inside the Imperial Door at a place specially marked in the pavement. Processing with the patriarch, he went directly into the sanctuary to offer gifts on the altar, and then retired to the *metatorion* (the imperial enclosure) in the eastern bay of the south aisle or to the throne in the mid-section, depending on the nature of the occasion. Paul the Silentiary described 'a space separated by a wall, reserved for the Ausonian emperor on solemn festivals. Here my sceptered king, seated on his customary throne, lends his ear to [the reading of] the sacred books.'[15] On leaving the church, the emperor received his crown from the patriarch on a pavement marked in the same way as the one by the Imperial Door; while in the church, he was in the religious domain of divine sovereignty.[16] Removing the crown in any sacred place was a recognition that sovereignty ultimately belonged to the King of kings and was only given in stewardship

Figure 6. Hagia Sophia, Istanbul: pavement inside the Imperial Door

until resumed at the Second Coming. It was a theme to be taken up again in the west by Charlemagne at his imperial church in Aachen.

To assume imperial authority, the new emperor had been elected by the army, proclaimed by the people, and ratified by the Senate, but he needed divine election too. The ancient ceremonial, described in *The Book of Ceremonies* by Constantine VII Porphyrogenitus in the tenth century, mimes the whole process, traversing the territory of each, transforming from a military display of the assumption of power outside the city at the Hebdomon military parade ground, to an *adventus* as triumphal entry through the Golden Gate, to various political encounters receiving homage, to a religious rite in Hagia Sophia celebrating divine election. The emperor of the earthly realm was subject to the Emperor of Heaven, but furthermore, within the Eusebian theological model developed for Constantine, the kingdom of this world was a direct reflection of the heavenly kingdom and divine rule. The Great Church was the bridge. The emperor was the personal embodiment of the empire, as mimed in the ceremonial; and the Great Church was the structural embodiment of both the earthly and the heavenly kingdoms.

Since the mob had reduced the seats of Justinian's power and legitimacy to charred ruins, giving the distinct appearance that divine favour had been withdrawn, it had been essential that Justinian demonstrate that this destruction was providential, that what would arise was divinely inspired, and that it should be accomplished quickly. Astonishingly, it took just five years and ten months to create this most wonderful building. To accomplish this, there were 10,000 men divided into two competitive teams, one on the north and one on the south. The logistics of the procurement of tons of materials and distributing them as needed to keep this army of workers on such a punishing schedule is nothing short of astonishing. The result was seen as miraculous: as Procopius wrote of the new Hagia Sophia: 'God permitted them to accomplish this impiety, foreseeing into what an object of beauty this shrine was destined to be transformed... The Christians... would have prayed that they might see their church destroyed forthwith, in order that the building might be converted into its present form.'[17] The scale is sublime, with the dome more than a hundred feet across. Justinian had the dome and the vaults covered in gold mosaic, the walls lined in polished coloured marbles, and the sanctuary sheathed in forty thousand pounds of silver. The reflected shimmering light of the candles, and the deeply drilled patterning of the 'basket' capitals, denied the massive materiality of the structure seen on the outside, and added to the impression of the effortless rise of the floating dome in the interior.

> Who could recount the beauty of the columns and the stones with which the church is adorned? One might imagine that he had come upon a meadow with its flowers in full bloom. For he would surely marvel at the purple of some, the green tint of others, and of those on which the crimson glows and those from which the white flashes, and again at those which Nature, like some painter, varies with the most contrasting colours. And whenever anyone enters the church to pray, he understands at once that it is not by any human power or skill, but by the influence of God, that this work has been so finely turned. And so his mind is lifted up toward God and exalted, feeling that He cannot be far away, but must especially love to dwell in this place which He has chosen.[18]

These sumptuous reflective surfaces made the church appear to generate its own light from within. Suspended silver discs holding numerous candles added to the dazzling effect. Still now, with the candles, the silver, and most of the gold mosaic covered or removed, and the chanting silenced, the heart still leaps as one steps through the Imperial Door.

Rebuilding an Ideology and Theology of Empire

In 557, an earthquake weakened the dome and in 558, it collapsed. While it was being repaired, on 7 May, part of the vault over the sanctuary collapsed, destroying the altar and the ambo. By 562, a much higher dome had replaced the very flat and less stable earlier dome. All was fully restored, and the church was reconsecrated on 24 December 562.[19] Not long after, Paul the Silentiary recited a long *ekphrastic* poem praising the aesthetic, and technical, accomplishment of Emperor Justinian and his architects. Most striking of all is the emphasis Paul places on the geography of empire built into the church (Plate 6): purple columns from the crags of Thebes, porphyry columns from Egypt, surmounted by green from Thessaly, emerald green Haimonian columns, Thessalonian columns with dashes of yellow, others from Haemus and Proconnesus, wavy-veined Carian marble with streaks of red and white 'from the Iasian peaks', green Calystus, speckled Phrygian flecked with white, purple, or silver, green of Laconia, yellow with swirling red from Lydia, and golden stone from Libya. Many of these places featured in Procopius' earlier writings in *The Wars*, and notably, events in Thessaly and Libya were illustrated in the mosaics of the Chalkê Gate. The veins of the marble in the wall panels, redolent of those conflicts, are used to create painterly patterns. Further, 'the ridge of Pangaeus and the cape of Sunium [in Attica] have opened their silver veins'.[20] The geography of empire is built into the fabric and shimmers in the light of the divine presence.

The pavement too is remarkable, laid in stone from Proconnesus in the Sea of Marmara. Its veins were described as the waves of the sea washing against the isthmus of the solea, a veritable Mediterranean Sea, which by now had become a virtual Roman lake, surrounded by the coloured marbles of empire. Green lines in the pavement and (later) large coloured discs at one and the same time delineate liturgical movement and hierarchical separation.

Two centuries later than *The Book of Ceremonies*, an ekphrastic text delivered by Michael, rector of the Patriarchal Academy (at the annual celebration of the reinauguration of Hagia Sophia by Justinian),[21] describes the approach from the *milion*, which gathered the main roads of Constantinople together in the Augusteion, where the great bronze column held the equestrian statue of Justinian aloft. From there, a gentle rise took the procession to the south entrance to the narthex, vaulted in gold and lined with coloured marble panelling. To the left was the exo-narthex and the great atrium; to the right, five brass doors. Even at that late date, Michael's text dwells on the freshness of the architecture and on the richness of the colouring of the marbles that 'in many respects convicts the flowers of being easily withered'.[22] He is also struck by the order of the architecture and the billowing of the interior space, both laterally in the sweep of the *exedrae*, and vertically in the vaulting and the remarkable innovation of the rise of dome and semi-dome, saying: 'and so does this work of art imitate the whole universe.'[23] The veined marble of the pavement he likens again to the waves of the sea breaking on the gulf of the sanctuary, sheathed in silver.

> The floor, the sea out of which I have said the holy sanctuary has been scooped, as the sea would do it, from there is a certain isthmus; at this spot there is a passage, and the holy tribune comes to shore at the isthmus, just as though it were a cargo vessel, and that it may rest untossed by the waves, it lowers from above its anchors of silver, the columns, down to the ground.[24]

The pavement being like the great waters under the firmament is an enduring image, one that was used six centuries earlier by Paul the Silentiary of the paving around the ambo: 'some wave-washed land, extended through the white-capped billows by an isthmus into the middle of the sea.'[25] Indeed, the marble of the paving looks strikingly like the rippled sand of the sea shore. The 'isthmus' leads from the ambo to the chancel screen, beyond which is the *synthronon* (the tiered benches for the clergy round the apse), like the one that still exists in the apse of Hagia Irene.

Ceremonial: Enacting the Ideology of Empire

The fabric of the church was saturated with the ideology of empire. When Constantine was baptized, it was not just an individual being admitted to the faith; in his writings, the contemporary and friend of Constantine, Bishop Eusebius of Caesarea, had been preparing for the Christianization of the office of emperor. He created a theology of empire that unshakably characterized the governance of the Byzantine Empire for a thousand years. Even in the reign of Julian the Apostate, when the majority of the population was still pagan, he made little progress in returning the structures of state to the old Roman imperial and pagan ways. Eusebius presented Constantine as the vicar of Christ on earth. In a panegyric oration before Constantine on the thirtieth anniversary of his becoming emperor, Eusebius said:

> The only begotten Word of God reigns, from ages which had no beginning, to infinite and endless ages, the partner of his Father's kingdom. And our emperor, ever beloved by him, who derives the source of imperial authority from above, and is strong in the power of his sacred title, has controlled the empire of the world for a period of years. Again, the Preserver of the universe orders the whole heaven and earth, and the celestial kingdom, consistently with his Father's will. Even so our emperor whom He loves, by bringing those he rules on earth to the only begotten and saving Word renders them fit subjects for his kingdom…He who is the pre-existent Word, the Saviour of all things, imparts to His followers the seeds of true wisdom and salvation, makes them at the same time truly wise, and understanding the kingdom of their Father. Our emperor, His friend, acting as interpreter to the Word of God, aims at recalling the whole human race to the knowledge of God; proclaiming in the ears of all, and declaring with powerful voice the laws of truth and godliness to all who dwell on the earth.[26]

Here is the origin of the Christian notion of the divine right of kings—a ruler ordained with 'authority from above' who rules his subjects, as Christ is the ruler of the universe. Christianity here offers to an emperor legitimacy that the ancient gods never could. Rule by divine pattern and by divine will meant that rebellion against the sovereign was rebellion against God himself. It is a way of thinking that is alien to the modern western mind, but not in fact far removed from British history and institutions. The sovereign is anointed during the coronation ceremony to be given a quasi-priestly status; the preamble to royal documents still reads: 'Elizabeth II, by the Grace of God, Queen'; and the Accession Service in the *Book of Common Prayer* says: 'We yield thee unfeigned thanks, for that thou wast pleased as on this day to set thy Servant our Sovereign Lady ELIZABETH upon the Throne of this Realm.' The Byzantine conception went far beyond this, using Trinitarian theology to justify monarchy and condemn democracy:

Lastly, invested with a semblance of heavenly sovereignty, he [that is Constantine, or the New Constantine] directs his gaze above, and frames his earthly government according to the pattern of that divine original, feeling strength in its conformity to the monarchy of God. And this conformity is granted by the universal Sovereign to man alone of the creatures of this earth: for He only is author of sovereign power, who decrees that all should be subject to the rule of one. And surely monarchy far transcends every other constitution and form of government: for that democratic equality of power, which is its opposite, may rather be described as anarchy and disorder. Hence there is one God, and not two or three, or more: for to assert a plurality of gods is plainly to deny the being of God at all.[27]

Hagia Sophia was not a dual symbol of divine and imperial rule; for Justinian, as for Constantine, the two were one and the same. This church and the emperor himself dissolved the boundary between earth and heaven. God's will was to unite the peoples of the earth under his own rule. The Church was to serve that end by its teaching and in its sacraments; the emperor was called to do that militarily and politically, as Justinian outlined in a text added to his great Code of Law of 528:

> There are two great gifts which God, in his love for man, has granted from on high: the priesthood and the imperial dignity. The first serves divine things, while the latter directs and administers human affairs; both, however, proceed from the same origin and adorn the life of mankind. Hence, nothing should be such a source of care to the emperors as the dignity of the priests, since it is for their (imperial) welfare that they constantly implore God. For, if the priesthood is in every way free from blame and possesses access to God, and if the emperors administer equitably and judiciously the state entrusted to their care, general harmony will result and whatever is beneficial will be bestowed upon the human race.[28]

Interestingly, according to Constantine VII in his *Book of Ceremonies*, the emperor was crowned not by the patriarch, but by a military official when proclaimed by the army, or by the hand of the senior emperor when the succession was dynastic. It could be delegated to the patriarch by the senior emperor, but it remained an imperial, not an ecclesiastical, right. The prayer preceding the crowning was for divine election. The emperor was vicar of Christ, unmediated by the Church. At his crowning, the emperor was proclaimed 'New Constantine'. Constantine the Great, as presented by Eusebius, was Constantine VII's model, and the Sacred Palace was replete with memories of Constantine, its reputed builder; even the relics reinforced Constantinian and Eusebian images. The combined ceremonial use of the Cross of Constantine and the rod of Moses (the latter still to be seen in the Topkapi Palace just north of Hagia Sophia) called to mind Eusebius' comparison of Constantine's victorious crossing of the Milvian Bridge to Moses crossing the Red Sea.[29]

When preparing to process from the throne room, or *Chrysotriklinos* (now probably under the eastern edge of the Blue Mosque near the Mosaic Museum), to Hagia Sophia after his crowning or on the great feast days of the Church, the emperor was presented with the Cross of Constantine, and this very special and significant relic, Moses' rod. It is an ancient thumbstick, polished by the hands of long successions of emperors and patriarchs. This very ordinary looking walking stick carries in itself the journey from Egypt to the Promised Land, having gauged each step of the way. That was the journey that delivered the Hebrews from slavery in the land of Egypt and established them as the people of God, the elect of God (Exod. 3:1–10). It is the rod that became a snake when placed on the ground to demonstrate Moses' power and authority (Exod. 4:1–5). It turned the waters of Egypt to blood (Exod. 7:14–21) and did other miracles in Egypt to gain the freedom of the Hebrews from Pharaoh. After the Passover, when Israel fled from Egypt, this was the rod that parted the sea before them (Exod. 14:16–31). It is the stick with which Moses struck the rock in the desert to provide water miraculously for the people of God (Exod. 17:5–7). The emperor was the new Moses ruling over the new Israel, providing for the new people of God, and in this ceremony leading them into the heavenly kingdom within the walls of the Great Church.

In his *Life of Constantine*, Eusebius described how Constantine had declared to some assembled bishops that he was himself a bishop: 'You are bishops whose jurisdiction is within the Church: I also am a bishop, ordained by God to overlook those outside the Church.' Emperors, as New Constantines, viewed themselves likewise, and Constantine himself presided over the Council of Nicaea. Despite a quasi-episcopal status and the rule of the Christian kingdom by divine authority, the emperor's removal of his crown on entering a church was recognition of a limit on his power where Christ reigned. This was the only limit of his power, but it could be manifested in a remarkable way. There were instances of an emperor being refused entry into a church, even Hagia Sophia. In 390, Theodosius I was refused entry by Ambrose of Milan to his cathedral following the emperor's massacre of the people of Thessalonica for rebellion. Theodosius' legitimacy was restored by his compliant penitence; similarly, Leo VI was twice refused an imperial entry to Hagia Sophia itself at Christmas 906 and the following Epiphany. He was required to enter discretely by the south side-aisle to reach his apartments in the imperial enclosure or *metatorion* in the south aisle. Leo appears to have remained a penitent for the rest of his reign.[30] The mosaic above the Imperial Door is probably an image of Leo as a penitent prostrating himself before Christ. It is an arresting image with an emperor in such a posture, and it served as a permanent reminder of the limits of imperial power.

Hagia Sophia was, along with the Hippodrome and to a lesser extent the Hebdomon military parade ground, an essential seat of the emperor's power and legitimacy, and they were all significant arenas for the ceremonial enactment of that power and legitimacy. Approaching and entering those spaces could pose problems that had to be negotiated carefully, but in the end it was Hagia Sophia that preeminently embodied both the earthly and heavenly empire and could potentially change the character of a reign.

The Fall of New Rome

Even two centuries later than *The Book of Ceremonies*, in the oration delivered by Michael, rector of the Patriarchal Academy, the living newness of the Great Church is celebrated. The Great Church was at that time the living heart of Byzantium, with the old Palace of Constantine reduced to a theatrical shell, and by this time even the games of the Hippodrome had become staged set pieces relying on the tradition of dramatic and musical entertainments shown in relief on the obelisk base of Theodosius I, rather than being for sport.[31] By the tenth century, the factions of the Blues and the Greens, far from being hooligans, had become choirs to sing the praises of the emperor. *The Book of Ceremonies* describes these acclamations and the elaborate imperial ceremonial.[32] There was no longer danger in the confrontation between populace in the Hippodrome and the emperor in the imperial box or *kathisma*. All had been tamed, except the patriarch and the clergy of Hagia Sophia. Much of the meaning of the functional layout of the old palace, and of the stages of the ceremonies themselves, was slipping from memory, which was presumably why it was necessary in the middle of the tenth century for Constantine VII to indulge in the antiquarianism of the compilation of the *Book of Ceremonies*—in a vain attempt to revive a sense of purpose and meaning to the complex rituals and the architecture of the palace. No such revival was needed for the liturgy and architecture of Hagia Sophia. By this time, the horizons of empire had drawn in, encompassing only two-thirds of the Balkans and half of Asia Minor, and the ceremonial core of Constantinople was crumbling, but Hagia Sophia then, and even later as the Great Mosque, would confer the image of the sacred imperium on the Ottomans in turn; and even now as these words are being written (24 July 2020) Hagia Sophia, by the renewal of prayers for the first time since its secularization in 1934, is being turned from a museum and World Heritage Site back into a mosque within President Erdogan's vision of a broader Islamic 'renaissance'. Hagia Sophia retains its religious, and political, potency.

Hagia Sophia was a statement of power and unity. When the statement is on such a scale, the question must have been equally great, and so it was, rising out of the mayhem, riot, and flames of the Nika Riots striking at the very heart of empire. The building that arose became the embodiment of empire in its very materials gathered from across its whole geography. It was also the meeting point between the heavenly and earthly kingdoms within a particular theology of empire beginning with Eusebius: the emperor and the empire were the reflection of God's rule in the Kingdom of Heaven and it was by God's will that the emperor ruled on earth. Rebellion against the emperor was rebellion against God. The only brake on this absolute power was the Church, in the person of the patriarch, who could, and did, forbid the emperor's entry into Hagia Sophia and communion. This was not mere symbolism; it was ultimate power of censure. The Church was in every way a parallel structure to the administrative rule of New Rome, Constantinople. The imperial rule lasted more than a thousand years before disappearing in the siege of 1453; the Orthodox Church adapted and survived the collapse of the Byzantine Empire and the capture of Constantinople, 'New Rome', finding new expression in a 'Third Rome', Moscow.

Figure 7. Facade of the Cathedral of the Dormition in the Moscow Kremlin

4

'The Third Rome'

The Cathedral of the Dormition
in the Moscow Kremlin

A second line of development in the history of the Orthodox Church began with simple trading links between the Byzantines and the Slavs in the region of Kiev from the time of Justinian in the sixth century CE. These would become formal religious and dynastic links under Grand Prince Vladimir of Kiev on his conversion to Orthodox Christianity in 988 and marriage to Anna, sister of Emperor Basil II. Probably in 1037, Jaroslav, Vladimir's son, began the Church of the Holy Wisdom in Kiev, as a reflection of Constantinople. From 1045, his son Vladimir of Novgorod built the Cathedral of St Sophia in Novgorod, finishing by 1052. It is said that, around 1046, Vsevolod I married another Byzantine princess, daughter of Constantine IX Monomachos. The couple's son was known as Vladimir Monomakh, prince of Kiev. His descendants, as grand dukes of Moscow, made much of this supposed imperial heritage. Constantinople, 'New Rome', fell to the Ottomans in 1453. Ivan III married Sophia Paleologos, a Byzantine princess, in a temporary structure on the site of the old Cathedral of the Dormition in the Moscow Kremlin in 1472, and he began to build the present cathedral in 1475. In form, the new cathedral was a lineal descendent of those in Kiev and Novgorod. A year after completing the new cathedral in 1479, Ivan broke the Tartar dominance over Russia, only a quarter of a century after the fall of Constantinople. Moscow would reconceive itself as the 'Third Rome', assuming the imperial mantle and the protection of Orthodox Christians. The Cathedral of the Dormition became the coronation church, and its throne, known as the Monomakh Throne, was dedicated in 1551 by Ivan IV, the Terrible.

The Distant Prospect

During the cold-war era, the Kremlin, and the golden domes of the cathedrals within its walls, bristled in the background of endless news reports from the Soviet Union and acted as a backdrop for the May Day parades displaying the latest rocket launchers and massed military might. Buildings often become iconic of cities or nations, but this visual association of the Kremlin and its cathedrals with the Soviet Union was double-edged. In the first place, it was jarring to have so many churches at the heart of the seat of government of a not only secular, but an avowedly anti-religious, state. Secondly, the Cathedral of the Dormition in particular had been built as a symbol of the authority and might of the grand princes. It had been at the heart of government since its foundations were laid, and its continued survival there tells not only of the history of the Russian Orthodox Church, but also of its improbable present and potential future. The architectural, political, and religious heritage of this remarkable building can be traced back through Novgorod and Kiev to Hagia Sophia itself, at the heart of the east Roman Empire in Constantinople.

Early Contacts with Byzantium

The Russian Primary Chronicle, compiled in the eleventh and early twelfth centuries, describes the response of a delegation of Prince Vladimir of Kiev to Hagia Sophia in 988:

We knew not whether we were in heaven or on earth. For on earth
there is no such splendour or such beauty, and we are at a loss how to
describe it. We only know that God dwells there among men, and
their service is fairer than the ceremonies of other nations. For we cannot forget that beauty.[1]

This was presented as the decisive moment in the conversion of
Russia. The 'Tale of the Spread of Christianity in Russia', of which
this story forms an important part, reveals some of the earliest aspirations to Russian self-determination. Analysis of the composition of
this text peals back layers connecting to Novgorod, Kiev, and perhaps
even to the Sagas of Scandinavian Varangians who served in the
Byzantine military and ruled the region of Kiev.[2]

Legend has it that St Andrew, patron saint of Russia, came to the
place where Kiev was to be built and blessed the hills, saying: 'See ye
these hills? So shall the favour of God shine upon them that on this
spot a great city shall arise, and God shall erect many churches therein.'[3]
In fact, eastern Slavs had moved up the river Dnieper to the area
around Kiev about the time of the founding of Constantinople, and,
from around the time of Justinian in the sixth century, Greek trading
settlements on the Black Sea had been engaged in trade with them.
Kiev had been an important link in the relationship between
Constantinople and the Rus', Scandinavians who dominated the territory stretching from the Black Sea north to the Baltic. That relationship was vexed, and as early as 860 the Rus' swept down from
their stronghold in Kiev and attacked Constantinople. The *Primary
Chronicle* relates how a miracle by the Virgin saved the city:

> Askold and Dir attacked the Greeks during the fourteenth year of the
> reign of the Emperor Michael. When the Emperor had set forth against
> the infidels and had arrived at the Black River, the eparch sent him
> word that the Rus' were approaching Tsargrad [Constantinople], and
> the Emperor turned back. Upon arriving inside the strait, the Rus'
> made a great massacre of the Christians, and attacked Tsargrad in two
> hundred boats. The Emperor succeeded with difficulty in entering the
> city. He straightway hastened with the Patriarch Photius to the Church
> of Our Lady of the Blachernae, where they prayed all night. They also

sang hymns and carried the sacred vestment of the Virgin to dip it in the sea. The weather was still, and the sea was calm, but a storm of wind came up, and when great waves straightway rose, confusing the boats of the godless Rus', it threw them upon the shore and broke them up, so that few escaped such destruction and returned to their native land.[4]

In a sermon in Hagia Sophia, Patriarch Photius described the same attack and lamented:

A people has crept down from the north, as if it were attacking another Jerusalem...the people is fierce and has no mercy; its voice is as the roaring sea...Woe is me, that I see a fierce and savage tribe fearlessly poured round the city, ravaging the suburbs, destroying everything, ruining everything, fields, houses, herds, beasts of burden, women, children, old men, youths, thrusting their sword through everything, taking pity on nothing...O city reigning over nearly the whole universe, what an uncaptained army, equipped in servile fashion, is sneering at thee as at a slave![5]

The Scandinavian rulers of Kiev were greatly feared, but not long after this attack a Byzantine Christian mission was sent to the Rus', though it seems to have had little enduring effect.[6] In 911, a treaty was signed between 'the Christians' and 'the Rus'', indicating that they had not yet been evangelized. It was quoted extensively in the *Primary Chronicle*, and no reference was made to Christians among the Rus'. Between this treaty and the next signed by Igor in 944, much had changed, and there were clearly many Christians among the Varangians and the Slavs of Kiev. In the following year, Grand Prince Igor was murdered, and his wife Olga acted as regent for their son Svjatosláv until 962. Olga was baptized, it is said, in Constantinople in 954–5, and she was given a sovereign's reception by Constantine VII Porphyrogenitus at court on 9 September and 18 October 957. Archbishop Anthony of Novgorod in 1200 recorded

a large gold disc for the mass, given to the Patriarch by Olga, a Russian princess, when she came to the imperial city to be baptized. In this disc there is a precious stone which displays the image of Christ, and the seal impressions of this are used as charms; but on the upper side the disc is adorned with pearls.[7]

It was she who built the first Church of the Holy Wisdom in Kiev.[8] Svjatosláv did not become a Christian; however, his son Vladimir became Grand Prince of Novgorod in 969 and eventually Grand Prince of Kiev by deception and murder of his half-brother Iaropolk, and would become a Christian by a long diplomatic route. He badly needed legitimation.[9]

The Conversion of Vladimir

In 988, Vladimir provided 6,000 troops to Constantine VII's grandson Basil II. The troops helped Basil to secure the Byzantine throne, and for his support Vladimir would receive Basil's sister Anna as a bride. As told in the *Primary Chronicle* under the year 986–7, emissaries of the various higher religions came to Kiev to argue the case for Vladimir's conversion. Bulgars from the Volga argued for Islam, there were Latin and Greek Christians, and Jews. There is independent evidence of Jews living in Kiev at this time, and probably Muslims too.[10] The chronicler records that Vladimir then sent his own emissaries to observe their various worship practices: 'send them to inquire about the ritual of each and how he worships God.' They were disappointed with what they found, until arriving at Constantinople.[11] There the glories of Hagia Sophia overwhelmed his envoys.

Vladimir confirmed his alliance with the empire by converting, along with all his people, to Christianity. An imperial bride for Vladimir, and alliance with the Byzantine Empire, gave him every reason to follow his grandmother's path into Orthodoxy. As a consequence, in 990 Greek missionaries were converting and baptizing his subjects, 'who did it not for love, did it for fear of him who had commanded it, because both were united in him—true belief and power', as Hilarion (appointed Metropolitan of Kiev in 1051) wrote in his

Discourse on Law and Grace.[12] This is the oldest extant Slavic/Rus' text, and its subject is the providential conversion of the Rus' in the context of biblical and world history. The conversion to Christianity was seen as a major step towards the creation of a Rus' state.[13] Vladimir is presented in the *Primary Chronicle* as 'the new Constantine of mighty Rome, who baptized himself and also his subjects'.[14]

Whatever the mix of his motivations, Vladimir was canonized as founder of Russian Orthodoxy. He set up a Greek hierarchy, gradually to be replaced by Russians, and from the earliest days there was a Slavic liturgy. By 996, the first brick and stone church in Rus', Vladimir's 'Tithe Church', was built on a Byzantine model with an interior of marble, mosaic, and fresco.[15] Art, architecture, and religion, indeed the whole cultural identity of Russia, stem from this single root, with consequences that echo still. Christianity and culture quickly spread from here throughout his realms. The growth of Christianity, culture, and political authority were closely identified in Rus'. In the middle of the eleventh century, Antony, a monk of Athos, established a hermitage in a cave, from which developed the great Kiev Monastery of the Caves. Russian monasticism spread rapidly, becoming a vital element in Russian Orthodoxy. The growing strength of Church and State and their recognition abroad are shown at this time by the marriage alliances achieved by Prince Jaroslav through his daughters to King Henry I of France and Harald Hardrada of Norway, and of his son Vsevolod to a Byzantine princess.[16]

The Cathedral of the Holy Wisdom, Kiev

When Vladimir died in 1015, there was civil war among his sons, and Rus' was divided. The decisive battle took place near the walls of Kiev in 1016 between his sons Jaroslav and Sviatopolk with his nomadic allies the Turkic Pechenegs. Jaroslav was victorious, but he faced still more challenges to his rule, especially from another brother, Mstislav, and became sole heir only on the death of Mstislav in 1036. Then, in

1037, Jaroslav began building a new Cathedral of the Holy Wisdom on the site of the battle against Sviatopolk at Kiev, the same year a metropolitan was appointed for Kiev.[17] Kiev was conceived as a Christian city in the image of Constantinople, with a 'Golden Gate' in its walls like the walls of both Constantine and Theodosius. The plan form of the cathedral too was probably derived from Constantinople. Just as Hagia Sophia in Constantinople was the mother church of Greek Orthodoxy, so the Cathedral of the Holy Wisdom was at this time the mother church of Russian Orthodoxy, and its impressive form was a reflection of the growing prominence of the Orthodox Church. The original church was of five aisles, each ending in an apse. The outer aisles have open galleries that may originally have been exterior galleries continuing round the west end. The wider central nave and crossing were surmounted by a dome with windows around the drum admitting light to the centre of the church, recalling the Church of the Holy Sepulchre in Jerusalem. All four arms reaching out from the central dome are of equal length, creating a cross-in-square. The interior is largely intact, but on the exterior only the five apses can still be seen; the rest is seventeenth-century encrustation, and many more have sprouted besides the original central dome. Where the original construction can be seen on the main apse, it is strongly reminiscent of Byzantine building methods at churches such as Chora, with alternating courses of brick and stone. This tradition continued in Russian architecture into the early thirteenth century.[18]

The spatial effect of the interior of the Church of the Holy Wisdom, Kiev, is very different from its namesake and model in Constantinople, but its atmosphere and its stunning decorative programme reproduce faithfully the experience of Vladimir's envoys in Hagia Sophia. The gold and frescos, and especially the glittering mosaics, combine with the natural light high in the crossing to create an uplifting and spiritual interior peopled with serried ranks of icon saints; architectural, ecclesiastical, and social structures were rigidly hierarchical. Hovering in the semi-dome of the apse is a shining Mother of God, with her hands raised in prayer. Below her is a 'Communion of the Apostles',

Figure 8. The Cathedral of the Holy Wisdom, Kiev

with a doubled image of Christ communicating the apostles, with bread to his right and wine to his left, from an altar magnificently vested under a silver canopy. Saints and angels hover on the walls below the four evangelists (of whom St Mark is original) in the pendentives of the dome, while in the dome itself the magnificent mid-eleventh-century image of Christ as Ruler of the Universe is surrounded by four cherubim with *flabella,* or liturgical fans. The physical structure of the church dissolves into the theological structure of the Church, a structure shaped in Constantinople by theologians such as St John Chrysostom and Gregory of Nyssa, who appear in the lower register of figures on the south side of the apse. There are references to the secular life of Constantinople as well in the frescos, including musicians and jugglers in the Hippodrome, which was still functioning at this date in the eleventh century. The images are glossed with text to articulate the message further and drive it home. The building itself was created as an instrument of evangelism and learning for, 'having written many books, Jaroslav placed them in St Sophia'.[19] It also served as the tomb of Jaroslav 'the Wise', whose sarcophagus is under the semi-dome of the apse of the inner north gallery.

Not surprisingly, the decorative programme did not come down to us wholly intact.[20] It was badly damaged by the Mongol Tartar armies of Batu Khan in 1237, when the centre of political and religious life transferred to Moscow. The Church of the Holy Wisdom in Kiev was disused for long periods during the thirteenth to sixteenth centuries. It was reconstructed and extended during the second half of the seventeenth century, when the Ukraine was reunited with Russia. The whole of the exterior was plastered, giving it an appearance that was more Muscovite than Byzantine. The grand dukes of Moscow had seized their independence from the Tatars by the second half of the fifteenth century, just when Constantinople had fallen to Turkish rule, leaving the grand duke as the sole sovereign Protector of Orthodoxy; New Rome had fallen, allowing Moscow to reconceive itself as the Third Rome.[21]

Cathedral of the Holy Wisdom, Novgorod

Vladimir the Great sent Bishop Joachim of Kherson to Novgorod. He took an aggressive approach to evangelization, tipping pagan idols into the river, and building a church dedicated to SS Joachim and Anna (no longer extant), and the wooden Saint Sophia. Traditional building in the whole of Russia had been in timber, which suffered terribly from fire, but the new masonry buildings not surprisingly inherited spatial treatment and forms from this tradition, including the variety of treatments of the dome. The first Cathedral of St Sophia in Novgorod was built in the citadel in wood at the end of the tenth century and had 'thirteen tops'—presumably bristling with domes. It stood for sixty years before being destroyed by fire.

Though ruled from Kiev through a governor, often a son of the grand prince in Kiev, the city of Novgorod was famously independent, to the point of telling Prince Vsevolod: 'We do not want you. Go wherever you want.' The prince remained, but power was exercised by merchants and the archbishop.[22]

The new stone cathedral of Novgorod was begun in 1045, shortly before the destruction of the original and eight years after the start was made on its namesake in Kiev.[23] The building of two cathedrals dedicated to the Holy Wisdom expressed strong links between Prince Vladimir and Constantinople, and indeed the Novgorod Third Chronicle records that 'icon painters from Tsargrad'—that is to say, Constantinople—were working in the cathedral soon after it was finished, and eleventh-century full-length images of Constantine the Great and Empress Helena have been found.[24] The building was completed by 1052. It is complex in form, with an equally complex building history. On plan it has a strong relationship with the Kievan Sophia, with five apses, but two extra narrow aisles, but the wider outer aisles with apses were built later. The walls were of uncoursed stone with a crushed red-brick mortar and regular brick window surrounds—rather different from the more clearly Byzantine building in

Figure 9. The Cathedral of the Holy Wisdom, Novgorod

Kiev.[25] Greater distance was already encouraging greater autonomy from Constantinople. The Russian Orthodox Church wholly rejected the Council of Florence of 1439, where reunion of eastern and western churches was agreed, and in 1448 the Russian hierarchy elected a metropolitan of Moscow without consulting Constantinople, so establishing their independence.

The interiors of the two contemporary churches of the Holy Wisdom in Novgorod and Kiev have similar spatial arrangements with very tall naves and galleries. The lower cells in the side-aisles are very dark, but the crossings are brightly lit by the dome, and even the upper galleries borrow a significant amount of light. The fragmentary twelfth-century remains of the iconographic programme and its materials are simpler at Novgorod than at Kiev, with fresco rather than golden mosaic and marble. The iconostasis in front of the altar is from the sixteenth century with icons of the Moscow School, revealing a shift in political dominance. From January 1478, Novgorod had lost its independence when captured by Ivan III, grand duke of Moscow, but resistance continued at least until the end of the fifteenth century. A series of repressive measures was taken, culminating in the confiscation of all church lands in 1499, which were then granted to important Muscovites in service to the grand duke.[26] This ensured the political dominance of Moscow.

The historic fabric of St Sophia in Novgorod was extensively damaged between 1941 and 1943 by occupying German forces, and artillery fire destroyed the central dome and the painting of the Pantocrator. Restoration began in 1949 and continued through the 1960s.[27]

Cathedral of the Dormition in the Moscow Kremlin

In the heart of the Kremlin in Moscow is the Cathedral of the Dormition, begun in 1475 by Ivan III and Metropolitan Filip I, and completed four years later. The Dormition, or 'Falling Asleep of the

Virgin', is the Orthodox equivalent of the Assumption in the western church. The Kremlin itself was being rebuilt at the same time. This is precisely when Moscow was assuming a dominant role over the whole of Russia, until now a constellation of principalities. It was Moscow that defied the former demand for tribute by the Tartars when Ivan III tore up the Khan's proclamation of suzerainty here in the cathedral, asserting independent nationhood. Under him, Tartar control of central Russia was broken in 1480.[28] Religious, political, and cultural aspirations were focused on this building. It was the coronation church of the tsars and the burial place of first the metropolitans and then the patriarchs of Moscow. Curiously, it was built by an Italian architect, Alberti ('Aristotle') Fioravanti, brought in specially in January 1475. He had worked with the great Antonio Averlino Filarete on the Ospedale Maggiore and built the Palazzo del Podestà in Bologna.[29]

Building had been virtually impossible under the domination of the Tartars, because of the heavy tribute they exacted. The only early thirteenth-century building left in the Moscow Kremlin is the small Church of the Saviour 'in the Forest', built by Ivan Kalita ('Moneybags'), who must have been particularly adept at extracting tribute money from his people, and who was styled grand prince of Moscow with their approval and ruled with the *iarlyk*, or seal of authority, from the Mongols. Besides the grand princes of Moscow, Metropolitan Peter made Moscow his official residence in 1325. The grand prince and Peter together laid the first stone of the foundations of the first Cathedral of the Dormition there in 1326. The status of the city and the church was enormously enhanced when Peter was canonized in 1339.[30] That early church was on the point of collapse when Ivan III came to the throne in 1462. Rebuilding began with the laying of the first stone by Metropolitan Filip in the presence of Ivan on 30 April 1471 on the model of the Cathedral of the Dormition in the city of Vladimir. In May of 1474, the shell was complete up to the great drum, but on the 20th of the month most of the structure collapsed.

With a gap of almost two and a half centuries in a strong tradition of building in most of Russia in the fifteenth century, Ivan III was eager to re-establish links with tradition, and so sent Fioravanti to the city of Vladimir to study the Cathedral of the Dormition, which had been the coronation church of the grand princes of Moscow. The Cathedral of the Dormition, Vladimir, was begun in 1158 by Prince Andrei Bogoliubsky, who, in the familiar phrase of the chronicler, gathered 'craftsmen from all parts of the earth'. Not long before the cathedral was begun, the prince had brought the miraculous Byzantine icon, which was to become known as the Virgin of Vladimir to the city, and it was housed in the new cathedral. A decade after beginning this church, Bogoliubsky petitioned Constantinople to have a Metropolitanate established here in Vladimir to enhance the political prestige of his principality. In 1164, he built a 'Golden Gate' in the city walls, in imitation of Constantinople, and the cathedral was at that time the tallest building in Rus', giving physical form to Bogoliubsky's ambitions with its shining golden domes visible from a distance of a dozen kilometres. But the Orthodox Church in Russia was seen as a single unit by Constantinople, dashing the prince's aspirations.[31] The cathedral had a central helmet dome on a tall drum, and after a fire of 1185 had been given similar but smaller domes on the corners, a format copied at the Cathedral of the Dormition by Fioravanti in Moscow, dedicated three centuries later in 1479.[32] Ivan was exploiting all the symbols of political aspiration provided by the tradition in the creation of a suitable setting for his sole rulership. Until Ivan III in 1460, coronations were in the Cathedral of the Dormition in Vladimir, where the great icon-painter Andrei Rubliev restored the interior along with Daniil Cherny in 1408. Two bays of this cycle of fresco icons are still extant (Plate 7). The miraculous Virgin of Vladimir is thought to have been brought from here to Moscow later that century in 1480. By now, it was regarded as the palladium of the Russian state, saving Moscow from the Mongol hordes in 1451 and 1480.

While Fioravanti was in Vladimir, the old church in Moscow was demolished, a temporary wooden structure was built in the place of the new chancel when Ivan married a Byzantine princess, Sophia Paleologos, there in 1472.[33] These links with the Byzantine Empire and the glories of the earlier Russian inheritance, and his taking of the title of *tsar* after throwing off the Tartar yoke, were all part of crafting a new ideology and theology of empire by Ivan III. The tsar became Protector of Orthodox Christians, and finally in 1589 the Moscow Patriarchate was established. The 'historical' basis of these aspirations coalesces in a remarkable object in Moscow's Cathedral of the Dormition, the 'Monomakh Throne' of Ivan IV, better known to history as Ivan the Terrible. Under a canopy that rivals the exuberance of the pinnacles of St Basil's Cathedral (just outside the Kremlin at the south end of 'Red Square') is the throne decorated with carved panels showing battles of Vladimir 'Monomakh', prince of Kiev, and scenes from the legendary granting of imperial insignia to him by his grandfather the Byzantine emperor Constantine Monomachos, who had in fact died long before Vladimir was crowned. The throne was dedicated on 1 September 1551, coming up to the centenary of the Fall of Constantinople, and it clearly reinforces the tsar's claim as successor to the east Roman Empire. The text carved on the right door is from the *Tale of the Princes of Vladimir* and describes the scene on the last panel on the south side of the throne facing the entrance:

> And from this time forward you are to be called Emperor crowned by God. Crowned by the hand of the most holy metropolitan prelate Neophyte and the bishops with this imperial crown, from that very time on Prince Vladimir Vsevolodovich would be called Monomakh and tsar of Great Russia, and thereafter he remained in peaceful and loving relations with Emperor Constantine and to this day the princes of Vladimir are crowned with that very same imperial crown.[34]

The throne originally stood in the middle of the nave below the main dome facing the Holy Doors, since this church had no galleries, where grand princes were usually accommodated. Later, it was placed just inside the southern entrance facing the iconostasis, after Byzantine precedent and the arrangement of Hagia Sophia in Constantinople. In most circumstances, a throne would face the people, but here it faced the iconostasis and the liturgy, so that the emperor would not be the focus, as in a throne room, but would lead the worshippers. The presence of an emperor at a liturgy had been a problem since Constantine, because the focus of any ceremony was normally on them, but facing the throne eastwards turned his focus, and that of the congregation, towards the action of the liturgy. The patriarch's throne is against the east side of the south pillar, and, like Charlemagne's throne in Aachen, the patriarch's was built to house a reliquary. The physical relationship between the thrones of the tsar and of the patriarch is a model of their political relationship. From the time of his coronation in 1547, they had cooperated in the framing of both a new Code of Laws in 1550 and the Manual of Church Governance in 1551. In the cathedral treasury is an object that in form relates directly to the form of the Monomakh throne, the 'Small Zion' representing the Church of the Holy Sepulchre.[35] The Small Zion was a ciborium, or container for the consecrated bread, the Body of Christ, so modelling the throne on the Small Zion emphasized the Byzantine notion of the emperor ruling on earth as Christ was emperor in Heaven.

Architecture and Identity

The building Fioravanti produced in the Moscow Kremlin was related in external form to its predecessors in Vladimir, Novgorod, and Kiev, and it became a pattern for many other Russian churches through the sixteenth and seventeenth centuries, and even very recently. On the exterior, the east facade with its five apses continues upwards with a further level of painted surfaces sheltered with corbelled arched canopies, before reaching the matched set of five glistening helmet-shaped domed pepper pots. Despite the similarities to its predecessors, there were also significant differences. Unusually the approach, including the formal processional approach, was always intended to be from the main square on the south side, so entry is directly into the crossing. Other than the introduction of the seventeenth-century iconostasis

(Plate 8) and the removal of the Corinthian capitals from the pillars, the interior is intact, though there was some considerable loss in the iconographic scheme (Plate 9).

On plan, the Cathedral of the Dormition, Vladimir, had a five-aisled plan like the two St Sophias in Kiev and Novgorod, producing multiple small, dark units in the corners of the plan. But the Cathedral of the Dormition, Moscow, has been reduced to a pair of side-aisles as broad as the nave itself, and units the size of the main crossing. On the interior, aisles and nave are of a uniform height, so the interior space is much more open and unified than the traditional Russian church interior, and the light is more evenly dispersed through the space. The chronicle provides an admiring description, despite its departure from prototypes: 'Of a truth this church is very wonderful in its dignified serenity, height, lightness and in its fame and renown, such as there has never been in Russia before, except in the churches of Vladimir.'[36] The Italian architect had obviously introduced just the right qualities of western Renaissance architecture in the building to relieve the more usual dark and constricted space.

Entry is into a square open space before the iconostasis with a dome on either side of the four round pillars. The upper volume just manages to squeeze over the seventeenth-century iconostasis beyond the crossing, with the central great dome creating a kind of canopy over the Holy Doors. The five registers, or levels, of icons on the iconostasis spill onto the walls, surrounding the visitor with all the hosts of heaven, and paintings on the columns people the space itself with yet more holy figures and events. Every surface is covered, including pilasters, arches, squinches, and domes. The Deesis, the register of the feast days and the series of prophets in the decorative scheme, was commissioned in 1481 as a victory thank-offering by the tsar from 'the icon painter Dionysius, the priests Timofey, Yarets and Konya'. Above the south door are images of Emperor Constantine and his mother, St Helena, and correspondingly above the north door by the throne are St Vladimir and Olga, his grandmother. The rest of the walls were covered in fresco between 1514 and 1515 but had decayed to such an extent by the mid-seventeenth century that they had cartoons copied from the original images; the walls were replastered and repainted between 1642 and 1644, carefully reproducing the previous scheme. This was commissioned by Tsar Michael Romanov, who died the following year. The work was done by 150 icon painters in the state icon workshops. Successive restorers' overpainting has been removed by conservators in an attempt to return the interior to its original quality.[37] Despite the ideological antagonism of the Soviet state to religion, this aspect of Russian ecclesiastical patrimony at the seat of state power was treated with considerable pride by the Soviet Department for the Care of Monuments.

The overall effect of the scheme is organized and theologically didactic, rather than patterned and decorative. Its narrative is concerned, naturally, with the Assumption of the Virgin and other doctrines of the Church. The domes all have representations of Christ, dominated by the Pantocrator in the main dome; figures of the patriarchs and prophets stand between the windows in their drums; the evangelists occupy the pendentives of the main dome, as at Kiev, with one of the Virgin towards the east; feasts of the Church in the vaulting; and the Dormition in the semi-dome of the main apse.[38] This is in complete opposition to Soviet ideals, yet enormous effort and resources were expended in enhancing legibility. It would appear that the message was that, powerful as this vision and institution had been, they had been completely overwhelmed by the Soviet state. The monuments of the national culture were to become the 'soil' for the growth of the new people's art, as proclaimed by the Executive Committee of the Council of Workers' and Soldiers' Deputies:

> Citizens, the old masters have gone, leaving behind a vast heritage. Now it belongs to all the people.
>
> Citizens, take care of this inheritance, take care of the paintings, statues, buildings—it is the embodiment of your spiritual strength and that of your forefathers. Art is something wonderful, that talented people were able to achieve even under the yoke of despotism, that bears witness to the beauty and strength of the human soul. Citizens, do not

even touch one stone, protect the monuments, the old buildings, articles, documents—all this is your history, your pride. Remember, all this is the soil from which will grow your new, people's, art.[39]

In an exhibition catalogue of 1964 entitled *Preservation and Restoration of Monuments of Architecture in the USSR*, the official party line was laid out:

> No rapid progress of Soviet socialist culture would be conceivable without a profound and critical study of the world's cultural heritage of the past, that of the peoples inhabiting this country first and foremost.
>
> Great Lenin, the founder of the Soviet State, pointed out that new socialist culture could only be developed on the basis of exact knowledge and the working over of 'the culture created by the whole development of mankind'...
>
> In October 1918 the Soviet Government issued a decree on the registration and preservation of artistic monuments and antiquities; the decree envisaged a series of measures aimed at the 'preservation, study and best possible acquaintance of the broad masses of population with all the treasures of art and antiquity that can be found in Russia'. It was the first revolutionary decree in this field: for the first time in history the State declared all the outstanding monuments of culture to be part of the national property, assuming full responsibility for their safety...
>
> An enormous, and in many ways irreparable, damage to the cultural heritage of our country was inflicted by the fascist barbarians during the Second World War. They strove not only for the destruction of national cultural monuments on the territories of the USSR temporarily occupied by them. Field Marshall Reichenau's order of October 10 1941, which was approved by Hitler, stated that 'no historical or artistic values in the east have any real importance', and demanded their unhesitant and complete annihilation. Architectural masterpieces in Kiev, Novgorod, Pskov, Chernigov, Riga, Vilnius, Leningrad suburbs and other old cities were utterly or partly destroyed with unprecedented cruelty by Hitler's hordes retreating under the pressure of the Soviet Army's attacks.[40]

The catalogue opens with the Moscow Kremlin, Cathedral Square, and the Cathedral of the Dormition. The cathedral had ceased to be a place of worship in 1918, after the revolution, and became a museum.[41]

Ironically in this post-communist era, the Russian Orthodox Church has re-emerged as a power in the land.

A Thanksgiving Service was held here on 13 October 1989, the first since the Mass at Easter 1918. Churches across the country have been reopened, and even the Cathedral of Christ the Saviour, on the opposite bank of the river to the Kremlin, has now been rebuilt at vast expense. It had been destroyed by Stalin, and a swimming pool built on the site. On 26 September 1997, Boris Yeltsin signed the Freedom of Conscience and Religious Association Act, which recognizes a number of churches, but only those that worked alongside the regime between 1917 and 1991. Churches are growing, and the Orthodox alone claim eighty million members, more than half the population of Russia.

There has been a remarkable religious revival in the twenty-first century, but it is, at least in part, the revival of a particular aspect of Russian identity. Since 2009, priests have been allowed back in the Russian army, and, by the end of 2019, 269 of them were being trained at Patriot Park outside Moscow as full-time military chaplains. In the park, a grand cathedral of green metal, glass, and golden domes 95 metres high is to 'symbolize the spiritual values of the Russian army'. The defence minister, Sergei Shoigu, 'said its steps would be cast of metal from captured Nazi armour. Slated to open on the 75th anniversary of the Second World War victory in 2020 [which indeed it did], the church will include exhibits of key battles and an "alley of memory" with the names of 30 million war participants.'[42] It is intended to be the National War Memorial, laden with architectural symbolism, for the Great Patriotic War. Military units are to be equipped with 'mobile churches' in tents and trailers with icons and golden domes. But there are competing historic Christian identities in what was the land of Rus'. In Kiev and the Ukraine, there was the Russian Orthodox Church and a self-styled Ukrainian Orthodox Church represented by two bodies, one of which added the term 'Autocephalos'. The Ukrainian bodies planned to merge into a single patriarchate. Recognition by the Ecumenical Patriarch of Constantinople (Istanbul) following a synod in October 2018 was crucial, but so is recognition by other Orthodox Churches, and certainly that is not forthcoming from the Russian Orthodox Church. A council of the unified Ukrainian Church elected Epiphanius as Patriarch of Kiev and All Ukraine in December 2018. Where religious and political identities have been so closely aligned historically, shifts in one or other can easily lead to schism, conflict, and even war. On 5 January 2019, the document was signed by the Ecumenical Patriarch, Bartholomew I, in Istanbul, granting independence of the Orthodox Church in the Ukraine from the Russian Orthodox Church. The religious symbolism is freighted with politics. The President of the Ukraine was at the ceremony, doubtless enjoying this declaration of independence. As reported in the *Financial Times*: 'Attaining religious independence is a victory for Ukraine in its wider struggle against Russia that encompasses Crimea and support for separatists fighting Kiev in the east of the country.'[43] These are potentially dangerous escalations in 'spiritual warfare'.

Figure 10. Church of the Holy Mother of God across the Katschhof

5

Renovatio Romani Imperii

Charlemagne's Church of the Holy Mother of God at Aachen

*T*he Basilica of the Holy Mother of God in Aachen was considered, even *by contemporaries of Charlemagne, to be one of the greatest monumental works of the age. Fortunately, it is also one of the most complete survivals. The building was begun after 794, and by 798 the structure was ready for the wholly decorative ancient marble columns to be added. It appears not to have been consecrated until 804, during a visit by Pope Leo III. Charlemagne had been crowned emperor on Christmas Day 800 in St Peter's in Rome. He was said to have been surprised by the crowning, but, with such an imperial setting for his throne either complete or very nearly so, Charlemagne cannot be said to have been wholly unprepared. The form and the very material of the palace church in Aachen are redolent of imperial references, providing a suitable set-ting for the imperial throne. Charlemagne had by no means been 'born in the purple', since his father, Pepin, was crowned king only after having effectively deposed the puppet Merovingian King Childeric III in 751. Pope Stephen himself anointed Pepin, and his heirs, Charles (later to be known as Charlemagne) and Carloman, were given the title Patrician of the Romans. Imperial titles and imperial architectural settings establish the claim to Romanitas and Charlemagne's declared aim:* RENOVATIO ROMANI IMPERII. *If* *we look back over the eighth century, so much seems to fall into place into an ambitious programme to re-establish the western empire.*

The Approach

Coming round the eastern end of the Rathaus in Aachen from the market square past the *Granusturm* gives a spectacular view, across the Katschhof, of the whole of the north elevation of today's cathedral, originally Charlemagne's Church of the Holy Mother of God. The Rathaus of Aachen itself is built on the foundations of Charlemagne's *Aula Regia*, which rises a few metres above ground in what was the western apse, and the eastern tower or *Granusturm*, archaeologically investigated from 2007, is a complex arrangement of rooms and stairs possibly providing security for the royal apartments or the treasury.[1] These excavations along the north side of the square were only partly archaeological, the main purpose being to install an urban heating system using the hot springs that Charlemagne loved so much.

A walk towards the cathedral along the west side of the Katschhof retraces the covered north–south axial approach to the palace chapel from the *Aula Regia*. Following the royal route, from his throne on a dais in the apse of the *Aula Regia* to his then palace chapel, took Charlemagne through the central *porta*, or main gateway to the palace complex, and on to the royal entrance in the north stair tower of the church's proto-westwork. This gave him access to the throne in the first-floor gallery. Today, instead of the entrance opening off this great square as might be expected, or from a cathedral close, the only public access is through the cathedral's large western entrance courtyard, or atrium, which harks back to the atrium in front of old St Peter's in Rome. This memory of St Peter's was intensified by the presence of a large bronze pinecone fountain in the middle of the atrium. Instead of a decorative west facade showing off refined architectural stylistic display and sculptural symbolism, as on so many mediaeval cathedrals, there is a small projecting porch with a massive tribune dominated by a great conch framing the place of the throne.

Charlemagne and his Church

Inside, instead of a long nave for liturgical precessions, it is a powerful three-storey octagon, which was lined with sumptuous marble in the nineteenth century, and beyond is a very different filigreed Gothic choir. All these remarkable characteristics, their dating, and how they relate to other periods are full of significance for understanding developments in the western Church and its relationship with a renewed empire, a weakened papacy, the advance of Islam, and an embattled Byzantine Empire. After Charlemagne had died, the scholar and prominent member of the court, Einhard, wrote of the chapel as chief of all the emperor's works:

> This king, who showed himself so great in extending his empire and subduing foreign nations, and was constantly busy at that kind of activity, also undertook very many works calculated to adorn and benefit his kingdom, and brought several of them to completion. Among these, the most deserving of mention are the basilica of the Holy Mother of God at Aachen, built with wonderful skill, and a bridge over the Rhine at Mainz five hundred paces long...above all, sacred edifices were the object of his care throughout his whole kingdom.[2]

Einhard was to Charlemagne what Procopius was to the emperor Justinian, working within the same genre with similar tropes. Already in Einhard's biography, the image of the recently deceased emperor as presented by his ecclesiastical buildings was being carefully manipulated to influence the present and future shape of the empire. Later changes to this church would do the same, and no period was more blatant in its manipulation than the nineteenth century.

There has been an argument as to whether this should really be called a chapel, since it was not strictly for the use of the ruler and the intimates of his court. It has always been a collegiate church, staffed by canons, similar to St George's Chapel in Windsor Castle. By the same token, the palace was not simply the residence of the ruler; it was a seat of government. The historic functions of the palace and chapel simply do not fit easily into the categories of today, expressed in one or other language, though, in the case of this church, it does fit more easily into the English understanding of the function of a chapel than the German.

The people could enter the atrium through a door on its axis opposite the chapel, so the atrium itself acted in a way as a nave and the chapel as a royal chancel, and this was certainly the case in later coronation liturgies. Behind the tribune in the gallery was the throne with six steps (Plate 10), modelled on the throne of Solomon described in the First Book of Kings (10:19). The main axis of the palace complex was a royal processional way between thrones of Charlemagne's temporal and spiritual power, and the cross-axes too centred on the thrones. With its embracing towers, the entrance ensemble of the chapel was an early example of the westwork that would characterize the great Carolingian churches. The remarkable 4-metre high double doors, which have been moved from the Carolingian entrance below the throne forward to the entrance of the eighteenth-century porch, are a finely cast late-eighth-century neoclassical design from the foundry in Aachen. On the bronze doors there are lion's-head bosses, perhaps referring to the Holy Sepulchre, since early Christian ivories show such devices on its doors, left ajar to show the empty tomb and folded grave clothes. The first hospital of the Order of St John also had bronze lion-headed door knockers, which are still to be seen in the Museum of the Order in London.[3] Evidence of bronze casting has been found nearby in the Katschhof. These became known as the 'Wolf Doors' because of their proximity to a Roman or Hellenistic first-century bronze sculpture of a wolf, recalling the Roman she-wolf that suckled Romulus and Remus, legendary founders of Rome. The sculpture is first mentioned at Aachen in the fifteenth century, but, even if it cannot be proven to have been brought by Charlemagne from Italy as a sign of his revival of the Roman Empire, it is certainly consistent with, and reinforcing of, that theme. It could, of course, have been brought by one of his successors to intensify the theme visually, something that happens all over this building.[4] This political use of art and architecture is to be found everywhere in both the Rathaus and the church. The full significance of Rome, Ravenna, and Jerusalem for Charlemagne will become evident as his history unfolds.

Historical Background and the Mirror of the Kingdom

Already in the first century CE there were Roman baths in nearby hot springs just to the east of the church, and, soon after that, baths were built where the cathedral now stands. Recent research confirms that Aachen was continuously occupied between the fifth and the eighth centuries. Charlemagne's father, Pepin, had a villa in Aachen, and there was already a small church on an adjacent site. This magnificent octagonal chapel was built for Charlemagne's palace by Odo of Metz. A coin from 794 has been found in the area of the foundations of the central octagon, and wood from the foundations has been dated to within five years of 798. A letter to Charlemagne of July 798 refers to the marble columns having been installed, so the progress of building has been securely dated. The building was probably consecrated only during the visit by Pope Leo III in 804.[5]

These were pivotal years in Charlemagne's reign. Before this time in northern Europe, stone churches were usually small and unaisled, as in the example at Bradford-on-Avon from the late seventh or early eighth century. It was probably under Charlemagne's father, Pepin, that work began to rebuild the Abbey of Saint-Denis north of Paris as a large aisled basilica with a monastic choir and ring-crypt reminiscent of the one at St Peter's in Rome. Under Charlemagne, just as under Constantine, builder of Old St Peter's, a massive increase in political power would be consolidated in an imposed unity of the Church, and displayed culturally in massive and opulent architectural projects; liturgy and pilgrimage made an important contribution to the project of unification in both the Constantinian and Carolingian contexts. This is supremely manifest in the palace chapel at Aachen as the 'mirror' of the kingdom.

Aachen itself does not appear to have much to recommend it as a capital, and indeed it did not function that way. It was one of a network of palaces across the realm, from which justice was dispensed, grants were made, and kingly power was exercised and on display. Often this was performed personally by Charlemagne, but to a great extent it was done in his name by his *missi dominici*, who carried royal authority. This was, however, clearly a favourite among Charlemagne's palaces, and he spent increasing amounts of time there towards the end of his life. He enjoyed its hot springs, and bathing could be a highly social affair, involving as many as a hundred members of the court. The growing prestige of this palace at Aachen was further enhanced when Charlemagne was finally hailed as 'imperator and basileus' by a Byzantine embassy in 812, and, during the reign of his son Louis the Pious, the *Annales Regni Francorum* recorded impressive embassies from Islamic Spain, Persia, the Avars, Venice, Jerusalem, and Northumbria.[6] Not all great embassies were received at Aachen, but many were, including those from Constantinople, from the Caliph Harun of Baghdad, and from 'the King of the Africans' in Libya. The architecture, especially of the chapel, lent a special grandeur to such diplomatic occasions.[7] It may be that architectural and artistic references to Rome, Ravenna, and Constantinople were lost on many of his own people, but those who travelled with him, and those who travelled to him in these embassies, would have recognized, or have had pointed out to them, the similarity of Charlemagne's palace and the governance of his realm to the greatness of those capitals and the Roman Empire that they represented.

Charlemagne and his forebears had long defended both the Church of Rome and Christian lands. His grandfather, Charles Martel, had stopped the Muslim advance into Gaul that had begun as early as 718. Muslim armies had pushed up through the Visigothic kingdom in

Hispania to create al-Andalus, and then pressed on into Gaul. By that time, Muslim forces were also at the gates of Constantinople. In 732, a force of at least 30,000 Muslims was moving towards Poitiers under their *amir* 'Abd al-Rahman al-Ghafiqi. At Poitiers, they ransacked the shrine of St Hilary, and Charles Martel raced across Europe to meet them just south of Tours. After a week of fighting and the death of the *amir*, the Franks were victorious.[8] The victory secured Charles's position, and, when he died in 741, the territory over which he held sway, nominally under the Merovingian sovereign Childeric III, was second only to the Byzantine Empire. Charles's son Pepin III, or Pepin the Short, was not so reticent about power, and in 750, probably at the instigation of St Boniface, the petition was put to Pope Stephen II 'whether it was good or not that the King of the Franks would wield no royal power'. With papal blessing, the then king, Childeric III, was deposed in 751, and the former Mayor of the Palace, Pepin III, became King Pepin I. He was anointed and enthroned by St Boniface at Soissons. In 753, Pope Stephen II was forced to cross the Alps to appeal to King Pepin for his support against the Lombard threat. Pepin's eldest son, the 6- or 7-year-old Charles (to become known as Charlemagne) was despatched to meet the pope as a gesture of respect and to accompany him on the last leg of his journey.[9]

After his effective usurpation of the throne, the legitimacy of Pepin's kingship came from papal blessing, which was reinforced with a second anointing by Pope Stephen himself at Saint-Denis, where Pepin and his sons, Charles and Carloman, were given the title Patrician of the Romans. Sacral kingship became firmly established in the west with his anointing of Pepin and his heirs. The first anointing by St Boniface could be considered to be a post-baptismal unction, which he would not have received in the Gallican rite, but the second anointing was a royal 'priestly' anointing, and in 794 Paulinus, bishop of Aquileia, pressed Charlemagne to be *Dominus et pater, rex et sacerdos*, 'Lord and father, king and priest'.[10] Spiritual and temporal power had much to offer one another.

The Significance of Building Materials

The throne in the gallery of the chapel emphasizes the religious side of Charlemagne's kingship. When compared to the opulence and refinement of the exotic marble columns, and the capitals (some ancient and some very competently copied by Carolingian masons), the throne looks cobbled together with relatively crude stonework. The paved 'carpet' beneath includes stone that had to be imported, red and green porphyry and grey Egyptian granite. This, then, was probably part of what had been collected from Ravenna. The shape of the steps reveals that they were cut from a single column, which has *graffiti* with crosses. The side-panels, bound with simple bronze brackets, also have ancient *graffiti* with crosses, calvaries, and even a board game. These materials had not been used for their aesthetic value; there must have been some other intrinsic worth. Beneath the back of the throne is a cupboard, and part of the structure is wooden, dated by dendrochronology to 800. Small nails and holes in the wood of the base have been identified as fitting precisely the base of the purse reliquary of St Stephen, protomartyr, now in Vienna.[11]

In 799, a monk of Jerusalem had arrived with blessings and relics of the Holy Sepulchre from the patriarch in Jerusalem. The nature of the *graffiti* and analysis of the red-veined stone of the steps and the panels make it extremely likely that these stones are the very relics from the Holy Sepulchre, too sacred to be worked further, other than to be shaped in the most basic way.[12] The position of the throne in the gallery elevated on steps gave a view of the altars of the Virgin and of St Peter below and of the altar of the Saviour directly opposite in the gallery. Directly above the altar of the Saviour was the apocalyptic image of Christ enthroned, surrounded by the symbols of the evangelists and offered the crowns of the twenty-four elders. The crowns belong to Christ, and it is only a small theological (and political) step to conceive of the imperial crown itself as received directly from Christ, as shown in the painting of the crowning of Otto III in the treasury of the cathedral. This theological side-lining of the pope became a recurrent theme in the politics of empire.[13]

Charlemagne had been anointed king and was crowned emperor on Christmas Day 800 in St Peter's in Rome by the pope. The iconography of the chapel proclaims that he occupied the throne by divine right, but, like his crown, it would be surrendered when Christ came again to judge the living and the dead. That time was constantly before the eyes of the emperor in the decoration of the dome. This was like the vision of the 'Son of man' granted to Stephen the protomartyr, whose relic of bloodstained earth was kept within the throne (Acts 7:55–6). It may only have been earth mixed with blood, but it was kept in a purse reliquary studded with jewels and mounted in gold. The rarest, most beautiful, and costly gems yielded by the earth were mere decoration for the earth and blood within, which bore witness to the 'Son of man standing on the right hand of God'. When Christ came again in power, he would occupy the throne in judgment. Meanwhile, Charlemagne was 'king by the grace of God' and occupied the throne as 'vicar of Christ'—as he was called in the earliest literary 'Mirror of the Ruler' (*Fürstenspiegel*). This throne was an intermediary place between earth and heaven. At the entrance to the palace chapel, the great conch marks the significance of the place of the throne in the gallery, making a great reliquary of the palace chapel itself as a protective chamber for these relics. Here sat Charlemagne on a throne made of stone taken from the Holy Sepulchre, the centre of the world. The image would not have been lost on the ambassadors from the emperor in Constantinople, where the source of the marbles was considered to be of such significance.[14]

Material, Form, and Meaning

The plan and general form of the whole palace chapel is based on San Vitale in Ravenna, built in the 540s during the reign of the Byzantine emperor Justinian I, who is famously portrayed in its mosaics, which

were the last known great imperial works of art before iconoclasm. San
Vitale was built by Bishop Maximian with finance provided by Julianus,
a wealthy local banker, soon after the reconquest of the area by Justinian.
Another intriguing formal similarity is with the first- to second-century
Praetorium not far away in Cologne. It has a fourth-century ceremonial
hall, which is octagonal on the exterior and round on the interior and
of comparable dimensions to the palace chapel in Aachen. The ceremonial
hall was destroyed in an earthquake around 780–790, just before
Charlemagne built the palace chapel at Aachen.[15] It is not certain
whether the dome of the palace chapel was covered in mosaic or
paintings, but the theme of the images was certainly the same as the
present mosaics, an apocalyptic vision of Christ as Pantocrator, with a
lower register of the four and twenty elders offering their crowns. The
images of the dome mediated in the iconoclastic debate, though there
was a general sympathy for the iconoclasts. The Carolingian theology
in the *Libri Carolini* denies that the images should be venerated as having the same spiritual qualities of their original, but it upholds their
usefulness in teaching, citing Gregory the Great.[16]

Both San Vitale and Justinian's somewhat earlier palace chapel of SS
Sergius and Bacchus in Constantinople, which was completed in 536,
have the arched bays of the octagon billowing outwards to columned
screens at both ground floor and gallery levels, whereas Charlemagne's
palace chapel has column screens at both levels in arched bays that on
plan are straight. This creates much less visual movement, a suitable
visual structural stability as a 'mirror' for the political stability of the
kingdom. On the other hand, it also creates the uncomfortable junc-
tion between a capital and the underside of an arch. That the columns
are structurally unnecessary was amply demonstrated by the occupying Napoleonic forces, who removed the magnificent marble and
porphyry columns to the Louvre. Many, but by no means all, were
returned, and, generally speaking, it is the columns in the arches in the
cardinal directions that are ancient. There is another pair of green
porphyry columns in the cathedral treasury. These columns are the
spolia brought back from Rome and Ravenna by Charlemagne, as

described by Einhard. Sometime between 788 and 791, Pope Hadrian had given permission for mosaics and marble to be removed from Ravenna by Charlemagne.[17]

When Charlemagne also obtained permission from the pope to bring a bronze statue of Theodoric from the pediment of the palace in Ravenna to his palace in Aachen, he was weaving together strands of imperial history. Marble columns, finely carved capitals, and marble paving from the palace of the last emperor in Ravenna made the message very clear by providing a material connection with the imperial past. In Charlemagne's palace of Ingelheim, Ermold records that the great hall contained a series of portraits of historical rulers. There, Augustus, Constantine, and Theodosius provide the types for Charles Martel, Pepin, and Charlemagne. Ermold commented that 'the Franks and their wondrous deeds continue the acts of the Caesars'.[18] Like Constantine, Charlemagne was founding a *Roma Nova*, as his contemporaries said. These *spolia*, or recovered materials, constitute the building that is to be seen today. Interestingly, if the bronze wolf and pinecone are later additions, as are certainly the elaborate nineteenth- and twentieth-century marble panelling and the mosaic of the drum of the dome, then successive generations have very consciously intensified the messages of *Roma Nova* to suit their own political agendas. Those capitals, which were newly carved by Frankish craftsmen, show that they were as skilled as Ermold, Einhard, and their political masters at the imitation of the antique.

The Byzantine emperor Justinian was able to order materials from all over his territory to embody the empire in the building of Hagia Sophia in Constantinople. This was not an option for Charlemagne, but he was able to establish continuity with the Roman Empire and demonstrate similarities and differences between his empire, Byzantium, and the glory of Rome. Porphyry had long been associated with the emperor, and there had been unsuccessful attempts to limit it to imperial use.[19] There are, of course, aesthetic aspects to this; purple is a noble colour, used to trim senatorial togas, and, as a hard, rare, beautiful stone, purple porphyry was particularly appropriate to embellish imperial buildings. As soon as status, geography, history (with the politics attached), and other associations begin to cling to materials, their use takes on symbolic meaning. Architectural form can certainly do that by making references to other significant Christian buildings, such as the Holy Sepulchre, St Peter's in Rome, San Vitale, and the Imperial Church of SS Sergius and Bacchus in Constantinople. The materials likewise can be charged with meaning— imperial porphyry, Roman columns from the Palace of the Exarchs in Ravenna, and stone slabs from the Church of the Holy Sepulchre in Jerusalem. Significantly, other Carolingian artistic images of the Holy Sepulchre bear a strong resemblance to the palace chapel.[20] These are a combination of historic and religious relics used in an age that understood their significance.[21]

The value and beauty of these stones, rather like the precious stones on the purse reliquary of St Stephen, point to something of even greater worth and deeper significance. The dimension of the chapel measured round the inner octagon is 144 Carolingian feet, which has been compared to the measurement given for the New Jerusalem in the Book of Revelation as 144 cubits. The biblical passage goes on to say that 'the wall was built of jasper, while the city was pure gold, clear as glass. The foundations of the wall of the city were adorned with every jewel.' The columns of the chapel were precious stone of every kind, including purple, red, green, and black porphyry. These columns are not only bearers of *Romanitas*; they also contribute to the apocalyptic vision of the New Jerusalem. The iconography of the decoration of the dome is drawn from the Revelation of St John:

At once I was in the Spirit, and lo, a throne stood in heaven with one seated on the throne! And he who sat there appeared like jasper and carnelian, and round the throne was a rainbow that looked like an emerald. Round the throne were twenty-four thrones, and seated on the thrones were twenty-four elders, clad in white garments, with golden crowns upon their heads ... And round the throne, on each side of the throne, are four living creatures ... the first living creature like a lion, the second living creature like an ox, the third living creature with the face of a man, and the fourth living creature like a flying eagle...[22]

The architectural form, the decorative imagery, and even the materials themselves present a religious message placing Charlemagne just a little lower than the angels. This was a direct expression of his sovereignty, being exalted above all his subjects. He ruled over the Franks as the *populus Dei* who were building the Church as the city of God, the New Jerusalem, manifest both in this building, but also in the kingdom for which it was the 'mirror'.[23]

Ravenna looking East and West

The architecture of Charlemagne's palace chapel mediates between east and west, and between the imperial past and his vast European realm that was emerging. San Vitale has magnificent mosaics of the Byzantine Emperor Justinian and the Empress Theodora, shown in offertory processions for the dedication of the church in 547. Even if the imperial couple was not at the dedication itself, the gifts represented in the image will have been tokens of imperial approval and the authority of Bishop Maximian, imposed by Justinian against the wishes of the people of Ravenna. That building and its decoration assert Byzantine imperial authority. Charlemagne's chapel contains further memories of the Mausoleum of Theodoric, Constantine's Palatine Chapel, the Golden Octagon at Antioch, and the imperial throne room in Constantinople, the Chrysotriklinos, where there was a mosaic of Christ enthroned above the imperial throne. As at San Vitale, Aachen blurs the line between basilica and *martyrium*. Both churches are shaped like *martyria*, but their function was primarily basilican, with aisles wrapping around octagonal naves. When Charlemagne was entombed in the palace chapel the day after his death—indeed, when relics were permanently housed in a basilican church—a memorial function would be immediately added to the

church, justifying the development of the ambulatory on both functional and symbolic levels.

At the beginning of the fifth century, Italia had nominally still been
under the rule of Roman emperors, but they had become puppets of
the Goths, who had come to dominate their Italian hosts. Finally, the
Gothic ruler Odoacer deposed the last Roman emperor, Romulus
Augustulus, in 476. Theodoric (king of Italy 493–526) was the son of
the king of the Goths and grew up as a hostage at the imperial Byzantine
court. When Theodoric himself became king, Emperor Zeno encouraged him to invade Italy as an imperial ally. Though a German,
Theodoric maintained the Roman legal and administrative structures
of the state, saying that his governors should 'obey the Roman cus-
toms. You are now by God's blessing restored to your ancient freedom;
put off the barbarian; clothe yourselves with the morals of the toga;
unlearn cruelty, that you may not be unworthy to be our subjects.'

Since Theodoric was king of Italy with the sanction of the Emperor
of the East, Charlemagne considered that the western imperial mantle
had fallen to Theodoric, who even minted his coins in the name of
the Emperor of the East.[24] In this sense, he restored imperial rule
and was greatly admired by Charlemagne, who had an equestrian
statue of Theodoric taken from the palace at Ravenna and brought
back to Aachen. In bringing the columns for his palace chapel from
Ravenna, Charlemagne continued a policy of Theodoric, who wrote
to his officials:

> We wish to build new edifices without despoiling the old. But we are
> informed that in your municipality there are blocks of masonry and
> columns formerly belonging to some building now lying absolutely
> useless and unhonoured. If it be so, send these slabs of marble and col-
> umns by all means to Ravenna, that they may be again made beautiful
> and take their place in a building there.

Theodoric used *spolia*, not in his churches, nor in his mausoleum, but
in his palace as an image of his government: 'Much do we delight in
seeing the greatness of our Kingdom imaged forth in the splendour
of our palace.' 'Thus do the ambassadors of foreign nations admire our

power, for at first sight one naturally believes that as is the house so is the inhabitant.' For Charlemagne, as for Theodoric, the qualities of material, antiquity, and provenance, all reflected on the government, character and power of the ruler.[25]

In 536, Justinian sent his general Belisarius to retake Italy from the Goths. In 540, Belisarius entered Rome, and by 554, after a long and gruelling campaign, Italy had been freed from Ostrogothic rule. The Church could now reassert its authority and combat the Arian heresy of the Ostrogoths. But there was only a short respite from invaders, with the Lombards arriving in 568.

Charlemagne's father, Pepin, was highly successful in his military campaign against the Lombards, who were threatening Rome in 754 and again in 756. When Pepin regained lands in northern Italia, the Byzantine emperor expected the return of what had been former Byzantine possessions, but instead Pepin presented them to the pope, establishing the territorial and temporal power of the papacy on the basis of the fraudulent document known as the 'Donation of Constantine'. That was a document purporting to transfer the land of Italia from Constantine to the papacy. The Byzantine emperor was infuriated by the passing of former Byzantine territory to the pope and demanded the return of the Exarchate of Ravenna to him, so Pepin himself confirmed a 'donation' of his own. This was a grand Constantinian gesture by the most powerful ruler in the west. The marble and statuary that were later removed by Charlemagne for his palace chapel at Aachen were redolent of associations with the last Emperor of the West, with Theodoric, with the Frankish defence of Rome, and with the establishment of the papal territories.

Before he died, Pepin captured Narbonne from the Muslims. He already enjoyed immense prestige for having saved Rome and secured the papacy, and that prestige was transferred into temporal and spiritual power. Unity was essential in a diverse realm with a powerful local nobility, which is why the king and his court were constantly travelling between his many palaces, and why he was anxious to conform the diversity of local Gallican liturgy of the Church within a recognizably Roman practice. In 767, the year before he died, like Constantine Pepin presided over a Church council concerning the portrayal of saints in art: 'the Lord King Pepin then held a great council at Gentilly with Romans and Greeks about the Holy Trinity and the image of the saints.'[26] He was dabbling in the Iconoclastic Controversy, now spilling much blood in the east, and in the Trinitarian controversy that divided the churches of east and west. He was clearly a hugely powerful figure on the world stage. As he died, an embassy arrived from the Abbasid Caliph of Baghdad, who was clearly seeking advantage over the hated Umayyad *amir* of al-Andalus, who was also a constant threat to the Franks.

Military action was an ever-present reality in the Kingdom of the Franks. In 772, Charles, king of the Franks since 768, waged a war against the Saxons on his north-eastern flank. He destroyed a key fort at Eresburg and their main pagan cultic shrine of the Irminsul.[27] Forced conversion followed. When Desiderius, king of the Lombards, threatened Rome again in 773, Charles led a Frankish army against them, laying siege to their capital, Pavia. Leaving Pavia encircled, he made a triumphal entry into Rome to celebrate Easter there. Leaving Easter and Rome behind, Charlemagne forced Lombard Pavia to surrender in June 774, and Lombard power in Italy was broken. Charlemagne was now king of the Franks and of the Lombards.[28] He restored papal lands and annexed northern Italia for himself. By contrast, in the sixth century, Byzantium had only temporarily regained its Italian lands.

Charlemagne proclaimed his own achievement of what Byzantium had only temporarily managed by using the architectural form of Justinian's church in Ravenna for his own palace chapel in Aachen. Clearly, the accomplishments of Theodoric, the Gothic king of Italy, and Justinian, who had liberated Italia from the Goths, retaking former Byzantine possessions, were being compared with those of Charlemagne, who had annexed northern Italia, destroyed the power of the Lombards, and removed their threat to the Church in Rome and the Papal States.

The Ravennate architectural forms, the marble and the statuary that were removed by Charlemagne for his chapel at Aachen, were redolent of associations with the last Emperor of the West, with Justinian, Belisarius, Theodoric, with the Frankish defence of Rome and the establishment of the papal territories. Much of this history is embedded in the architecture of the palatine chapel at Aachen. It was a fresh integration of ancient forms, looking to sources perhaps nearby in Cologne and certainly in Ravenna, including the mausoleum of Theodoric, whom Charlemagne saw as the first German emperor.

The Relationship with Islam

In 777, Charlemagne continued the war in the far north-east against the Saxons. The territories were regained, and the inhabitants were either killed or converted to Christianity at the sword's point. He called an assembly at Paderborn in his new lands in Westphalia, to discuss the governance of his rebellious new territories. During the assembly, ambassadors arrived from al-Andalus. The semi-autonomous Arab rulers of Barcelona and Zaragoza[29] asked for Charlemagne's help to contain the expansionism of 'Abd al-Rahman and the incorporation of these independent territories into the emirate. It was said that the Abbasid Caliph of Baghdad would contribute forces against this hated ambitious Umayyad prince in Cordoba (see Chapter 8).[30] Charlemagne's relations with Damascus were very different from his military opposition to the expansionism of the Amir of al-Andalus. In his *Life of Charlemagne*, Einhard records:

He had such friendly relations to Harun-al-Rashid, the king of the Persians, who held almost all of the East except India, that he held him in favour more than all the kings and princes in the world and thought that he alone was worthy of his honour and generosity. Indeed, when Charles' representatives, whom he had sent with gifts to the most holy sepulchre of our Lord and Saviour and to the place of His resurrection, came to him and told him of their lord's wishes, he not only allowed them to do what they requested but even granted him that holy and salvific place so it might be thought to be in his power. He sent his own legates back and sent magnificent gifts to Charles, robes and spices and other riches of the East, and a few years before he had sent an elephant, the only one he possessed, to Charles, who had asked for one.[31]

With rebellion likely in either Saxony or restive Lombardy during his absence, it is a wonder that Charlemagne could be drawn beyond the farthest south-west corner of his dominion. On the other hand, his family had a history of fighting Arab incursions—his grandfather Charles Martel at Poitiers, his father, Pepin, in south-western Gaul, and his capture of Narbonne, all of which were to hold back Arab expansion. Moreover, the promise of territories beyond the Pyrenees proved too tempting. In 778, having crossed the Pyrenees, Charlemagne found both his erstwhile allies in Barcelona and Zaragoza had barred the gates to him. As 'Abd al-Rahman's forces swept towards him, Charlemagne had to retreat across the mountains to Francia. The destruction of his rearguard by Basques is memorialized in the *Chanson de Roland*. Meanwhile, the Saxons had indeed rebelled, and the king sped towards the north-east to suppress it. Charlemagne had very nearly overreached himself. In consolidating his realms, he had his sons crowned in 781 by Pope Hadrian, Carloman as King of Italy, and the younger Louis as King of Aquitaine. It was the first crowning of Frankish kings, probably a ceremony again borrowed from Byzantine ritual.[32]

The Symbolic Function of the Building

Much of this history of the intimate relationship between Church and State is embedded in the architecture of what is now Aachen Cathedral. The palace chapel at Aachen was a fresh integration of ancient forms. The building materials were historic relics of imperial continuity, and the main religious relics, besides those of

St Stephen, were the cloak of St Martin, the greatest of Frankish saints, and the robe of the Virgin, given to Charlemagne by the Byzantine emperor—this was visibly the heart of a revived western empire allied to the Roman Church. His chapel at Aachen was the exemplar of this ideal. He showed his personal devotion by adorning it 'with gold and silver and lamps, and with railings and portals made of solid bronze' and marble brought from Ravenna and Rome.

The success of the image projected by the palatine chapel at Aachen is attested by its emulation by princes both of the Church and of the realm. Early and evocative copies were produced in Nijmegen and one at Liège by Bishop Notker (972–1008) as his chapel and mausoleum. Another comparable example was in Croatian Zadar, founded by Bishop Donatus, who had been both ambassador for the Byzantine emperor at the court of Charlemagne and also an ambassador for him in Constantinople. Much later, the west end of Essen Cathedral was modelled on three bays of Aachen, with an imperial throne in the gallery. At the nunnery church of St Maria im Capitol in Cologne, one bay was used as a screen across the west end of the nave. An octagonal nunnery church at Ottmarsheim in Alsace, consecrated in 1049, is the best preserved of the successors to Aachen. The nunnery churches were probably more interested in the fact that the chapel was dedicated to the Virgin and housed the relic of her robe than in the imperial connection, which testifies to the possibility that the image can be read in different but complementary ways.

The architectural forms adopted in the imitations bore a variety of meanings. Charlemagne's Visigothic courtier Theodulf, now abbot of Fleury and bishop of Orléans, built an oratory during his abbacy between 799 and 818 within a Roman villa at Germaniacus, now Germigny-des-Prés near Fleury. About a century later, the *Catalogue des abbés de Fleury* is explicit about how

> he vied in this with Charlemagne, who, at this time, had built at his palace of Aachen a church of such splendour that its like could not be found in all of Gaul. Theodulf consecrated his oratory to God,

Creator and Preserver of All Things and had a master artist represent, above the altar, cherubs covering the mercy seat of Divine Glory with their wings.[33]

The *Catalogue* gives detailed information about Theodulf's building of the oratory. There is an inscription around the eastern apse that reads: 'Beholder, gaze upon the holy propitiatorium and cherubim: and see [how] the ark of the covenant of God shimmers. You, perceiving these things and ready to beset God with prayers, add, I implore you, Theodulf to your invocations.'[34]

Though there appears to have been conscious emulation of Charlemagne and the architecture of his chapel, in formal terms the emulation was rather free. Theodulf's oratory is a centralized building, but it is square with apses on each wall, and tri-apsed to the east in the Visigothic tradition, perhaps going right back to the Byzantine domination of Hispania. The bishop's throne was housed in the western apse. There are also horseshoe arches from the same tradition, and the mosaic in the eastern apse is Byzantine in influence. The building establishes Theodulf's connection with the royal court, its glories and reforms. It also draws on his own Visigothic origins in Spain and their architectural forms which were also being adopted by the Muslims of al-Andalus. It must be said that the relative contribution of the Visigoths and Muslims to this tradition has become highly controversial, but the visual references in the chapel are clear. There is a hint of this in the palace chapel in Aachen too, in places where the Carolingian stonework is still in evidence—for example, the alternating coloured bands of the *voussoirs* of the arches recall the architecture of Muslim Spain, the Amirate in al-Andalus, and also the Caliphate in Damascus.[35] Charlemagne had been at war with the first and had established useful relations with the other, making him Protector of the Holy Places and holding the keys to the Holy Sepulchre.

Despite there being peace at this time, clearly it was not an easy relationship between Christianity and Islam in the Holy Land, and many Christians lived in exile, including at Rome. Pope Theodore I (642–9) himself was born in Jerusalem, and Sergius I (687–701) seems to have introduced the feast of the Exaltation of the Cross on 14 September jointly commemorating the return of the Cross to the Holy Sepulchre by Emperor Heraclius and the original 'Finding of the Cross' by Helena. As the premier shrine of the Christian faith under Muslim rule, the Church of the Holy Sepulchre was vulnerable and in need of powerful friends. A Jerusalem monk brought 'blessing and relics from the Sepulchre of the Lord and of the place of Calvary, also the keys of the city and of the mount, with a banner' to Charlemagne, the Frankish king.[36] In his *Life of Charlemagne*, Einhard wrote:

> When [Charles's] representatives, whom he had sent loaded with gifts for the most Holy Sepulchre of our Lord and Saviour [in Jerusalem] and the place of his resurrection, came before [Harun] and informed him of their lord's wishes, he not only allowed them to complete their mission, but even handed over that sacred and salvific place, that it might be considered under Charles's control.[37]

In 800, a delegation from the Patriarch of Jerusalem presented the keys to the Holy Sepulchre, Calvary, and Mount Zion to Charlemagne. He was crowned emperor later the same day. This unsettled the Byzantine emperor in Constantinople, who suspected that Charles might have even grander ambitions. That whiff of suspicion may have been intended by Caliph Harun al-Rashid, who had been exchanging envoys with Charlemagne. It was all part of an early 'Great Game' of empires, but it was more than just that. Four years earlier, when Pope Leo III was elected to follow Pope Hadrian, Leo sent ambassadors with flags of the City of Rome and the keys to the tomb of St Peter. Such gifts emphasize the temporal and spiritual aspects of Charlemagne's rule, and crucially his responsibility as the protector of the Church, of both Rome and Jerusalem. Charlemagne was allowed to create a Christian quarter in Jerusalem, with a monastery and pilgrims' hostel. He also paid a handsome tax on behalf of the Christians to the caliph. This arrangement suited everyone at the height of their strength. The first political dealings between Charlemagne and the Muslim overlords of Jerusalem had a happy outcome; the next would not. Al-Rashid died in 809, and the civil war that followed brought extensive damage to the churches of Jerusalem, and in 810, the capitulary of Aachen records the decision to send money to Jerusalem 'for the restoration of the churches of God'. In 813, there was an earthquake that brought down most of the roof of the rotunda around the Holy Sepulchre. It was restored with the support of a rich Egyptian, who paid for a double-shell wooden dome to be built and covered with lead.[38] The mutually beneficial relationship between the empires of Charlemagne and the caliph was gone, and the next encounter between the Caliphate and the Franks would be a murderous confrontation during the Crusades.

The Church and the Kingdom

Every aspect of Charlemagne's whole palace was loaded with meaning, including the overall plan. A parallel has been drawn between the palace at Aachen and the pope's Lateran Palace in Rome, which was an imperial palace, given by Constantine himself early in the fourth century to the bishop of Rome.[39] Pope Hadrian sent Charlemagne a collection of books in 774 to assist in the king's drive to bring the Church in his lands into closer liturgical harmony with Rome, and in 781, Charlemagne invited the English scholar Alcuin of York to establish a school at Aachen. Alcuin, who was a pupil of the great intellectual Bede, was at court for most of the decade following his arrival in 786. He led ecclesiastical and liturgical reform, along with Benedict of Aniane, who was the leader of monastic reform.

A recognizable Romanization of the liturgy was an important part of the new Carolingian order and the unity of the realm.[40] Those reforms emanated from the chapel at Aachen. The liturgy was an instrument of orthodox religious education, it was a unifying link with Rome as the guarantor of orthodoxy, and it created and reinforced the new political order with the new rites of anointing kings and with constant prayer on their behalf. The liturgy enacted social relationships that were then embodied in religious architecture. The earlier Gallican liturgy, on the other hand, was rich, and varied in use from place to place. Such richness is attractive and bound to persist, but that variety was reflected in belief as well, which is why both Pepin and Charlemagne pressed towards a Roman standard. All this took decades to move forward. Round about 784, Charlemagne received a Roman sacramentary from Pope Hadrian I, but a papal mass book needed revision to be useful in rather more ordinary contexts. The revision has traditionally been attributed to Alcuin of York but was more probably prepared by Benedict of Aniane. Throughout his life, Charlemagne himself kept a strong religious discipline.

> As long as his health allowed, he regularly went to church both morning and evening, and also to the night offices and to Mass. He was especially concerned that everything done in the church should be done with the greatest dignity and he frequently warned the sacristans that nothing foul or unclean should be brought into the church or left there. He supplied the church with such an abundance of sacred vessels made of gold and silver and with such a great number of clerical vestments that in the celebration of the Mass not even the janitors, who hold the lowest of all the ecclesiastical orders, found it necessary to serve in their ordinary clothes. He corrected the discipline of reading and singing most carefully, for he was skilled in both. But he himself never read publicly and would only sing in a low voice with the rest of the congregation.[41]

In *The Deeds of Charlemagne*, Notker the Stammerer confirms the care that the king took in his chapel and the eagerness of all there to read and sing well: 'they all took such trouble to familiarize themselves with what was to be read that when they were unexpectedly ordered to read they were found blameless by him.'[42] Notker's anecdotes make clear how offices in Church and State, high and low, were held at Charlemagne's pleasure, naturally including those in his palace chapel, and they were granted as honours and revoked at whim. He would distribute these offices, lands, and titles carefully and spread them widely, and usually on a temporary basis as *beneficia* or benefices, only for special reasons granting more than one to any individual, as he did to Theodulf, bishop of Orléans and abbot of Fleury. He did this because, 'with that estate or that, with that little abbey or that church can secure the fidelity of some vassal, as good a man as any bishop or count, and perhaps better'.[43] On the other hand, they could be as easily be removed for any sign of disloyalty, lack of wisdom, or any other cause for displeasure.[44]

In terms of the Church, the reforms included both the harmonization of the liturgy with the Roman model and the education and regulation of the clergy and people in orthodox belief. Theodulf issued *Statutes* that required his clergy to explain the liturgy to the people, and he gave clear instructions concerning the sacraments, as well as religious and moral education. His *Statutes* were a very early set and were widely used in Charlemagne's realms. The Church was highly effective in disseminating Carolingian ideals throughout his lands, where citizenship and being a Catholic Christian were synonymous. Theodulf regarded Charlemagne as St Peter's vicar, and, since the king ruled 'by the Grace of God', disobedience to the laws promulgated in his name was rebellion against God. Theodulf emulated Charlemagne in the way gifts—spiritual gifts in Theodulf's case—bound the clergy to the bishop: 'Know that your rank is second to our rank and almost joined to it. For as the bishops hold in the church the place of the apostles, so the presbyters hold the place of the other disciples of the Lord.'[45] Religious belief and practice were essential as civilizing forces to the radical and complete *RENOVATIO ROMANI IMPERII*, Charlemagne's motto. The gifts and the reforms focused loyalty ultimately on the person of Charlemagne and the pope. The one could not do without the other, Charlemagne's royal authority was sanctioned by the pope, and the pope needed Charlemagne's military power to defend his temporal rights.

In his reform and rebuilding, Charlemagne saw himself as the Old Testament King Josiah, who rebuilt the temple of Jerusalem and reformed its worship.[46] Sitting on his elevated throne in the western gallery, he had a view directly down to the altars of the Virgin and that of St Peter below. He was perfectly positioned to see the action of the liturgy and other ceremonial before the altar in the centre of the octagon, but he himself could not be seen except by the intimates of the court in the galleries at his side. Invisibly he dominated all that took place. The interior gleamed with the polished marble, imperial porphyry, and classical columns brought from Ravenna. The Roman imperial associations are extremely important here to establish the legitimate inheritance of imperial institutions and authority, which were *de facto* when building began on the Church of the Mother of God in Aachen, and *de jure* when it was complete.

The building integrated all these material connections with political, cultural, and religious realities to establish the identity and credentials of Charlemagne, who, having been crowned emperor on Christmas Day 800, was the embodiment of the RENOVATIO ROMANI IMPERII by the time the building was complete. Grandson of the powerful, but illegitimate, Mayor of the Palace to impotent Frankish kings, and son of a papally sanctioned 'usurper', Charlemagne was asserting his own legitimacy as the wearer of the imperial crown. The very fabric of the building shouted that he had done this by using his military might to defend Christians and the Church, by defending its orthodoxy and establishing its unity throughout his realms as 'a New Constantine, a New David'. When Pope Leo III built the *Aula Leonina* in the Lateran Palace, he installed a mosaic to the left of the apse showing St Peter presenting the pallium to Leo on his right and a banner to Charlemagne on his left. Both have square haloes showing the sanctity of the living, and Charlemagne is wearing the imperial crown and mantle. The inscription below read: 'Blessed Peter, give eternal life to Leo and to Charles the Crown, life, and Victory.'[47] This showed a shared spiritual and temporal authority, with slight precedence given to Pope Leo, placed on St Peter's right as his successor. Even the Byzantine emperor finally recognized Charlemagne's imperial title, after twelve years and some threat to Venice, the last

Byzantine foothold in the west. With advancing age, Charlemagne spent increasing amounts of time in Aachen, and, when he died, all agreed

> that he could be buried nowhere more suitably than in that basilica which he had built at his own expense for the love of God and our Lord Jesus Christ and to honour his mother, the holy and eternal Virgin. He was buried there on the same day on which he died and a golden arch was erected over his tomb with an image and an inscription. The inscription was written as follows: 'UNDER THIS TOMB LIES THE BODY OF CHARLES, THE GREAT AND ORTHODOX EMPEROR, WHO GLORIOUSLY INCREASED THE KINGDOM OF THE FRANKS AND REIGNED WITH GREAT SUCCESS FOR FORTY-SEVEN YEARS. HE DIED IN HIS SEVENTIES IN THE YEAR OF OUR LORD 814, IN THE SEVENTH INDICTION, ON THE TWENTY-EIGHTH DAY OF JANUARY.'[48]

He may have been buried initially just in the earth at the entrance to his chapel, much as he had buried his father, Pepin. There is a possibility that he may have been entombed in the antique Proserpina Sarcophagus, still in the treasury of the cathedral, as part of a more elaborate tomb at the east end.

Einhard recorded that there had been portents before Charlemagne's death, including a lightning strike on his chapel, sending the golden apple set in the apex of the roof spinning off and striking the bishop's house next door. And, in the year that he died, some said that, in the inscription recording Charles as its builder round the cornice at gallery level, the word PRINCEPS became almost invisible. Charles ignored the portents. On hearing news of his father's death, Louis the Pious immediately marched north from his subkingdom of Aquitaine to Aachen to take over the levers of power.[49]

Charlemagne (Plate 11) had used architectural form, the significance of the type and source of materials, iconography, the power of holy relics, and the literary genres associated with imperial aggrandizement to recreate a western Roman Empire in alliance with the Church at all levels. He had saved the pope when threatened by barbarian Lombards and established the Papal States, and also sheltered him when the pope was personally under attack by factions within the Church itself;

he imposed Christianity on his belligerent neighbours the Saxons. He presided over the reform of the monasteries and of the liturgy, bringing it more into conformity with Rome. The liturgy was to be a means of education, and his zeal for education was carried forward by Alcuin in the school at Aachen and by Bishop Theodulf in his *Statutes* for the education and conduct of his clergy, which took reform in education right through to parish level. To be a citizen of his empire was to be a Catholic. To be outside the Church was to be outside the law.[50]

Figure 11. Facade of the Abbey of Saint-Denis

6

'Transported from this inferior
to that higher world'

The Abbey of Saint-Denis

*T*he Abbey Church of Saint-Denis has its origins in a funerary chapel for
the martyred first bishop of Paris, St Denis. According to Gregory of
Tours, St Denis died in 251 CE, just before the end of the year-long Decian
persecution, but, according to The Golden Legend, compiled by Jacobus de
Voragine in the 1260s, he was martyred under the emperor Domitian (81–96
CE).[1] Abbot Suger of Saint-Denis was of the latter tradition, conflating Denis
with Dionysius (Denis) the Aropagite, mentioned in the Acts of the Apostles,
and the writings of Pseudo-Dionysius. Under royal patronage from the sixth
century, notably by Dagobert I in the 630s, the abbey grew in reputation and
as a place of pilgrimage, partly in response to the legend that it was consecrated
then by Christ and St Denis together. When Pepin removed the Merovingian
king Childeric from the throne, it was at Saint-Denis that he and his sons
Charles and Carloman were anointed by Pope Stephen as a new royal line in
754. Pepin began rebuilding Saint-Denis, which was completed by Charlemagne
with a new west front in 775. Saint-Denis would become the favoured burial
place of the kings of France. For some time before Suger became abbot in 1122,
he had seen the consequences of the crush of pilgrims gaining access through
the narrow west front built by Charlemagne. By 1144, Suger had transformed the
abbey church into an environment he experienced as 'some strange region of the

universe which neither exists entirely in the slime of the earth nor entirely in the purity of Heaven; and that, by the grace of God, I can be transported from this inferior to that higher world'.[2]

The Pilgrims' Approach to the Abbey in the Early Twelfth Century

During the first half of the twelfth century, the pilgrim approaching the Abbey Church of Saint-Denis just to the north of Paris may have been both disappointed in the architecture and daunted by the difficulty in gaining access. The abbot of the time, Suger (b. 1081, abbot 1122–51), described the approach, saying that 'in the front part, toward the north, at the main entrance with the main doors, the narrow hall was squeezed in on either side by twin towers neither high nor very sturdy but threatening ruin'.[3] Pilgrimage had burgeoned all over Europe, most especially since the millennium, and, since Saint-Denis had been granted the fair, the 'Lendit', by the king, the pressure of pilgrim numbers on the old basilica had become enormous, with distressing results.

> Through a fortunate circumstance attending this singular smallness— the number of the faithful growing and frequently gathering to seek the intercession of the Saints—the aforesaid basilica had come to suffer grave inconveniences. Often on feast days, completely filled, it disgorged through all its doors the excess of the crowds as they moved in opposite directions, and the outward pressure of the foremost ones not only prevented those attempting to enter from entering but also expelled those who had already entered. At times you could see, a marvel to behold, that the crowded multitude offered so much resistance to those who strove to flock in to worship and kiss the holy relics, the Nail and the Crown of the Lord, that no one amongst the countless thousands of people because of their very density could move a foot; that no one, because of their very congestion, could [do] anything but stand like a marble statue, stay benumbed or, as a last resort, scream.

The distress of the women, however, was so great and so intolerable that [you could see] how they, squeezed in by the mass of strong men as in a winepress, exhibited bloodless faces as in imagined death; how they cried out horribly as though in labor; how several of them, miserably trodden underfoot [but then], lifted by the pious assistance of men above the heads of the crowd, marched forward as though clinging to a pavement; and how many others, gasping with their last breath, panted in the cloisters of the brethren to the despair of everyone. Moreover the brethren who were showing the tokens of the Passion of Our Lord to the visitors had to yield to their anger and rioting and many a time, having no place to turn, escaped with the relics through the windows. When I was instructed by the brethren as a schoolboy I used to hear of this; in my youth I deplored it from without; in my mature years I zealously strove to have it corrected.[4]

Suger has painted a vividly alarming picture, but it was also by way of a retrospective justification for the radical solution he carried out. It may not seem particularly radical to expand architecturally to meet the huge increase in demand, but when the current building had been built by a succession of the king's royal forebears and moreover was reputed to have been consecrated by the hand of Christ himself, Suger had a lot of explaining to do and had to proceed with extreme caution to a solution that demonstrably respected both the sacred fabric and the long history of royal benefactors and, before them, their patron saints. The west front itself had been built by Charlemagne over the grave of his father Pepin and consecrated in 775, but that is exactly where Suger would begin his work.

The Royal Patron Saints

St Denis, or Dionysius, was one of the 'seven bishops' listed by Gregory of Tours as having been sent to evangelize various parts of France in the middle of the third century. Denis was the first bishop of Paris. Suger calls him the 'Apostle of All Gaul', and he and his companions

Rusticus and Eleutherius were martyred during the Decian persecution in 251 CE. Their funerary chapel in the Gallo-Roman cemetery
just north of Paris became an early site of pilgrimage. From as early as
the sixth century, the church enjoyed royal patronage, and, during an
epidemic of dysentery, Dagobert, the younger son of King Chilperic,
died and was buried there.[5] In the 630s, King Dagobert I lavished
patronage on the church, and the ninth-century *Gesta Dogoberti* claims
that he doubled the building in size, but earlier documents refer only
to magnificent refurbishment. In any event, in the twelfth century,
Abbot Suger of Saint-Denis considered Dagobert to be the Founder,
writing:

> When the glorious and famous King of the Franks, Dagobert, notable
> for his royal magnanimity in the administration of his kingdom and yet
> no less devoted to the Church of God, had fled to the village of
> Catulliacum in order to evade the intolerable wrath of his father
> Clothaire, and when he had learned that the venerable images of the
> Holy Martyrs who rested there—appearing to him as very beautiful
> men clad in snow-white garments—requested his service and unhesi-
> tatingly promised him their aid with words and deeds, he decreed with
> admirable affection that a basilica of the Saints be built with regal
> magnificence. When he had constructed this [basilica] with a marvel-
> lous variety of marble columns he enriched it incalculably with treas-
> ures of purest gold and silver and hung on its walls, columns and arches
> tapestries woven of gold and richly adorned with a variety of pearls, so
> that it might seem to excel the ornaments of all other churches and,
> blooming with incomparable luster and adorned with every terrestrial
> beauty, might shine with inestimable splendor. Only one thing was
> wanting in him: that he did not allow for the size that was necessary.[6]

As so often, this text tells us as much about Suger and his transformation of Saint-Denis as it does about Dagobert and its past. There
was a legend that a leper had secreted himself in the church at night
on the eve of the consecration of Dagobert's church. A great light
broke the darkness in the middle of the night, and he saw both St Denis
and Christ himself together celebrate the rite of consecration. Christ
told the leper to inform the king what had happened. The Saviour
released the poor man from his leprous skin and cast it against the

wall, where it remained for centuries as proof of the miraculous event. Dagobert had richly endowed the Abbey of Saint-Denis, and it is no wonder that when he died in 639 he was buried there. The intervention by the Saviour himself at the consecration of Dagobert's church gave special prestige to the fabric, but it also created a dilemma for Suger. If he wanted to rebuild on a greater scale, consecration by the hand of Christ himself really did raise the very stones to the level of relics. Destroying such fabric was bordering on sacrilege, and he recognizes this in writing his *De Administratione* by repeating the building's consecration 'by the Hand Divine',[7] but he also emphasizes the providential role of the Hand of God in the completion of his new work with 'unexpected resources',[8] including the miraculous provision of quarries, columns, timber,[9] and, in 'one merry and notable miracle', gems, ironically acquired from the Cistercians, who disapproved of such riches.[10]

The Eighth-Century Abbey

The towered western facade was in fact not Dagobert's work; rather Suger recognizes elsewhere[11] that, in the middle of the eighth century, King Pepin the Short had begun a rebuilding of the church, which was completed by his son Charlemagne. At that time, in the Kingdom of the Franks, to be a citizen was to be a Catholic, and the king and the pope needed each other.[12] From 741, Pepin, like his father, Charles Martel, from 717, had held power as Mayor of the Palace to the puppet King Childeric III of the ancient Merovingian line. In the end, Pepin had petitioned the pope in 750 to be able to end the political charade by removing Childeric and assuming the throne himself. The embassy to Pope Zacharius included Abbot Fuldrad of Saint-Denis. With the approval of Pope Zacharius, St Boniface anointed and enthroned Pepin at Soissons. Then, in the winter of 753, Pope Stephen III (sometimes referred to as Stephen II, since 'Stephen II' died only four days after his election), having lost hope of aid from the emperor in

Constantinople, travelled across the alps to plead for Pepin's aid against the Lombards, who were threatening Rome itself. Stephen personally anointed Pepin again at Saint-Denis on 28 July 754 along with his sons Charles (later called Charlemagne) and Carloman, and conferred on them the title of Patrician of the Romans. Rather than being viewed as usurpers, this was a new Pippinid royal line. Pepin went to the pope's aid in 755, defeated the Lombards, and established a papal state.

Pepin probably began rebuilding Saint-Denis as a response both to his victory over the Lombards and to celebrate his anointing there at the abbey. Both Charles Martel and Pepin were buried in Saint-Denis. Charlemagne completed his father's rebuilding of the church by extending the nave and erecting a new west front over his father's grave. Suger described this as an 'addition asserted to have been made by Charlemagne on a very honorable occasion (for his father, the Emperor Pepin, had commanded that he be buried, for the sins of his father Charles Martel outside the entrance with the doors, face downward and not recumbent)'.[13] He was buried in a western porch flanked by the towers.[14] Charlemagne attended the dedication of the renewed Saint-Denis on 24 February 775. It had been refashioned as the first truly Carolingian building with its towered facade as a proto-westwork, giving access to a Roman-type aisled basilica. It had a relatively large monastic Choir, with access to an annular crypt on either side of the single eastern apse. It was certainly one of the first churches built according to this Roman custom north of the Alps.[15] Father and son had tried to harmonize the liturgy with Rome to strengthen the unity of their realms in much the same way that Constantine had imposed credal unity on the Church for the sake of imperial unity. Likewise, the architecture made obvious gestures to Roman practice, most particularly in the ring crypt at the east end.

These strong Roman references also called to mind that in 773 Charlemagne led a Frankish army finally to crush the continuing Lombard threat to Rome and to recover land from them for the pope.

This was celebrated in 774 by Charlemagne's triumphal entry into Rome for Easter. Charlemagne was indisputably the most powerful leader in the west, and in 795, on the election of Leo III as Pope, Charlemagne could write to him:

> My duty is by Divine aid to defend everywhere with armed might the Church of Christ from the inroads of pagans and from ravaging of infidels from without; from within to fortify it by the learning of the Catholic Faith. It is your part, holy Father, to support our fight by hands raised to God as those of Moses, so that, through your intercession and the guidance and the gift of God, Christian people may ever have victory over his enemies and the name of our Lord Jesus Christ be glorified throughout the world.[16]

There is a kind of equivalence here between the sacred and secular servants of God, and in this light it hardly seems surprising to us (though he himself claimed to have been surprised) that five years later, at Mass on Christmas Day 800, Charlemagne was crowned emperor in St Peter's. An imperial coronation may belong in St Peter's, but, as king of the Franks, Charlemagne's son Louis the Pious was again crowned in Saint-Denis. After he was deposed in 833, and subsequently restored, he was crowned and reinvested in Saint-Denis, which clearly had become indispensable to the Frankish royal line. In 867, Charles the Bald assumed the title of lay abbot, and on his death he was buried there, as was Hugh Capet in 996. Thereafter all but three kings of France were buried there, Philip I, Louis VII, and Louis XI.[17]

Monasticism

Saint-Denis was one of the first two basilical monasteries in Gaul. The earliest was St Martin at Tours.[18] Martin, bishop of Tours, had died on 11 November 397 CE,[19] and from early on the two monasteries were in competition for royal favour. A basilical monastery is one where a church is built beside a shrine for offices and Masses to be sung in its

service by the monks. A small chapel had been built over the shrine
of St Martin soon after his death by St Bricius in the early fifth century, but the number of miracles, and consequently the number of
pilgrims, was so great that a successor, Bishop Perpetuus, replaced it
with a very large church *c.*472. In 496, Clovis, king of the Franks, was
baptized a Christian along with his followers after a victory over the
Alamanni in answer to his prayers. After his victory over the Gothic
king Alaric II outside Poitiers in 507, Clovis gave rich gifts to St
Martin after wintering in Bordeaux. His military successes had made
Clovis ruler over the greater part of Gaul, and he was recognized by
the Eastern emperor Anastasius with the title of consul, or Augustus.
He took the title in a ceremony in St Martin's, where he crowned
himself with a diadem. St Martin's had benefited greatly from his
royal presence and patronage, but he then left Tours and moved
his government to Paris, near the rival monastery of Saint-Denis.[20]
Gregory of Tours recounts in great detail how Clovis's power
continued to grow.

   Naturally, the fortunes of the nearby basilical monastery, dedicated
to the blessed martyr and apostle of Gaul, St Denis, would prosper in
like measure. Here the pious were able to enlist the powerful intercession of the saint and dedicate gifts at his shrine. Royal patrons were
also able to be buried *ad sanctos* so that nearness to the saints in death
might bring his spiritual power and protection for their souls, 'the
favourable intercession of our Holy Protectors with God'.[21] Pilgrimage
to both Saint-Denis and Saint-Martin had grown enormously in
response to the spiritual power of the places and the sanctity of their
relics, at Saint-Denis including the 'Nail and Crown of the Lord', a
fragment of the Crown of Thorns, itself still in Constantinople (see
note 4). On the saints' days in particular, great crowds would come: at
Saint-Martin 'You should observe this feast-day on 4 July; and you
should remember that Saint Martin died on 11 November. If you
celebrate this faithfully you will gain the protection of the saintly
Bishop in this world and the next.'[22] This pattern of building over
the tombs of saints was repeated at other locations in the late fifth

century. The priest Eufronius, before becoming bishop of Autun in 456, built a church over the tomb of the martyr St Symphorian.[23] In the early 480s, a basilica was built over the tomb of St Julian at Brioude, and Duke Victorius later enhanced the architecture with columns.[24]

The purpose of the basilical monasteries was to maintain a constant round of liturgy to ensure the intercession of the saints, and Saint-Denis adopted the perpetual liturgy of Agaune as suitable to a royal abbey. This distinguished it from houses of the monastic orders and may go some way to explain the criticism by St Bernard, as a Cistercian, of Suger and Saint-Denis: the gorgeous ornament appropriate to a royal burial church had no place in the austere spiritual life of the Cistercian and reformed Benedictine cloister living according to the rule of its founder. As St Bernard wrote of pilgrimage to the Abbot of St Thierry:

> Thus wealth is drawn up on ropes of wealth, thus money bringeth money; for I know not how it is that, wheresoever more abundant wealth is seen, there do men offer more freely. Their eyes are feasted with relics cased in gold, and their purse-strings are loosed. They are shown the most comely image of some saint, whom they think is all the more saintly that he is the more gaudily painted. Men run to kiss him, and are invited to give. There is more admiration for his comeliness than veneration for his sanctity. Hence the church is adorned with gemmed crowns of light . . . O vanity of vanities, yet no more vain than insane! The church is resplendent in her walls, beggarly in her poor; she clothes her stones in gold, and leaves her sons naked; the rich man's eye is fed at the expense of the indigent.[25]

The monasteries of the orders were intrinsically inward-looking, while basilical monasteries were there for pilgrimage, the liturgy, and the intercession of the saints on behalf of the living and the departed.[26] Their churches were therefore open to welcome the laity who sought the intercession of the saints. It was a practice well known in fifth-century Rome and probably had roots in the pattern of worship seen in the late-fourth-century Anastasis in the Jerusalem of Basil of Caesarea and Egeria, and also deep in the early church.

From the Material to the Immaterial

To say that the difference between Abbot Suger and Bernard of Clairvaux centres around the use of decoration, whether in terms of sumptuous material or carved stone, is superficial to say the least. Suger put it like this:

> Thus, when—out of my delight in the beauty of the House of God— the loveliness of the many-colored gems has called me away from external cares, and worthy meditation has induced me to reflect, trans- ferring that which is material to that which is immaterial, on the diversity of the sacred virtues: then it seems to me that I see myself dwelling, as it were, in some strange region of the universe which nei- ther exists entirely in the slime of the earth nor entirely in the purity of Heaven; and that, by the grace of God, I can be transported from this inferior to that higher world in an anagogical manner.[27]

This is part of his description of the high altar of Saint-Denis, which is now lost, but an indication of its glory is shown in a painting of about 1500 in the National Gallery, London, by the Master of St Giles. Rather fancifully, it shows Charlemagne at Mass in Suger's new Choir of Saint-Denis (Plates 12 and 13). Just as an icon is not just a painting, but points beyond itself, placing the viewer in the very pres- ence of what is depicted, so, for Suger, the sumptuous material of this golden altar and cross studded with gems (many ironically acquired from the Cistercians, Suger records[28]), 'the radiance of delightful alle- gories', the 'verses expounding the matter', and the architecture itself, all mean that the viewer 'can be transported from this inferior to that higher world'.[29]

Though the altar itself has not survived, a considerable amount of the stone carving, much remarkable stained glass, and a few astonish- ing liturgical objects, including the Eleanor Vase, Suger's chalice of a solid piece of agate, which he refers to as 'sardonyx', and Suger's porphyry Eagle Vase, all still exist.[30] These objects in particular were singled out for special mention by the abbot:

Another vase, looking like a pint bottle of beryl or crystal, which the Queen of Aquitaine had presented to our Lord King Louis as a newly wed bride on their first voyage, and the King to us a tribute of his great love, we offered most affectionately to the Divine Table for libation. We have recorded the sequence of these gifts on the vase itself, after it had been adorned with gems and gold, in some little verses:

> As a bride, Eleanor gave this vase to King Louis,
> Mitadolus to her grandfather, the King to me, and
> Suger to the Saints.

We also procured for the services at the aforesaid altar, a precious chalice out of one solid sardonyx, which [word] derives from 'sardius' and 'onyx'; in which one [stone] the sard's red hue, by varying its property, so strongly contrasts with the blackness of the onyx that one property seems to be bent on trespassing on the other...

And further we adapted for the service of the altar, with the aid of gold and silver material, a porphyry vase, made admirable by the hand of the sculptor and polisher, after it had lain idly in a chest for many years, converting it from a flagon into the shape of an eagle; and we had the following verses inscribed on this vase:

This stone deserves to be enclosed in gems and gold.
It was marble, but in these [settings] it is more precious than marble.[31]

To have both the personal words and the objects of Suger allows an intimate share in his evident excitement at doing something beautiful for God, like the woman who anointed Jesus in the Gospel of Matthew (Matt. 26:7–10).

St Denis, the Martyr

Not surprisingly, if one considers these sparkling objects and the large areas of stained glass made possible by the architectural innovations, Suger's theology places a great emphasis on light and was based, he believed, on the theology developed by St Denis himself. A manuscript of 'The Works of Dionysius the Areopagite' (now in the

Bibliothèque Nationale) was given by the Byzantine emperor to Louis the Pious and by him to the abbot of Saint-Denis in 827.[32] Eusebius, in his *History of the Church*, mentions Dionysius (Denis) the Areopagite,[33] who was converted by Paul, as also reported in the Acts of the Apostles. Eusebius adds, on the authority of Bishop Dionysius of Corinth, that Dionysius the Areopagite then became the first bishop of Athens. Suger must have known the tradition that identified Dionysius the Areopagite with St Denis, since Hilduin, Suger's predecessor as abbot of Saint-Denis in the early ninth century, was the first translator in about 838 of the *Corpus Areopagiticum* into Latin and also wrote a 'Passion of the Most Holy Dionysius' that identified the two.[34]

The lives of the saints contained in *The Golden Legend* continues the tradition, relating that Dionysius the Areopagite, along with Rusticus and Eleutherius, were sent by Pope St Clement to France, where he converted so many by his sanctity that the devil provoked Domitian (emperor 81–96 CE) to persecute the Christians. This resulted in a spectacularly bloody martyr's death by scourging, prison, roasting on a grill, crucifixion, and finally decapitation.

The association of St Denis with Dionysius the Areopagite was controversial even then, with critics pointing out the temporal discrepancies. De Voragine concludes with the demand that the reader

> note also that Hincmar, bishop of Rheims, says, in the letter that he wrote to Charles, that the Dionysius who was sent to Gaul was Dionysius the Areopagite, as was said above. John Scotus makes the same assertion in a letter to Charles. This cannot be questioned, therefore, on the ground that the dates are contradictory, as some have tried to argue.[35]

You can hear in his petulant tone that he did not expect many doubters to be convinced. In Saint-Denis it was a sensitive issue.[36] The identification was part of the ascription of the writings to the patron saint, and those writings 'illuminated' the abbey and Suger's plans for it:

> The great, shining, ever-lighting sun is the apparent image of the divine goodness, a distant echo of the Good...

So it is with light, with this visible image of the Good...Every perceptible thing seeks it, as they seek to see, to be moved, to receive its light and warmth, to be kept together by it. The old myth used to describe the sun as the provident god and creator of this universe. I do not say this. But I do say that 'ever since the creation of the world, the invisible things of God, the eternal power and deity, have been clearly perceived in the things that have been made'.[37]

It is easy to imagine the sense of revelation for Suger as he handled the shining gold and glowing sardonyx of the chalice during Mass, or walked in the pools of light that form in the ambulatory of the miraculous newly transformed east end of the abbey church. As though to prepare the pilgrim for this, the gilded doors showing the Passion and Ascension of the Saviour are dated 1140, and are inscribed with the verses:

Bright is the noble work; but, being nobly bright, the work
Should brighten the minds, so that they may travel,
        through the true lights,
To the True Light where Christ is the true door,
In what manner it may be inherent in this world the golden door defines:
The dull mind rises to truth through that which is material
And, in seeing this light, it is resurrected from its former submersion.[38]

Abbot Suger and Reform

Suger obviously had a deep aesthetic sensibility, and he found a strong theological foundation in writings he believed to be by the patron both of the abbey and the Crown, but he did not participate in the main theological debates of the day—for example, with Abelard. His own native strengths lay in administration and statesmanship. He had been a child oblate from a poor family, dedicated to the abbey as a small boy from a 'small' family. The abbey, like so many, had a school where he was educated along with Princes of the Blood, including Louis, who would become Louis VI, the Fat, and a lifelong friend. Having been educated on a level with princes clearly put Suger at ease with all manner of men, and he served as an envoy to Henry I of England and also to Rome, while still a humble monk.

Suger was also adept at the administration of small daughter houses of the abbey, which had been established to develop and defend its lands and possessions—by force if necessary.[39] He opens the *De Administratione* by describing his reason for writing in response to the request of the Chapter of Saint-Denis, to lay out, in the first place, the economic reforms he had carried out after the laxity of his predecessor, Abbot Adam, especially in the improvements of the abbey's properties and possessions, and, secondly, the building programme and the accumulation of gold, gems, and textiles for furnishing. He had clearly faced a good deal of criticism, not only from the likes of St Bernard of Clairvaux as a radical reformer, but from among his own brethren. Eventually, the reforms carried out by Suger were sufficient by the sixth year of his abbacy, 1127, for him to be sent a congratulatory letter from the abbot of Clairvaux that reveals the depth of the previous criticism:

> It was at your errors, not at those of your monks, that the zeal of the saintly aimed its criticism. It was by your excesses, not by theirs, that they were incensed. It was against you, not against the Abbey, that arose the murmurs of your brothers . . . This was the one and only thing that moved us: that, if you were to continue, that pomp and circumstance of yours might appear a little too insolent . . . Finally, however, you have satisfied your critics and even added what we can justly praise.[40]

These can be seen as a continuation of the Gregorian Reforms, recently championed by Gregory VII, pope from 1073 to 1085. These were aimed at the discipline of the clergy and the standard of their education and liturgical and pastoral competence. On the side of the laity, the reforms were opposed to their interference in ecclesiastical appointments. This last might at first sight seem the least significant, but when the higher clergy, such as bishops, were invested with the insignia of their office by a lay authority, such as the king, they effectively became a vassal of the lay authority, compromising the autonomy of the Church. In 1124, this came to a head in the Investiture

Controversy when France was being threatened by Henry I of England and the Holy Roman Emperor, Henry V. Louis VI had to rally the factious French nobility, and in a ceremony at Saint-Denis he swore on the relics of the patron of France and the monarchy that he would make great gifts to the saint for his support. Suger gave the *oriflamme*, the banner of the saint, as a battle standard to rally the nobility. The emperor was poised for attack, but, astonishingly, withdrew. Louis fulfilled his oath, and the saint then had the wealth for Suger to rebuild the abbey. The king also returned the 'Crown of the Lord' and the Holy Nail, increasing the revenue from pilgrimage, and passed the *Lendit* fair and its revenues to the abbey as a steady income for the rebuilding. The king was a vassal of the saint and the Church. What he received in return was the unity of the Church and the nobility under him as visibly the chief vassal of the Apostle of All Gaul.

In the ceremonies associated with laying the foundations in 1141 and consecrating the saint's new abbey church in 1144, the bishops, the king, abbots, and monks all laid stones in the excavations, and others gave precious stones and gems. The powerful of France were literally being cemented together into a renewed nation state. Later, at the consecration of the altars, the king himself carried the relics of the Apostle of All Gaul, and 'the bodies of the holy martyrs and confessors, out of the draped tents and on the shoulders and necks of bishops, counts and barons, went forth to meet the holy Denis and his Companions at the ivory door'.[41] This great procession of saints was carried by those who held spiritual and temporal power in the land to their temporary rest on the old altar, while the twenty new altars were consecrated by nineteen prelates. The united power of this heavenly host was to be arrayed around these new altars in the *chevet*, centred around the patron saint of France and the monarchy. The function of the royal abbey was not merely as the burial place of kings; it had become the symbolic seat of regal power. While not the coronation church, which was at Rheims, it was the permanent depository of the crown and sceptre, and Saint-Denis's banner had become the king's battle standard.

It was fitting in this role that the architecture of the abbey should have the splendour found in the tradition of the magnificent Abbey of Cluny, rather than the austerity of the Cistercians. Suger protested that he initially was timid and intended a modest frontal for the altar of the patrons' shrine; but not only was he encouraged by gifts of jewels from the king and from bishops of their very episcopal rings; 'the holy Martyrs themselves handed to us such a wealth of gold and most precious gems—unexpected and hardly to be found amongst kings—as though they were telling us with their own lips: "Whether thou wantst it or not, we want it of the best."'[42] Who could resist the demands, and miraculous provision, of the saints themselves?

The Second Crusade

In 1145, the year after the consecration of the new east end of Saint-Denis, the militant Bernard was preaching the Second Crusade for the forgiveness of sins and the liberation of the Holy Places. What was to become the First Crusade had been proclaimed towards the end of 1095 by Pope Urban II to liberate the Holy Sepulchre, and on 15 July 1099 Jerusalem fell to the crusaders. In 1143, a former monk under Bernard became Pope Eugenius III, and in 1144 Edessa again fell to the Muslim atabak Zangi.[43] In response to the new call to the east, Louis made his vow and received a cloth cross sent by the pope on 31 March 1146 at Vézelay. Wearing his cross, he then appeared before the crowd with St Bernard, who preached a rousing sermon on salvation for those who take the cross, to enormous effect, with huge numbers responding. After a year's preparation, on 11 June 1147, at Saint-Denis, the pope himself presented the king with the pilgrim's purse and the *oriflamme* to carry into battle in the Holy Land.[44] From June 1147 to November 1149, Suger's master Louis VII of France led the Second Crusade to the Holy Land along with Conrad III of Germany.[45] During the absence of the king, Suger became regent of France. The prolonged absence of a king threatens to produce a power vacuum, and at the age of 68 Suger was faced with an attempted *coup d'état* by the king's brother, Robert de Dreux, which Suger 'put down in the name of righteousness and with the confidence of a lion'.[46] He governed justly, and, as at the abbey, his fiscal care filled the treasury. At the end of his life, his biographer Willelmus tells us, 'the people and the prince called him the Father of the Fatherland'.[47]

The *Liber de Rebus in Administratione Sua Gestis* and the *Libellus Alter de Consecratione Ecclesiae Sancti Dionysii* (to give these important writings by Suger their full titles) in many ways resemble the panegyric on Hagia Sophia written by Procopius in *The Buildings* (see Chapter 3). Unusually for a patron of the arts, Suger left nothing to chance and wrote the panegyric himself, deflecting the praise away from himself as builder to St Denis as patron saint. The *De Consecratione* was written after the event itself, of course, which took place on 11 June 1144, and was completed before the *De Administratione*, which mentions it in passing. The latter mentions the death of Evrard de Breteuil, which took place while on crusade to Jerusalem, so the text could not have been fully completed before late 1148 or early 1149.[48] It was, then, still in hand late in Suger's life, probably while he was still regent of France.

The Modern Approach

In *The Golden Legend*, after being beheaded, 'instantly the body of St Dionysius stood up, took his head in its arms, and, with an angel and a heavenly light leading the way, marched two miles, from the place called Montmartre, the hill of martyrs, to the place where, by his own choice and by God's providence, he rests in peace'.[49] To trace an equivalent route today to Saint-Denis would mean descending from near the Sacré-Coeur in Montmartre away from the direction of Paris towards the north on the Rue Lamarck into the narrow Rue du Mont-Cenis, down its length past the Mairie and the Église Notre-Dame de Clignancourt, into the Boulevard Ornano, then the Avenue de la Porte de Clignancourt and across the Périphérique into the Avenue Michelet. After that, the area is poor and run down. The successive boulevards Ornano and Anatole France lead to the centre of the district, at which point left into the Rue Gabriel Péri, then the Rue de la Légion d'Honneur and on the right finally is a view of Suger's west front of the abbey church, now a basilical cathedral. The distance from Montmartre must be at least double the two miles claimed by *The Golden Legend*.

The abbey church is a magnificent sight; when it was first built, the specific combination of elements would have been very distinctive as the cradle of the Gothic. Most of the elements are not in themselves innovations; in fact, many of the elements are consciously historicizing, referring back to, or even reusing, Merovingian forms—for example, columns, capitals, and even the door to the cemetery reused from the old building.[50]

The building itself and its style are intimately bound up with the emergence of monarchical power, as are the other great near-contemporary structures of Gothic, all in the Île de France.[51] Fittingly, since it faced the town, the western section, or narthex, was paid for by 200 livres, a significant sum, given by the local inhabitants to secure their release from a burdensome tax, mortmain, payable annually to the abbey. The form of the narthex owes something to its predecessor, the towered entrance, or westwork, built by Charlemagne over his father Pepin's grave. Suger added crenellations to his new west front for both decorative and potentially defensive reasons. There have been significant changes to the facade since the time of Suger. Perhaps most striking is that the north tower has been removed above the line of the parapet. The level of the pavement was also raised in 1806, which severely reduced the proportions of the once-lofty doors. The sculpture of the portals has also been extensively restored, in particular the heads and some of the other fine detail, but the magnificence of the sculptural programme can still be appreciated.

As a space for the performance of the rituals of kingship, and the special favour of the saints and martyrs, no other could compete with Saint-Denis. The site itself had been chosen by the Apostle of All

Gaul, the patron of both France and the monarchy. The new building was on a magnificent scale: its stylistic references were redolent of the illustrious kings and emperors of the past, through Charlemagne to Clovis. The primary concern was not to exhibit stylistic novelty, but rather to establish continuity, which is the denial of the transitory, emphasized by Suger when he writes: 'The recollection of the past is the promise of the future.'[52]

With Gallo-Roman origins, Saint-Denis was a celebration of the arrival of Christianity in Gaul, brought by St Denis as one of the seven bishops, and recognised by Suger to be the Apostle of All Gaul. Worship at the site had always been associated with pilgrimage to seek the intercession of the saints. As the pilgrimage grew, it made the monastery rich, the collection of relics expanded, and under royal patronage the abbey flourished. Its school educated both the nobility and poor child oblates, including Suger, who, though from a humble background, was educated with Princes of the Blood. He became a royal emissary while still a lowly monk and as abbot he created contexts, including liturgical ceremonial, that united a factious nobility around the king and the *oriflamme*, the banner of St Denis himself, against both the king of England and the emperor. While King Louis was away on the Second Crusade, Suger acted as regent of France, successfully defending the throne from usurpation. Before his death, he was hailed as the Father of the Fatherland. Rebuilding the French polity and rebuilding the abbey were his two great projects. The building project, like the political one, brought together existing elements and fused them with historical references and theological depth. The result was, on the one hand, a remarkable new architectural style, the Gothic, that would dominate Europe for centuries, and, on the other hand, the emerging nation state. The building of Saint-Denis can reveal an intimate level of detail about the Church in the history of the period.

Figure 12. Distant view of God's House at Ewelme

7

'To the increce of oure merites'

God's House at Ewelme, Oxfordshire

*T*he buildings discussed in the previous chapters have been some of the greatest in the world, royal and imperial foundations demonstrating how political and ecclesiastical power were bound together at the very top of the social and ecclesiastical order. In the countryside, at parish level, an attenuation of that relationship might well be expected, but the interlacing of royal and noble lines in great landowning families means that theology and politics shaped local life, even in parish churches in the depths of the countryside, and even for the poor. In 1437, the Foundation of God's House was established in the tiny village of Ewelme in the Oxfordshire countryside by Alice Chaucer (granddaughter of the poet, Geoffrey) and William de la Pole, then Earl and later Duke of Suffolk as chief advisor to Henry VI. The foundation provided a school for the local children, an almshouse for the local poor, and a chantry chapel for the grand family. Both the good works and the prayer were to meet the 'tariff' to smooth the way for the founders through Purgatory. Comparable foundations ranged from the grand dual foundation of Henry VI at Eton College (1440) and King's College Cambridge (1441) to almshouses in market towns like Abingdon (1441), not far from Ewelme. The pattern of patronage developed and changed, with the emphasis shifting from the chantry, though Henry VIII's own will would provide for one, towards education, with Henry's grandmother, the Lady Margaret Beaufort, founding two colleges in Cambridge and Professorships of Divinity in both Oxford and Cambridge.

The Approach to Ewelme

In a fold in the landscape on the edge of the Chiltern Hills lies the village of Ewelme in Oxfordshire, just a third of the way between Oxford and Windsor. The gentle incline of The Street runs past the watercress beds, the Manor, then the King's Pool at the heart of the village, where the aquafers rise. A little further, where the road branches towards Henley and Windsor, on the left is a medieval school, which very remarkably remains the local parish school, unlike its contemporary establishment at Eton. The school is a four-square brick building, once free-standing but now part of a range of build-ings mounting the side of the little valley. Facing the road on the facade of the school are the gilded coats of arms of Roet and Berghersh belonging to Alice Chaucer, and of De la Pole, the family of William, Duke of Suffolk, her husband. William had fought in Henry V's wars in France, and between 1428 and 1429, he was in command of English forces against Joan of Arc, later negotiating a peace on behalf of Henry VI.

The surrounding lands came through Berghersh, Alice's mother's side of the family. Alice was granddaughter of Geoffrey Chaucer, who wrote the Canterbury Tales. She, at least, must have preferred this part of the country to the ducal lands in Suffolk and Hull, and, for William too, a seat here was placed conveniently near both the royal court at Windsor, and Oxford, where he was made Protector of the University at the height of his power in 1447.[1] The university wrote to William after the death of Duke Humphrey, the previous protector, asking him 'to be good lord and protectour to us and to owr sayd Universite, for the good rest and tranquillite of the study, to the honoure of God, maintenance of C[h]ristyn faith, wyrschip and profet of the realme of Engelond. And we and oure successours of the say[d] Universite schal pray for yow for evermor'. They had been swift in writing to William to get his help in receiving Duke Humphrey's books, promised by him to the university, since at his death all his property was seized by the Crown. Instead, Henry VI gave the books to his own foundation, King's College, Cambridge.[2]

Adjacent to the school up the hill is a block joining it to School House through a medieval crenelated brick gateway with a late-fifteenth-century four-centred arch. Above School House is another gateway, this time within the range. It has a stepped gable with blind tracery within the large tympanum. On the other side of this gate is a through passage opening onto a cloister and a pretty little quadrangle containing thirteen modest almshouses. In the centre of the opposite range is a broad, steep stair to the height of the upper storey, where there is a large door to another cross passage. There are more stairs opposite, and the west doors of St Mary's Parish Church.

This whole sequence of buildings is the Foundation of God's House, and at the far end of the church, between the high altar and a magnificent chantry chapel, now stands the tomb of Alice Chaucer (Plate 14), with that of her parents nearby. Alice's tomb has been cut down to fit the arch and was perhaps moved from another location, such as the middle of the chancel. All the elements of the foundation continue in their original practical function set out in the Founders' Statutes written between 1448 and 1450 by the duke and duchess[3] that 'we woll and orden principaully to goddes worshyp', though the worship that continues has been decoupled by the Reformation from the intention that the chantry in particular shall be 'to the increce of oure merites'.[4]

Religious Foundations in Late-Medieval Society, Local and Royal

Though God's House at Ewelme is a remarkable survival, it is by no means unique, with hundreds of schools, colleges, and almshouses of medieval foundation continuing to function throughout England, though usually under new statutes and often in reduced circumstances. Henry VI granted the then Earl and Countess of Suffolk the licence to found the almshouse on 3 July 1437, when Henry was just 15. On 11 October 1440, aged 18, Henry himself founded 'the Kynges college of oure Ladye of Eton beside Windsore to the praise, honour and glory of the Crucified and the exaltation of the most glorious Virgin Mary, his mother'. As perhaps the premier public school in the land, Eton is the prime example of a school that did not escape the fate avoided by the foundation at Ewelme. The provost, priests, clerks, and choristers of the foundation at Eton were

> to serve there daily in the celebration of divine worship, and of twenty-five poor and indigent scholars and also of twenty-five poor and indigent bedesmen, whose duty it shall be to pray there continually for our health and welfare ... and for the souls of Henry V, Queen Catherine and all their forefathers and the faithful departed; together with one master or teacher in grammar, whose duty it should be to instruct the said scholars in the rudiments of grammar.[5]

The royal foundation was twice the size of God's House, but constitutionally very similar, and what has survived at Ewelme is much closer to the original first intention than at Eton, where the king's plans quickly grew in their scope.

Six months after founding Eton, on 12 February 1441, Henry signed the Letters Patent for the King's College of our Lady and St Nicholas at Cambridge, but it is possible that two foundations were conceived together, since the king's commissioners bought part of the site for his college in Cambridge as early as 14 September 1440.[6] The original foundation was modest, a rector and twelve scholars, as were the original buildings, now the Old Schools of the University of Cambridge, just north of the present chapel. By July 1443, the then provost and scholars petitioned for a larger site, and the purchase began by August. The scale was to be truly regal, with grants of numerous manors, priories, estates, and lands, and immunities from ecclesiastical authorities by nine papal bulls.[7] Henry himself laid the

Figure 13. The Chapel of King's College, Cambridge

first stone of the new chapel on St James' Day 1446, and among his commissioners to visit the next year was William de la Pole, by then elevated as Marquess of Suffolk.

The magnificent Chapel of the King's foundation at Cambridge was to function as a chantry for the king, and it was designed to provide yet more chantries between the great buttresses down either side. Provost Robert Hacombleyn, who died in 1538, established a chantry in the second chapel from the west on the south side in the reign of Henry VIII, and Provost Robert Brassie endowed a chantry during the return to Roman Catholicism in the reign of Mary I.[8] An eighteenth-century *Account of King's College Chapel* recounts that:

> the Vestries (which are eighteen in number, nine on each side of the Chapel) had long since covered in, and one, if not more, of them already *endowed*. For it is a well-known circumstance, that these Vestries were formerly called *Chantries*: that they were employed in the ceremony of singing or saying Mass for the souls of the deceased: and that any Superior of the society, who was inclined to have that service

performed for his soul after death, endowed one of these Vestries for that purpose.

It appears from the Founder's Will...that Altars would have been erected in all the Vestries, had not the laws of the Reformation, which followed some few years after the finishing of the Chapel, abolished all superstitious rites belonging to the ancient religion: among which may very justly be numbered the ceremony of singing Mass for departed souls.[9]

In 1448, William de la Pole literally bought into the magnificence of Henry's dual foundation by pledging 1,000 marks towards the building of the chapel at Eton, and, considering the impressive buildings he provided for his school at Ewelme, he may have had larger plans of his own to link the school to one of the colleges in his university of Oxford.[10] The sheer scale of the two-storey school building, the fashionable brickwork, and the quality of the detailing of the windows in the west elevation, at the time more to be seen in Suffolk than in Oxfordshire, all indicate greater ambitions, but his fortunes were about to turn. He had been created duke of Suffolk in 1448, but by 1450 parliament prosecuted him for treason, and before the end of the year he had been executed. Next up the hill from the school is the Grammar Master's House, now connected by a later low building. The house was originally also a substantial residence of three bays on two floors, with the addition of an annex wrapping round the north-west corner of the almshouses.

William de la Pole's Wider Patronage:
The Fraternity of the Holy Cross, Abingdon

William was involved in other similar foundations, mostly on his family's estates, including the college at Wingfield in Suffolk. But another near Ewelme is of particular interest: since 1416–17, the modest Fraternity of the Holy Cross at St Helen's Church in Abingdon, just south of Oxford, had been attempting to rebuild the bridges over the

River Thames. The fraternity was partly religious, but largely a practical association of townspeople, men and women, for their mutual
help and to protect their interests in relation to the extremely powerful Abingdon Abbey. A Licence from the Crown was secured by the
Commonality of Abingdon for this major project and an Act of
Parliament in 1422. The fraternity was incorporated under Royal
Charter in 1441, granted, among others, to the earl of Suffolk. There
had been a long-standing family connection, since his wife Alice's
father, Thomas Chaucer, had been a leading member of the guild.[11]
This involved the earl in the fraternity's activities, including in the first
place the building of the Long Alley Almshouses opposite the west
end of St Helen's Church for 'thirteen poor sick and impotent men
and women', and his patronage also crucially placed him at the centre
of the town's commerce. There are architectural similarities between
the Long Alley and the cloistered almshouses at Ewelme, and they
were built at pretty much the same time, as far as records show. In all
likelihood, William de la Pole was directly involved in building both.[12]
In 1484, a confirmatory Royal Charter was granted by Richard III,
addressed to John, Duke of Suffolk, and in 1536, Henry VIII issued
Letters Patent approving their objects and confirming them in their
possessions. Henry suppressed Abingdon Abbey, and a decade later, in
1547, Edward VI suppressed the Abingdon Guilds, the Fraternity of the
Holy Cross and the Guild of Our Lady. However, in 1552, an Abingdon
man, Sir John Mason, as Clerk to the Privy Council, secured the return
of the lands to the people of Abingdon as being outside the compass
of the Chantries Act. Christ's Hospital was founded as a successor to
the guilds and continues to operate the almshouses in the town.[13]

The Church of St Mary, Ewelme,
and its Chantry

Away from the tranquillity and comfort of the almshouse quadrangle
at Ewelme, up the steps on the right is the Master's dwelling, and on

the left the Common Hall, corresponding to the hall in the Long Alley almshouses. Through double doors and a cross-passage, up some steps are the west doors of the mid-fifteenth-century church. The tower is all that remains of the earlier fourteenth-century church, left perhaps to establish the antiquity of the place and the family, though in truth Duke William's great-grandfather, Sir William de la Pole, had been a merchant of Hull, and became very rich lending vast sums to Edward III, despite various turns of fortune.[14] The beautifully elegant nave arcades regularly pace towards the east, with bright windows in the bays of the clerestory above, and corbels supporting the moulded trusses of a shallow-pitched roof. The north aisle is the result of a pre-1434 building campaign, while the south aisle was post-1437. The proportions of the chancel screen tell of a lost rood-loft (doubtless as a result of the Reformation), which is confirmed by more recent replacement angel-stops above the adjacent piers.

The crossing is in the bay immediately next to the tower, and the font is attached to the first pier of the northern arcade. Its wooden cover is a marvel, a suspended pinnacle more than 10 feet tall consisting of radiating carved wooden buttresses and carved ogee arches (added in the nineteenth century) in diminishing tiers. It is topped by a feathered Archangel Michael, and its counterweight is a multiple rose, a device that appeared on Alice Chaucer's signet. Detailed inspection has shown close resemblance to East Anglian work, especially the font cover at Salle in Norfolk, perhaps even by the same craftsman, indicating the East Anglian base of the De la Poles.[15]

At the eastern end of the south aisle of Ewelme Parish Church is the Chapel of St John the Baptist, the Chantry Chapel of Alice de la Pole and her parents, Thomas Chaucer and Maude Berghersh. As it is a family chantry, heraldry plays an important role, and early descriptions by heralds and antiquarians indicate that it once played an even greater role, both in the chapel and in the church itself. What remains are fragments of stained glass in the east window of the chapel and coats of arms on and near the tombs.

Thomas Chaucer, who fought at Agincourt in 1415, was MP for Oxfordshire in most parliaments between 1400 and 1431, became Speaker of the House of Commons, and locally was Constable of Wallingford Castle.[16] He died in 1434 and his wife, Maude Berghersh, in 1436. Their tomb is a large plain stone chest with a brass showing the pair, him in armour, and their coats of arms above them. His father, Geoffrey, the poet, may not himself have had arms, so Thomas took the arms of Roet (three golden wheels on a red field), his mother's older and more prestigious family. The Berghersh arms displayed a golden lion rampant on a white shield with a red chief. The descriptions are unheraldic, but of strikingly simple devices.[17] Connections with the great families of the land, including royal connections, are shown in brightly enamelled heraldic achievements in the blind tracery on the ends and side of their tomb. One of the most important connections was that Geoffrey's wife, Philippa Roet, had a sister, Catherine, who married John of Gaunt, so their third-generation heir, Margaret Beaufort, was a distant cousin whose arms also appear on the tomb. Though the De la Pole line was not related by blood to John of Gaunt, Michael de la Pole, 1st Earl of Suffolk, had been a close ally, further binding the families together.

The connection with Lady Margaret Beaufort was more than just distant consanguinity. As the Hundred Years War dragged on into the reign of Henry VI, in 1443 John Beaufort, Duke of Somerset, grandson and heir of John of Gaunt, was preparing to lead a major offensive in France when his only child, Margaret, was born on 31 May. The campaign was a disaster, and on his return in 1444, charges of treason were being drawn up when he died suddenly on 27 May. Margaret was made a ward of William de la Pole, King Henry's chief minister and negotiator for peace in France. William's fortunes were still on the rise and he was created duke of Suffolk in 1448. Besides the Beaufort heiress, William also had the wardship of Anne Beauchamp, daughter of the late Henry Beauchamp, Duke of Warwick. These two young girls were both enormously rich heiresses, and, as their guardian, William had control of their marriage prospects. He also had a son,

John. It appears that William's first intention was to marry his son John to Anne, but she died on 3 January 1449 at the age of 5.

Though he retained the favour of the king, William de la Pole had made many enemies. When parliament insisted on prosecuting William in his turn for treason as a result of what they considered to be the disastrous consequences of his negotiations, they also blamed him for Henry's ceding Maine to the French Crown.[18] In his increasingly desperate situation in 1450, William had his son John, by then aged 7, married to Margaret Beaufort, aged 6. The marriage was dissolved three years later. The king made her the ward of his half-brothers Jasper and Edmund Tudor, Earl of Richmond. Margaret was married to Edmund and bore him a son. Edmund died in 1456, before the boy was born, leaving Margaret a widow at the age of 12.[19] The boy would become Henry VII.

Alice Chaucer's Wider Benefactions

Alice displayed the family's arms more publicly, more prominently, and in very different company through her gifts to the University of Oxford. During the fourteenth and fifteenth centuries, the family is recorded as having sent more than one of its sons for a time at least to the university.[20] She was repeatedly thanked in letters from the university, which show that she continued benefactions after her husband's death in 1450, and in 1454 she is recorded as having donated £20 towards the Divinity School.[21] Those thanks were memorialized in stone in the vaulting of the Divinity School, where there are heraldic bosses showing her family arms of Roet and one that appears to be of Berghersh. Contributions to the building had been invited as early as 1423, when work was probably already under way, but it had certainly begun by 1427. The arms appear amongst those of bishops, including William of Waynflete, Founder of Magdalen College, Oxford, John Kemp, Cardinal Archbishop of Canterbury (formerly of London), who gave 1,000 marks,[22] and a boss with the words 'Edwardus

Quartus Rex'. In the first south side-bay her arms appear between a boss with a bishop's mitre and the motto of William of Waynflete and others of the five wounds of Christ, the university, and Archbishop Kemp. In the third north side-bay on the other side may be a representation of her Berghersh[23] coat of arms above the door, and her Roet coat of arms of three wheels appears among a boss of the Virgin and Child, the arms of the university, Kemp as archbishop and as bishop of London, and on the south side-bay of the fourth bay from the entrance are the arms of her son John de la Pole, appearing beside that of Waynflete. In the west end (fifth) side-bay on the north, three wheels appear again above William of Waynflete.[24] This is a high-profile family presence, with four, or more probably five (if the lion is indeed of Berghersh), family armorial bosses along with those of a select few of the highest in the land at the heart of the developing university, representing significant benefactions to the teaching of Divinity. The university arms themselves appear six times, only once more than Alice's family, so hers is a very significant presence indeed.

Figure 14. The vaulting of the Divinity School, Oxford University

The vaulting was added to the Divinity School, probably beginning at the west end,[25] between about 1480 and 1483, so Alice will not
have seen it, though her son John probably did, as steward of the university from 1472.[26] On 24 September 1481, King Edward IV himself,
whose arms are on the boss in the middle of the central bay, is recorded
as having been 'present at public Disputations...to the hearing of
which, he about this time had sent his Nephew Edm. Poole [Edmund
de la Pole, Alice's grandson] (whom the University in their letters do
highly commend) and other young men of his blood'.[27] At this date,
the vaulting was probably still under construction. Directly above the
vaulting is Duke Humphrey's Library (completed between 1483 and
1490), the same duke whose downfall and perhaps even death were
probably the responsibility of William de la Pole as the king's chief
advisor.[28] In her benefactions, Alice is amassing self-perpetuating
good works to the benefit of her soul. That was also a key aim in
founding God's House in Ewelme for the education and relief of the
poor, along with prayer in her chantry chapel.

Alice Chaucer's Chantry Chapel

On Alice's own tomb, angels carry the arms of the extended family;
the first angel facing into the chapel carries the arms of her son John
impaling those of his wife, Elizabeth Plantagenet, sister to both
Edward IV and Richard III, whose claims to the throne also came
through John of Gaunt. John de la Pole and Elizabeth were buried
together in the church at Wingfield in Suffolk, on the lands of the De
la Pole side of the family. Their effigies are fine portraits carved in
alabaster, and, like his mother's, he wears a ducal coronet and the robes
of the Order of the Garter. Their son, John de la Pole, the grandson
of William and Alice, through his mother Elizabeth was recognized as
heir presumptive to the throne in 1484 but was left in peace by Henry
VII after the death of Richard III. Later, though, he was central to
Lambert Simnel's plot and was killed at the battle of Stoke.[29] A family

coat of arms appears in a contemporary window of the late fifteenth century in the Church of St Mary the Virgin, Iffley,[30] near the road to Oxford from Ewelme. The manor of Iffley was part of the endowment of the almshouses at Donnington near Newbury in Berkshire, of which John was also patron. The window shows his father's arms impaled with his mother's royal arms, demonstrating his claim to the throne. The family had had a meteoric rise, and fall.

The heraldry of the chantry chapel is not just about family pride; it is also about identity and where these people fitted into the fabric of medieval English society. Heraldry is less about the individual than their connections and, to some extent, the honours they brought to the family. Life was precarious, and, by the time Alice's tomb was being carved, her husband William had been dead more than two decades, executed at sea after capture on his way to banishment in 1450. He had escorted Margaret of Anjou to England in 1444 for the royal marriage, and been created duke of Suffolk only in 1448, but by 1449 English losses in France placed him under suspicion, and there were political disorders directed against him.[31] Though he still had the support of Henry VI, he was banished and was murdered on the way, captured at sea and beheaded. The awful story of that dreadful day in May 1450 is recounted in one of the Paston Letters:

> Some say he wrote much thing to be delivered to the King, but that is not verily know. He had his confessor with him, &c. And some say he was arraigned in the ship, on their manner, upon the apeachments, and found guilty &c.... And in the sight of all his men he was drawn out of the great ship into the boat, and there was an axe and a stock; and one of the lewdest of the ship bade him lay down his head, and he should be fair ferd with, and die on a sword; and took a rusty sword, and smote off his head within half a dozen strokes.[32]

Family connections were a stabilizing influence in the shifting fortunes of this uncertain and violent world; he was accompanied by his confessor so as always to be prepared for such sudden death, and the prayers of the faithful and good works 'to the increase of our merit, by which we hope for salvation' in the next, were the work of the chantry.

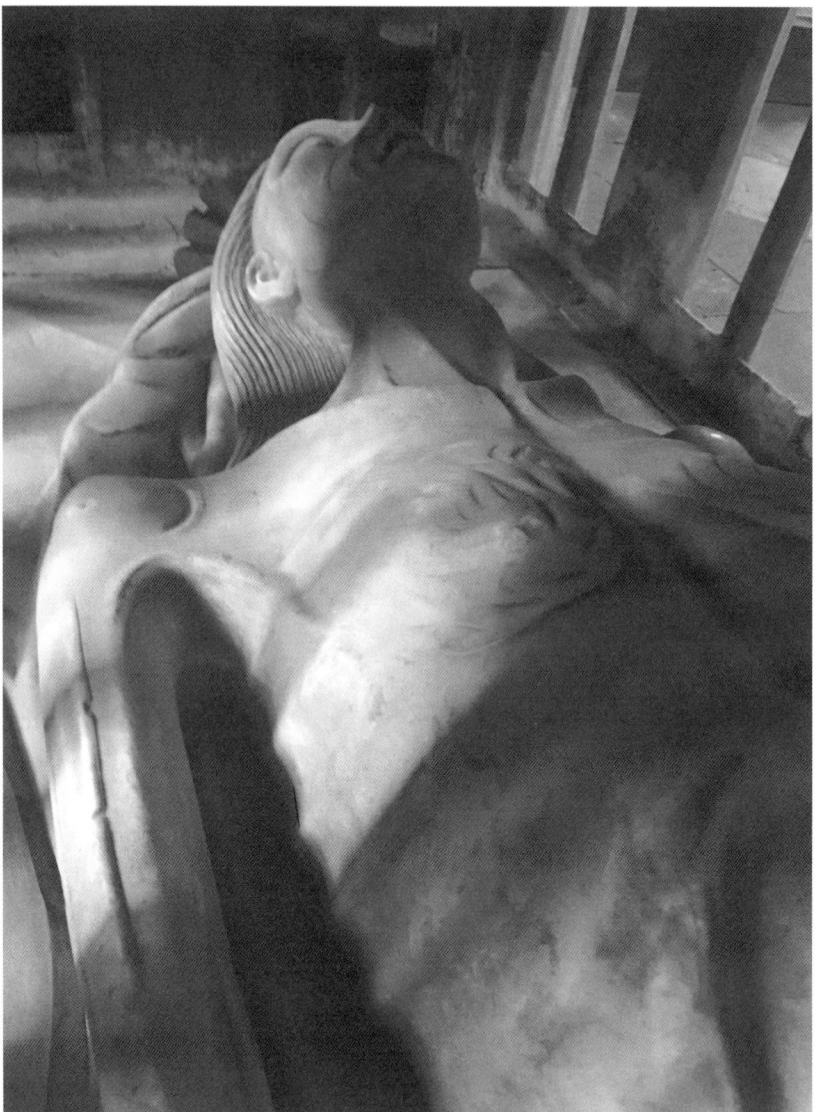

Figure 15. Cadaver effigy of Alice Chaucer

There is a canopy above Alice's effigy on the tomb (Plate 14). The opening in the wall above the effigy is carved with late-Gothic panelling surmounted by a magnificent canopy that covers the whole of the tomb. Alice herself is dressed simply but wears a coronet, and she wears the Garter on her left arm as a member of the order in her own right. Her pillow is cradled by angels, and her feet are guarded by her heraldic beast. She rests on a tomb chest with ranks of angels down either side holding coats of arms demonstrating her connections with the most powerful families in the land. This is worldly grandeur, but round the top of the walls run biblical texts, one of which reads: 'He has bestowed on him the name which is above every name, that at the name of Jesus every knee should bow, in heaven and on earth and under the earth' (Phil. 2:9–10). It is a call to humility, and under Alice's tomb chest through the open tracery can be seen another effigy of Alice in death. She is an emaciated figure loosely covered in her shroud, suffering final humiliation. This and the other texts emphasize salvation in the name of Jesus: 'And you shall call his name Jesus, for he will save his people from their sins' (Matt. 1:21) The sacred monogram of Jesus as Saviour, IHS, covers the walls. Though restored in the nineteenth century, it appears to replicate the original programme, as seen in a section left unrestored.

Interestingly, the imposing Alice above prays with formal dignity, while the weight of the hand of the cadaver below is all that holds the shroud closely enough to maintain her modesty. Eyes partly open, she faces the images of Mary Magdalen and John the Baptist painted above her on the soffit of the tomb chest. The images are relatively crude and 'seen' only by the deceased, so it is a very private and reassuring appearance by her patron saints and intercessors. The whole ensemble is a show of public dignity and, at the same time, private humility, faith, and hope.

Prayer, the Work of the Chantry

The members of the Foundation of God's House would have been worked hard in return for their support, if the foundation documents were ever carried out to the letter. The Statutes stipulate that prayers be offered by the residents on waking for the king, William, and Alice, then further that matins, prime, and other canonical hours be said. After the daily Mass, everyone is to gather round the Chaucer tomb:

> Also wee woll and ordeyne that ev[er]y seide maystyr minister and pore men ev[er]y day to come the which may well doo it and ev[er]y holy day the techer of gra[m]mer aftyr the saide masse to be sayde by the seide maystyr shall gadir them self to gedir abowte the tow[m]be of our fadyr and modir Thomas Chawcer and Mawte his wyfe where they shall say this psalme Deus misereatur with the comyn suffragijs used to be sayde for the quyk w[ith] this Colle[c]t Deus qui caritatis. And thoo of them which shall not conne say it shall say .iij. Pater n[ost]ris .iij. Aves and a Crede the which I done the Maystyr if he be p[re]sent or the techer of gram[m]er or the minister or one of the brotheris shall openli and distinctly say in the Englissh tong duryng the lives of our seide soverayne lord and of us both. God save in body and sowle oure soverayne lord the kyng my lord Will[ia]m Duke of Suffolk my lady Alyce Duchesse of Suffolk his wyfe oure founders my lord John theire son and all cristen pepill the brotheris answeryng Amen.[33]

The English prayer specified here is of the same simple format as the prayer that continues to be said daily in St George's Chapel, Windsor, home of the Order of the Garter.

The founders of the chantry, living and departed, effectively employed the poor of the parish to pray for their souls, and, for their hire, the round of prayers extracted the maximum spiritual capital from their employ. Jesus said, 'Blessed are the poor in spirit, for theirs is the kingdom of heaven' (Matt. 5:3), so their prayers would be especially effective intercession for the salvation of the souls of the founders and their families. The ubiquitous practice of attaching chantries to parish churches, cathedrals, schools, and colleges meant that the dead became major employers of the living in the industry of institutionalizing perpetual good works, almsgiving, and intercessory prayer in this literal 'economy of salvation'.[34] The foundations were to pray for the souls of the founders, their parents, and their heirs—that is, the family across time. The chantry chapel placed the founder within a very specific generational, social, political, and religious context. That is what the heraldry is about. The chantry became a liminal space, where the normal barriers became diaphanous and blessings flowed across them from generation to generation.

The Cost of Salvation

There were many theological, and social, difficulties with this system of atonement 'by the upholding and mayntenyng of divine service. And by the exercise of warkes of mercy.'[35] Practical 'warkes of mercy' aside, an obvious question was about the required amount of prayer—that is to say, the tariff—to see a soul through Purgatory. This was less of a problem for the founder of a perpetual chantry like Ewelme, their family, and possibly even their bedesmen. For others of limited means, the question of an adequate tariff was crucial; their immortal soul was at stake.

At Ewelme, the required offices and Masses were minutely specified in the *Statutes* along with Lady Psalters, Hail Marys, Our Fathers, Creeds, 'Our Lady Matins with the Seven Psalms and Litany OR Placebo and Dirge with Commendations OR several Nocturnes of the Psalter OR reading'. This was to be followed daily by a Mass followed by gathering round the Chaucer tomb for prayers, saying the *Deus Misereatur*, the common suffrages, and the collect *Deus qui Caritatis*. Those who did not know those prayers were to say three Our Fathers, three Hail Marys, and three Creeds. Anniversaries were to be kept with *Placebo* and *Dirge* with commendations and a Requiem Mass. In the evening after Compline, they were to gather round the tomb again, adding the *De Profundis* and its suffrages. It was a stringent daily round, and spiritual superfluity to give a reasonable degree of security to the founders and their family. This daily liturgical life of the chantry was paid for by the foundation, but the services and the mass-priests were a benefit to the parish as well, here, at the chantry college at Wingfield on the De la Pole lands in Suffolk, and up and down the country.[36] The parishes also benefited from enhanced pastoral care, the support of the poor, and the education of the young.

Many ordinary people concerned for the health of their souls joined guilds such as the Holy Cross in Abingdon to ensure at least the proper funeral rites were observed. Five Masses might be commissioned in honour of the Wounds of Christ,[37] or a 'Trental', which is thirty Masses, might cost 'upwards of ten shillings. For five or six pounds, one could "wage" an "annualer", a priest who would sing for one's soul for a whole year.'[38] These were temporary chantries, but there was no telling how much within this range of spiritual work was sufficient for salvation. Not long before the chantry at Ewelme was established, in 1422, in a text called the 'Revelacyone schewed to ane holy woman', two sets of Masses are specified as fully sufficient, an elaborate set of three hundred Masses, and the other, more modestly, of thirteen Masses plus days of repetition of the *Miserere* and *Veni Creator*.[39] Either of these required not only financial resources, but also religious establishments of a considerable size to carry them out. Even at God's House at Ewelme it would take at least a year to carry out the major cycle. It is no wonder that works of mercy gradually received greater emphasis in the face of this liturgical inflation.

Changing Emphasis in Atonement

There are significant differences between this version of 'God's House' and the collegiate foundation of this earlier generation, and the 'God's House' or collegiate foundation of the succeeding generation. The earlier model was a small inward-looking foundation concentrating primarily on prayer and perhaps providing a single master to teach. The later foundation was much larger, with a broader outward-looking theological focus. The change can be detected in the development of Henry's double foundation of Eton and King's, and even more clearly in Lady Margaret Beaufort's foundations at both Oxford and Cambridge. In the early sixteenth century, Lady Margaret Beaufort had made the conventional provision on a regal scale for a chantry in Westminster Abbey, but her long involvement in sending young men from her household, and particularly her chapel, must have made it relatively easy for her progressive confessor and advisor, Bishop John Fisher of Rochester, to convince her to divert the chantry funds to educational ends.[40] Through him, she began in 1497 to establish Chairs of Divinity in both his University of Cambridge and at Oxford, and he was the first incumbent of the Cambridge Chair in 1502. Like Alice's benefactions to the Oxford Divinity School, these were good works of a practical, humanist type. Through Fisher's good offices, she also founded two colleges in Cambridge: Christ's College as a kind of seminary, 'created out of a run-down Chantry-cum-grammar school, God's House', and St John's College, later in 1524 helped further by his suppression of two nunneries. There was to be study of secular subjects, but an emphasis on theological education, and at St John's a quarter of the Fellows were to be involved in preaching in the parishes in English.[41] The emphasis had been taken off intercessory prayer and masses for the founder and placed on the new Humanist learning. The living were still to be employed by the dead, but this shows a slowly growing tendency for wealth to be diverted towards extending the Kingdom of God in this world by good works, and a new educational industry. It was through Fisher that Erasmus was brought to Cambridge in 1511, which further encouraged the study of the Bible in the original languages. Fisher was a leader of both educational and religious reform. As the premier English Catholic theologian, he refused the Royal Supremacy, and was made a cardinal in May 1535, and beheaded on 22 June.[42]

Antiquity in Action: God's House since the Reformation

Huge wealth was tied up in the chantry system, and Henry VIII was preparing to seize it to refinance his wars in France, which had all but bankrupted him. Descendants of the founders had sometimes suppressed chantries themselves, but in December 1545 a bill was introduced in parliament to transfer to the Crown such illegally privatized assets, and further it allowed Henry to seize remaining endowments; consequently 'patrons and parishes made their own pre-emptive seizures, often for church or village needs'.[43] The fortunes of the living and the dead were legally severed by the Chantry Act of December 1547, dissolving the chantries, abolishing prayers for the dead, seizing their assets, and even resulting in the physical destruction of the monuments.[44] The proceeds were used this time for war against the Scots. Thereafter wills seldom left money for Masses (though Henry's did, as well as for the establishment of a chantry at St George's, Windsor). Instead of Masses, there was a growing tendency to leave money to the poor, and other 'warkes of mercy'.[45]

Clearly, the worst and most destructive consequences of the Chantry Act did not occur in Ewelme. In a sense, the foundation did not need to be suppressed, since the estates were already in the possession of the Crown. Edmund, second of the seven sons of John de la Pole and Elizabeth Plantagenet, remained a possible Yorkist claimant to the throne after the death of his brother John, Earl of Lincoln, at the battle of Stoke on 16 June 1487 in a rising against Henry. Edmund himself was created Earl of Suffolk by an indulgent Henry VII in 1493 and remained loyal until he fled to Flanders in 1499. This disconcerted Henry, but Edmund was again received back at court until 1501, when he and his brother Richard defected to the Emperor Maximilian to seek his aid, a threat that Henry took very seriously. Royal favour towards the family was at an end. Their brother William was committed to the Tower, where he remained for the rest of his life. Edmund was outlawed, then finally in 1506, as a bargaining chip in a treaty negotiation, he was returned to Henry and imprisoned in the Tower of London.[46] On Henry VIII's accession in 1509, a general pardon was issued, excepting Edmund, who remained an inconvenient potential Yorkist rival until 1513, when Henry VIII was about to embark with 40,000 troops for war against France. The last surviving brother, Richard, had recently joined the French; Edmund was executed without trial before Henry embarked.[47]

Plate 1. Detail of *The Temptations of Christ*, by Jacob Cornelisz van Oostsanen, Netherlandish, before 1545, since the Crusader tower of the Church of the Holy Sepulchre still has its upper stages and cupola

Plate 2. Apse Mosaic, Santa Pudenziana, Rome

Plate 3. The Dome of St Peter's with inscription: 'You are Peter, and on this Rock shall I build my Church . . . I will give you the keys of the kingdom of heaven'

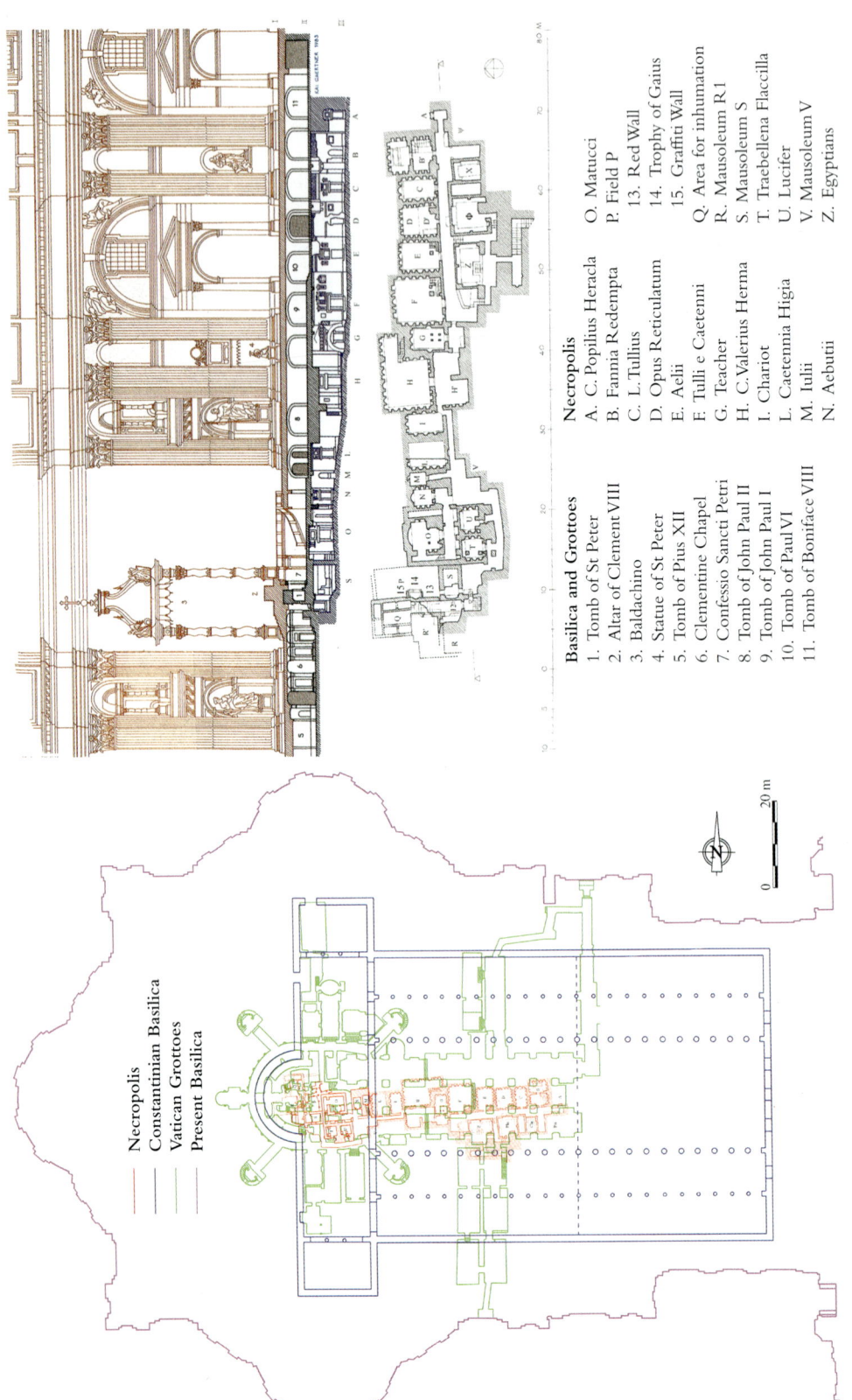

Necropolis
A. C. Popilius Heracla
B. Fannia Redempta
C. L. Tullius
D. Opus Reticulatum
E. Aelii
F. Tulli e Caetenni
G. Teacher
H. C. Valerius Herma
I. Chariot
L. Caetennia Higia
M. Iulii
N. Aebutii
O. Matucci
P. Field P
13. Red Wall
14. Trophy of Gaius
15. Graffiti Wall
Q. Area for inhumation
R. Mausoleum R1
S. Mausoleum S
T. Traebellena Flaccilla
U. Lucifer
V. Mausoleum V
Z. Egyptians

Basilica and Grottoes
1. Tomb of St Peter
2. Altar of Clement VIII
3. Baldachino
4. Statue of St Peter
5. Tomb of Pius XII
6. Clementine Chapel
7. Confessio Sancti Petri
8. Tomb of John Paul II
9. Tomb of John Paul I
10. Tomb of Paul VI
11. Tomb of Boniface VIII

Necropolis
Constantinian Basilica
Vatican Grottoes
Present Basilica

0   20 m

Plate 4. St Peter's Basilica, plans and section

Plate 5. Hagia Sophia, Istanbul: interior

Plate 6. Hagia Sophia, Istanbul: coloured marble of the revetment

Plate 7. Rubliev, frescoes in the Cathedral of the Dormition, Vladimir, 1408

Plate 8. Interior of the Cathedral of the Dormition, Moscow Kremlin, showing the iconostasis

Plate 9. Interior of the Cathedral of the Dormition, Moscow Kremlin

Plate 10. Church of the Holy Mother of God, Aachen: the Throne of Charlemagne

Plate 11. Church of the Holy Mother of God, Aachen: gold bust of Charlemagne

Plate 12. Abbey of Saint-Denis: interior of the Choir, rebuilding and strengthening of the upper part of the choir were needed after a collapse in 1231

Plate 13. 'The Mass of St Giles', showing the High Altar of Saint-Denis with Charlemagne kneeling to the left

Plate 14. Alice Chaucer Monument

Plate 15. Cathedral of Cordoba: interior of the Mezquita

Plate 16. Cathedral of Cordoba: vaulting joining the Cathedral to the Muslim arcading

Plate 17. Bernini, *Cathedra Petri*, St Peter's Basilica

Plate 18. Andrea Pozzo, painted ceiling in Sant'Ignazio, Rome

Edmund's estates were appropriated by the Crown (Richard, 'White Rose', was killed, still fighting for the French, outside Pavia on 14 February 1525), and Ewelme Manor became a Tudor palace but was gradually reduced to a ruin, with only part of the accommodation wing now surviving behind a Georgian outer skin. The church and its fittings survived not only the Reformation, but also the Civil War, thanks to a local parliamentary landowner, Francis Martyn.[48] Though God's House was not suppressed, and its buildings survive, clearly the chantry must have ceased to function. One fifteenth-century pew remains in the corner at the entrance to the chapel; it was re-pewed in 1637, and again in the 1840s, and, with increased use by the school in the twenty-first century, extra seats have been inserted between the pews in what had been a narrow central aisle, so the chapel has continued to be well used, now weekly for the school (with the crush of major festivals in the nave), though presently there is only an annual service specifically for the Almsmen, now including women. After just over a century under Crown patronage, in 1617 the Mastership was attached to the Regius Professorship of Medicine at Oxford, which is still the case.[49] The Master ceased to be resident, but even now the incumbents continue to take a serious interest.

Church and Society

In its original form, God's House was an example of how the Church permeated every aspect of society. The font was where infants were baptized into the faith—as soon as possible, because to die unbaptized was to die in original sin. The magnificent font cover trumpeted the importance of this fundamental sacrament of initiation. The children of the manors of Alice's lands were educated at the school. Some might even go on to the university and study in the Divinity School, the recipient of other De la Pole munificence. The old and the poor among Alice's community could be housed in the almshouses, and all were enjoined, or even contracted, to pray for the souls of the founders and their families and for all Christian people. The Church was involved in the lives of its members from cradle to grave, and beyond, through Purgatory to the Day of Judgement.

The fifteenth century was a politically and socially unstable period when family fortunes and honours were amassed only to be seized, the holders to fall from power, often resulting in prosecution and sometimes execution. Yet that was not the end, with Purgatory still to be endured before the Day of Judgement. The Church had a role in all stages of this life, and in the form of a foundation like God's House there was relative stability in a community rooted in place but extending over generations of the living and the dead. Charity and liberality continued from generation to generation through the wealth of the endowment, and the thankful prayers of the living shortened the purgation and pains of the dead, and the provision of priests for chantries strengthened the ministry of the parishes.

At the end of the fifteenth century, there were new forces at work. Some were religious, but there were even more desperate political, dynastic, and financial forces in play. Reform in religion and education could be driven by other ends. Early in the process, until 1524, monastic houses had been suppressed as a means of endowing the colleges of Oxford and Cambridge.[50] Later, Cromwell may have had religious reform as his deepest motivation, and in the monasteries there was much that needed reform, but Henry needed ever more money for his wars, so they were all suppressed and their wealth seized—likewise for the chantries. God's House in Ewelme survived, probably because along with the manor it had already been seized from the final generation of De la Poles as Plantagenet claimants to the throne, and was already in the possession of the Crown. The alms-houses in Abingdon survived because the charity was essentially refounded as Christ's Hospital through the efforts of loyal people of the town.

There is a sense in which the objects of the chantry at Ewelme did survive. It was never just about Purgatory, but also about the grandeur and display of an aristocratic family demonstrating their connections to other noble and royal lines—almost forgetting the distinction of Geoffrey Chaucer. This remains, and cannot fail to impress on first discovering the chantry chapel—such an array of coats of arms and such a distinguished and elaborate tomb of the highest quality, beautifully carved in alabaster, in a parish church deep in the English countryside. And this is also a sign of the interlacing of the living and the dead, of religion and secular society, of the power structure and pattern of patronage of the aristocracy, and how it was based in the land and their local communities. Because it retains so many of the characteristics of the original foundation, and perhaps also because of those things that have changed as well, God's House today reveals the completely different relationship that existed in the fifteenth century between Church and society on the cusp of radical change.

Figure 16. Cathedral of Cordoba: view across the bridge

8

The Western Caliphate and the Christian Monarchs

The Cathedral, Cordoba

From the middle of the sixth century, the Basilica of St Vincent in the heart of Cordoba was the seat of a bishop. In 711, Muslims from North Africa seized power in southern Spain and made Cordoba their capital. The church of St Vincent was used as a mosque and may also have continued in partial use as a church. Soon, however, the building was demolished, and a new mosque was begun in 785–6 by 'Abd al-Rahman I. As power, wealth, and numbers of worshippers grew, so did the mosque, with building programmes under 'Abd al-Rahman II between 833 and 848 and 'Abd al-Rahman III from 939. In the 960s, al-Hakam II, son of 'Abd al-Rahman III, added a remarkable library said to be of 400,000 volumes, and between 965 and 971 (roughly contemporary with the magnificent mosaic of Constantine and Justinian in Hagia Sophia) he brought Byzantine mosaicists to decorate the royal maqsura area and the mihrab wall. When al-Hakam died in 987, his grand cadi, al-Mansur, added a further eight aisles. A decade later he went on to capture Santiago de Compostela itself. The western caliphate came to an end in 1031, but Cordoba was not under Christian control until 1235, when the mosque became the cathedral. The Muslim Kingdom of Granada was the last to be conquered, in 1492 by Ferdinand and Isabella, the 'Catholic Monarchs'. The mezquita/cathedral in Cordoba was used for Christian worship with only the integration of a number of chapels within the fabric until 1523, when permission was finally given by Emperor Charles V to destroy a section at the core and build a full choir within it. The axis of the cathedral cut directly across the main axis of the mosque, like a standing metaphor of the two religious communities. The choir was complete by 1598. This part is a sixteenth-century building, but the whole of the former mosque has been consecrated as the cathedral, and Christian claims to priority of occupation are visually presented by the exposed archaeological excavations of the Basilica of St Vicente in the corner near the entrance. Still, architectural and cultural history and archaeology are being challenged and contested throughout the country. Contested history is literally written into the DNA of modern Spain.

The Approach

If you cross the Puente Romano from the south over the Guadalquivir River, which divides the Province of Cordoba into two, the view is dominated by the lateral expanse of the square walls of the mezquita or the Great Mosque of the caliphs of al-Andalus. The walls define the core of the city of Cordoba. At the heart of the mezquita rises the vertical mass of the choir, repeating the rhythmical march of the arched bays of the Muslim building into which it has been wedged. The Christian building was clearly meant as a symbol of historic, cultural, and religious victory, but just as clearly the mezquita was too fine a cultural achievement to be destroyed, and the 'dominant' cathedral is architecturally inferior in every way. The juxtaposition is unintentionally revealing, and the architecture of the complex charts the relationship between Christian and Islamic culture in Spain.

This site was at the highest navigable point on the river, and this Carthaginian territory was taken by the Romans in 206 BCE. The original Roman bridge carried the Via Augusta, the main artery of the province of Baetica, and this key geographical site became the location of its capital. The city was religiously important too from Roman times, when there was a temple to Janus on the site, and the remains of another temple are to be found near the Roman city wall. Bishop Fructuosus of Tarragona (Tarraco) was martyred during the Valerian Persecution in 259 CE in the amphitheatre of that city, and in the sixth century a church was built on the spot. As the Roman Empire was Christianized, the province became strongly Catholic, and the pilgrim Egeria, who was in Jerusalem between 381 and 384, may have come from a religious community in Spain.[1]

Visigothic Spain and Conversion to Catholicism

The Visigoths and other Germanic peoples invaded, or immigrated, depending on how you look at it, into the western empire in the late fourth and early fifth centuries.[2] Barbarians had always provided mercenary troops, but in the fifth century large numbers were under their own Gothic leadership, and the disgruntled mercenaries then became dangerous for their masters. Alaric was the first Visigoth to serve in this way in 394 for Theodosius, emperor in Constantinople. The alliance did not go well, and Alaric sacked Rome itself in 410. In 476, the Goth Odoacer deposed the last emperor of the west, the young Romulus Augustulus in Ravenna. By 500, the western empire was divided into Gothic kingdoms, including Visigothic Spain, run in Roman ways by barbarian elites, but with local Roman aristocrats still in place.[3] They notionally recognized the Byzantine emperor, but remained fiercely Arian and a continuing threat to the bishop of Rome and the Latin Church.

Spain had been hit by a series of waves of Germanic invaders, Vandals after 409, the Suevi after 439, and finally the Visigoths in 456. The Visigothic kingdom at this time was still ruled from Gaul, even after their defeat by Clovis in 507. From 511, Theodoric acted as regent, ruling from Italy, for the child-king Amalaric until Theodoric died in 526. One coup followed another, until Athanagild (551–68) asked for help from the Byzantine emperor Justinian in his civil war against the rule of Agila.

The Visigoths dominated the region, but Emperor Justinian's troops established a foothold (Spania) from 552, and the Byzantines remained until 628. Depending on the level of the Visigothic influence, there are some characteristics of the architecture of Iberia that were introduced either early by them or later by the Ummayads from the end of the eighth century.[4] The question is whether there was a flourishing high point in artistic and architectural achievement under the Visigoths, or whether it was reuse and spoliation, with the fine work achieved later under the Muslims. The religious and cultural dimension of this uncertainty makes it highly controversial, which has led to disputes about the dating of buildings. From 572, Cordoba was possibly the capital of the Byzantine province of Spain, but the Byzantine Metropolitan bishop dependent on the Patriarch of Constantinople was installed in Cartagena.

Cercadilla was originally the seat of Bishop Osio, but in the middle of the sixth century the see was transferred to the Basilica of St Vincent in nearby Cordoba, excavated in the 1930s on the site of the Mezquita.[5] During the mid-sixth century, the Visigothic kingdom was fragmenting, but from 569 Leovigild ruled the Spanish part of the Visigothic kingdom. He tried to impose unity on these fragments, and unity would have meant greater uniformity between the Arian Visigothic elite and the majority Catholic Romans. When Leovigild's son Reccared inherited the kingdom in 586, he quickly converted to Catholicism the following year, and Arianism was finally outlawed at the Council of Toledo in 589. After the death of Reccared in 601, instability followed, with a quick succession of kings, partly due to the tradition of elective kingship among the Goths, whereby succession could be to any member of the nobility. Powerful contenders would have to wipe out opponents to secure the throne. Despite this, the kingdom retained centralized government, and in about 628 King Suinthila finally managed to remove the Byzantines from all Iberian territory.[6]

Byzantine influence continued and can clearly be seen in church architecture, as at San Juan de Baños, dated by an inscription to 652 or 661–2 by King Recceswinth. When Recceswinth converted, Pope Gregory the Great sent him relics, including fragments of the True Cross, of the Chains of Peter, and hairs of John the Baptist, which perhaps explain the dedication of the church.[7] This has a four-bay nave with side-aisles, transepts, and chapels to either side of the sanctuary, recalling the *prothesis* (where the bread and wine were stored and prepared for Mass) and *diaconicon* (space for the offerings) of churches of the Byzantine rite. Such tri-apsed basilicas became the dominant form for churches in the region, though there was considerable variation in detail.

The now-Catholic Church in Spain was governed by councils called frequently by Visigothic kings at Toledo. These councils were a particular characteristic of the Spanish Church and State, which was not seen in the Frankish church nor in Lombard Italy. The councils were presided over by the king and enacted both ecclesiastical and secular legislation.[8] There were thirteen of these councils by 683, and they provided what stability there was during a quick succession of coups in the first half of the seventh century, when Isidore of Seville was bishop for much of this period (599–636). This dominance of the Catholic Church in the politics of the region was soon to be shattered. Though Catholics would retain a numerical majority of the population until the tenth century, their influence in society was to be frustrated by the Islamic conquest.

Seventh-century Arab expansion had quickly overwhelmed Byzantine Syria, and Islam found a rich quarry for architectural forms, which were transformed in early masterpieces like the Dome of the Rock, the first great architectural achievement of Islam built between 687 and 692.[9] Byzantine possessions in North Africa fell successively to the armies of Islam, and, even before the region was fully absorbed, in 710 the governor of Tangiers, Tariq ibn Zeyad, made an initial advance into Visigothic Spain, called al-Andalus by the Muslims. He was aided by Count Julian, a Goth who provided ships for transport.[10] Tariq built his fortress on 'Jabal Tariq'—Gibraltar, as it is still known.

Muslim Conquest

Initially, the Byzantines had been invited in to support a contender to the throne, and in 711, a similar invitation was sent by the sons of the last king, Wittiza, to the Muslims of North Africa for their support in a struggle against King Roderic. Internal rivalry makes a kingdom vulnerable to external forces, but the Visigothic kingdom was still the strongest in western Europe.[11] With the defeat and death of Roderic on 19 July 711[12] by Lake La Janda in Medina Sidonia, the Muslims seized power. Cordoba resisted their advance but was taken by Mugayath-al-Rumi, and it was later to become their capital, but the whole of Spain did not fall into their hands; a kingdom was left in the north. Count Pelayo was the focus of Visigothic resistance and managed to harry the invaders from the mountains in the northern area of Murcia. Typically, those Visigothic leaders who were under Muslim domination, including Theodemir, ruler of Murcia in 713, by treaty, remained in control under certain general conditions:

> We will not set special conditions for him or for his men, nor harass him, nor remove him from power. His followers will not be killed or taken prisoner, nor will they be separated from their women and children. They will not be coerced in matters of religion, their churches will not be burned, nor will sacred objects be taken from the realm, [so long as] he remains sincere and fulfils the [following] conditions that we have set for him.[13]

At this early period, Christians and Jews were protected under the *dhimma*, giving them religious freedom as 'Peoples of the Book'. In terms of life and society among Christians, the Church itself governed their daily lives, and even presided over internal legal matters within the Christian community. These generous terms meant that they were easily absorbed, albeit as second-class citizens, into Muslim al-Andalus.

In a little over two decades, Muslim holy war took Islamic armies north as far as Poitiers, where they were defeated by Charles Martel, Charlemagne's grandfather, at the place called by Muslims the 'Plain of the Martyrs' between 25 and 31 October 732.[14] Charlemagne's father, Pepin, recaptured Narbonne in 751, and in 758 the Muslims were forced back to the south beyond the Pyrenees. In 777, Charlemagne himself was invited into Spain by northern Muslim governors to help in an internal power struggle, resisting absorption into 'Abd al-Rahman's Emirate. In his dealings with the Bagdad caliphate, Charlemagne enjoyed 'friendly relations to Harun-al-Rashid, the king of the Persians, who held almost all of the East' (see Chapter 5).[15]

This was a game of global politics, with potential prizes in both east and west for players, including two Christian emperors, the Abbasid caliph as 'Commander of the Faithful', and the Umayyad (descended from Muawiya, secretary to the Prophet Mohammed) Emir of al-Andalus. Charlemagne arrived with an army in Spain in 778, but was soon forced to withdraw because of a revolt in distant Saxony, and the expedition ended in the slaughter of his rearguard at Roncevalles, memorialized in the epic poem the 'Chanson de Roland'.[16] In 785, the Franks established themselves in the territory around Barcelona as the 'Spanish March'.

Church and Mosque in Al-Andalus

In the middle of the eighth century, 'Abd al-Rahman established a western emirate with Cordoba as its capital. He was the sole survivor of the Umayyad ruling family after the usurpation of the Damascus caliphate in 750. He fled across North Africa, finding sympathizers in the western Islamic world. Supporters rallied to this Umayyad prince over the next five years, and, following a military victory at Musarah over the Abbasid governor of al-Andalus, Jusuf al-Fihri, he entered Cordoba and in 756 proclaimed himself emir in the Friday mosque of Cordoba.[17] He ruled over the first territory to secede from the caliphate now installed in Baghdad.

At first, the Visigothic palace and nearby Basilica of St Vincent appear to have served adequately as mosque and Emir's palace in his

capital at Cordoba. But his growing wealth and power and the growing population of the city pressed for a radical architectural solution.
The basilica may have been shared by the two religious communities,
and the thirteenth-century writer Ibn Idhari maintained that the
emir then bought the Christian half of the church complex to create
his mosque, it is said for 100,000 dinars, and the Christians were to be
allowed to build other churches in the city.[18] He levelled the church
to the ground and began building the mosque in 785–6. Partly to
establish his credentials and partly in direct competition with Baghdad,
he appears to have brought masons from Syria who maintained practices and used architectural elements recalling the Syrian Byzantine
past. 'Abd al-Rahman surrounded himself with memories of Umayyad
Damascus, but they were mixed with the Visigothic and Roman forms
and materials that were to hand. This created a breathtaking and original style epitomized in the mosque he built in Cordoba, which still
forms part of the Cathedral complex.

Roman columns and capitals, the technique of stacked arches, borrowed from the old Roman aqueduct at nearby Mérida, and the
horseshoe arch perhaps borrowed from the local Visigoths, enriched
the new architecture of the mosque. The church was opposite the old
Visigothic palace, and the Bab al-Wuzara, or Ministers' Gate, now
called the St Stephen Gate, which is still in its original form, gave
access to court officials from this side. An inscription dates it to 786. It
is a relatively modest door, surmounted by a huge horseshoe arch
under a canopy that breaks forward carrying stepped battlements. The
usual entrance for the populace was through what was then a smaller
courtyard on the northern side. The gate was on the central axis of the
eleven-aisled mosque, of which the central aisle was about a metre
wider than the others, giving the interior direction without undue
hierarchy. The courtyard was a roofless prayer hall, and the building
itself originally was probably open to the courtyard.

With quantities of *spolia* on site, the mosque was said to be ready
the next year. Other sources attribute the completion to Hisham I,
'Abd al-Rahman's son and successor in 788. His expedition against

Gerona, Narbonne, and Carcassone provided a fabulous 'royal fifth' of the booty to pay for the Great Mosque. Not only that, but Roman carved stones from the walls of Narbonne are said to have been carried to Cordoba on the backs of Christian captives and used in the eastern foundations of the building.[19] The mosque was approached through a broad courtyard. and on plan the mosque and its courtyard were roughly square, measuring approximately 74 metres along each side. The building itself consisted of a nave, running roughly north–south, and ten slightly narrower aisles, which were 37 metres long and divided into twelve bays.[20] The outer aisles are narrower and may have been separated from the main body of the mosque by grilles and reserved for the use of women. The simplicity of the plan recalls the al-Aqsa Mosque in Jerusalem, as does the double-tiered arcading. The stacked arcading had horseshoe arches below on the lower tier and round arches above, and the reuse of Roman columns and capitals, with some faithfully copied, creates a revolutionary antiquarianism, redolent of both Umayyad and local history, yet new in its integration of these elements of diverse origin into an emerging Hispanic art. The horseshoe arch has both common Visigothic and even some rare Umayyad precedents, as at the mosque at Damascus. An antiquarian approach may have been encouraged by friendly links between Cordoba and Constantinople, where there were dynastic reasons for indulging an antique revival.[21]

All adult male Muslims were required to attend prayers in the main mosque at noon on Fridays. The preaching by either the ruler or his appointee was both religious and political, just as the ruler was both a religious and a political figure. The mosque and its message were thus a direct expression of the ruling dynasty, so 'Abd al-Rahman's Great Mosque had to express his royal and historic Syrian legitimacy, as well as his dominance, and even absorption, of the local populace and its historic culture (though this is currently disputed). The style and materials of the architecture accomplish that magnificently, repeating the long-established ability of the Umayyad dynasty to borrow forms, methods, and craftsmen from the rival Byzantine Empire, as they did in the Dome of the Rock, built a century earlier between 687 and 692 as the first great architectural achievement of Islam.[22] There the vegetal mosaics and the marble panelling show an obvious debt to Constantinople.

With continued prosperity and growth of the population of Cordoba, and with numbers of converts to this attractive and highly cultured religion increasing, 'Abd al-Rahman II (822–52, great-grandson of the first of that name) extended the mosque by a further eight bays towards the south, making the building itself almost square. The project was carried out between 833 and 848. The same architectural strategy was followed in the reuse of material, especially columns, and mostly classical capitals were copied.

Up to this point, the Christians of al-Andalus continued to be in the majority, even where they were under Muslim rule. The Berbers, who came as troops in the first conquering wave, and the Syrians, who came as a paid army in the 740s, both began settling the land and intermarrying with the local Visigothic families, and the population slowly began converting to Islam. It was a slow but inexorable erosion, however, and late in the reign of 'Abd al-Rahman II, though Christians continued their religious observance, apparently with little harassment, it is said that it was a symptom of frustration when a group of about fifty activists known as the 'martyrs of Cordoba', led by Alvar and a priest called Eulogius (who died in 859), began insulting Islam in public in the 850s, deliberately provoking their own deaths.[23] Communicating with the Christian kingdoms in the north, they appealed to the early Roman martyrs as their model, while many other Cordoban Christians, including the hierarchy, saw them as senseless suicides.

Christian and Muslim during the Caliphate

'Abd al-Rahman III came to the throne in 912, when he was just 21, and declared himself caliph on 16 January 929. In 939, he led an enormous army against the Christian north, but was defeated near Samancas. Politically, he was much more successful, finally exacting tribute even from Castile and Barcelona. Awash with tribute, the ransom of Tunis, and political success in establishing good diplomatic relations with both Constantinople and Otto the Great's Holy Roman Empire, he again extended Cordoba's Great Mosque and built a minaret beside the main gate of an enlarged courtyard.[24] This expansion of the mosque was necessary as a result of the huge expansion of the city (probably much larger than present-day Cordoba), combined with mass conversions to Islam. The Church was now in decline, becoming a minority for the first time. As caliph, and claiming to be the rightful successor to Mohammed, 'Abd al-Rahman III had assumed a title fitting his increasing political glories, reflected in newly elaborated ceremonial and architectural settings. He built a new palace–city, Madinat al-Zahra, a few miles north of the burgeoning city of Cordoba. In this new palace, the complexity of the seemingly endless series of indoor and outdoor architectural spaces mirrored the social and official complexity of the court. It was decorated and furnished to the same glittering degree as the Great Mosque, to dazzle both his subjects and the embassies from his expanded sphere of diplomacy, including the Christian kings and emperors of his day. Though religious communities were clearly separate at this date, linguistic and ethnic boundaries were certainly porous. Christians and Jews spoke Arabic and were to be found in high office. There was much intermarriage, and the caliph himself was bilingual in Arabic and Romance. Though descended from the Umayyad caliphs of Baghdad, the mothers of the royal line were frequently Christians from the northern kingdoms. 'Abd al-Rahman's own mother was Basque.[25]

   'Abd al-Rahman's son and successor al-Hakam II (961–76) was immensely cultured and learned, establishing a library in Cordoba said to be of 400,000 books—an astonishing collection when compared to monastic collections that tended to be in the order of a few hundred. This was the apogee of Islamic culture and political power in Spain. In the Great Mosque, this was manifest when he began construction of the *maqsura* area, including a gilded and carved wooden enclosure, for himself as caliph, beneath magnificent domes, and the decoration of the *mihrab* wall with gold mosaic between 965 and 971. The entrance to the *mihrab* is flanked by small columns of lapis lazuli. A walk along the axis of the Great Mosque was now a walk through the history of the dynasty of the rulers of al-Andalus. Craftsmen were brought from Constantinople to create the magnificent mosaics in front of the *mihrab*, which unusually opened into an octagonal room. There are comparable mosaics in the Hagia Sophia, including the Virgin and Child in the apse, thought to be from 867, the penitent Leo VI on the tympanum above the Imperial Door, from between 880 and 900, and Constantine and Justinian above the door to the narthex of the tenth or perhaps early eleventh century, while the Cordoban mosaics have been directly compared with the mosaics of Saint Sophia in Kiev. Though comparable, they were not of the same technical brilliance. The Cordoban mosaics were Byzantine Christian in origin and secular in their forms and themes, all of which was adapted to a Muslim religious context while integrating local traditions. It is a perfect cultural fusion of Byzantine and Arab, Christian and Muslim.

In his enhancement of the mosque, Caliph al-Hakam set out to demonstrate that his own magnificence was comparable to, perhaps even greater than, his contemporary, the Byzantine emperor Nicephorus II Phocas himself.[26] The mosaics also covered the cupola of the *maqsura*, the area immediately in front of the *mihrab*. The *mihrab*, being a dark octagonal room without windows rather than a mere niche indicating the direction of Mecca, becomes a place beyond, the hereafter, the enveloping mystery of God. Its door is surrounded by mosaic *voussoirs*, framed with carved spandrels and running bands of Kufic script.

The double arcading surrounding the *maqsura* bristled and fluttered into multi-foil cusped arches, effectively giving the impression of a high-level screen for the area reserved for the caliph in front of the *mihrab*. The enclosed southern aisle also gave direct private access to the palace, in much the same way as the emperor's *metatorion* (royal enclosure) in Hagia Sophia gave discreet private access to the Great Palace of Constantinople. The eastern rooms of the *maqsura* may have been the treasury, and the rooms above the private aisle and *mihrab* housed the library. The caliph's magnificence and his religious role are suitably emphasized here. The *maqsura*, as the place of the caliph, identifies this building uniquely with the Caliphate of al-Andalus, and its dominant geographical position within Cordoba would present a problem when the city was again taken by Christian armies. It had to be reused as the cathedral, or replaced by a cathedral.

The separation of the *maqsura* area later made it ideal for Christian tombs and side-chapels at the former focus of the building. Acting like canopies sheltering the caliph, the ribbed domes are magnificent and highly original creations, covered in gold mosaic perfectly fusing Islamic and Byzantine forms, and providing the model for repetition in Christian architecture throughout the Middle Ages. A dome of similar form is to be found far to the north on one of the French pilgrim routes to Compostela in the Church of Notre-Dame-du-Port at Clermont-Ferrand, where the early eleventh-century dome uses squinch arches to fit the dome onto the square space. There are also horseshoe arches at tribune level, coloured voussoirs, and coloured tiles, all reinforcing the sense of Islamic influence.

The composition of the facade of the Church of Notre-Dame, Le Puy-en-Velay, relates to Cordoba, and inside there are cusped arches, coloured voussoirs, patterned panels, decorative use of kufic inscriptions, and a great many carved capitals of Muslim type. As far away as Vézelay, at the start of one of the most important routes through France to Compostela, the transverse ribs of the vault have alternating coloured voussoirs characteristic of the Great Mosque of Cordoba.[27]

At al-Hakam's death in 976, al-Mansur, who had been al-Hakam's grand *cadi*, or palace master, dominated the new Caliph Hisham II, still only a child, keeping him under virtual house arrest. Like the Caliphs, al-Mansur was highly cultured, and even more successful militarily. In 988, he plundered León, and the booty would help to pay for a huge project adding a further eight aisles on the southern side of the Great Mosque, visibly placing him on an all but equal standing to the caliphs he 'served'. His rule clearly aligned with all that came before and demonstrated his piety. Like previous rulers, he is reputed to have laboured personally on the building site.[28] His huge extension continued the style of the earlier work without any significant new development. This re-created the square plan on a vast scale, thirty-two bays long and with nineteen aisles. The columns stretch off into the darkness, giving the sense of a limitless expanse, an architecturally delimited place in 'forever' (Plate 15). The courtyard was planted with trees in a continuation of the bay system, reinforcing the impression of a forest of columns.

In 995, al-Mansur inflicted a significant defeat on the Christian armies, and, in 997, he captured Santiago de Compostela, dedicated to St James, the 'Moor Slayer', and destroyed the city and its shrine. It stuck in Christian memory, and fuelled abiding resentment, that he had the bells transported back to Cordoba on the shoulders of his Christian captives, to be used for the lighting of Cordoba's Great Mosque. When Cordoba was retaken by the Christians, they were carried back to Santiago by Muslim captives.[29] In 1000 he sacked Burgos, and in 1002 he died returning from a campaign against Castile.[30] By 1031, the last caliph of Cordoba had abdicated, and al-Andalus fragmented into separate Taifa kingdoms.

The Christian kingdoms that clung to power in the north-west, though constantly vigilant against Muslim military encroachment, were very open to cultural influence. Theirs was a highly characteristic early Romanesque architecture, and the clear articulation of mid-ninth-century buildings like Santa Maria de Naranco near Oviedo can be traced back to the clarity of both the interior and the exterior articulation of the eighth-century Great Mosque at Cordoba.

The Mosque as Cathedral, and the New Building

Cordoba was not back in Christian hands until 1235, and the Great Mosque was then used as the cathedral after the Chapter gained control of the former site of the cathedral of St Vincent. The existing mosque was, of course, unsuited to Christian worship, but they had to make do while disputes raged over the future of the building. From early on, Christian altars and chapels were introduced into the existing fabric, including the original Villaviciosa Chapel and the Capilla Real by Alphonso X (r. 1252–84). In 1401, it was decided that the twelfth-century mosque of Seville would be swept away in building a stupendous Gothic cathedral to be second only to St Peter's in Rome in size. It was under construction throughout the century and completed in 1506. The fourteenth and fifteenth centuries were the great age of the Gothic cathedral, especially in reconquered cities.

The Catholic monarchs Ferdinand of Aragon and Isabella of Castile were married in 1469 and assumed power in 1474 and 1479. In 1492, they conquered the last Muslim kingdom, Granada. At first, Muslims were allowed to continue to practise their religion. But, after continued harassment, they rebelled, and in 1500 Isabella demanded that all Muslims convert to Christianity. In Spain, religion and politics were volatile, with so many *conversos*, recent converts to Catholicism from Judaism and Islam, and expectations of the 'end times' were rife. In the region of Cordoba in 1499, a wave of millenarianism brought a particularly savage response from the Inquisition and almost 400 victims were burned.

Spain's very diversity of ethnicity, religion, and culture was seen as incompatible with the project for unity. The grandson of Ferdinand and Isabella, Charles V, became emperor in 1519, and Spain was set to dominate Europe for the next century. During that century, cathedral building in Spain continued in the Gothic style. The cathedral in Seville, like that in Cordoba, had been in the old mosque, which was demolished in 1401 to make way for a new Gothic cathedral. It was dedicated in the same year that Charles V ascended the imperial throne, 1519.

In 1523, the cathedral Chapter in Cordoba finally gained permission from Emperor Charles V himself to build within it. The roof in the centre of the complex was to be raised, and more than sixty columns were removed to clear the central area, destroying the sense of infinite regression through the forest of columns. As the building then stood, in lateral views the double-height arcading made it impossible to see the roof, giving apparent 'lift' to this extensive spatial grid. Only along the axis in the direction of worship did the roof press the spatial focus towards the spiritual focus. This was further emphasized by the addition of 833–48 by 'Abd al-Rahman II, where the red columns of the central aisle ended with two chamfered white marble columns in front of where the *mihrab* would have been. It was a large portion of this mid-ninth-century addition that was destroyed in building the cathedral, with its axis cutting right across that of the Great Mosque.

There was surprising resistance to this triumphalist gesture, even breaking through the pride of the *Reconquista*. There are tales of stoppages of work by outraged labourers, and confrontations among them, the city fathers, and the cathedral Chapter. It had been under the authority of the emperor, Charles V, that work finally proceeded, but when he saw the result, he is said to have lamented: 'Had I known what was here I would never have dared touch the old structure. You have destroyed something that was unique in the world and added something one can see anywhere.'[31]

The architect of the cathedral was Fernán Ruiz, who completed the *capilla major* (or chancel), the crossing, and the transepts. When the columns were removed from the heart of the mosque, the walls of the transepts and eastern chancel, and piers for the crossing and the buttressing, had to be set in place. The piers of the flying buttresses rise on the grid of the arcading of the mosque. After Ruiz the elder died in 1558, his son built the *coro*, or Choir, over four decades, completing it in 1598, and added the cupola over the crossing.

The architecture is most extraordinary. The eastern wall of the chancel rises as a Renaissance reredos under a fan vault covered in geometric Renaissance panelling. The piers of the crossing rise as Gothic clustered colonettes supporting round main arches east and west and slightly pointed arches over the north and south transepts, which are vaulted in a similar way to the nave. The ribbed and coffered cupola is pure Renaissance classicism. The nave has Renaissance cross-vaulting. The whole is a Gothic structure in Renaissance dress, but to call it transitional seems wrong, since the architects seem fully capable in either style, rather than interpreting elements of a new style within the constraints of the old. Only the elder Ruiz's vaulting can be seen as transitional in that sense, suggesting that the original scheme was for an elaborate late-Gothic structure, but that a change of intention came with the insertion of the east wall of the chancel in pure Renaissance classicism. That vaulting bears an interesting comparison with the purer Gothic of the cathedral in Seville, but even there craftsmen from many countries together produced an exotic hybrid.

At Cordoba Cathedral, the great crossing arches appear to have been intended to support a square tower, but instead received squinches to support a dome. The integration to the surrounding mezquita is interesting. In the transepts, large relieving arches rise above and embrace the open double arcading left visible as obviously Muslim motifs embedded in the eclectically European structure (Plate 16). It is as though in that very Spanish (not to say Moorish) *horror vacui*, nothing was overlooked from the stylistic and decorative history

Figure 17. Cathedral of Cordoba: vaulting and dome of the Cathedral

of the intervening period between the glories of the caliphate and
the triumphalism of the Roman Church that was gearing up for
the Counter-Reformation (or Catholic Reformation) over precisely
this period.

Outside, at the entrance to the courtyard, a minaret had been built
by 'Abd al-Rahman III beside the main entrance to the mosque, but it
was replaced in the sixteenth century by a bell tower for the cathedral.
Of course, both minaret and bell tower call the people to enter for
prayer, so the position beside the main entrance was entirely appropriate.

The Cathedral of Astorga was begun in flamboyant Gothic in 1477
and was still being built in 1559. The Cathedral of Salamanca was
begun in 1513 under the great Juan Gil de Hontañón and is Gothic
with the exception of classical elements on the facade. Around 1521,
he was engaged with the Cathedral of Segovia, though he died not
long after that, and the strictly Gothic cathedral was not finished until
1617.[32] Such was the continued strength of Gothic in Spain, but, like
the Cathedral of Cordoba, the new Cathedral of Saragossa, built
between 1490 and 1550, was Gothic in plan but Renaissance in
decoration. The vaulting of its tower lantern related to cross-ribbed
vaulting of the *maqsura* of the Great Mosque of Cordoba. The cathedral in newly conquered Granada, begun in 1523 at the same time as
the Cathedral of Cordoba, is again a Gothic structure with Baroque
decoration carried out in a building programme continuing until 1703.

Put within this context, the Cathedral of Cordoba is more easily
understood. The vigour of the flamboyant Gothic style pushed the
boundaries of international Gothic, allowing the introduction of
Italian and Renaissance motifs. The architecture of the Caliphate had
been eclectic in its assemblage of architectural elements and forms,
and the new Spanish architecture remained eclectic in its sources and
mixture of European styles and forms. If flamboyance arose naturally
from the exuberance of Moorish patterning, then the Baroque would
also be easy. Though rooted in Spanish traditions, Church and society
were outward-looking at this period. It was a dominant European
power and was becoming rich in developing an empire in the New

World. Spain was forging a confident new European Christian identity, while stripping away essential aspects of its multilingual and multi-ethnic past. In 1391, pogroms tore into the Jewish community, prompting widespread conversion, and in 1492, the Jews were expelled from Spain. 'Purity of blood' became a requirement for joining many religious orders or holding high office in the Church, but ironically the nobility were often of mixed lineage and so excluded.

The Church in Imperial and Modern Spain

Though Spain was hugely powerful on the European stage during the sixteenth century, there were continuing rebellions amongst the Moriscos through the first half of the century, and in mid-century Ottoman fleets harried the central Mediterranean and besieged Malta in 1565. The siege was lifted eventually by a fleet sent by the Spanish viceroy in Naples. In 1566, Muslim Corsairs attacked Granada and its surroundings, capturing thousands of Moriscos. Cyprus was captured in 1571, and its Latin Gothic churches were converted into mosques. The Orthodox Church here had been oppressed for centuries, and Orthodox Christians were pleased to come through relatively unscathed while their rivals were brought low. The situation was desperate enough to bring an unusual unity of purpose to Venetian, Italian, Spanish, and Portuguese states, whose fleets destroyed the Ottoman galleys.[33] Constantinople had fallen more than a century before, in 1453, and Ottoman momentum continued until 1683 when they reached the gates of Vienna.

In 1614, the Muslims of Spain were in their turn expelled, which created the Christian nation and moved it towards its Golden Age of Empire. But the supposed purity that this was to re-establish was a chimera. The Cathedral of Cordoba embodies the story much more clearly. To walk into the Great Mosque and down the axis of its main aisle was to walk through the history of the caliphate, beginning with 'Abd al-Rahman I in 786–7, into the section by 'Abd al-Rahman II between 833 and 848, then that of his son al-Hakam II with its sumptuous gold mosaics created between 965 and 971, and finally turning left into the vast but cautiously derivative aisles of the *cadi* al-Mansur at the end of the tenth century before the decline of the caliphate. Though not completely obliterated, that historical walk has been interrupted by the east–west axis of the cathedral itself, occupying the greater part of the ninth-century section of the mosque. In the cathedral, the historical narrative is read vertically, with the Gothic footings in the grid established by the mosque, and the Gothic main structure clasping and supporting elements from Moorish arcading in the transepts, to Renaissance classicism in the reredos to late flamboyant/early Renaissance vaulting in the transepts and sanctuary, to the pure Renaissance dome at the end of the sixteenth century. The narrative is discontinuous and full of conflict, separated by religion, but culturally and ethnically irretrievably mixed.

The dual heritage physically embodied by the building continues to erupt into conflict. The twentieth century and increasingly the twenty-first have brought Muslim immigration from North Africa, especially Morocco, and a growing number of conversions. In Spain, there are now somewhere in the region of a million followers of Islam, or two per cent of the population. There are newly built mosques, but the modern one in Cordoba is too small for the 500 or so Muslims in the city, and they have requested the right to pray in the cathedral/mezquita from both the local bishop and the Vatican. An appeal to Canon Law forbidding prayer by other religions is generally met by incomprehension by those politically sympathetic to accommodation, but after 9/11 and the terrorist attacks in Madrid on 11 March 2004 that left 191 dead and 1,800 injured, toleration is hard.[34] On 3 May 2004, the *Guardian* newspaper reported the response of Archbishop Michael Fitzgerald, president of the Pontifical Council for Inter-Religious Dialogue in the Vatican:

> 'The Holy Father visited the Ummayad mosque in Damascus, praying in front of the tomb of St John the Baptist. But he did not ask to celebrate mass,' he said. 'One has to accept history and go forward.'

He pointed out that Hagia Sophia in Istanbul, another important building with a past as both a Christian place of worship (in its time centre of the Orthodox church and the biggest church building in the world) and a mosque, was now a museum: 'It is difficult to have Christians and Muslims mixing and sharing a common [civic and religious] life, despite being driven by wanting to go back in time or take some form of vengeance.'[35]

The cathedral/mezquita of Cordoba is of particular significance to Muslims, and to pray there is a growing aspiration. In 2006, the *Guardian* reported the local Muslims' persistent appeal to be allowed to pray in the building. Predictably, it was seen by some members of the public as a bid for 'reconquest', while others asked when Christians would be allowed to pray in mosques, but the Muslim council maintained that the request had been 'very well received', with support from some local politicians, particularly among the left. An official request submitted on Christmas Day 2006 was intended to take advantage of attempts by the Vatican to assuage Muslim anger at Pope Benedict's quotation of a Byzantine emperor's harsh remarks about the Prophet Mohammed.[36] On 1 April 2010, during Holy Week, violence erupted when a group of Muslims from Austria began a protest by unrolling rugs and beginning to pray. Those at prayer were surrounded by others in their group, and, when security guards asked them to move on, scuffles broke out, leaving two guards injured. The situation was enflamed because the protest coincided with the Holy Week parades of penitents dressed in robes, distinctive conical hats, and floats bearing statues of Christ and the Virgin Mary in the city.

The debate resurfaced the following November with the visit of the pope to Spain.[37] Aspirations hinge on the fact that the old Visigothic cathedral of St Vincent was once shared between the two religions. The histories of the two religious communities, Church and mosque, are inextricably bound by these buildings of the cathedral/mezquita, but they are proving as difficult to reconcile religiously as the buildings are visually.

Figure 18. Sangallo's wooden model, in the Fabbrica di San Pietro

9

Ultimate Authority
under Attack

The Building of Renaissance St Peter's

*O*ld St Peter's Basilica was a formidable presence in Rome, but, less than
a century after its completion, the former capital of the empire was sacked
in 410 CE by Alaric the Goth. The basilica seems to have come through the
disaster relatively unscathed, but it was a severe cultural shock. The papacy
soon recovered, and new churches, including Santa Sabina, were being built in
the 420s and 430s. Leo the Great became pope in 440, establishing the
authority of his office as the inheritor of the Prince of the Apostles and obtain-
ing a rescript from the emperor in Constantinople, giving him authority over
the western empire. However, in 455 Rome was again taken, this time by
the Vandals. From the late sixth until the mid-eighth centuries, the Exarchate
of Ravenna was the Byzantine toehold in Italy. The exarchate fell in 751, and
Rome was under pressure from the Lombards. The same year, the pope gave his
assent to Pepin, then Mayor of the Palace, to remove the last Merovingian king
of the Franks, and take the throne for himself. Pepin's military support for the
pope relieved the Lombard threat to Rome, and his son, Charlemagne, continued that support, establishing the Papal States. Charlemagne was crowned
emperor on Christmas Day, 800, in St Peter's, a tradition that continued with
successive emperors. The relationship between pope and emperor had great
potential for conflict. Under Henry III, it flared, and under his son, Henry IV,
there was open warfare, which kept Rome under siege for two years. The pope's

secular and political power in the west brought him into frequent conflict with the emperor. The Frenchman Clement V moved the papacy to Avignon in 1309, where it remained until Martin V returned to Rome more than a century later in 1420. By that time, St Peter's was in a bad state of disrepair. No satisfactory solution was found until 1505–6 under Julius II and his architect Bramante. It was not until 1510 that destruction of significant parts of the ancient Constantinian fabric had to be destroyed, giving Bramante the nickname 'Ruinante'. The new basilica was to be even larger and much grander than its predecessor, with its financing on a similarly colossal scale. In 1514, an indulgence was to be granted to the Archbishop of Brandenburg and also newly of Mainz, and half the proceeds would go towards the building of the new basilica. The indulgence drew protest from a young Augustinian friar named Martin Luther. The building of the basilica continued, with the completion of the dome in 1593, by which time the Reformation had riven the western Church.

The Approach

For well over a thousand years from the death of Constantine the Great, Old St Peter's Basilica had been the colossus whose presence dominated Rome as the *caput mundi*, but a series of threats would finally reduce the great basilica to a state that required its total replacement. The size of the Constantinian basilica was overwhelming: the nave was just under 300 feet long, more than 77 feet wide, and almost 125 feet to the ridge of the roof.[1] The exterior had changed little during that millennium: to a visitor approaching from the west, the height of the platform on which the whole complex sat, and the size of the eastern range of the atrium, meant that it was only on reaching its huge open space that the enormity of the basilica was revealed.

A broad monumental staircase led up to a terrace in front of the eastern range of the large atrium, which was paved with marble. At its centre was a bronze pinecone fountain under a bronze domed canopy.

Intimidating authority was exuded, not only by the scale of the basilica, but by its sumptuous materials and the great antiquity of many of the coloured marble architectural elements recycled from ancient monuments. There was also the iconography: there was a double cycle of narrative paintings on the nave walls (probably dating from at least the end of the fifth century), there were the apse mosaics, and then there was the gold, including the great cross of Constantine. All this reinforced the authority of the Church and the bishop of Rome as the successor of Peter. Even during the fourth century, there had been significant pagan survival within Roman society, but from 391 CE, sole religious authority had been vested in the Church with the final suppression of all pagan cults. Christianity was triumphant.

The Sack of Rome by Alaric the Goth and its Aftermath

Despite the city's declining political and military importance, Rome maintained its prestige as a cultural emblem, so, when it was sacked in 410 CE by Alaric the Goth, the shock waves were felt throughout the empire. In Palestine, St Jerome was at that time engaged in his commentary on the book of the Prophet Ezekiel, where he wrote: 'The Brightest light of the whole world is extinguished.'[2] The pagan cults may have gone, but there were still some old pagans among the aristocracy in particular, and they attributed the fall of Rome to the desertion of the old Gods who had protected the city. This was the problem addressed by St Augustine in his book *The City of God*, written between 413 and 426. Augustine denied that Christianity was responsible for the fall of Rome. What really mattered was the citizenship of heaven, and the Sack of Rome had to be seen in that divine perspective. Besides, the disaster could have been much worse, considering the mercy shown by the Goths to those who sought sanctuary in 'the graves of the martyrs and the basilicas of the

Apostles'.[3] These buildings did indeed command great respect. Four years before the sack, Jerome had used the example of the two basilicas of the apostles to refute those who denied the sanctity of relics: 'So does the Bishop of Rome do evil, when he offers sacrifices to God over what to us are the hallowed bones but to you is the miserable dust of the dead men Peter and Paul, and when he treats their tombs as the altar of Christ?' So there were protests against the cult of relics even then, but St Peter's basilica and St Peter's successor were by then the measure of orthodoxy. Still, confidence had been so shaken by the sack, and the questions raised were so large, that it took someone of the stature of St Augustine and a work of the gravity of *The City of God* to give an adequate answer.

The suffering endured by the people of Rome at the hands of the Goths has always been a contentious matter. Augustine seemed surprised by the degree of mercy shown by the barbarians, and the Romans did refer to these incomers as 'barbarians', though modern scholars more often use the more neutral term 'Germanic peoples'. Only a few years after the sack, between 417 and 418, the Spanish priest Orosius too wrote that few were killed because there was little resistance. Besides, he argued, things had been worse in every way in pagan times. The Visigoths may have been Arian heretics, but they were still Christians and were under instruction not to loot the churches. If that is true, it must have taken unbelievable restraint and discipline to resist carrying off the gold cross weighing 150 pounds given by Constantine to St Peter's. In the intervening century, between the magnificent gifts of Constantine and Alaric's Sack of Rome, the Church had grown enormously in terms of both numbers and wealth. Edward Gibbon in *Decline and Fall* and more recent historians too have blamed the Church itself for the fall of Rome, just as contemporary pagans had—not such a change really. Where we are standing changes our perspective on history. Early in the twenty-first century, the point has been made very forcibly:

> The changing perspectives of scholarship are always shaped in part
> by wider developments in modern society. There is inevitably a close

connection between the way we view our own world and the way we interpret the past. For instance, there is certainly a link between the interpretations of the Germanic invaders as primarily peaceful, and the remarkable (and deserved) success that modern Germany has had at constructing a new and positive identity within Europe, after the disastrous Nazi years. Images of the fifth-century Germanic peoples and their settlement in the western empire have changed dramatically since the Second World War, as ideas about modern Germans and their role in the new Europe have altered...

The Roman empire on its own, although in some ways a wonderful precedent for much that modern Europe aspires to (with its free-trade zone, its common currency, and the undoubted loyalty that it inspired), has also never been entirely satisfactory as an ancestor for the European Union. Roman power was used too recently (by Mussolini) as part of a specifically Italian national and imperial agenda.[4]

Clearly, great care must be taken when we project ourselves back into history, but it does not seem very likely that the pope standing on the steps of St Peter's or the other citizens of Rome experienced the approach of Alaric and his Gothic troops as the approach of a peaceful transition. Zosimus, writing after 425, tells of great suffering during the siege; starvation was followed by plague, but then he is writing from an anti-Christian perspective so he would want it to be seen as a great disaster and the fault of this upstart religion.

There is no doubt that the fall of Rome to these barbarians was traumatic, and not only for those in the city. The citizens of the empire called themselves Romans. Its sway had been universal, and its essence was distilled in the city itself. Augustine theologized the problem: the earthly city and its citizens were beset by sin as inheritors of fallen Adam; the heavenly city, the Kingdom of Heaven (for which the pope held the keys as direct inheritor of Peter), was the objective of the Church. With his spiritual authority, and growing secular authority in Rome and the west, the pope became the guardian and purveyor of an enhanced *Romanitas*, or sense of what it is to be Roman. Ironically, the Sack of Rome in some ways worked to the advantage of the pope. Rivals to his wealth and power among the aristocracy were even more devastatingly affected than himself; he may have lost revenues from

Italian estates, but he still had revenues in Africa, Sicily, and the east, so he had the means to assume the patronage and charitable work of the senatorial families. His political gain was immense, and, as far as finance was concerned, the Church was soon able to build again, including the exquisite Santa Sabina from 422 to 432, which perhaps gives the best impression of what the interior of Old St Peter's was like.

In 440 CE, a new pope was elected who would further enhance the standing of the papacy and who refurbished the basilica, Leo the Great. He strengthened the papal claims based on Matthew 16:18, where Jesus says: 'Thou art Peter, and upon this rock I will build my church; and the gates of hell shall not prevail against it.' He used concepts rooted in Roman law—that an heir assumes all the rights and obligations of the testator, and in a legal sense *is* that person. The bishop of Rome as successor of Peter *is* the rock on which the Church is built. Without actually adding anything to the notion of papal authority, this was clarified and put on a legal basis.[5] Leo was also granted a rescript from the emperor, Valentinian III, recognizing his jurisdiction over the whole of the west. This would cause disputes with the Holy Roman emperors in centuries to come. For the time being, doctrinal disputes in the east meant that the pope was courted by the rival factions, enhancing his influence, though not establishing the direct authority that would naturally flow from his Petrine claims. This question of authority opened a rift between east and west that would eventually lead to schism. Leo's political skill extended beyond doctrinal dispute, and he was effective in negotiating concessions when the Vandals in their turn took Rome in 455.

A Holy Roman Empire

Up until the eighth century, most of northern Italy was governed by the Lombards, while the Byzantine emperor still claimed Ravenna and the south under the governorship of the exarch. In fact, the exarch was powerless to defend Rome when under threat, and the popes had to make their own accommodation with the Lombards, as Gregory I (the Great) did as early as 593, which is probably also when the Choir area of St Peter's Basilica was reorganized.[6] Pope Zacharias again negotiated with the Lombards in 742. Just the year before that, in 741, Pope Gregory III had built a screen of six twisted columns, a gift of the exarch, in front of the seventh-century screen of similar columns that defined the front of the *confessio* in St Peter's Basilica. He crowned his six columns with beams sheathed in silver. Significantly, these interventions were at the focus of the whole architectural complex, the grave of the Prince of the Apostles. Only a decade later, the exarchate fell in 751,[7] leaving Rome and its territories surrounded and under serious threat.

No support could be expected from his overlord, the Byzantine emperor, so Pope Stephen took the dangerous step of travelling late in the winter of 753 to seek help from Pepin the Short of the Franks. Pepin had not been king of the Franks until 751; before that he had been Mayor of the Palace, as his father, Charles Martel, had been. But he had been the effective ruler, placing the powerless Childeric III on the throne. Pepin had written to Stephen's predecessor, Zacharias, essentially asking whether it would not be appropriate to recognize the actual situation and had received the reply 'that it was better to call him king who had the royal power than the one who did not'.[8] When Pepin took the throne for himself in 751, he was anointed by Boniface. Stephen removed any shadow on the legitimacy of his kingship by anointing Pepin again at Saint-Denis on 28 July 754. He also anointed his sons, Carloman and Charles (the future Charlemagne), and he pronounced that the Franks were,

> on pain of interdict and excommunication, never to presume in future to elect a king begotten by any men other than those whom the bounty of God has seen fit to raise up and has decided to confirm and consecrate by the intercession of the holy apostles through the hands of their vicar, the most blessed pontiff.[9]

Stephen duly received the military support he needed. That support continued under Charles. At Easter 774, Charles visited Rome. He was met 30 miles from the city by a delegation bearing the papal standard, and a mile from the gates by a military escort led by papal crosses. There Charlemagne dismounted and walked to the steps of St Peter's. He kissed each step as he climbed and was met by Pope Hadrian at the bronze doors he had recently installed. They exchanged the kiss of peace before entering the basilica hand in hand in conscious imitation of Byzantine imperial ceremonial. In the *confessio* they swore mutual oaths before the apostle.[10]

Hadrian was succeeded by Leo III, who announced his election to Charlemagne, as previous popes had customarily done to the Byzantine emperor, showing the shift in power relations. Leo was soon deposed by rivals who attempted to blind him and cut out his tongue. He fled to Charlemagne. His rivals made serious accusations against Leo. Charlemagne's advisor, Alcuin, maintained that the pope could be judged neither by a secular court nor, as Peter's successor, by his inferiors. In the summer of 800, Leo was taken back to Rome after publicly swearing his innocence. In November of that year, Charlemagne arrived in Rome, and during the Mass in St Peter's on Christmas Day, he was crowned emperor. Charlemagne issued a new seal with an image of Rome and the text *Renovatio Romani Imperii*.

'Binding and loosing' by Peter and his successors as bishops of Rome, represented by the emblem of the keys, applied to sin and to the giving or denying of access to heaven, so Rome and St Peter's Basilica were naturally supremely important goals of the pilgrim. But pilgrimage required considerable resources of time and money. Those without could go only in heart and mind. Though not all the people could travel, images of St Peter's and Rome could, as signs of ultimate authority. Those images and Roman liturgical practices were replicated far and wide. Seventh-century Canterbury and its churches were laid out as a replica of Rome. From Northumberland, where he founded the twin monasteries of Monkwearmouth, which was dedicated to St Peter, and Jarrow, dedicated to St Paul, Benedict Biscop travelled to Rome a number of times, returning with masons, glaziers, singers, and ceremonial books and clothing 'to build a church of stone for his people after the Roman fashion, promising that it should be dedicated in honour of the blessed chief of the apostles'.[11]

'Binding and loosing' also extended to authority. Prelates and princes travelled to Rome to have their authority recognized and affirmed. Prelates might return with a highly prized pallium (a woollen mantel left in contact with the very grave of Peter, conveying some of his sanctity, charisma, and Petrine authority on the wearer). They might return with relics, if only 'contact relics', from Rome. Or they might return with plans to build in imitation of St Peter's Basilica, with its distinctive reliquary annular crypt below the apse. Symbolism, relics, patterns of worship, and architectural patterns are all highly portable and can be used to produce powerful evocations. In times of very special need, as when Pope Stephen sought the military aid of Pepin or Leo III of Charlemagne, the pope might be forced to travel himself, and all he had to offer were blessing, recognition, anointing, and, most importantly, authority. Secular and religious power had need of one another. That power was operated not so much by levers as by delicate negotiation.

At Easter 1027, in St Peter's, the most powerful secular and religious men of Europe gathered together; there was Cnut, king of Denmark and England, Rudolf III of Burgundy, the German King Conrad II, the nobles of Germany and Italy, archbishops, bishops, abbots, and, of course, the pope, John XIX. Conrad was crowned emperor in St Peter's by the pope and led out in procession by the kings. A role in such an occasion was both an honour and an affirmation of position. There was intense diplomatic activity surrounding the coronation. Charters and agreements were negotiated, and the exchange of diplomatic gifts reinforced relationships.[12] The effectiveness of such a gathering with its acts and agreements was greatly enhanced by being held in the presence of the Prince of the Apostles, presided over by his successor, in his basilica. It is well to remember in this context that the word *basilica* means 'hall of the prince', a Roman law court where oaths were sworn and bargains struck before the image of the emperor in the apse. In this sense, the Christian coronation ceremonial in St Peter's

Basilica in 1027 had not departed greatly from the original secular use of the Roman imperial basilica. Still, most of these dignitaries were not there solely for the coronation; the journey would also be a pilgrimage, and Cnut was clear about his intentions: 'I have learnt from wise men of the great power which the holy Apostle Peter had received from our Lord of binding and loosing, and that it is he who bears the keys of the Kingdom of Heaven; and for this I thought it very profitable to seek his advocacy in particular with God.'[13] The appeal to Matthew 16:18–19 has had wider implications than ever could have been anticipated by Pope Stephen I, long before, in the middle of the third century, in his appeal to the text.

St Peter's Deserted: Avignon and the 'Babylonian Captivity', 1309–1377

In 1046, the preamble to another imperial coronation would loosen the connection of the pope to Rome and begin the irremedial decay of the Old St Peter's Basilica. On his way to his coronation, the Holy Roman Emperor Henry III presided over the synod of Sutri. Pope Gregory VI was charged with corruption and removed. Henry appointed Clement II, a German, in his place. His name is revealing; Clement I was Peter's immediate successor, so Clement II was clearly expected to restore the apostolic purity and authority of the Roman See. For the next eighty years, only one of the popes was from Rome itself. Previously popes had usually been from the Roman aristocracy, and their concerns had for the most part revolved around Rome and the lands given to them by Charlemagne's father, Pepin, the Patrimony of St Peter. Now that popes came from much further afield, their concerns, likewise, extended more widely, and included authority and rights over clerical appointments in distant England, France, and Germany. The German king Henry IV was equally determined to maintain his right of investiture, making direct appointments to high, and often lucrative, clerical office. The result was that Pope Gregory

VII forbad lay investiture in 1075. The next year, Henry IV convened synods at Worms and Piacenza that pronounced the pope was to be deposed. The pope, in turn, pronounced excommunication and deposition against Henry. A true son of Henry III, Henry IV laid siege to Rome itself for two years, finally taking the city. The pope was freed but died soon afterwards. Henry eventually appointed an anti-pope, Clement III, who crowned him emperor in 1084.

This imperial policy was continued by Emperor Frederick Barbarossa in the second half of the twelfth century. Contemporary popes from Innocent III to Gregory IX countered with pointed iconographic display in a mosaic in the apse of St Peter's showing Innocent III wearing the *phrygium*, the headwear said to have been given by Constantine in his 'donation' to Pope Sylvester symbolizing his transfer of temporal power over the west to the pope.[14] With the support of the French Crown, the papacy was successful in its struggle against the empire, but that resulted in a similar dispute between Pope Boniface VIII and Philip IV of France. After Boniface's death, a French pope, Clement V, was elected in 1305. The pope moved to Avignon in 1309, abandoning Rome and St Peter's. A series of French popes followed, and the College of Cardinals also became dominated by the French. Rome, the See of Peter, and his basilica fell into neglect.

Rebuilding St Peter's, the Fuse for the Reformation

The Lateran Palace had been burnt in 1308, so, on the return of Martin V to Rome in 1420, the fortified, but now terribly dilapidated, papal residence in the Vatican was the only even vaguely appropriate place for him to live. The basilica was also in disrepair. Remedial work was carried out by Martin on the narthex, but Nicholas V began a project to build a large new Choir beyond the altar. It halted at foundation level at his death in 1455. This was the first project to build a new St Peter's, and it was abandoned.[15] Half a century later, Julius II still pondered how the by now sacred fabric could be consolidated. The walls were leaning alarmingly—not a good image of papal authority.

It was no use. Old St Peter's would have to be demolished, and it would have to be replaced by a building to astonish the world and reassert the authority of the Chair of Peter. Like the empire at the time of Constantine, the Catholic Church was threatened by fragmentation. As so many times before, and since, power, authority, and unity were to be demonstrated in a great iconic building project, but such powerful symbols can reveal more than originally intended; a monumental answer implies a question of similar proportions. Pope Julius II, who ruled from 1503 to 1513, was temperamentally suited to initiating a project of these dimensions. He was also well served by artists of genius. Michelangelo completed the Sistine ceiling between the spring of 1508 and October 1512 and had begun work on Julius's tomb in 1505, which was to continue sporadically until 1545. Also during Julius's reign, Raphael produced the Stanze, and Donato Bramante began work on a new basilica.

The work that had been initiated under Nicholas V (1447–55) was behind the western apse, and care was taken to ensure it did not necessitate the destruction of any of Constantine's building. Julius and his architect Bramante were made of sterner stuff, and new work began with foundations for the piers of the dome at the crossing. There are drawings dating from 1505–6, and Julius had a foundation medal struck in 1506 showing the intended design. Five hundred years later, the date of the laying of the first stone on 18 April 1506 by Julius was celebrated when a commemorative medal was struck with Benedict XVI on the obverse, and Peter receiving the keys before the completed basilica on the reverse.

Excavations had started with the south-west pier, outside the existing building, but, when the eastern piers and the first of the nave were begun in 1510, large parts of the crossing and transepts—the heart of the basilica—had to be destroyed.[16] Contemporaries were horrified, and progress was slow. Julius died early in February 1513, and Bramante died the following year. He had designed a dome to sit on the great

Figure 19. Maerten van Heemskerck, views of the Vatican Basilica, *c.*1536

piers, but left it unrealized. In broad terms, if not in detail, this conception would govern all subsequent designs. Though executed somewhat later, drawings by Maerten van Heemskerck give an impression of what had been accomplished—Bramante had set the scale even higher than had Constantine, but had left a vast building site.

Julius was not just occupied with artistic and architectural projects. He was a warring pope, the *pontifice terribile*. In 1504 he was at war with Venice, in 1505 with Bologna and Perugia, and in 1506 he personally led the army, taking Perugia without significant opposition and then occupying Bologna. He defeated Venice in 1509. He was operating on an imperial scale, but, unlike Constantine when he built St Peter's, or Justinian when he urgently rebuilt Hagia Sophia, Julius did not have resources on a similarly imperial scale, but that did not dispel the vision. Julius was succeeded by a Medici pope, Leo X (1513–21), and Bramante by Raphael.

From 1506 and the selection of Bramante's design for the rebuilding of St Peter's, the greatest architects of the Renaissance worked on the vast project that was to dwarf even its predecessor. A building on a scale and magnificence appropriate to house the main shrine of the western Church and on the scale set by Bramante's vast crossing piers would absorb huge resources that simply were not immediately available to the pope, but the political situation in Germany presented an opportunity that the papal curia at least thought had great potential. Election to a bishopric or archbishopric required papal confirmation, to which a fee was attached. When Albert of Brandenburg, the 24-year-old Archbishop of Magdeburg (from 1513) and administrator of the diocese of Halberstadt, was elected Archbishop of Mainz in 1514, he wanted to continue to hold his other episcopal offices at the same time. Holding two bishoprics was not unknown, but two archbishoprics was an entirely different matter. It was uncertain whether it was possible under canon law. The issue was not simply a matter of Church politics; it was key to the secular politics of the Holy Roman Empire.

The holder of the office of the Archbishop of Mainz was also an Elector of the Holy Roman Empire. Albert's brother was the Elector of Brandenburg, Joachim I. This would concentrate immense power in the hands of the family. Confirmation of his election would already entail a huge fee; dispensation to hold the three offices, an entirely novel proposition, would take exceptional measures, on an exceptional scale. Rome came up with an answer. Albert would be granted an indulgence for eight years, applying to Magdeburg, Mainz, and Brandenburg, in all about half of German lands. The proceeds of the indulgence would go half to the archbishop and half towards the building of a new St Peter's Basilica. This meant that no fee was actually paid for confirmation of the dispensation of 1514, but a huge amount of money would be generated for both parties. If this was not simony, then it would escape the charge on a mere technicality, and still be condemned as an ecclesiastical abuse. The bull for the indulgence, *Sacrosanctis Salvatoris*, was issued in 1515. The young archbishop was such a success that he was made a cardinal in 1518.[17]

Already in 1515, Martin Luther, a young academic Augustinian friar, was giving a lecture course on St Paul's Epistle to the Romans, in which he came upon a verse that would ring across the millennia to throw an almost accidental challenge against the 'binding and loosing' authority of the papacy. That verse was Romans 1:17: 'the righteousness of God is revealed through faith for faith, as it is written "he who through faith is righteous shall live."' The reference was to the prophet Habbakuk (2:4) in the Hebrew scriptures. Justification came through faith alone, directly through the grace of God. At the time, Luther was hardly a revolutionary, though eventually the logic of his argument drove him to the position where justification—righteousness—was entirely unmediated by confessors, not even by the 'binding and loosing' of the Church, let alone the pope as successor of Peter. For now, the exactions of the sellers of indulgences, especially the preacher of the new indulgence announced in *Sacrosanctis Salvatoris*, Johann Tetzel, attracted Luther's protest. As an academic inviting debate, Luther nailed ninety-five theses to the door of the local castle church in Wittenberg on 31 October 1517. Three of the theses were directly aimed at what he saw to be the cruel, and useless, sale of indulgences to finance the building of St Peter's Basilica:

> (50). Christians should be taught that, if the pope knew the exactions of the indulgence-preachers, he would rather the church of St Peter were reduced to ashes than be built with the skin, flesh, and bones of his sheep.

> (51). Christians should be taught that the pope would be willing, as he ought if necessity should arise, to sell the church of St Peter, and give, too, his own money to many of those from whom the pardon-merchants conjure money.

> ...

> (86). Again: Since the pope's income to-day is larger than that of the wealthiest of wealthy men, why does he not build this one church of St Peter with his own money, rather than with the money of indigent believers?[18]

There is an urgent call for an answer, but it was as yet by no means a call to revolution. There is still an implicit confidence in the structure and order of the Church. From the strength of the response, it would appear that the Church itself realized better than Luther the scale and consequences of the challenge.

First called to account before his own order, Luther won support, and until 1519 continued to believe that the pope was unfortunately isolated from the truth of the situation. He was then called before the emperor at the Diet of Worms to recant, but his reply was: 'Here I stand. Unless I am convinced by Scripture or by plain reasoning, I will not recant.' He had turned from the Chair of Peter to a different absolute authority, the Word of God, *sola scriptura*. In June 1520, Pope Leo X issued the bull *Exsurge Domine*, in which he excommunicated Luther. There was now no turning back; at the end of that year, December 1520, Luther publicly burned *Exsurge Domine* at Wittenberg.[19] In 1521, Henry VIII of England himself wrote a book attacking Luther, *Assertio Septem Sacramentorum* ('Defence of the Seven Sacraments'), earning him the title of 'Defender of the Faith', and Luther's books in turn were burned in London.

Rebuilding, Reform, and Reformation

Leo X died in 1521, and the papacy was itself briefly reformed by his successor, the Dutchman Adrian Dedel, Hadrian VI, formerly tutor to the future Emperor Charles V and mentor of Erasmus of Rotterdam. His frustrated efforts to reform the curia lasted not much longer than a year, and he was succeeded by Leo's cousin, Giulio de' Medici, as Clement VII. He began well, founding the Fabbrica di San Pietro, to control and bring order to the project, and building went forward with the south transept. Though an upright character, he badly mishandled the Reformers, Emperor Charles V, and the divorce of Henry VIII,[20] allowing greater fracture of the Church, the brutal Sack of Rome itself by the emperor's troops in 1527, and the alienation of the 'Defender of the Faith'. The project to rebuild St Peter's was beginning to look like an image of hubris.

Bramante had died in 1514, leaving only the crossing arches and choir apse finished, but providing enough shelter for papal Masses to resume over the grave of the Prince of the Apostles.[21] He was succeeded by Raphael. Late in 1516, Antonio da Sangallo the Younger, former assistant to Bramante, was brought in as associate architect. Financial constraint meant that little could be accomplished on the massive construction site, so architects were left to experiment with design possibilities until construction could resume in 1519. On the death of Raphael in 1520, Sangallo took his place as first architect. He was critical of the designs of Bramante and Raphael, and all that had been built. The great piers of the crossing and the apse had started to crack because of inadequate foundations.[22] Baldassare Peruzzi was appointed as Sangallo's assistant. Both architects provided their own remarkable versions of the design, and the building project edged forwards under Clement VII from 1523, with work on the south transept. Building came to a complete standstill again in 1527 with the devastation of the Sack of Rome by imperial troops.

While things had ground to a halt at St Peter's, Protestants were necessarily only adapting buildings to reformed worship. This was successfully and conservatively done in Lübeck, for example, from 1531, where a rich inheritance of religious art is still to be found. In England, it was accompanied with considerable iconoclast violence. Here, as elsewhere, the traditional arrangement of nave and choir were allocated respectively to Word and sacrament, as demonstrated in Langley Chapel, Shropshire, fitted out in the early seventeenth century with fixed seating with kneelers and desks surrounding the Lord's table at the chancel end, and a densely pewed nave with pulpit. The arrangement is perfectly suited to the rubric in the 1549 *Booke of the Common Prayer*:

> Then so manye as shalbe partakers of the holy Communion, shall tary still in the quire, or in some convenient place nigh the quire, the men on the one side, the women on the other syde. All other (that mynd not to receive the said holy Communion) shall departe out of the quire, except the ministers and Clerkes.[23]

The Church Ordinances of Braunschweig and also of Wittenberg of 1533 provided for the same separation of Word and sacrament in existing churches.[24] A Netherlandish painting of the mid-sixteenth century shows *Christ Preaching in the Temple*, sitting at the base of a column preaching to a contemporary crowd in a familiar church interior. The focus had changed from altar and sacrament to the Word of God in scripture and preaching.[25]

Protestants were also just beginning to design buildings to reflect radically renewed theology. Their natural model was the hall church, dating from the thirteenth century, where the preacher could be heard and seen. With high windows in aisles almost as high as the nave, they provided bright, open spaces. Their successor, the auditory church, was, as the name suggests, an acoustic space for sitting and listening, so such churches were often centrally planned with no need for ceremonial movement or liturgical processions. This was not sacred space. God was present in the preaching of the Word and in the hearts of the congregation, not in the building, and certainly not in relics.

In building a new church, there had to be appropriate space for the distribution of communion, good lines of sight, and a good acoustic to hear the preaching of the Word. These were clearly the driving principles when Nickel Gromann from 1532 designed a new castle church for Torgau, a Protestant enclave since 1520.[26] The Torgau Articles, the basis of the Augsburg Confession, had been drafted there by Luther, Melanchthon, and Jonas in 1530. The church is a square hall with two levels of arcading covered by a groined ribbed vault. A stone table altar is elevated on a platform at one end, and a pulpit hangs between two bays at the side. On 5 October 1544, Luther himself dedicated the church, setting it apart, but with preaching, prayer, and praise. The pulpit from which he preached has carved stone reliefs with New Testament scenes: the 'Cleansing of the Temple by Jesus' facing the entrance; the 'Woman Taken in Adultery', with Moses in the background, to show that forgiveness is by grace, not adherence to the Law; in the middle panel 'The Boy Jesus Teaching in the Temple'. It is a standing paradigm of Protestant preaching. In 1534, a similar pulpit was to be found in Lübeck's Marienkirche, with carved panels of 'Moses with the Tablets of the Law and Adam', 'The Preaching of John the Baptist', 'Jesus as the Good Shepherd', 'The Sending out of the Apostles', and 'Jesus Preaching'.[27] Here the facets presented of Protestant theology are: forgiveness, preaching the advent of the Word, the grace and love of the Son, the Apostolic mission, and the preaching of the Word. It can be read as an appeal to biblical authority for a new Protestant apostolic mission to preach the forgiveness of sins through the new dispensation of faith in the love and grace of Christ.

After the Sack of Rome of 1527, it seemed almost inconceivable that the huge fragment of the new basilica would ever be finished. In 1534, Alessandro Farnese became Paul III. He then promoted Peruzzi in 1534 to be equal to Sangallo. Peruzzi immediately set about producing drawings for a design of his own, with a facade related to that on the reverse of the foundation medal, but lacking the corner towers.[28] In 1539, a gigantic wooden model showing Sangallo's whole scheme in detail was commissioned. When completed, seven years later, it included the towers and dome, and opened to show the interior.[29] In the realization of the model, it was necessary to produce an enormous number of detailed drawings to resolve various aspects of the design, including the problem of the massive dome. The model is still preserved in the Fabbrica di San Pietro. In these fallow years since the Sack of Rome, the model kept the dream alive. In a practical move, Sangallo closed off the eastern part of the existing nave with a wall to restore it for liturgical use. It remained in this arrangement until 1614.[30] Sangallo died in 1546.

The Council of Trent and Architecture

The Council of Trent was a pivotal moment in so many ways. Convened in 1545, it would continue to meet until 1567, deliberating on the means of Catholic reformation. In the face of schism and fragmentation, the short answer was centralization and unity. Priestly formation was to be improved and closely regulated, and the liturgy was to be standardized under the control of Rome. The theology and teaching of the Church were reaffirmed, with practice strengthened or reformed. Luther had questioned the teaching on the sacraments in *The Babylonian Captivity of the Church* of 1520:

> *The first thing* for me to do is to deny that there are seven sacraments, and, for the present, to propound three: Baptism, penance, and the Lord's Supper. All these have been taken for us into a miserable servitude by the Roman curia and the church has been robbed of all her liberty. If, however, I were to use the language of Scripture, I should say that there was only one sacrament, but three sacramental signs of which I shall speak in detail in the proper place.[31]

Penance, he says later, as a sacrament, is 'a return to baptism', but it lacks the 'divinely instituted visible sign' of a true sacrament, so his number is reduced to two. This initial blast against sacramentalism was echoed by Ulrich Zwingli in his *Commentary on True and False Religion* in 1525. The Council of Trent in the Canons issued at the seventh session on 3 March 1547, on the other hand, not only defended the seven sacraments (baptism, confirmation, eucharist, penance, anointing of the sick, holy orders, and matrimony) as 'necessary unto salvation' (Canon IV) but emphasized the effective operation of the ceremonies (Canons VI and VIII). This theological emphasis on ceremony would, of course, have consequences for the way the sacraments were performed, for their architectural context, and, in the case of the eucharist, for its manifestation in terms of the bread. The performance became highly elaborated visibility, the architecture a gorgeous and glorious setting, and the bread was not just to be received by the worshipper, as the Body of Christ; the host would now be displayed in a monstrance, a 'reliquary' of its own, for contemplation and worship.

In late medieval liturgy, the consecrated host had already become mobile, carried in a pyx in Palm Sunday processions as at Wells Cathedral or in a crucifix placed in the Easter sepulchre or in a gold and crystal shrine with relics on Corpus Christi in the Durham rite.[32] But the host in a monstrance was a sustained visible assertion of sacramental presence in denial of Protestant objections, which were refined and tightened by John Calvin in chapter XIV of his *Institutes of the Christian Religion* in 1559: 'I make such a division between Spirit and the sacraments that the power to act rests with the former, and the ministry alone is left to the latter—a ministry empty and trifling, apart from the action of the Spirit, but charged with great effect when the Spirit works within and manifests his power...'.[33]

The nature of the sacraments and especially of the eucharist was of central concern for Catholic and Protestant alike, with repeated treatment in articles, catechisms, and the canons of the Council of Trent. In the twenty-second session at Trent on 17 September 1562, the canons included: 'VII—If anyone saith, that the ceremonies, vestments, and outward signs, which the Catholic Church makes use of in the celebration of masses, are incentives to impiety, rather than offices of piety: let him be anathema.'[34] Theology, outward signs, ceremonial, liturgical space, and architectural treatment are coextensive here; one is made manifest and visible in the others.

Michelangelo Moves the Basilica towards Completion

In 1546, Pope Paul III ignored Michelangelo's protests and com-manded him to take over the building of St Peter's. Michelangelo despised Sangallo's model, likening it to a dark alley where all manner of mischief might occur.[35] Michelangelo began work on his own large wooden model as early as December 1546. This would not be completed until September 1547, but he quickly made a smaller sketch model to show his intended developments. He appreciated the purity of Bramante's design, and revised and developed the present plan as a magnificent statement of unity, retaining most of what had already been built, including the lines of piers and the vaults of the nave to the east and the south transept. He deleted the ambulatories round the apses in Sangallo's plan, removing the obstacles to the penetration of natural light.[36] A dome was always an integral part of the design, though its form and integration with the developing architectural concept were also continuously evolving. Between 1559 and 1561, Michelangelo produced a large wooden model of his design for the dome, still in the Fabbrica di San Pietro.[37] Only the drum had been finished by 1564, and there was a rethinking of the project before Carlo Maderno took over. Maderno extended the nave and produced the massive portico. Michelangelo's magnificent design for the dome, somewhat revised, was finally brought to completion in 1593 by Carlo Fontana and della Porta.

In the dome (Plate 3), as the image of perfect unity, is the papal answer to Luther's challenge. On the interior is the scriptural seal, in letters 6 feet high, of the authority of the successors of Peter: 'You are Peter, and upon this Rock shall I build my Church...I will give you the keys of the kingdom of heaven.' Below that, behind his great baldacchino, between 1657 and 1666, Bernini created the baroque extravaganza of the 'Cathedra Petri', the Chair of Peter (Plate 17), between the four doctors of the Church, two Latin, two Greek. It was a reliquary to house the chair associated with Peter himself (though probably of Carolingian origin)[38] and the concrete symbol of his authority. It visually drove home the point made by Pope Paul IV when he revived the mid-fourth-century liturgical feast of Cathedra Petri (22 February). The purpose was clearly to establish the focus of ecumenical Christian authority, east and west, on the present occupant of the Chair of Peter, and to confound the Protestants.[39]

Again in the twentieth century when the Church was under threat from across the Tiber, *Summi Pontificatus*, the first encyclical by Pius XII on 20 October 1939, appealed to the same two sources of papal authority, the verse from Matthew and the chair. The dome and Bernini's triumphal sculptural composition in the apse express this as a monumental answer, but, just as mixed memories of bitter division slumber in the Via della Conciliazione as a monument to reconciliation, so are they also dormant in the seemingly irrepressible sculpture and in Michelangelo's dome as images of perfect unity. Despite their emphatic denial, they also tragically memorialize the fracture of the Church in the Reformation, for which the building of the Basilica of St Peter in the Vatican was itself an unintended, but powerful, cause.

Figure 20. Facade of Sant'Ignazio, Rome

10

The Iberian Empires and the Evangelization of the World

The Church of Sant'Ignazio, Rome

*I*gnatius of Loyola founded the Society of Jesus in 1539 along with *Francis Xavier and Peter Faber. The Society was approved the next year by the pope, Paul III. The Council of Trent met between 1545 and 1563 to discuss the reform of the Catholic Church. The Church of the Holy Name of Jesus, Il Gesù, was built as the Mother Church of the Jesuits in 1568. Education and mission were their two prime objectives, and its Collegio Romano was one of its key institutions. The Church of Sant'Ignazio, begun in 1626, just four years after the canonization of Ignatius, was built as the chapel of the college. It was completed in 1650, and between 1691 and 1694 the Jesuit mathematician and painter Andrea Pozzo created a highly animated fresco ceiling in the church. It shows the apotheosis of St Ignatius, in which souls of all races are drawn upwards from the four continents where the Society had been active in educational and missionary work. Its influence spread within, and beyond, the advance of the Iberian empires and placed it in the context of imperial conquest and pillage of resources and indigenous peoples. The Church was often in collusion with, but frequently in opposition to, imperial policies. When immense wealth and power were at stake, as in a confrontation between Pope Paul III and Emperor Charles V, it was the pope who gave way. In the second half of*

the sixteenth century and the early seventeenth, in the context of the
empires of Japan and China, the nature and the means of mission were
questioned in particularly interesting ways.

Piazza Sant'Ignazio

The Piazza Sant'Ignazio is an exquisite late baroque square in Rome
designed by Filippo Raguzzini in 1727 as a prelude to the drama to be
found within the Church of Sant'Ignazio. The piazza billows and
breaks surprisingly, but symmetrically, around the facade of the church,
begun a century earlier in 1626. The whole composition has a dynamic
but measured instability, perfectly scaled to contain the urban space, yet
the movement of the facades produces a centrifugal force that bursts
out in indeterminate directions: as the architecture, so the institution
it contains. The Church of Sant'Ignazio is the chapel of the Jesuits'
Collegio Romano, and is in many ways the heart of the Society. It is a
simulacrum of Ignatius's teaching and preaching, as the spearhead of the
Catholic Reformation, not to say Counter-Reformation. The facade
closely resembles that of the nearby Il Gesù, or Church of the Holy
Name of Jesus, begun in 1568 as the mother church of the Jesuits. That
design is a model of incised clarity, but the paired pilasters add a dynamism to the composition held under control by the strong horizontals
of the deep cornices. The facade of Sant'Ignazio is similarly laid out,
but much more vigorously modelled, with the elements pulled into
higher relief and so casting stronger, more dramatic shadows.

The entrance to the church opens into the vast nave, bound by
paired white fluted Corinthian pilasters and the horizontal white
entablature (Plate 18). Their capitals define a horizontal band of putti
with swags of flowers and fruit. These are linking elements for arches
and pendentives sitting on disengaged columns all in red, green, and
white marbles. Together they form three great bays surmounted by a
deeply modelled unbroken entablature below a shallow attic storey, and
above that a clerestory within a barrel-vaulted ceiling.

The Painted Ceiling

And what a ceiling! Above the four pairs of pilasters of the nave are labelled personifications of the four continents, Europa, America, Africa, and Asia, evangelized by Ignatius de Loyola, founder of the Society, and his companions. Nearest the entrance door is Africa, riding on a crocodile and holding an elephant's tusk like a sceptre. Below her, a register of large figures and ferocious animals represent the wild state of the continent, and above her some figures sit looking down to engage the visitor while others fly up with the help of angels from an illusionistically painted entablature. The swirl of figures is led by a Jesuit on a cloud beholding an overwhelming heavenly scene. Each of the four continents is treated this way as part of an allegory of the Triumph of Ignatius, as he encounters Jesus in dazzling heavenly light. It is a theological reflection on the accomplishments of the Jesuits in the reform, revival, and expansion of the Catholic Church in the wake of the Protestant Reformation.

The creator of this magnificent work, Andrea Pozzo, is the quintessential baroque artist, who squeezes every drop of dramatic effect out of his preferred medium, the frescoed ceiling. This is his greatest achievement, painted between 1691 and 1694. There he develops a highly sophisticated visual narrative presentation of the Apotheosis of Saint Ignatius that draws into its vortex, the theological, political and cultural programme of the saint, his early companions, and the missionary society he founded.

Pozzo's narrative technique is completely different from Michelangelo's in the ceiling of the Sistine Chapel in the Vatican, painted between 1508 and 1512, where major events of the biblical narrative are arranged historically in the series of cartouches created within the subdivisions of the vaulting, culminating in the Last Judgement on the east wall. Pozzo, on the other hand, develops a theological structure that is to be read simultaneously across the whole of the work, rather than sequentially from west to east.

Between these two great works came the shock of the Reformation. Stated contentiously, the proximate cause of the Reformation was architectural, insofar as it was the rebuilding of St Peter's Basilica in the Vatican that gave rise to the sale of indulgences on an industrial scale, which in turn sparked reforming protest. A prime example of the Roman Catholic Church 'coming off the back foot' to return to the religious and cultural offensive is the early history of the Jesuits. The theology and politics of this 'Catholic Reformation' addressed the matter of indulgences and related abuses, and art and architecture were key instruments in communicating and effecting radical transformation in the spiritual life of the Church and spreading its faith and teachings around the globe.

In architectural terms, the classicism and balance of St Peter's had given way at Sant'Ignazio to fluidity, dynamism, and deliberate visual instability. Both Andrea Pozzo and the architect of Sant'Ignazio, Orazio Grassi, were Jesuits. The artistic narrative and stylistic features of the Church of Sant'Ignazio and its decorative programme reveal the explosive energy being released in the theological, political, and cultural ideals of Counter-Reformation Rome and being carried round the world by the Jesuits through the trading systems of the Iberian empires of Spain and Portugal. Readings of the art and architecture of the Counter-Reformation can reveal much about this project of evangelization, sometimes more than originally intended when subjected to a close and contextual consideration. The problem is to align the rhetoric and the reality, the heroic drama of the artistic monument and the reality of its political and theological circumstances.

In 1548, the first Jesuit College opened in Messina in Sicily; in 1551, a few decades after the completion of the Sistine Ceiling, the Collegio Romano was founded by Ignatius as an early teaching institution run by the Jesuits, and it quickly became the model for their core activity, both in Europe for the spiritual renewal following the Council of Trent, and for the worldwide mission. A new chapel for the foundation, dedicated to Ignazio, recently canonized in 1622, was begun in 1626 by the college's mathematician, Fr Orazio Grassi. The designs were approved on 7 April 1627, and the building completed in 1650.

It closely resembles the mother church of the society, Il Gesù, not far away, which was, after a few false starts, designed and begun just over half a century earlier in 1568 by Giacomo Barozzi da Vignola with later revisions by Giacomo della Porta. Both churches are essentially all nave, with no intermediary zone at the entrance and interconnecting side chapels rather than aisles.

The overall iconographical structure of the churches is very similar, as visual responses to similar architectural structures, but the narrative techniques are very different. At Il Gesù, the painter Giovanni Gaulli has opened up a great central cartouche in the roof to reveal the 'Triumph of the Holy Name of Jesus', closely modelled on a Last Judgement, as seen from below. The dramatic scene-painter's craft blurs the line between reality and art by using high-relief sculpture, free-floating clouds, and figures on panels spilling out of the heavenly realm within the frame of the cartouche into the earthly realm of the viewer below. Clearly, these figures are falling to perdition. This places the viewer within the drama of a suspended moment before those grotesque figures thunder past.

In terms of Jesuit preaching and spiritual practice, as taught by Ignatius in the *Spiritual Exercises*, the painting sets the viewer within the 'crisis' of the scene (what Ignatius calls 'composition of place'[1]), inviting a state of prayer before the Glory of the Holy Name of Jesus (IHS) and, as he says in the *Spiritual Exercises*, 'to ask for knowledge of the Lord *from inside*, Who for me has become human that I may more love and follow Him'.[2]

This image in Il Gesù was painted by Gaulli from 1669 to 1683; only eight years later, Pozzo extended the narrative techniques and theological rhetorical structure very considerably in the ceiling of the Church of Sant'Ignazio. The layered complexity and expansive movement of its composition had to be kept under strict visual control to enable a clear theological reading. The controlling structure was provided by geometry. He gave a first demonstration of the dramatic possibilities of perspective by producing a *trompe-l'oeil* dome on the ceiling of the crossing of the Church of Sant'Ignazio, where a real dome had been intended, but had to be eliminated because of financial constraints.

Pozzo outlined the geometrical method he used for this ceiling in his book *Rules and Examples of Perspective Proper for Painters and Architects*.[3] Significantly, in the 1707 English translation, there is an 'Approbation of this Edition' that says: 'We have perus'd this Volume of Perspective; and judge it a WORK that deserves Encouragement, and very proper for Instruction in that ART.' This is signed by Christopher Wren, John Vanbrugh, and Nicholas Hawksmoor, the three giants of English baroque. Vanbrugh in particular, as a former stage designer like Pozzo, would have been interested in the scenographic possibilities.

The first thing Pozzo did in the design of the nave ceiling was to reproduce an illusionistic 'New Church' above Grassi's as a kind of antechamber to heaven. It is in this (literally) intermediary *fictive* space that he would present the Jesuit theology of mission as an extension of the salvific act of Jesus. Remember that he had already painted a fictive dome (still shown as real in figure XCIV in his book), and now he further blurred the line between design and reality (or perhaps he would prefer to say 'extended visible reality by design') by creating a

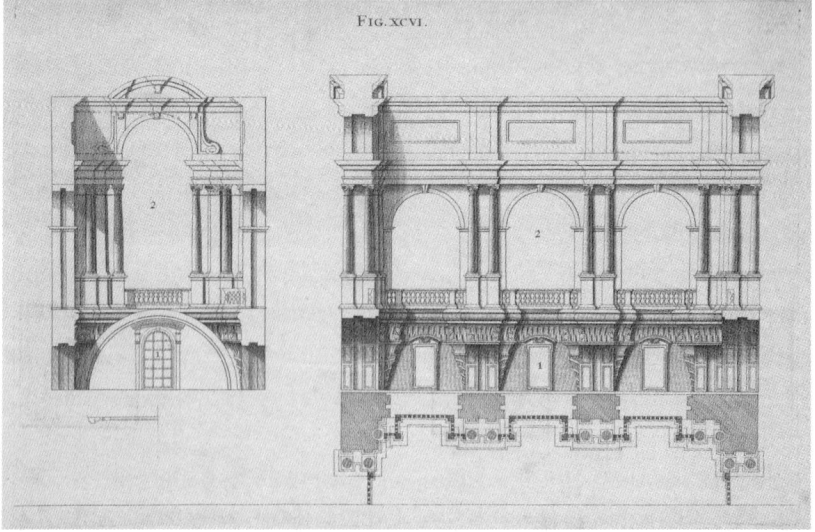

Figure 21. The 'fictive' upper storey, engraving from Andrea Pozzo's *Rules and Examples of Perspective*

perspective projection of that *fictive* second storey in the same way as he had for the dome, as though they simply could not pay for that either. The perspective exercise was vastly complicated by the fact that the ceiling was not flat, but rather a barrel vault, which caused deformation of the lines in the projection. Entrance to the church via a small draft-porch places the student of the college (or the visitor) off-axis, causing the fictive second storey to appear to lean menacingly, and it continues to shift alarmingly while the visitor progresses across the floor. The perspective resolves laterally when the visitor reaches the main axis. At a single point on the axis, directly below the shining figure of Christ, the whole perspective is perfectly resolved.

A ray of the light of Christ reflects off Ignatius and is *refracted* into rays that pass through groups of flying figures, clustered around mainly identifiable Jesuit priests above allegorical figures of the four continents of Jesuit missionary activity. A fifth ray is reflected off a round mirror, with the Holy Name of Jesus held by an angel on the axis directly in front of the viewer. It is as if all those rays reconverge on the individual standing on that fateful spot. The theological structure—that is to say, the *preaching*, of the ceiling—is focused (like the personal *mis-en-scène*, or 'composition of place', of Ignatius's *Exercises*) on the individual, challenging him or her to respond directly to the immediate presence of the Light of Christ.

This swirling vortex of humanity is based on a Last Judgement, as at Il Gesù, but with a rather limited division of 'sheep and goats', so to speak, between the real architectural entablature below the clerestory windows, and Pozzo's painted entablature above the windows. In this liminal zone, Pozzo continues to play with what is real and what is mere architectural conceit by painting cherubs above his painted entablature of the 'New Church', with some near a cartouche in living colour, and many below the painted entablature in *grisaille* as an illusionistic part of the mundane architecture below. The character of the visual 'preaching' of the two ceilings is rather different. In this intermediary zone, some of the figures below the continents, in the 'savage' register, strain upwards; some fall, or are beaten back by spears or torches. The 'New Church' Pozzo projected above the painted entablature is clearly the place of salvation, in its direct encounter with the Saviour, and there is Pozzo sitting on his entablature in the middle of the north side staring quizzically down. In summary, the ceiling at Il Gesù is preaching conversion through a personal encounter with Jesus, and Pozzo is preaching to a specific text that reveals more.

Europa

On the axis below the mirror with the Holy Name is a cartouche with the text 'IGNEM VENI MITTERE IN TERRĀ[M]', from Luke 12:49: 'I came to cast fire upon the earth,' and an angel to the left is handing an incendiary to a figure standing on the painted entablature and another incendiary is already in flight directly above the text. The paired columns of this 'New Church' rise from the corbels of the continents. If one continues to read clockwise from the text, one comes to Europa, resting on a horse, with her left hand on an azure globe borne up by a putto, while, on her right, another putto holds an overflowing basket of fruit, representing prosperity. During the seventeenth century, the Jesuits were vigorously re-evangelizing Europe, in the poverty of the towns, in the depths of the countryside, in areas such as Lower Bavaria under Protestant pressure. There was a fertile mission field even in the traditionally Catholic heartlands.[4] The project of re-evangelization would often start with the establishment of a Jesuit college on the model of Sant'Ignazio, and from there preaching missions would go out into the countryside. Groups of two or three Jesuits would spend months on the road moving from parish to parish. Many were charismatic preachers creating sustained dramatic spectacles with catechetical teaching as their aim. Shortly after the conclusion of the Council of Trent, a standardized missal was issued, including the texts for the other sacraments.[5] Another characteristically Jesuit contribution to renewed Catholic piety was the establishment in 1563 of the Marian Congregations by Jean Leunis, studying at the

Collegio Romano. They were confraternities most often based in a Jesuit college encouraging regular religious observance and the deepening of spiritual practice. The congregations were to be found throughout Europe and were affiliated to the original in Rome. These were important local anchors for the Catholic Church.

Below the figure of Europa, under the painted entablature, are one very pale figure and another very dark one, who appears to have a leg shackle. The latter looks very like other figures to be seen under the personification of Africa, one of which also has his ankles bound with cloth. Could this be a first reference to slavery, which was then a foundation of the prosperity of Europe, though largely invisible to its inhabitants? The meaning of this shadowy character is ambiguous, but Europa's mount is certainly obstructing the light of Christ for him. On a cloud above Europa is a vested priest (showing the importance of the renewal of sacramental worship), whose face is turned obliquely upwards, and who is unrecognizable, so perhaps he represents those many in whose hands (lighted by a ray) the Church was being renewed. Sharing his cloud are two young religious, one perhaps St John Berchmans, who had entered the society via one of the Marian Congregations in Mechelen, and the other undoubtedly St Luigi (Aloysius) Gonzaga, who as a young man died tending the sick during a Roman epidemic, holding his attribute, a white lily. St John Berchmans's remains were subsequently placed in the church after his beatification (in May 1865), and the chapel in the north transept just beyond the arch near this part of the composition is now dedicated to the Annunciation and to St John Berchmans. Its altarpiece, designed by Pozzo with all the most 'bizarre' flourishes of the baroque, corresponds to that of Luigi Gonzaga opposite in the south transept, and to his altarpiece for the Chapel of St Ignatius in Il Gesù. These 'bizzarrie', as they were called at the time before the use of the term 'baroque', were the flourishes that broke all the rules, destabilizing Renaissance classical order.[6] The fluid, twisting entablatures and pediments of the executed altarpieces were not as 'bizarre', in the sense of 'extravagantly unconventional', as in his original design, which proposed elevating the ashes of the saint to an urn borne up by four angels sitting on a fractured quadripartite pediment high above the altar rather than more conventionally below the altar. In terms of religious iconographic convention, this was another 'bizarre', even triumphalist, flourish that broke all expectations.

If you continue clockwise round the ceiling composition, there is Pozzo himself leaning over his entablature looking down, with perhaps his assistants either side of him, the one on his left pointing at him, and the one on his right with his right index finger, precisely on the cross-axis of the composition, pointing down at us. Was this some in-joke in the studio, or perhaps an indication of the whole purpose of the narrative—Pozzo's 'preaching' of the Jesuit mission?

America

Beneath the next pair of columns in the 'New Church' is the figure of America, a scantily clad native woman with a feathered headdress. She has a quiver of arrows and in her right hand a spear with which she pushes back a savage jaguar, on which she is seated, and two males, one tumbling back and one reaching up. She is assisted in warding them off by an angel thrusting a firebrand at them, the fire of conversion. Above is a swirl of figures, one in semi-native dress, others having mounted the next entablature of the 'New Church'.

Of course, the Jesuits worked with the indigenous populations in the Americas, founding churches and colleges. The architecture of those buildings reveals inculturation as part of the working methods of the Society in its mission in the New World. On the one hand, a building like the Igreja de Jesus, in Salvador, Bahia, Brazil, has a facade that is closely modelled on the mother church of Il Gesù and Sant'Ignazio, with the addition of flanking towers from the Portuguese tradition, along with an array of sculpted altarpieces and paintings, including a ceiling painting in the library of the college based on Pozzo's manual of perspective. On the other hand, the Church of Santiago in Arequipa, Peru, has a baroque facade thickly overlaid with the indigenous decorative work typical of the mestizo, or 'mixed', style.[7]

The Jesuits had a strong identity, but they had a policy of adapting to the local situation. Here in the Americas they were able to follow this policy only to a limited degree within the royal Spanish and Portuguese policy of Europeanization. Pope Julius II had granted a *Patronato real*, which gave exclusive rights to preach the gospel in New Spain to the Spanish monarchy, and likewise a *Padroado real*, for the Portuguese Crown. These paper grants ensured that religious policy was always subordinated to imperial commercial interests and a policy of assimilation. One example was that native elites in Mexico were being educated by the Franciscans in Latin for colonial government administration. The earliest such Latin text still existing was written to Emperor Charles V on behalf of (perhaps by?) Don Pedro de Montezuma, son of the murdered Aztec emperor. He was trying to secure the return of land in 1541. The result of the plea is unknown, since this remains an isolated record, but it is known that Dom Pedro had received the grant of a coat of arms from Charles V the year before.[8] This is evidence of a remarkably successful policy of Europeanization, but, contrary to the policy of the Crown, more generally the native population in New Spain was being educated in Nahuatl, the majority native language, by the Franciscans.[9] By contrast, the native elites were being successfully Europeanized and to some extent integrated, with Martín García de Loyola, the nephew of Ignatius, deposing and executing the last Inca ruler of Peru and later marrying Beatriz, his great-niece. But at the same time, under the native notion of the *mita*, thousands of Indians were used as forced labour in the mines, a system widely condemned by the Church.[10]

Africa

In Pozzo's ceiling in Sant'Ignazio, as the swirl rises from the figure of America, it begins to collide with another ascending from Africa. That collision was happening on the ground as well, with Jesuits working among the slaves arriving in the New World. Bartolomé de las Casas arrived in the New World as early as 1502 and was originally a slave-owner. He became a Dominican and was ordained in 1507. He was sickened by the forced conversion and brutalization of the indigenous population and wrote forcefully against their exploitation:

> Laws are silent, human feelings are mocked, nowhere is there rectitude, religion is an object of scorn, and there is absolutely no distinction made between the sacred and the profane ... For if things which are gentle, mild, and pleasing cause a man ... to listen to new matters willingly ... and to lend faith to what he ... hears, contrary things must produce a contrary effect. Therefore, this method of subjecting pagans by war to the rule of the Christian people so that the Gospel may be preached to them is contrary to the natural and gentle method described earlier.[11]

Needless to say, the exploitation of New World native labour was a highly controversial subject, since vast wealth was at stake. Pope Paul III supported the stance taken by Las Casas in the bull *Sublimis Deus* of 2 June 1537:

> the said Indians and all other people who may later be discovered by Christians, are by no means to be deprived of their liberty or the possession of their property, even though they be outside the faith of Jesus Christ ... The said Indians and other peoples should be converted to the faith of Jesus Christ by preaching the word of God and by the example of good and holy living.[12]

He censured the conquistadors, but Emperor Charles V pressurized him to withdraw it. A year later, the pope softened his stance by removing the censures, but he maintained his support for Las Casas. Unfortunately, at one point Las Casas suggested the import of African slaves for the plantations, replacing one exploitation for another.[13]

A very close look at the black figure in the collision reveals what appears to be a shackle on his left leg. The two Jesuits at the top of the rising Africans may represent the Jesuits Alonso de Sandoval and the sainted Pedro Claver, who for years in the early seventeenth century had ministered to and converted West African slaves who landed in Cartagena, Columbia, one of only two slaving ports in the Spanish New World.[14]

The dominance of the *Padroado* of the Portuguese and their deep involvement in the African slave trade meant that Christian missions on the African continent were fatally compromised. Many missionaries worked tirelessly to mitigate the suffering of the slaves, but little could be accomplished to stem the flow of the millions from the African interior, who were caught up in this lucrative trade and mostly received little more than mass baptism before being shipped off to plantations in the New World. The Jesuits also had a brief mission in Ethiopia after the Portuguese helped defend the country and its Church in a war against the Islamic Emir Ahmed Granj. Despite their policy of assimilation to local custom and inculturation, the Jesuits found it more difficult to accommodate to differences of custom with other Christians in Ethiopia than with other religions in India, the Americas, and Asia. They were outraged by what they saw as Judaizing elements in keeping the Sabbath, male circumcision, and not eating pork. Cultural and inevitable doctrinal differences resulted in a complete failure of the mission.[15] That mission was manned from Goa, the hub of the Asian mission, and in late 1579 Francesco Pasio asked for permission to be sent to the Ethiopian mission, but by 1580 the situation was such that no more Jesuits were to go. Pasio was made Procurator of the Asian Province instead.[16]

Asia

The fourth and final allegorical figure on Pozzo's ceiling is Asia, sitting on a camel and reaching up to receive in her hand the beams of light passing the upstretched arm and staff of St Francis Xavier, Apostle of Asia. Beside Asia are two cherubs gathering a basinful of light. Only angels and Ignatius himself are closer than Xavier to the divine source of light, establishing their hierarchical position within the Jesuit narrative.

Xavier arrived in Portuguese Goa in 1542, but it was not even at this relatively early date what could be called a fresh mission field. He had been sent in response to a request to Ignatius from João III of Portugal for priests to work in his eastern territories. Xavier was supported in this by Pope Paul III, who also wanted him to look for further opportunities for missionary expansion in the east. This would eventually take him outside the *Padroado* of the Portuguese monarch, to Japan and China, and return ecclesiastical initiative, and control, to the Roman pontiff.

The port of Goa had been conquered in 1510, and the Franciscans had established a permanent house there by 1518. Since 1534 it had been a bishopric. The Portuguese had taken their responsibilities under their *Padroado* both seriously and successfully. Here the policy was aggressively assimilationist, with mosques and temples levelled to the ground and replaced by churches in the Portuguese national Manueline Gothic style. When the Jesuits themselves engaged in building, as at the baroque Church of the Bom Jesus in 1594–1605, this was related to Portuguese precedent, but they also declared their Roman allegiance with the structure of the facade and the interior planning, which were strongly reminiscent of the Gesù and Sant'Ignazio.[17] Bom Jesus has the typical box-like interior with a pulpit to the side, suited to missionary preaching, and an open chancel giving an unobstructed view of the action of the Mass. Again, the structure here was Roman, while the decorative overlay was strongly influenced by local artistic traditions. It is as if the Jesuits provided the grammar, and the locals provided the vocabulary, even encroaching on the syntax. This is visual confirmation of the Jesuit 'way of proceeding' that in later stages in China would amount to full-blown inculturation. Over the next decade, Xavier evangelized the poor Paravas, then the Macuans on the south-western coast of India, then among the Malays, and ultimately, on 15 August 1549, he entered the port of Kagoshima, Japan.

The Japanese were highly cultured, which called for a very particular kind of missionary activity. Within two short years, Xavier had met with remarkable success, having established five communities. Always aware of the wider eastern mission, he attempted to gain access to China, but died on the island of Shangchuan off the coast of China on 3 December 1552. Xavier, the Apostle of the East, is buried in the transept of the Church of the Bom Jesus in Goa. Matteo Ricci, who would later become central to the mission to China, in January and again in November 1580 wrote to his professor at the Collegio Romano about hopes for the conversion of Oda Nobunaga, a warlord and patron of the Jesuits in Japan, and the Mughal emperor Akbar in India, who had sent to Goa to ask that learned Christians be sent to him: 'We are all very apprehensive, with great hopes for nothing less than the conversion of all India, if everything goes well. But everything has its difficulties...'.[18]

The Jesuits' encounter with a culture as sophisticated as the Japanese raised anew the glaring question of inculturation and what that meant for mission and theology. In 1575, a suffragan bishopric to Goa had been established in Macao, and in 1588, another had been established in Funai in Japan; their first bishops were Jesuits. In Japan, Otomo Yoshishige, the local lord, had met Xavier himself, and, a decade before the establishment of the bishopric in Funai, had converted to Christianity. Over that short span of time, the Jesuit mission had met with enormous success, with fewer than 1,000 converts when Xavier had left now grown to more than 150,000 by the time the bishopric was established.[19] Among those converts were many high-ranking aristocrats. Unfortunately, this was a time of intense civil war in Japan, with tragic results for the Christian community. Alessandro Valignano was appointed Visitor to the East of the Society of Jesus by the Superior General Everard Mercurian, and between them they appear to have loosened the hold of the *Padroado* over the operation of the Jesuits in the east, and its identification of the mission of the Church with the interests of the Portuguese Crown.[20] Valignano arrived in India in 1574 and travelled the Eastern Province until his death in 1606. In 1580, he established a Jesuit novitiate, a school, and, in Funai (Bungo), a college where both European and Japanese classics, philosophy, and theology were taught. Engravings published in 1596 show that the buildings for these foundations were very substantial and designed on European models. The engravings are rather rough, but the one of the Professed House in 'Uxuqui' (Usuki in the territory of Yoshishige) shows an austere church on a simplified Serlian model with a single tower on the right side of the facade. Again, the decorations of the typical Jesuit models appear to have been influenced here by the restrained simplicity of local practice.[21] In 1587, only seven years after Valignano had founded these key teaching foundations, the Jesuits were very nearly expelled from the country. The situation cooled, but they had to keep a low profile. Then, in 1596, suspicion of European motivation in supporting a Christian mission in Japan resulted in persecution, and the crucifixion of twenty-six Christians in Nagasaki in 1597. Anti-Christian legislation followed in the early seventeenth century, with expulsion, martyrdom, and suppression, until finally the Church was driven underground.

Xavier had seen the Japanese mission as part of a larger mission to include China. A major problem was the prohibition by the Ming emperor for foreigners to reside in the empire, which had prevented him from establishing the mission himself. The Jesuits were also dependent on transport with Portuguese traders, and Xavier had died in 1552 before managing to get himself smuggled in. The situation was eased five years later in 1557, when Macau was founded as a Portuguese concession. For the Jesuits, it also functioned as a staging-post for strengthening the fledgling mission in Japan. Valignano took the Chinese mission forward by sending first Michele Ruggieri to learn Mandarin and prepare the ground, then Matteo Ricci, who in 1582 sailed to Macao, then joined Ruggieri in the permanent house he established in Zhaoqing. They began to dress as Buddhist monks to remain clerical but appear less exotic. Developing the mission was a slow business, and conversions were few. They cultivated good relations with local mandarins, whose postings were relatively short, leaving the Jesuits' position rather unstable. If they were to make progress in their mission among the poor, the patronage and protection of the imperial court were needed.[22] Ricci learned the Chinese classics and abandoned the robes of the lowly Buddhist monk in favour of the garb of the traditional Chinese scholar. In 1595, he completed his *Treatise on Friendship*, based on Cicero, which became a Chinese classic.[23] That same year he travelled to Nanjing, and in 1597 he made a first trip to Beijing.

Ricci was ordered by Valignano to make another attempt to become established in Beijing and make contact with the court. Ricci managed to arrive at the turn of the year in 1601. There he approached members of the emperor's court on their own terms as a sage and *literatus* with the intention of converting them and, if possible, the emperor himself. The 'bait' was western science. Ricci charmed the emperor with the presentation of a mechanical clock. The Jesuits were well received and given a residence in the capital and a prestigious imperial stipend as a sign of favour.[24] Ricci's fame spread, and he received a steady stream of mandarins from the court and also from those in Beijing for the equivalent of civil-service examinations. He made many politically powerful and influential friends, but relatively few converts. Ricci impressed the emperor with a world map showing China at its centre, and he translated western mathematical and scientific works into Chinese. Few, but very significant, friends converted; one of these was Xu Guangqi, who took the baptismal name of Paul. Ultimately, Xu reached the rank of Imperial Grand Secretary. Along with Xu, Ricci translated Euclid's *Elements of Geometry* among other mathematical texts. Xu Guangqi is still revered in China for this work, especially in his home city of Shanghai, where there is a memorial hall celebrating his achievements. His impressive burial mound is nearby. He established the meteorological bureau there and bequeathed land nearby, where St Ignatius Cathedral was eventually built.

Ricci had written *The True Meaning of the Lord of Heaven* in 1595 before arriving in Beijing, but as a consequence of his conversations with scholars in the capital he brought out a revised version in 1603. It was a synthesis of Christian and Confucian teaching, showing their common teaching as a dialogue between a western and Chinese scholar. The collaboration between Ricci and Xu Guanqi was emblematic of this Christian–Confucian accommodation, and Xu's main career was spent in the Ministry of Rites. It was, in the end, this accommodation, particularly in the matter of the possibility of converts continuing to observe Confucian rites, that would drag on and fatally weaken the Jesuit mission in China. At given points, mandarins were required to pay ceremonial honours to their ancestors, and there was a question whether these rites were religious or civil. There were also questions of translation for key Christian concepts, as there had been in the Japanese mission. Even the Jesuits themselves were divided on these issues, and, when they became political issues within the Chinese court itself after Ricci's death, the result was an imperial edict expelling the Jesuits. Fortunately at this time the edict was only partially enforced. By the time Pozzo painted the great ceiling in Sant'Ignazio in Rome, the single Jesuit remaining at court, Ferdinand Verbiest, was a mathematician who had recently been reinforced in 1688 by some French members of the Society. The year after Pozzo began his great work there was a decree of toleration by the emperor, but within a century there would be widespread persecution of Christians.

The Fire of Conversion

If you turn from the allegorical figure of Asia on the ceiling of Sant'Ignazio and proceed down the axis, you see, in a second cartouche over the pediment of the window above the entrance, the second half of the text: 'ET QUID VOLO NISI UT ACCENDATUR' ('And would that it [the fire] were already kindled!' (Luke 12:49b)). An angel above is armed with a spear tipped with a firey light, thrusting it downwards, while other angels prepare to throw incendiaries. It appears as an exhortation to us to catch the fire of conversion, as Ignatius had—hence his name, a cognate of *ignis*, fire. In the Gospel of Luke, the text comes after a long discussion between Jesus and the crowd, and with the disciples. There Jesus pressed the point that nothing matters but God alone and his Kingdom. To be alive to God is *all*. The text is followed by Jesus proclaiming that 'I have a baptism to be baptized with; and how I am constrained until it is accomplished'. That 'baptism' was his crucifixion, and in the ceiling we see that it is accomplished; the central figure in light is Jesus bearing his cross in triumph, with the Father and the Holy Spirit behind him. Troublingly the passage continues: 'Do you think I have come to give peace on earth? No, I tell you, but rather division; for henceforth in one house there will be five divided...they will be divided father against son and son against father...'. Indeed, the House of the Church *was* divided—the coming of the Son of Man brings crisis and division and, the ceiling preaches, all that matters is the Kingdom of God, encapsulated by Jesus' reply to Peter immediately before this outburst:

> Peter said 'Lord, are you telling this parable for us or for all?' and the Lord said, 'Who then is the faithful and wise steward, whom his master will set over his household, to give them their portion of food at the proper time? Blessed is that servant whom his master when he comes will find so doing' (Luke 12:41–3).

This exchange between Jesus and Peter (who in Catholic teaching represents the Church), indicates how their ministries are intertwined— graphically represented by the divine light irradiating the scene, and reflected down to us.

The theological challenge of the ceiling is to produce a *personal* crisis in the student of the college, to face the division and choose the service of Christ in serving other members of the household of faith, as had Ignatius, Frances Xavier, Alonso de Santoval, Pedro Claver, John Berchmans, and Luigi Gonzaga in so many and varied ways in so many lands. The *earth* should be set on fire with 'the fire of conversion', the *individual* should be set on fire by preaching and by art and architecture. The rules of geometry and perspective could produce astonishing effects, especially when cool Renaissance classicism is set on rhetorical fire with the deliberately bizarre manipulation of the baroque.

The Counter-Reformation, or Catholic Reformation, was full of vitality in its reassertion of Catholic truths in Europe and its determination to spread them across the globe, both within and beyond the Iberian empires. Within the Jesuit mission beyond Europe, the impetus encountered the problems of any cross-cultural encounter, including the questions of inculturation, indigenization, translation of both texts and doctrinal concepts, and the meaning of ceremonial within different cultural contexts.

Figure 22. Crimean Memorial Church, Istanbul: photograph of the situation

11

English Parish Churches Exported

The Crimean Memorial Church, Istanbul

*I*n 1852, the sultan in Constantinople confirmed the authority of the *Orthodox Church in the Holy Sepulchre and the other Holy Sites. Christians in the Ottoman Empire were under the protection of the Russian tsar, who was also encouraging the Greek war of liberation from the Turks. As the diplomatic situation deteriorated between Russia and the Ottoman Empire, Russia mobilized, Turkey declared war, and Britain and France (who feared that Russia had designs on their interests in the Middle East) declared war in their turn, and the Crimean War began. During the 1850s, there was a growing English community in Constantinople/Istanbul, and missionary societies were becoming increasingly concerned for its pastoral care. The embassy chaplain was overwhelmed, and the lack of pastoral provision was seen as a national disgrace. Being in a Muslim society brought religious sensitivities and even dangers regarding conversions. The war was over by early 1856, at which point the demand for a national memorial and the need for an English church were brought together, and fundraising began for a Crimean Memorial Church. An architectural competition was organized, with the submission date set for 1 January 1857. The architectural style should appropriately represent the English community. This remarkable Crimean Memorial Church is part of a much wider phenomenon of English communities around the world, both* *within the empire and, as here, beyond, with parish churches being built as communities became established. Moreover, it was a particular kind of church that was thought appropriate to be built abroad.*

The Approach

It is a relatively short walk from Istanbul to Karakoy, ancient Galata, a walk that takes you over the bridge at the entrance to the Golden Horn, with the Bosphorus opening on the right. The traffic on the bridge is busy, so it is a pleasure to slip into the quiet of the narrow streets of buildings, cheek-by-jowl, and wind up the hill until reaching a bushy garden. Over its high stone wall loom a minaret, which is not unexpected, and a Gothic spire, which is arresting. A little further up the little cobbled lane with its stepped pavement, you can peer down into an isolated, rather overgrown English sub-urban churchyard, with the vicarage on the right. This is the Crimean Memorial Church, discreetly crowded by trees. An elevated view from a nearby building reveals the profile of an English church against the Bosphorus, and Hagia Sophia lifted against the distant sea. The grey stone of the church, which comes from the nearby island of Yeni Oyah in the Sea of Marmara, is roughly coursed with yellow sandstone dressings, imported from Malta. The natural slope of the site creates a large crypt area at the east end, which is a dream for a parish, if there are enough resources for its development. The church was closed in 1976, but it was reopened in 1991 with the support of a little congregation of Sri Lankan refugees who had been given shelter in the crypt, and since then it has been brought back from the brink. The period of closure took its toll on the fabric, but this is gradually being disentangled from the garden. Anyone entering the interior will find it is beautifully proportioned, with polychrome striped ashlar walls and ribbed vaulting.

The Holy Sepulchre and War in the Crimea

How did such a church, more at home in leafy north Oxford, come to stand here in Galata? Curiously, the story goes back to the Holy Sepulchre in Jerusalem. In the middle of the nineteenth century, there was tension between the Catholic and Orthodox traditions concerning the control of and access to the Holy Sites in Jerusalem, and none more so than the Holy Sepulchre. In 1690, the Catholics had been granted authority in the churches of Jerusalem, Bethlehem, and Nazareth by the sultan in Constantinople, but in 1757 the sultan gave pre-eminence to the Greek Orthodox. The majority of Christians under Muslim rule were Orthodox, and, in the eighteenth century, Russia was given protection of Christians in the Ottoman Empire. In 1852, Napoleon III petitioned Sultan Abd-ul-Majid to restore Roman Catholic rights in the Holy Places. Russia made a strong diplomatic response, and in February 1852, the sultan decreed in favour of the Orthodox, a decision that was confirmed in another edict of May 1853, stating: 'The actual status quo will be maintained and the Jerusalem shrines, whether owned in common or exclusively by the Greek, Latin, and Armenian communities, will all remain forever in their present state.'[1] In 1853, there was rioting in Bethlehem, and a number of Orthodox monks were casualties in the fighting with French Franciscans.

Tsar Nicholas thought the Orthodox should enjoy his protection, and at the same time he was also encouraging the war of liberation in Greece. When he sent representations to the Turkish government in Istanbul and his demands went unheeded, Nicholas mobilized his army. Britain and France were concerned that Russia had designs on their interests in the Middle East. After aggressive moves by Russia, Turkey declared war, and within months, in March 1854, Britain and France also declared war on Russia, which resulted in the disaster of the Crimean War. The Ottoman Empire was in decline, and the great powers were positioning themselves.

As far as the Holy Sepulchre is concerned, the Russian Orthodox Church still has no rights in the church, except through the Greek Orthodox, but the Russians are now a large and highly visible pilgrim constituency, exerting considerable pressure, some of it very physical, within the building. As a proximal cause of the Crimean War, the Holy Sepulchre was recognized as a continuing flashpoint for international conflict in the modern world, and in 1878 the Treaty of Berlin declared 'that no alterations can be made in the Status Quo in the Holy Places', making it a matter of international law.[2] This situation still prevails into the twenty-first century and is carefully observed as a truce among the communities that share the site. One of the resident Franciscans, with a clutch of relevant documents and a video camera, carefully monitors the site to ensure that events 'will remain forever in their present state'—modern technology in the service of the deepest conservatism.

The Pastoral Need for an English Church in Constantinople

Even before the outbreak of hostilities in the Crimea, as early as 20 April 1852, Alfred Child, who had been acting in the capacity of embassy chaplain in Constantinople, replied to enquiries from the Society for the Propagation of the Gospel in Foreign Parts (SPG), which was

> requesting information with regard to the condition of British sailors at Constantinople, and suggestions as to the way of aiding them in spiritual matters . . . It is not only most deplorable as regards themselves, but a great reproach to our Church, and a direct hindrance to the cause of Christian truth amongst those with whom they are brought in contact . . . The conduct of the greater part of them on the Sunday, which is the only day they are not occupied in loading or discharging their cargo, is most shocking, notoriously far worse than that of the sailors of other nations who frequent the place. They spend the day in the Maltese wine shops which abound within a few yards of the

shipping, and in places of a worse character in the dark alleys around; and then, maddened by drink, are to be met continually fighting with others and among themselves, and assailing the ears of all around them with the foulest possible language.[3]

With the voice of someone immediately involved, Child reports Sunday brawling, wounding, and death. He continued:

> Soon after my arrival, I endeavoured to get the use of a Store near the water for divine service, but was not successful. Since then, having besides the duty of the Ambassador's Palace, another congregation 8 or 9 miles distant to attend to, the utmost I could do was to give a service in the afternoon of every alternate Sunday, until the winter set in, on the deck of one of the ships...To talk to them about going to the Embassy Chapel (or the room in the Palace used as a Chapel), even if it were within reach, wld be much the same as to instruct the sailors of Gravesend or Wapping to go to St George's, Hanover Square...But I am persuaded that if there were a building devoted to divine service, & close at hand, there wld be little difficulty in getting them to go to it.[4]

At that particular historical moment, the pastoral need was enormous for a church to serve the English community in Constantinople.

Child wrote similarly to the *Guardian* on 27 June 1854:'Disgraceful as it assuredly is to us, it is yet perfectly true as your report asserts, that "doubts have been expressed by the Turks whether we English have any religion at all" and not without good reason.' Not only was the behaviour of the sailors on a Sunday 'such as [the Turks] themselves would shrink from with disgust';[5] there was no church for any English residents, or travellers, for public worship, whereas all other Christians had theirs. This was a poor reflection of Britain's place in the world.

> What I now wish to urge upon those under whose control the building of an English church at Constantinople may fall, is the great necessity for making it a model of what an English church ought to be, both in its general plan and architectural character, and also in the strict and full observance of the ritual of its services. It ought to be so built, and its services so conducted as *to invite observation*, without descending to display.[6]

Figure 23. The Former British Embassy, Constantinople, now the British Consulate

Building an appropriate church was a matter of national pride, as well as of evangelism. He was advocating High Church, Oxford Movement worship, with its colourful and dignified ceremonial. The right sort of British presence in the capital of the Ottoman Empire was for him an important consideration. Religious practice was part of the projection of national identity. It was a sentiment that would be widely shared.

The religious sensitivities of the situation are highlighted in a second letter from him to the SPG of 12 November 1855 reporting:

> It is said that two Turks have suffered death for professing themselves Christians…Do you not think that the Government might be petitioned to instruct the Ambassador to *insist* on the abolition of it? This could not surely be called 'taking an unfair advantage of the necessities of the Turks to induce them to barter away their religion'. It would only be giving them that freedom in such matters wh. of right belongs to every man.[7]

He continues, rather dangerously, with a plan for conversion among the Turks.

A Crimean Memorial

When the dreadful war was over in 1856, *The Times* of London reported on 20 February that a committee had been formed to build a church in Istanbul as a memorial to those who had fallen. Its first regular meeting was reported on 6 March, there was a general meeting of the committee on 8 April, and a public meeting was held under the presidency of HRH the Duke of Cambridge on 28 April to raise money, which resulted in almost £25,000 being raised for a fund to be administered by the SPG.[8] The huge and moving list of donations that came in response to the appeal is testimony to the impact the war had had on the general population. The list includes pages of private individuals, including the queen herself,[9] Regiments, '15th Light Infantry | 1 day's pay from Officers 3.8[*d.*]', geographical areas, £20 from Mr Gladstone, 'a Thank Offering for the Preservation of a Son from the Perils of the War—£5', 'a Gloucester Post Boy, 5s.', 'a Grain of Mustard Seed from WB £5',[10] and 3 guineas from the Lady Charlotte Pepys in memory of Lord Raglan.[11] Lord Raglan was the Commander of British Forces whose lack of clarity issuing orders had resulted in the Charge of the Light Brigade.

In a letter of 23 July 1856, Charles Curtis, the newly appointed SPG chaplain at Constantinople, notes that he has received some donations, and in a letter of 7 August he refers to 'another sum in the hands of Miss Nightingale', whom he knows, of course, since from time to time he is required 'to bury the dead from the British Hospital', and she has also given him 'a good supply of copy books, slates, etc. for the school'. The sum held by Florence Nightingale was £50, which she divided equally between her hospital, near the port in Galata, and the building of the Memorial Church.[12] Curtis would serve in this post for another forty years until his death in nearby Pera in 1896.

On 14 June 1856, applications were invited in the *Builder* for an architectural competition to build the Crimean Memorial Church, and it was then advertised again in the High Church Cambridge Camden Society's journal the *Ecclesiologist* in its August issue. Submissions were to arrive with the SPG by 1 January of the following year. Prime considerations in judging the results were to be adaptation to the climate and architectural style.

As far as climate is concerned, the SPG already had experience in building around the globe, both inside and outside the British Empire. For example, a letter of 24 February 1849 from its missionary in Sarawak on Borneo contains a drawing of a simple wooden 'Early English' church with a three-light pointed east window and a note for the side wall indicating '5 doors opening onto verandah on east side', obviously to catch the breezes. Climate was also a consideration for the materials to be used here, with another note emphasizing that 'bricks I have proved will not stand the Climate—the best rot & crack & crumble away'. The little church was ready for consecration the next year, and the missionary invited the bishop of Calcutta to perform the ceremony. The bishop replied that, as the church was outside his diocese, he would need the permission of the Archbishop of Canterbury. English episcopal politics had a very long reach, and in matters of style so did the influence of the Cambridge Camden Society.

As regards style, the competition instructions for the church in Constantinople stipulated that the church

> must be a modification to suit the climate, of the recognised Ecclesiastical Architecture of Western Europe, known as 'Pointed' or 'Gothic;' and the neglect on the part of any architect of this provision will absolutely exclude from Competition.
>
> The numerous and beautiful instances existing in Southern Europe of this modification of Pointed Architecture amply justify the preference thus given to it. Any approximation to the specific features of Byzantine Architecture is prohibited, as being objectionable in many respects. Still more must the competitors abstain from the imitation of any forms connected with the religious architecture of the Mohametans, which is, indeed, at Constantinople based upon Byzantine models.[13]

Furthermore, 'no representations of human form or of the forms of animal life, are to be introduced, either externally or internally; at the same time architects are advised to avail themselves of the beautiful constructive materials which are so easily and cheaply procurable at Constantinople, particularly the Marmora marble'.[14] Unfortunately for the appointed architects, building would not turn out to be as cheap as the competition rules implied.

Stylistic considerations were obviously not purely aesthetic; there were religious, cultural, and political dimensions, but advice was at hand—at times more than was welcome. From 1839, there were two societies in particular that were very vocal in the practical, theological, and stylistic aspects of church building by the Church of England, both at home and in 'foreign parts'. They were the Oxford Society for Promoting the Study of Gothic Architecture, which later became the Oxford Architectural Society, and the Cambridge Camden Society, which later became the Ecclesiological Society.

Architecture and Ecclesiology

The Oxford Society for Promoting the Study of Gothic Architecture was founded in 1839, changing its name in 1848 to the Oxford Architectural Society and then in 1860 to the Oxford Architectural and Historical Society. In the early years, its membership included many heads of Oxford colleges, and before long Bishop Bagot of Oxford, peers of the realm, archdeacons (responsible for church buildings), and even the Archbishop of Canterbury himself were numbered among its supporters. Its purpose was the study of 'ecclesiology'—in this context understood to be building new, and improving existing, churches according to the correct principles of Gothic architecture. Many of the members were, broadly speaking, Tractarians, but the leaders of the Oxford Movement, Richard Hurrell Froude, Edward Bouverie Pusey, John Keble, and John Henry Newman, showed little interest in the accompanying architectural polemic.[15] Their more immediate concern was doctrine, but the ecclesiologists were intent on ensuring that doctrine and sacramentalism were visible in ritual gesture, ceremonial worship, and its setting. It was this High Church view of Anglicanism at that time that informed the ecclesiological brief, which was neatly summed up by Alfred Child's letter to the *Guardian* in 1854 regarding the English church for Constantinople: 'a model of what an English church ought to be, both in its general plan and architectural character, and also in the strict and full observance of the ritual of its services.'[16] He was interested in the moral state of the sailors, certainly, and of course in theology, and there were also overriding considerations of politics, national pride, and visibility in the mix. These ideas had widespread currency: a paper read to the society in November of 1845, the year that Newman converted, was on 'The Development of Roman and Gothick Architecture, and their Moral and Symbolical Teaching'.[17] A. W. N. Pugin, the author of the moralizing *Contrasts* (1836) and *True Principles of Pointed or Christian Architecture* (1841) and a prolific English ecclesiastical architect responsible for so much of what we see at the Houses of Parliament, was not the only one to connect morality, architecture, and theology.

The Cambridge Camden (or Ecclesiological) Society

The Cambridge Camden Society was also founded in 1839, the same year as the Oxford Society for the Promotion of Gothic Architecture, by two undergraduates at Cambridge, John Mason Neale and Benjamin Webb, and their views were considerably more strident than those of the Oxford group. The writings in their journal, the *Ecclesiologist*, were highly polemical in their advocacy of the reintroduction of medieval Catholic ritual to the Church, as far as could be justified within the theology of the Book of Common Prayer. They were also active in restoring ancient, and building new, Gothic churches according to the best 'approved' examples. A central ritual aim was to increase the frequency of the communion service and provide architecturally for its more elaborate celebration. This rested on a particular interpretation of the 'Ornaments Rubric' inserted under Elizabeth I into the 1559 Prayer Book and retained in 1662, which said 'that such Ornaments of the Church, and of the Ministers thereof, at all times of the Ministration, shall be retained, and be in use, as were in this Church of England, by the Authority of Parliament, in the Second Year of the Reign of King Edward the Sixth'. This clearly permitted vestments, allowed the revival of long disused ritual including the sign of the cross in blessing, and could also be used to smuggle in aspects of the late medieval Sarum liturgy as well, with its elaborate processions, vestments in colours according to the day and season, ritual and ceremonial for every detail, and the 'secret' prayers of the clergy at every stage leading up to and including the service. Even many of the more moderate changes, though commonplace now, including lighted candles and the wearing of a surplice to preach, were met with disapproval and even censure. The

Revd John Purchas, of Christ's College, Cambridge, in 1858 published the *Directorium Anglicanum; Being a Manual of Directions . . . According to Ancient Uses of the Church of England*, which put this programme on a sound basis, including legal judgments from court cases that took place just the year before, in 1857. Despite his attention to the relevant law, he was himself prosecuted in 1869, with the judgment going against him in 1871, and Benjamin Webb himself, as Warden of Sackville College, East Grinstead, had his orders inhibited by the bishop of Chichester for a full sixteen years.[18]

The Cambridge society was established on a strong foundation of scholarship. Neale and Webb published a translation of William Durandus' book *Rationale Divinorum Officiorum*, as *The Symbolism of Churches and Church Ornaments*, in 1843. It is about the theological basis of symbolism, form, and style in architecture. By this point, there were 700 members of the society, including distinguished architects, MPs, peers, archdeacons, sixteen bishops, and the Archbishops of Armagh and Canterbury. That list of politicians, peers, and prelates indicates that the Establishment recognized a strong force for the revival of the Church and probably also for the spread of its influence across the expanding British colonial system.

Significantly, the great architectural historian of both the University of Cambridge and Canterbury Cathedral, the Revd Robert Willis, resigned from the Cambridge Camden Society in 1841, because, as he wrote in a 'Remonstrance' published in the *Ecclesiologist*, 'it is in the highest degree improper' to 'convert the Society *into an engine of polemical theology*, instead of an instrument for promoting the study and practice of Ecclesiastical Architecture'.[19] Like the detached academic Willis, members of the Ecclesiological Society were interested in archaeology, but theirs was an archaeology with a very particular agenda. The thrust of that agenda is summed up in Neale and Webb's preface to their translation of Durandus' *Rationale*: 'we have considered it necessary to prefix an essay on the subject; in which we have endeavored to prove that Catholick Architecture must necessarily be symbolical; to answer the most common objections to the system; and to elucidate it by references to actual examples, and notices of the figurative arrangements of our own churches', and furthermore, they conclude, '*pointing out the sacramental character of Catholic art*'.

The whole space of the church thus becomes not only overlaid with symbolism, but a sacramental vessel of the doctrine of the Church. The revival of the Anglican Church led to a huge spate of church building in England alone, with 3,765 new and rebuilt churches being consecrated between 1835, when the permanent Ecclesiastical Commission was set up, and 1875.[20] By then, a third of English churches had been restored, almost universally according to ecclesiological principles. They were restored to what they *should* have been, to conform with current liturgical practices—as they *should* be. Doubtless some of this was driven by committed ecclesiologist architects as well as by devoted Tractarian clergy.[21] Though Pugin had converted to the Catholic Church, unlike Newman he was no 'Romanizer'; he championed a revival of the *English* Catholic tradition, including the late medieval Sarum Rite, and in that he was more perfectly aligned with the Anglican ecclesiologists of Cambridge and Oxford than with members of his adoptive church.

Architects and Missionaries

By 1841, the year of the establishment of the Colonial Bishoprics Fund by Bishop Blomfield of London, the reach of the influence of the Cambridge Camden Society was about to become global in extent. Bishop Blomfield was a High Churchman intent on enforcing the rubrics of the Book of Common Prayer. Because he was bishop of London, the colonial churches came under his auspices, so his ritualist views were hugely influential in the formation of the Anglican Church overseas. By 1838, there was correspondence between Blomfield and the Secretary of State for the Colonies concerning the allocation of land in New Zealand to provide an endowment for the soon-to-be-appointed bishop. The correspondents in this matter included the Revd George Augustus Selwyn, who was making preparations, as bishop elect, to go out to his See of New Zealand, and on 13 March 1840 the SPG passed a 'resolution to grant £100 towards the cost of erecting a church'.[22] In volume 1 number 1 of the *Ecclesiologist*, published in November of that year, there was a notice entitled 'Parish Churches in New Zealand', which began with the interesting news that the newly appointed Lord Bishop of New Zealand, Selwyn, wanted the Cambridge Camden Society to provide designs for the new cathedral and parish churches. The logic of the principles to be followed typifies the approach of the society:

> The ingenuity of the natives in carving is well known; and it is the Bishop's design to convert this faculty to the glory of God. For this purpose the Camden Society will furnish working models of the actual size, of Norman capitals, sections of mouldings, ornamented pier, door and window arches: and these, it is hoped, it may be easy for the natives to imitate in the stone of their own country, which is said is well adapted for building.
>
> One model of a parish church will at present be sufficient; because the churches will be, at first, two hundred miles apart. Norman is the style adopted; because, as the work will be chiefly done by native artists, it seems natural to teach them first that style which first prevailed in our own country; while its rudeness and massiveness, and the grotesque character of its sculpture, will probably render it easier to be understood and appreciated by them...
>
> It is indeed a matter of heartfelt delight to the Society, that it is enabled to be of service to so interesting a branch of the ONE Catholick and Apostolic Church as that about to be established in New Zealand...[23]

Clearly, on an ideological and stylistic level, Anglo-Norman architecture was suited to an assimilationist colonial project, and for the ecclesiologists its suitability was based on the Catholicity of the Church and the suitability of the form for the liturgy. The 'sections of mouldings' were supplied by the Cambridge Camden Society's sister society in Oxford, whose members took casts of beautiful surviving carved details from Iffley Parish Church on the southern edge of Oxford on the way to Littlemore, where Newman was vicar. It is uncertain whether the casts ever reached New Zealand. In any event, the influence of the two societies travelled with Bishop Selwyn in the two clergymen who accompanied him, the Revd William Charles Cotton, a High Churchman from Oxford, and the Revd Thomas Whytehead, from Cambridge and a member of the Ecclesiological Society.[24] In the end, New Zealand was not covered in Norman churches, even at distances of 200 miles. Only a few simple churches were built in stone.

Interestingly, in the missionary context, on the other hand, an architectural fusion began to appear in New Zealand. Missionaries were not simply aiming to 'civilize' and assimilate; they took an interest in local culture in their mission to convert. The architectural result can be seen in a building for both Māori and Pākehā (Europeans) at the Church Missionary Society Station at Ōtaki between 1848 and 1854. Like the little church in Sarawak, it was a wooden Early English parish church, but the interior was visibly Māori in construction and design. The *Ecclesiologist* was surprisingly positive about another similar Church Missionary Society church, but the principles of the *Ecclesiologist* remained assimilationist: 'it should have been developed so as to Christianize and improve the native taste and skill, not merely to admit its savage grotesque power, just as it is.'[25] They were clearly not about to 'go native'. In this sense, the New Zealand context provides an interesting comparison with the project in Constantinople regarding religious, cultural, and political sensitivities in relation to architectural style.

The Oxford Society published examples of liturgical furnishings and produced detailed studies of fine local churches, including St Giles, Oxford, and Newman's own church at Littlemore. It also advised on the restoration of churches, including Dorchester Abbey beyond Littlemore to the south of Oxford (towards Ewelme). Clearly, it was not just English parsons who wrote for advice; the society also advised on the building of Gothic churches throughout the colonies. Between 1845 and 1853, Snettisham church in Norfolk was copied as a cathedral in Fredericton, New Brunswick, hailed by the *Ecclesiologist* as 'the first pure cathedral in the Pointed styles that has ever been reared in a British Colony'. It was clearly recognized that there were special requirements imposed by different geographical contexts—for example, in answer to the bishop of Bombay's enquiry regarding the design of a local church, the Oxford Society replied:

> The church should be wide open so as to admit the sea breeze from south to north-west. Care should be taken to have doors on the sides to admit of soldiers easily getting out of the church. I would suggest whether it would not be preferable to give up the idea of a middle aisle (gangway), and have two side ones: by this arrangement the troops will be more immediately before the clergyman. It will be desirable to have at least one porch, and on the north side, for protection from the sun of ladies and others on getting out of their carriages. Moulding in this country, especially on the outside of a building, soon falls down...It will be necessary to have punkahs in the church.

Clearly, climate, social structure, and military security were considerations that might require adaptation of the style and organization of the church, but the architect's view of the Gothic was that the origin of the style arose from the efficient function of its elements—pinnacles and buttresses to counter the outward thrust of the roof; mouldings, parapets, and gargoyles to direct the flow of water off and away from the fabric. Even the pleasing effect of picturesque asymmetry allowed flexibility in the functional distribution of rooms, stairs, and windows, producing a pleasing, often dramatic, massing. In the Oxford Society, essays on the use of the Gothic in the colonies emphasized the necessary adaptability of style, while remaining true to its origins and its liturgical and sacramentalist doctrinal symbolism.

By contrast with Fredericton Cathedral, the hard environment and materials available in St John, Newfoundland, created a result that displeased the ecclesiologists. Bishop Aubrey Spencer announced that he had 'collected in St John's, 5 March [1841] £1430 in one day from *eighteen* contributors' towards the building of a cathedral to replace the 'parish church...built more than forty years ago and no longer worth repairing, on the contrary, this being the Bishop's See in New Foundland, and the Roman Catholics owning a cathedral and episcopal palace in the city it seems fitting that a Cathedral Church should be raised in the Capital'.[26] He made sufficient progress to be able to lay the first stone on 21 August. It was one of his last acts as bishop. He received his people's valedictory addresses on the 23rd, before moving to the more comfortable New Brunswick diocese (which he would continue to hold together with the diocese of Bermuda).[27] The building thus begun was destroyed by fire before its completion. George Gilbert Scott began its replacement in 1847. The ecclesiologists did not like him or his building, complaining of a 'most impracticable climate, no available native materials, an unpliant ritual . . . authority for every detail and phrase; it is learned and dignified, but perhaps cold'.[28] The impression given is that its real failing was architectural stylistic rigidity and the similarly 'unpliant ritual', and Catholic ritual along with the Oxford Movement's revival of Catholic theology were by then very potent forces in the Anglican Church in the middle of the nineteenth century. By 1852, Webb reported that advice had been given for churches in 'the Canadas, Bombay, Ceylon, Sierra Leone, Mauritius, the Himalaya, Tasmania, Guiana, Australia and New Zealand, Newfoundland, Egypt and Hong Kong'.[29]

In response to the strengthening influence of the Oxford Movement during the 1840s and 1850s and in a drive to improve the training of the Anglican clergy, the bishop of Oxford, Samuel Wilberforce, founded Cuddesdon Theological College opposite the Bishop's Palace in 1854. This further encouraged High Church Catholic vocations. Wilberforce's vision is encapsulated in two designs by G. E. Street, the Oxford Diocesan Architect: the lower part of the west window of Cuddesdon parish church and the theological college itself. The window, described in the *Ecclesiologist* as 'altogether the best specimen of the art'[30] and showing angels with trumpets heralding 'the holy city, the New Jerusalem, coming down out of Heaven from God', was built in Gothic style and had a remarkable resemblance to the college itself at the top of the hill. That was the purpose of both church and college—to bring in the Universal Kingdom of God. The tide of empire was still on the rise, and it seemed providential that its might could smooth the way for the advance of God's Kingdom. As the tide retreated, a lot of church communities would be left 'stranded', and, left to their own devices, would have to adapt or die.

Building the Crimean Memorial Church

The Crimean Memorial Church occupied a special place within the British imperial context. The eyes of the world had at least temporarily been focused here, and the acute pastoral need cast a hard and critical light on the British in Constantinople in the wake of the war. There were still restrictions on what could be done; religious sensitivities meant there could be no figurative iconography, style had to be Gothic with no Byzantine or Islamic references, climate had to be taken into account, and, unbeknownst to the competing architects, there were problems with the site and building was in fact especially expensive in Constantinople. Furthermore, Child's demand for 'full observance of the ritual' in his letter to the *Guardian* had already put sacramentalism firmly on the agenda.

The Sultan Abdülmecid (1823–61), grateful for British support, gave a plot of land, and the land was surveyed in June 1856. It was thought unsuitable, but a plan to sell it and buy something better was blocked because 'a grant of the Sultan could not be so transferred'. The ambassador, Lord Stratford de Redcliffe, tried in February 1857 to acquire land near the hospital, which commanded a view of the entrance to the Bosphorus such that any building would be a highly visible presence from the water. He failed, and on 2 March he wrote to the Earl of Clarendon in London:

> It is still out of my power to convey to Yr Ldp any reliable prospect of being able to realise the wishes of those who with so much religious & patriotic feeling have united their subscriptions for the construction of a Memorial Church in this Capital. The persons employed, under the joint direction of Reshid Pasha and myself, to find an appropriate site for the buildings, have continued to meet with difficulties which

are far from encouraging, as Y Ldp will learn from a perusal of the accompanying report…Since I last wrote to Y Ldp on this subject, I took occasion to mention our difficulties to the Sultan himself, and HM replied with his usual affability that he had pleasure in granting whatever was possible. I greatly apprehend that in this instance even the Sovereign's goodwill can do but little for us. The only sites in question are private property, belonging to numerous owners, some of whom will not and others cannot sell, while those who are willing & able to sell, refuse extravagant prices.

I have heard of one more situation which offers a chance of success, and, if that hope fail, I shall have nothing left but to make a final report, & wait for further instructions. It is to be remembered that the ground in hand, though secured for HM last, is altogether alien to the Conditions hitherto required.

I have—

S.de Redcliffe.[31]

Despite the problem being considered sufficiently important to be addressed at the highest levels of government in both Constantinople and London, it remained intractable. While the problem festered in Constantinople, 46 entries with a total of about 370 drawings had been submitted to the SPG in London by 1 January 1857. On 7 February, the results were announced in the *Builder*: the successful candidates were, first, William Burges; second, George Edmund Street; third, George Frederick Bodley; George Truefitt was among those specially mentioned. The judgement added 'that both the first and the third of the selected designs are founded on the church of St. Andrea, at Vercelli!'.

An exhibition of the successful designs was held on 13 February at the rooms of the SPG in Pall Mall, and one of the judges, Professor Willis, gave a descriptive talk about the submissions, reported in the *Builder* on 28 February: 'He then referred to the church at Vercelli, adopted as a study by two of the successful competitors, and which had been erected, as it was said, by English workmen and English money, or, at all events, for one who had lived in England…'. The *Builder* was highly critical of these as credentials of Englishness: 'they have awarded their chief premiums to designs which every one at first sight pronounces to be Byzantine. Thus the design to which they have given the second place [G. E. Street],—looking at their "instructions," is that which might have been expected to stand first.' They repeated their support for Street's design at greater length in an article of 21 March. Street did not comment at this point, but they had his 'memoir', or written description, which was a required part of the submission:

> The author of this design claims to have attempted to secure the object which the committee had in view by making his design avowedly monumental. He considered, therefore, that a fine simple chapel without aisles was the most suitable form to adopt...In his memoir Mr Street strongly argued against the impropriety and absurdity of taking a cathedral as a type for the proposed church, which ought rather to be considered as a chapel for the English residents of Constantinople than as the church for a future bishop. He considered also that the church should distinctly proclaim its English origin, and should not be an imitation of foreign buildings to such an extent to render it difficult to distinguish it from a building devoted to the use of Italians or others. He looked, therefore, to Italian buildings only for the best modes of securing his church against the heat of the climate. These he found to be, generally, very few and small windows placed at great height from the floor, groined roofs, and external cloisters or porches. Besides this, in Constantinople it is the custom to have large blinds in front of the windows. The windows in the design are therefore arranged with outer and inner traceries, and so narrow is the light and so high from the floor that the sun would never have fallen upon the people occupying the seats on the floor of the church. There was a passage round the walls also at the base of the windows to allow of blinds of lattice-work being put up and taken down if it were found necessary. The spaces between the buttresses were converted into a small cloister, which would protect the doors from the sun and keep the walls cool. No one who has not been in a hot climate knows how intolerable a large amount of window is in such a city as Constantinople, and in this case, it was useless to think of filling the windows with stained glass sufficiently rich in colour to subdue the light.[32]

The *Ecclesiologist* agreed, though was not fully won over by Street's 'thoroughly un-English . . . Teutonism':

> There is no architect in England, perhaps, better qualified than Mr Street, both by experience and predilections, to engraft Italianising features on Northern Pointed; but in the present very powerful and original design the artist seems to us to have preferred, by a process the very reverse of that pursued by his successful competitor, to clothe a Northern thought in the expression and detail of the South, rather than to borrow the original idea from the South, and translate it into a Northern dialect.[33]

Street spoke their language, and the design indeed fulfils the brief admirably, but for the time being he was on the sidelines, with the second place. The *Building News* disagreed and criticized the *Ecclesiologist*'s contention.[34]

The winner of the competition, William Burges, was in Constantinople, staying at the Hotel d'Angleterre, in June 1857, and noted

> that the present or rather the proposed site is a most unpopular one with all parties & if we can possibly get it changed (almost anywhere) it would certainly be for the better. For the street is very narrow on one side of the buildings for the medical school now erecting on the Galata Serai will pretty well shut out all views of the church (except of the tower or perhaps of the roof) from the sea.[35]

Burges was now actively involved in the search for a site. He was still there in July and remarked that 'building is so dear'.[36] The chaplain, Charles Curtis, wrote to Ernest Hawkins at the SPG in London:

> As Wm Burges has probably informed you, negotiations have been entered with regarding the site to which you allude, that on the brow of the hill. This site is, as you imagine, South of the granted one; about, I suppose, 1000 yards South of it. It is discernible both from the Golden Horn & the entrance to the Bosphorus.[37]

A major difficulty of this site was the proximity of a mosque that might preclude the building of the church. Problems continued to pile up for poor Burges. On 29 July 1857, Curtis again wrote to Hawkins that 'it will not, I suppose, astonish you that Mr Burges' plan could not be executed without exceeding the estimate by some thousands of pounds. You will have been prepared to imagine that no experience gained in England would qualify one for judging of the cost of a work here.'[38] A week later, on 6 August, Burges is clearly becoming frustrated:

> The last news is that the Vizier said that the vicinity of the Mosque was a great objection & that Lord Stratford must ask for the ground from the Sultan himself...The worst part of the affair is that the attaches think the Memorial Church a bore, especially the one who is charged with the business (a Mr Moore).[39]

Towards the end of the next month, on 24 September, he wrote 'on board the Carmel...I have at last left Constantinople to my very great joy—It happens that the Sultan has issued the edict (yradèe) granting the Tophana site to the English for the purpose of building a church—the only thing now wanting is for the Government to buy it.'[40] The proximity of the mosque had not in the end been an insurmountable problem. He was delighted to leave Constantinople, but he was returning to controversy in London.

Burges's design was typically elaborate, and he was required to simplify not once but four times, and in the end the Revd Ernest Hawkins of the SPG wrote to Mr Burges on 23 April 1863 to tell him that the Building Committee had finally decided to abandon his design and requested a statement of outstanding claims. It was not until 19 December that Hawkins wrote to Street to tell him that the committee had now approved his design, subject to minor amendment.[41]

Street's competition design showed a chancel perfectly suited to the ritualist celebration of the liturgy, so much so that an almost identical layout was published the following year in the *Directorium Anglicanum*. He had placed the altar up three steps within the apse, a large open sanctuary with choir stalls as far as the chancel arch. The perspective drawing showed how magnificent the space would have been, if in the end it had been built as designed, with the horizontally striped ashlar of the walls, the verticals of the colonettes soaring into the ribs of the vaults, and the groins of the apse. As demanded in the

Figure 24. Crimean Memorial Church, Istanbul: interior

competition brief, the design relied on the monumentality of the architecture and its elements to produce its effect. To mitigate heat, he provided a deep entrance porch, which he then wrapped around the nave as a cloister through the deep buttresses between the four bays of the nave and opening into the wider transept. In the event, the required amendments were far from minor. As built, the design was reduced to a square sanctuary, but with the altar retaining its three steps, while the beautiful sedilia remained on the south wall. The choir stalls are still there in his revised design, but on the revised plan they are shown occupying the better part of what was left of the chancel. The horizontal stripes of the ashlar have gone in the chancel (though not on the upper walls of the nave between the windows), but remain in the vaulting itself, which is of course very much simplified, with the sanctuary now being on a square plan. Verticality is still emphasized by soaring colonettes, but these are reduced in number with simpler vaulting, so Street picks them out in dark polished marble. Forced economy has cut the design to the bone, but the church maintains its dignity and even a kind of grandeur. Street retained the deep porch, and on plan it is shown wrapping round as a cloister through the buttresses, finally becoming small outward-facing rooms, on the south side leading to a vestry and stairs to the crypt. It remains an impressive accommodation to the prevailing circumstances, which Burges had found increasingly frustrating.

Expat Communities

Street was also active in building churches for English-speaking communities beyond the reach of the empire. When the Kingdom of Italy captured Rome from the papacy in 1870, it became possible for Protestants to build their own churches. In 1871, Street was commissioned by the Revd Dr R. J. Nevin to build the American Episcopal Church on the Via Nazionale in Rome. The site was purchased on

12 March 1872, and Street was there that month. Designs were ready for ground to be broken that November. Street was there in January of 1876 as the building neared completion. St Paul's Inside the Walls (its dedication) was consecrated on Lady Day, 25 March 1876. It was an altogether English work, with glass by Clayton and Bell and mosaics by Sir Edward Burne Jones.

In 1880, Street was commissioned by the SPG to build a second church, All Saints, in the Via del Babuino near the Spanish Steps in Rome. The site was obtained in January 1880, Street was there in March, and designs were ready by July. Street died on 18 December 1881 while the foundations were being prepared, and the church was built by his son, A. E. Street. It is another highly original design to cope with a difficult site and orientation. Again there was a slight variation on the liturgical chancel, which this time was itself raised an impressive five steps above the nave.

Expatriate communities in a city like Rome will remain pretty stable, and history has been kind to communities supporting the Anglican Church in many ex-colonies in Canada, Australia, and New Zealand, but in Constantinople—now Istanbul, of course—political and religious pressures have had their effects on even the hardiest of communities. In the wake of the First World War, the Ottoman Empire collapsed, and the Sultanate was abolished in 1922. Constantinople and the Middle East were dominated by Britain and France. Britain no longer occupies such an exalted position as then, nor as in the days when Lord Stratford de Redcliffe was ambassador to the Sublime Porte. The Memorial Church had rarely been used since the 1940s. In 1964, the embassy chaplain, Wilfrid Castle, wrote:

> It is shut in by buildings and shut out of the life of the community and rarely visited. In summer I hope to use it for evening services, but its existence poses a problem for our hundred-strong community now living in new suburbs up to seven miles away. The tragedy is—the British nation was offered a superb site now occupied by the Galata

Saray, a big secondary school, right in the centre of town, but then on the edge of the country. Equivalent to Piccadilly Circus! It would have been a marvelous site. Its actual site is little better than a dump and it takes an intimate knowledge of the place to find it.[42]

Whether the hundred-strong community could have supported the church on another site during the 1960s, even if it had been 'offered', as he maintained, is a moot point. The pastoral need was then different in the extreme from that which caused the church to be built, as were the political circumstances, while the religious problems had become extreme, not to say extremist. On 27 June 1975, the bishop of Fulham and Gibraltar, whose responsibilities included Istanbul, wrote to Sir John Betjeman as a champion of Victorian architecture:

> The church is indeed a masterpiece...I am desperately sad to see it in its present state of disrepair...We have, for a number of years, been trying to offer the church to some other Christian community in Istanbul, but no one has been able to take it on. As you know, the number of Christians living in Istanbul has dwindled rapidly in recent years because of pressure from 'certain quarters'...[43]

The church was deconsecrated in 1976, then closed, but reconsecrated in May 1993. It seemed that things could hardly get worse for the little community, but on 20 November 2003 a bomb exploded outside the British consulate in Istanbul, wrecking the building then being used as its chapel and killing the consul-general, Roger Short, who had spent the evening with the Archbishop of Canterbury, Rowan Williams, just two days previously. Yet the Memorial Church survived, and began to thrive, modestly, under the determined leadership of its incumbent, Fr Ian Sherwood, supported by a resilient core of members. The building reflects this, as it has always done. What began as a design for a grand national war memorial, represented by the more elaborate winning entry by William Burges, was then passed to the more economical G. E. Street, who produced a building of a somewhat more modest presence for the English community in Constantinople. It was then embattled, irrelevant, 'shut in', and 'shut out', and found a new, broader community to house and serve. The colonial tide has gone out, leaving these now–exotic structures beached as relics of a bygone age, but, in finding renewed and more diverse communities to serve, the building now stands for adaptability and sustainability of mission and service by the Church.

Figure 25. Coventry Cathedral, visit of Winston Churchill to the Ruins, 1942

12

'A Phoenix Too Soon'

Coventry Cathedral

The twentieth century became problematic for the Church as an institution and likewise as a builder. Its identity had been confidently expressed (appropriately or not) in the great neo-gothic buildings of the nineteenth century right up to the turn of the twentieth, when the architect of the last and mightiest neo-gothic cathedral—Liverpool Anglican Cathedral, built from 1901—Giles Gilbert Scott, began shifting his designs gradually away from strictly historical forms and increasingly towards an expressive rationalism. When Coventry Cathedral was destroyed during the Second World War on the night of 14–15 November 1940, Scott was commissioned to produce designs for its replacement. His final proposal was liturgically and architecturally very forward looking, even radical. He was supported by the hierarchy, but the circumstances behind the need for a replacement, involving destruction and loss of life, meant that the recovery and reconstruction were being used rhetorically by very different factions for very different ends. These different interest groups were represented on the committee for the architectural competition announced in October 1950. This resulted in a good degree of confusion, and the final choice of a compromise design was as much a reflection of the 1951 Festival of Britain as it was an embodiment of the Church reimagining itself for modern life.

First Impressions

The Cathedral Church of St Michael, standing in the square on Priory Street in Coventry, displays its dramatic history as a badge of honour, with the modern forms of the new cathedral dropping gently down the hill to the right and the ruined shell of the medieval cathedral still bristling on the other side of the entrance canopy to the left.

Coventry as a Cathedral City

The history of the Church in Coventry is complex, as it has been fed by different streams of Christianity, both Celtic and Roman. In the middle of the seventh century CE, it was part of the Celtic Diocese of Mercia, whose wandering bishop had no fixed cathedral at the centre of his diocese. King Oswy, at the Synod of Whitby in 664, Bede records, decided to follow St Peter as keeper of the keys of the kingdom of

Figure 26. Coventry Cathedral viewed from the Square

heaven (quoting Matthew 16:18), 'lest, perchance, when I come to the doors of the kingdom of heaven, there be no one to unlock them for me, if he is averse who is proved to have the keys.'[1] The immediate issue was whether to follow Celtic or Roman practice, especially concerning the date of Easter. St Chad, a monk of Lindesfarne, who became Bishop of Mercia in 669, decided on Lichfield for his cathedral. The diocese, which included Coventry, was huge, and out of it have come the dioceses of Hereford, Worcester, Lincoln, and Leicester.

The Abbey of Coventry was said to have been founded by the Countess Godiva and her husband Leofric in the middle of the eleventh century. At the end of the twelfth century, Bishop de Lymesey acquired the Abbacy of Coventry and installed a prior to administer it on his behalf, so he became Bishop of Coventry and Lichfield. This situation remained until the Dissolution of the Monasteries under Henry VIII. The church, dedicated to St Mary, had become a monastic cathedral, and so it remained until 15 January 1539, when the last prior surrendered the foundation to the Crown, and it was pulled to the ground. Coventry had lost its cathedral in the sixteenth century. In the seventeenth, having backed the wrong side against the King in the Civil War, it also lost its precedence over Lichfield, with the diocese becoming 'Lichfield and Coventry' after the Restoration of the Monarchy in 1661. It became part of Worcester Diocese in 1837, the year Victoria came to the throne. Birmingham became the cuckoo in that episcopal nest, which left Coventry isolated in the east of the diocese.

Various unsatisfactory arrangements were tried until, in 1908, when Bishop Yeatman-Biggs of Worcester constituted St Michael's Church, Coventry, as a collegiate church with plans for it to be the cathedral of a new 'Diocese of Warwickshire', slipping in the stream of the new dioceses of Chelmsford, Sheffield, and St Edmundsbury, which had been established in 1914. The First World War stopped all progress in that direction, but at the end of the war parliament passed the Bradford and Coventry Act, and Yeatman-Biggs became the first diocesan bishop of Coventry. Under the new constitution, he was also dean of the cathedral. It was only under his successor that a titular provost was installed in 1931. The second titular provost was Richard Thomas Howard, who did not become full provost until 1938. Only two years later, his cathedral would be the second cathedral in Coventry to be destroyed, on 14–15 November 1940. National, political, architectural, and religious voices can all be heard in the rhetoric surrounding its rebuilding and can be read in the visual rhetoric of the resulting building.

Twentieth-Century Architecture and the Church

If you pick up a general history of European architecture and flick through it, you would generally expect pride of place to be given to ecclesiastical architecture as the high-water mark of the art of building – that is, until you reached the twentieth century. Then, on the contrary, you would be surprised if the study were to give more than fleeting sidelong glances at isolated churches by the likes of Auguste Perret, Le Corbusier, Mies van der Rohe, and perhaps Antonio Gaudi. Until more recently, Giles Gilbert Scott, Frederick Gibberd, or Basil Spence were lucky to be mentioned, even disapprovingly. Ecclesiastical architecture has been marginalized in the twentieth century.

On his return from America and his encounter with the work of Frank Lloyd Wright, the great Dutch architect H. P. Berlage wrote a *Memoir of an American Journey (Amerikaansche Reisherinneringen)*, published in 1912. He argued that there had been a significant cultural shift, maintaining that the American-style office block was, for the twentieth century, what great religious buildings had been right up to the nineteenth century. As he wrote, they 'contain a spirit you may well call religious...While ancient architecture was based on the temple, offices and shops are the ideal built forms of modern architecture: they are placed to embody the highest cultural values.'[2] This constituted a radical discontinuity in the language required to express 'the highest cultural values', in Berlage's terms, decoupling them from the vocabulary of historic forms and allowing the modern, or Modernist, architect to explore a new tectonic language. For him, religious architecture was no longer culturally defining and was becoming an architectural backwater, though both Berlage and Wright would build singularly successful churches—Unity Temple in Oak Park, Illinois (1906), and the Christian Science Church in The Hague (1925).

If church architecture had become a backwater in twentieth-century European architecture, and Britain was to remain a backwater in European *church* architecture, then it is no wonder that even the greatest of twentieth-century British church architects remained largely unsung in the annals of modern architecture, though recently critical assessment has begun to shift. The most sympathetic reception these architects received until the 1980s at least, even in histories dedicated solely to English architecture, is found in the 'serious historicism' of Paul Thompson, who praised Sir Giles Gilbert Scott in particular as he 'handled Gothic with a conviction and on a scale equal to the boldest Victorian work'.[3] The status of church architecture was a reflection of the status of the Church itself in this era of increasing secularization.

History, Architecture, and the Liturgy

Scott did not restrict himself to the historic forms of English Gothic but developed a personal style that was always historically rooted, rather than slavishly historicist, as exemplified in the chapel that he built between 1932 and 1934 at Lady Margaret Hall, Oxford. This design looks back to his Church of Our Lady and St Alphege, Bath, which he designed in 1925 and which was built in stages between 1929 and 1954. There he brought the altar forward under a baldacchino, making it visually and physically accessible to the congregation. It very consciously takes Santa Maria in Cosmedin, Rome, as its historical reference, recalling the simplicity and authenticity of the liturgical practices of the early church. Gregory Dix published his magisterial liturgical study *The Shape of the Liturgy* in 1945. It was similarly intended to revolutionize contemporary Christians' views of ancient liturgical use in order to affect contemporary practice in the celebration of Holy Communion, or the eucharist: 'Slowly but certainly it will affect first what they think and how they pray in the central and vital act in fully Christian living, the corporate celebration of the eucharist.'[4] This was taken up during the 1960s by the Lambeth Committee report on the Book of Common Prayer in its 'suggested modifications or additions for the further recovery of other elements of the worship of the Primitive Church'.[5] But William Lockett, in 'A Lesson from Anglican History', complained: 'It is a popular misconception to think that the Liturgical Movement seeks to re-establish the liturgy of the Primitive Church or to imitate fourth-century buildings, as Sir Giles Gilbert Scott has in the Roman Catholic Church of St Alphege, Bath. Nothing could be further from the truth.'[6] There was obviously a subtle theological and historical argument in play here, and it had been variously rehearsed for decades, but the main issue was clearly the role of history in informing contemporary liturgical and architectural practice.

Scott's super-scaled personal development of Gothic at Liverpool Cathedral may not be to every architectural critic's taste, but it deserves, and is now coming to receive, better than being dismissed as 'emasculated Gothic'.[7] Scott had won the competition for Liverpool Cathedral at the tender age of 21, so young that it was thought necessary to appoint one of the judges, G. F. Bodley, an extremely distinguished Victorian Gothicist, to supervise the work, and Scott distinctly felt that Bodley cramped his style. When Bodley died in 1907, Scott was still only 27, but he seized his new-found freedom and significantly redesigned the treatment of the Lady Chapel, despite its construction already being well under way. He was a meticulous designer, using fine materials worked by the best craftsmanship. His work embodies his conviction that architecture is an evolutionary rather than a revolutionary art, and Liverpool Cathedral stands squarely in the great tradition. This is no mere pastiche, but rather a powerful rationalist analysis, gradually paring down decorative overlay to enhance the vision of structural force and architectural volumes but allowing detail and carefully articulated decoration to enhance those architectural qualities. The building of that cathedral spanned his whole career and continued nineteen years beyond his death in 1960. He remained consistent, but his idea of a cathedral and architectural style continued to develop throughout the years he spent on Liverpool Cathedral.

For a building to be a success, its form must meet and mesh with its function. In the case of a cathedral, the architectural vision must rise to, and fuse with, the theological vision. At Liverpool, these two visions developed side by side over a long period. The bishops and deans who oversaw the building clearly had huge vision. Not long after the completion of the cathedral, it was said of the deans that:

> Frederick William Dwelly . . . was the great innovator of the building's liturgical and ceremonial traditions. Then came Frederick William Dillistone, with his wide and expansive theological mission.
>
> Edward Patey is a deep thinker, but primarily a radical doer. He, perhaps more than anyone, has made Liverpool Cathedral a multi-racial, multi-media, multi conscious, multi-denominational laboratory. As a result, one of the thickest files on his desk is marked 'Letters of protest'.[8]

That spirit continues with the 2008 commission of Tracey Emin to create a work—a pink neon sign saying: 'I felt you and I knew you loved me.'

In 1933, when Liverpool Cathedral was roughly half-finished, Scott became the president of the Royal Institute of British Architects (RIBA) as a mediating influence between 'modernists' and 'traditionalists', the two warring parties into which British architects were increasingly falling. His churches were reassuringly traditional, but in his industrial work, such as Bankside Power Station and his involvement in the redesign of the exterior of Battersea between 1930 and 1931 (built in 1934), he was seen as a worthy modernist in the rationalist tradition of Berlage. Scott handled materials as a constructor, not as a theorist, so when it came to 'truth to materials', he said in his inaugural address as president:

> There is a lot of functional nonsense about extreme Modernism: for instance logical expression of materials is claimed as one of its fundamental principles, yet we find that buildings are designed to look as if they were of reinforced concrete, even when they are nothing of the sort...I am afraid it is a craving for striking effect rather than for functionalism expressing construction that leads the extreme Modernist to tell the same constructional lies that he condemns so heartily in the work of the extreme traditionalist.[9]

He was clear that what appeared to be the directly determined and functional new language of modern architecture could often be used as allusively and rhetorically as the most symbolically and archaeologically bound traditionalism.

The War, Destruction, Reconstruction

Between 1935 and the end of the Second World War, the Incorporated Church Building Society recorded 269 churches built in England, but only a dozen or so of these were built during the war. After the war, then, it was perfectly obvious that 'during the next few years church building on a large scale will be necessary to replace some of the churches completely lost by enemy action and to make spiritual provision for the vast new housing estates to come into being'.[10] The question was, with the division between modernists and traditionalists becoming even more entrenched, would the architectural community, and its clients, be ready to build churches that *spoke* coherently to post-war society?

The Second World War, with the huge destruction of the urban fabric of Britain and Europe, had provoked an acute architectural crisis in the face of necessary reconstruction. Fifteen years after the end of the war, Peter Hammond looked back over the way the Church and its architects had risen to this challenge:

> The results of all this activity have been depressing in the extreme. It is hard to think of any field of ecclesiastical investment where so much money has been squandered to so little purpose. The devastation caused by the war, the development of new and exciting techniques of building and a theological recovery within the Church of the full biblical meaning of the *ecclesia* and its liturgy together provided the Church with a splendid opportunity for creating a living architecture: an architecture firmly rooted in tradition and yet wholly of its time.[11]

He too has laid a claim to history and roots in tradition, as did other radical modernists, but it was on such an abstract level that the relationship with history was almost impossible for the client, not to say the public, to read in the designs themselves. Here was a different historical rhetoric that was read as a denial of history. This particular 'Battle of the Styles' would see its fiercest fighting in the competition for Coventry Cathedral.

Coventry Cathedral had been destroyed in the blitz of 14–15 November 1940, when there were also heavy casualties, with 568 people killed and 863 badly injured.[12] The death and devastation caused literally became an emotive byword for this tactic of urban destruction when the Nazis coined the word *Coventrieren*. In 1942, Scott was controversially commissioned by Provost Howard to produce a design for its replacement. In the decades between Scott winning the competition for Liverpool and the 1942 commission, his style had continued to evolve, as had his approach to cathedral planning and the liturgy. In *Post-War Church Building*, published in 1947, Ernest Short wrote of the resulting design:

> It will be for the architect to determine the size of altar or communion table so that it shall appear worthy of its high office and not be dwarfed in relation to the rest of the chancel. Sir Giles Scott carried this thought so far in planning the rebuilding of Coventry Cathedral, that he placed his altar in the centre of the congregation; in other words, he proposed to build the new cathedral round the altar. Commenting upon the scheme, the Provost of Coventry pointed out that a further object of the change is to confront the people, worshippers and visitors alike, with certain ideas which are of paramount value for the destiny of

mankind—namely, the reality and priority of God in all human life, the essential character of God as self-giving love, the Holy Communion as the deepest source of true community, and the hallowing of man's daily work and craft by the offering of it to God in worship. These are beliefs...better emphasised by an altar table visible to all at the centre than by one partially hidden from sight at the far end of the church.[13]

This was very advanced planning, very much in tune with developments within the Liturgical Movement, where the abiding theme was to place the eucharist at the centre of the worshipping community, which has architectural ramifications, creating (in contemporary terms) a *Domus ecclesiae* rather than a *Domus dei*—that is to say, a house for the gathered people of God would be a very different shape from a house of God.

Before the end of the war, there were only two Roman Catholic and two Anglican churches that, following such precepts, had centralized altars. The Roman Catholic examples were the Church of the First Martyrs, Bradford, of 1935 and Eric Gill's Church of St Peter, Gorleston-on-Sea, consecrated in 1939. In an essay published in 1940, 'The Mass for the Masses', Gill wrote: 'there is nothing whatever in the nature of an altar that implies that it should be anywhere else but in the middle. It began as a table around which people sat and partook of the consecrated bread and wine. It remains that thing.'[14] In the Anglican Church before the Second World War, only Cosham St Philip (J. N. and J. B. S. Comper, 1938), and an altar, again by Eric Gill, at Blundell's School for Neville C. Gorton (soon to become Bishop of Coventry) can in any real sense be considered to have centralized altars. Even Gorton's altar was not precisely in the middle of the congregation, but it was 'in the centre of the cleared space...not an architectural reform but a liturgical one'.[15]

There had been other radical designs that had been thwarted in the end, as built, including the best work of N. F. Cachemaille-Day at St Michael and All Angels, Wythenshawe, in 1937. He planned the church as two interlocking squares, producing a star shape. The original intention was revealed in the description in *Fifty Modern*

Churches (1947):'Large open space required with little or no obstruc-
tion by columns, congregation to be near altar. Diagrid reinforced
construction adopted, and star-shaped plan evolves from this.'[16] The
altar was intended to be among the congregation. In the event, it was
removed to the far point of the star, reputedly at the insistence of the
bishop.[17] (The anticipated liturgical development did not gain a
firm hold in England for another quarter of a century.) The tall,
still-traceried windows, the corona of lights echoing the plan of the
church, the colour scheme, together with the attenuated yet finely
articulated concrete structure, all combined to produce a soaring
space sparkling with light. Admittedly the interior is better than the
rather ponderous purple brick exterior, but it is still a very significant accomplishment.

   For the first quarter of the century, church building had been seen
in England as an unproblematic activity; the greatest difficulty was the
development of an appropriate decorative programme. In the years
between the late 1920s and the Second World War, the buildings produced by Scott and his colleagues were hardly revolutionary, but many
churches were adventurous, and sometimes there were glimpses of
fundamental new developments to come.

   Christianity is an incarnational religion; God is conceived of as
present in a very particular way in history, and this means that appeals
to the authority of tradition, as the history and experience of the
Church, are very powerful. There are architectural ramifications too
in relation to the growing traditionalist/modernist divide within
the British architectural profession. Sir Charles Nicholson, whose
churches are among the most conservative included in *Fifty Modern
Churches* in 1947,[18] wrote a chapter, 'Building the Church: Styles and
Requirements', in *Post-War Church Building*, of the same year, sum-
ming up what he saw as the choices:

> one is given a choice in building a new church—not a choice between
> Anglican or Roman Catholic or Presbyterian or Baptist or high church
> or low church arrangements—but between traditional and modern
> principles.

There is much to be said for both alternatives... There are, however, two distinct schools of modernism, one aims at pure functionalism devoid of style, and studiously disregarding all precedent, the other affecting modernism by reviving the forgotten styles of prehistoric, or ultra primitive, or perhaps even savage buildings, and presenting the results as artistic discoveries...if we are going to disregard traditional forms, do not let us proclaim our cleverness from the housetops by being aggressively functional or aggressively archaic or by wilful disregard of convention.[19]

From this point of view, Scott would have been the natural choice to redesign Coventry Cathedral, just as he had been the natural choice to be president of the RIBA in 1933. The designs as fully developed would have produced a worthy and dignified cathedral that would respond to contemporary theological and liturgical thinking. Characteristically the design was carried out in Scott's usual historically rooted idiom, but on a grand scale and with dramatic spatial and lighting effects.

Both Provost Howard and Neville Gorton, bishop of Coventry, were radical thinkers, but there were many other interested parties. There was officialdom, including both central government and the City Council, whose Lord Mayor wanted the old cathedral restored. The Central Council for the Care of Churches, whose chairman, F.C. Eeles, also proposed restoration, though the Esher Report, which was produced by the Central Council with A. E. Richardson and Sir Charles Nicholson, recommended that a new cathedral be built within the walls of the old and that it be bold, but harmonize. Donald Gibson, Coventry's city planner, favoured a modern design. With such divergence of opinion, no wonder that any appointment by Howard was so controversial. But the relationship to history and the tradition were key concerns, so perhaps Scott, as the old pilot, could navigate these waters, especially given the industrial nature of Coventry and his own industrial credentials. In the event, neither the city nor the public liked the design, and, significantly, Gorton put it to Scott that 'the only support we have is from the young and forward looking, whose plea is "why should [we] be tied to rebuilding old churches or building new ones on past formulas"'. Gorton was for a modern, even industrial approach, but Scott thought it out of place, even extreme, for the design of a cathedral.[20] Revised designs were prepared that showed a bold new interior, and these were approved by the Cathedral Council. In the event, Gorton would get a more modern stylistic idiom, at the expense of modern liturgical planning; the Royal Fine Art Commission saw the discrepancy between the new interior and the exterior and wanted the historic ruins to be preserved as far as possible, but Scott's scheme would sweep away a good part of them. This time, Scott the great compromiser pleased no one, and he resigned.

Different factions, within and without the Church, were all eager to use the cathedral for different purposes within their own rhetorical structures: preservation of the history and archaeology; recovery from the war and the continuity of social, civic, and religious life; or modernization of the Church and its worship and reconnection with the citizenry, especially the young. The Harlech Commission was instructed to address this diversity in its recommendations for setting the terms of an architectural competition, and it was at this point that a central altar and liturgical reform were removed from the agenda. Continuity and stability were the preferred rhetoric, and compromise was still the only practical way forward.

The Festival of Britain, 1951

The secular context had a very different mood. In June 1951, J. M. Richards praised the architect, Leslie Martin, and his team for their modern solution to technical problems posed by the newly completed Royal Festival Hall, in contrast to the approach at Coventry, where the design was bound to the past. But he had reservations about the modern style that was emerging: 'To give a building of this kind sufficient robustness of modelling and richness of architecture to produce an effect of monumentality is extremely difficult in view of an absence of a recognised modern decorative idiom ... an attempt to contrive such an idiom is liable to appear mannered and is soon dated.'[21] Form, even for the radical modernists, did not directly follow function to produce style, but had to be controlled to give an apparent functional transparency that was readable, while suppressing elements that were disturbing to the aesthetic balance of the massing. The logical solution to the technical problems did not directly produce an acceptable visual logic.

The Royal Festival Hall was inaugurated at the same time as the Festival of Britain, which surrounded it, but was a London County Council (LCC) project that would have been built in any case, and LCC architecture under Leslie Martin was radically modernist. The festival style was, as would be expected in the circumstances, exhilarating, optimistic, colourful, and modern. Roy Strong, who mounted a twenty-fifth anniversary exhibition at the V&A, ventured: 'It was the last really great stylistic statement this country made; it's still having repercussions even now.'[22] Not all assessments have been so positive, and the mix of contemporary aesthetic sensibilities, along with the social, political, and national importance and function of the festival can be glimpsed in a description by Gerald Barry, its director, of the opening ceremony, which took place at St Paul's Cathedral on 3 May 1951:

> With the Lord President, the Lord Privy Seal, and Lord Ismay, I stood at the entrance to the portico to await the King and Queen. Opposite us stood the Archbishop, Bishop of London and Dean and Chapter of St Paul's, medieval in their copes ... And here we stood at the top of the steps, a handful of men, privileged to occupy an almost empty grandstand to witness an instant of British history ...

> From my position next the centre aisle I could observe the procession at close quarters. The order of precedence in the programme reads almost like something from the age of chivalry. 'Portcullis Pursuivant, Bluemantle Pusuivant, Richmond Herald, Chester Herald, Lancaster Herald ... The Archbishop preceded by his Chaplain bearing the Canterbury Cross ... the Bishop of London ... vergers ... the Lord Mayor, the King and Queen, accompanied by nine members

of the Royal Family.'...Seeing these uniforms pass, one felt suddenly that St Paul's itself was too youthful a building for their presence. They demanded the antiquity of Gothic, not these renaissance rotundities.[23]

British society and its structure were there in emblematic form, and the uniforms by which he was so impressed (especially on the heralds!) connected these individuals to ancient offices, so ancient that the full depth of the history to which they were all connected was not sufficiently recognized by the relatively youthful St Paul's. Here was a man acutely aware of the rhetoric of style and the importance of a sense of historical connectedness—and this festival attitude would reflect on the rebuilding of Coventry Cathedral.

The Competition to Rebuild Coventry Cathedral

The conditions of the competition to design the new Coventry Cathedral set in relation to the ruins of the old were announced in October 1950. The emphasis with the Harlech Commission remained on continuity with the tradition and stability of institutions, but the compromise reached meant that the published conditions flatly proclaimed that 'no restrictions are placed on competitors as to style or materials to be used in any of the buildings'.[24] This appeared to leave the field wide open, but belied the complex politics and interests lying behind the competition. Thus began the distilled 'Battle of the Styles', with a vast number of competition entries of every conceivable type. As the press reported:

> The bulk of the field jibbed or refused. Many obviously had no belief that cathedral and contemporary could be reconciled at all—they sought their inspiration in the past. Others, in their anxiety to eschew past forms floundered in meaningless new ones. The result, therefore, was largely a parade of sterile, dreary, vulgar or stunt designs with, of course, the odd pipe dream or so.[25]

Tellingly, a restriction was placed on the architects who were eligible to compete. They had to be from Britain, Eire, or the Commonwealth. This was symbolically important. Defiance in the face of the enemy was symbolized by St Paul's; the destruction of British cities had become embodied in the ruins of Coventry Cathedral; and the new cathedral would stand for the reconstruction and recovery of the nation. The many continental architects who at this time were producing innovative new designs for churches built round the altar as a *Domus ecclesiae* were excluded for obvious reasons, since the foremost of these were German, pre-eminently Rudolf Schwartz. In the end, 567 copies of the Conditions were sent out and 219 entries received along with a total of 1491 drawings.[26] The brief was confused, attempting unsuccessfully to reconcile the demands of (and even within) various interest groups, traditionalist and Modernist, City and national, clerical and lay. A clarification document subsequently had to be provided in response to the resulting confusion on the part of the architects. The site itself also presented very particular demands in its size and shape, its relationship to Gibson's Redevelopment Plans for the City, and the remains of the old Cathedral, which had already found a ceremonial use including Bishop Gorton's enthronement on 20 February 1943.

The many entries tended to treat the relationship with Donald Gibson's plans in a picturesque way, but every conceivable treatment of the ruins was explored. The violence of the destruction of the old cathedral, the suffering and loss of life on that night and throughout the war, and the ceremonial use of the ruins during the intervening period, all made the ruins a powerful symbol. The symbolism of suffering and death had to be met by one of Resurrection in the rebuilding of the Cathedral; the Provost's emphasis on the symbolism of sacrifice and resurrection had been removed from the conditions, but was made explicit in naming the chapel for private prayer the Chapel of the Resurrection. The material relating to the redevelopment plan for the city made it clear that the ruins remained of great importance in the design.

The size and shape of the site meant that, if the ruins were to be preserved, a long narrow nave had to be oriented parallel to the old cathedral on its north side, or on a north–south axis abutting the ruins towards the east end. Otherwise a new design of any other shape would tend to have a more attenuated relationship with the fully preserved ruins. Of the three designs to receive awards, the third place was given to A. D. Kirby, who left nothing of the ruin except the magnificent spire itself, which he juxtaposed with his own rather fussy spike over the crossing. It was a traditional design, but rather more werlitzer than Gothic, a 1930s modernism. The assessors commented: 'The plan and composition of the masses are impressive, but the design lacks distinction in quality of architectural detail.'[27] The second prize went to a lecturer in the Cambridge Department of Architecture, W. P. Hunt, who removed all but the spire, apse (restored as the Lady Chapel), and south porch (again restored as a chapel), placing a glazed cloister 'of considerable charm'[28] where the south wall had been and the cathedral where the north stood. This left a cathedral-shaped void at the heart of the design. He too had a crossing spire, this time very plain. The style was direct and understated rather than severe and relied on the fenestration for rhythm and decorative effect, with relief and contrast provided by the Gothic of the ruins.

Radical Responses

Two radical plans, passed over without comment by the assessors, were produced by Colin (Sandy) St John Wilson and Peter Carter, and Alison and Peter Smithson. Wilson was a recent graduate of the Bartlett School of Architecture, then working at the LCC. He qualified in 1950, with a cathedral as an examined design. This is perhaps unsurprising considering he had a metaphysical, not to say spiritual, side, and he was at home in the cathedral world—his father was bishop of Chelmsford from 1929 to 1950. He wrote:

Figure 27. The Smithson Competition Entry

> Architecture is inevitably drawn to reach precariously out from its
> own discipline to make contact with a world that is other...and to
> make out of that contact a common cause, an in-between order that is
> neither the order of art nor the raw assimilation of day-to-day experi-
> ence, but the discovery of a common theme through which conduct
> begins to find its true rhythm, as stumbling feet are caught up in the
> measure of a dance.[29]

Within his Christian background,[30] such a conception might well be
transferred to the liturgy, and to explore these two axes of the idea
within the context of a cathedral becomes, with Wilson, a meditation
on the Anglican Church.

The Wilson and Carter entry looked like nothing so much as an
aircraft hangar. The huge cantilevered roof was supported by four
open webbed box-beamed columns that embraced the altar platform
and were founded on the walls of the Chapel of the Resurrection on
the lower level. It was like a vast, spreading baldacchino, sacralizing the

space not only of the altar, but of the congregation too. The huge glass walls were hung with polished aluminium louvres, which bounced light into the space while masking the view of the external world as you entered past the font; at the end of the service, as you turned from this numinous world to leave, the world of the city again became visible as you went to meet it. Wilson was explicit about the symbolism, saying:

> This was the only occasion on which I really became engrossed with the Miesian aphorism 'less is more'. However, this reduction of means was intended to bring maximum focus upon a few symbolic elements: the entrance ramp which circled round the baptismal font, and a roof structure springing from a slightly raised altar platform and spreading towards you in an enormous, all-embracing cantilever.[31]

Sandy Wilson had radically reconceived the Anglican tradition on a level of abstraction of a metaphysical poet, with which few people could identify. In an article entitled 'Towards a New Cathedral' (echoing Le Corbusier's revolutionary 'Vers une architecture') in his column in the Observer, he proposed that such great architectural compositions as the Piazza of St Mark in Venice were the result of great architects of different generations working in the '"modern" manner of his day', and clearly he intended to work in this great 'tradition' of discontinuity.[32]

The Smithsons' design was frequently mentioned in the ensuing years, but rarely in any detail until the original submission was given a special edition of *churchbuilding* in 1963 (until 1962 it was *Church Buildings Today*). The journal emanated from the circle of the New Churches Research Group, founded in 1957 and including at its core Bob Maquire, Nigel Melhuish, Peter Hammond, and Keith Murray, while contributors among the clergy were Basil Minchin, A. M. Allchin, and Victor de Waal. This particular edition reviewed *The Cambridge Movement: The Ecclesiologists and the Gothic Revival*. The review attempted to loosen the grip that the Gothic still had on the general mental picture of a church building. There was another review of Gilbert Cope's *Making the Building Serve the Liturgy*, and one entitled

'A Phoenix Too Soon?' by Basil Mitchell assessing Spence's *Phoenix at Coventry*.

In presenting the Smithsons' competition entry, 'The Editors' insisted:

> Although not recognised by the judges, and in spite of its meagre illustration, the fame of the Smithsons' design has been sufficient to make the anticlastic shell, or hyperbolic paraboloid, popular. Before 1951 it was hardly known. Since the competition it has become particularly popular among the 'advanced' church architects, who justify it as 'liturgical'; but as Alison and Peter Smithson point out, the form is quite unsuitable for a church unless handled in a very special way. The subtlety and beauty of their design are the result of the way in which this form has been used in careful relation to function.[33]

This design, too, removed all of the ruins except the tower and the apse, covering the greater part of the site of the ruined cathedral with the southern corner of a great square created by the vast tent-like canopy canted upwards towards the east. The huge white marble aggregate concrete shell would shine in the sunlight, and the architects described how the structure would have had tensioned mullions all along the edge beams 'achieving the dissolution of the wall, to which medieval builders aspired'.[34] The soaring shell would achieve that weightless sweeping ascent that was the highest achievement of the Gothic as understood by Schopenhauer in the nineteenth century.[35] This single pure and dominant form was not only intended to impose order on what was still a city centre in unredeveloped chaos. As the competition submission put it:

> The general lack of order and the size and scale of adjacent buildings seem to point to the cathedral being conceived as one large simple volume containing all the cathedral functions, rather than a series of small related volumes whose tensions would be slackened and confused by the existing chaos. This large simple volume should be placed on the site in such a manner to bring discipline and cohesion to the neighbourhood and the city.[36]

They had clearly anticipated the nature of many of the other submissions, and the Smithsons refused the bitty picturesqueness of the reconstruction plan. The main diagonal axis ran parallel with the axis of the old cathedral. The primary entrance on the main level was at the western corner, and an entrance to the upper-level Trinity Chapel was ramped up along the axis of the old cathedral through the tower. The main functional and liturgical elements of vestries, chapels, and ark (which, rather like an ancient *scola cantorum*—for example, as in St Clement in Rome—enclosed the altar, choir, and lectern) were all deployed within this free space, vertically as well as horizontally. The altar was a monolithic block of stone placed centrally—which must also have counted against them with the adjudicators. During more intimate services, the congregation could be accommodated within the 'ark', or *scola cantorum*, and on large diocesan occasions it would be occupied by the diocesan clergy. The Chapel of Unity, Lady Chapel, and Chapter House (all dimensionally related to the base of the surviving tower) would be held aloft within the space as a trinity and covered in brightly coloured frescoes 'whose chromatic joy will communicate itself to the whole congregation'.[37] The reference to 'chromatic joy' conjures up visions of Edwardo Paolozzi murals animating the major elements suspended in the vast free space.

Beneath the cathedral, the vaults of the surviving crypt would be partially uncovered, and the crypts themselves would receive the 'Cross of Nails and other relics' memorializing the old cathedral. The Smithsons appealed frequently in their report to history to justify their formal approach, going so far as effectively to repudiate Berlage's historical analysis cited at the beginning of this chapter. For them, ecclesiastical architecture had not been superseded by the great commercial building; at this point they still maintained that 'in churches the architecture of all periods reaches its highest expression, and in this cathedral the architecture of our time must find its fullest realisation'.[38] They drew their submission to a close saying:

> It is hoped by the competitors that the building of this cathedral will finally explode the fallacy that Modern Architecture is incapable of expressing abstract ideas and will prove that only Modern Architecture is capable of creating a symbol of the dogmatic truths of the Christian faith and 'thrusting them at the man who comes in from the street' with the dynamism that so great a faith demands. Christianity, upon

which Western civilisation is built, deeply influenced the Renaissance concept of total architecture, which, in the perfect relationship of the parts to the whole, reflects the perfection of the natural order and allows Divine law to reveal itself. Modern Architecture is the heir to this great tradition and has at its disposal means of expression that would have sent Brunelleschi wild with joy.[39]

Basil Spence: A Winning Compromise

First prize in the competition went to Basil Spence, who clearly considered himself to be a British modernist, and there is a similarity in the rhetoric of his understanding of modernism to that of both the Smithsons and Wilson and Carter. Sandy Wilson refers to the Piazza of St Mark, where architects of different periods boldly built in a contemporary style and created a great architectural and urban space; the Smithsons talk of modern architecture being in the 'great tradition' of bold contemporary work; and Spence, in the same vein, wrote:

> How is it, I wondered, that advocates of our national architecture consider a contemporary style to be completely wrong when applied to churches, when it is clear that the whole character of our churches in the past has depended on integrity and a sense of adventure?
>
> Many sincere people, little realising that our tradition is such an adventurous one, are shocked when architects think in this traditional way; they cannot see that the true traditionalists are people who think simply in their own era. The copyists, then, are surely the revolutionaries.[40]

So, a contemporary contrasting style is good, but it must be 'polite' and in sympathy, as he says: 'This conception, after all, can be accepted because the church stands for permanence, continuity and vitality—a living Faith.'[41] Here he departs from the ideas of the more radical competitors, but shows himself to be the man for the hour. He was a Romantic and was inspired by the ruins that seemed to him still a holy place and he was determined to keep as much of the old cathedral as possible. He describes having a vision while standing in those ruins before he began his design:

The picture I saw was a sparkling and beautiful altar at the end of a long vista backed by a great picture, the body of the nave spread out in front of the altar, but I did not see it clearly because in front of my eyes floated the bodies of the saints and the martyrs and it was through their bodies that the altar could be seen. We all know the price of this new altar—1200 people killed and many, many more maimed and injured for life, 5,000 homes wiped out even with the people in them, 60,000 homes damaged, apart from the tremendous industrial damage. So the new altar will be seen through the saints and the martyrs.[42]

The whole of the chapter from which this comes, 'A Contemporary Expression of Cathedral Traditions', is dedicated to historical precedents for his approach and how all of these 'were always modern when they were built'. He ends the chapter as he would later close his book, with a section dedicated to the works by the best contemporary British artists integrated into his design. It is small wonder that his more radical critics felt that the cathedral was a permanent monument to the Festival of Britain, frozen in that historical moment of recovery and unable to embrace the future.

Basil Mitchell quoted someone he described as 'a member of the Cathedral body' in his review of Spence's Phoenix at Coventry: 'If we had known at the beginning as much about liturgy as we have learnt during the building, we wouldn't have started with this building!'[43] Mitchell lays a good deal of the blame for the lack of focus on the altar on the great Sutherland tapestry. While the tapestry makes an almost evangelistic impact on the passer-by through the glass screen with its saints and martyrs (as originally intended both by the architect and by the brief), whether or not the visitor enters the space, the visual impact of the tapestry is so great that during a service it is very difficult to focus attention on the action of the liturgy.

Spence had a further dream, apparently occasioned by an anaesthetic in a dentist's chair, which inspired the zigzag walls with their very effective lighting. It is a charming, not to say naive, detail that is unlikely to have been made up, so is probably true. The form of these walls has a remarkable effect on the worshipper. Walking towards the

altar to receive communion takes you past all the texts on the otherwise blank walls (the 'zig', if you will); on reaching the sanctuary and
receiving the sacrament, you turn to be dazzled by the blaze of light
through the stained glass on the 'zag'. It is breathtaking. It was one of
the first buildings I visited the first time I came to Britain in 1969. The
building was then still very fresh, having been completed and consecrated only on 25 May 1962. The Whitsun number of Anglican World
of that year reached my family in Canada, where there was great
interest in the new cathedral; Basil Spence had come to Vancouver to
speak in 1954.[44] In the magazine, the then bishop of Coventry, Cuthbert
Bardsley, made the most of his new cathedral's modernity:

> The centrality of the altar is not merely something architectural, but
> rather will it be central in the whole life of this house of God. With
> this in mind, a great deal of time has been spent by members of the
> staff of the cathedral in thinking out ways and means of celebrating the
> liturgy to the glory of God in this contemporary building.

He goes on to describe a reformed and modernized form of liturgy
for the cathedral. The centrality of the altar may not be 'merely something architectural', but it still might be left to fight the architecture.
The rather lame defence by Bardsley and Spence was that the whole
cathedral was an altar at the centre of the life of the cathedral and
city.[45] It appears to be without any irony that Bardsley writes:

> Today, thank God, nobody could accuse the Church of being cowardly
> or merely imitative of a bygone age. We are beginning to realise that
> sham Gothic just will not do. Once again we must express our faith in
> terms that will be understood by a modern generation. The Church
> must be seen to be adventurous and forward looking.[46]

Modernity in both liturgy and architecture is more than mere style. In
his book *Liturgy and Architecture*, Peter Hammond was damning:

> The new cathedral at Coventry has already been hailed as a modern
> church, wholly of its time. I believe that this is a highly superficial
> judgement: that it is in fact a building which contributes nothing to
> the solution of the real problems of church design and perpetuates a

conception of a church which owes far more to the romantic movement than to the New Testament or authentic Christian tradition. The fundamental problem which we have to face today is one not of style but of *function*.[47]

For Hammond, as against Bishop Bardsley, the altar had to be in a tectonic, structural, and liturgically functional relationship with the built form housing it—that is to say, precisely, but not 'merely', 'something architectural'. This was the line of exploration taken by continental, especially German, architects such as Schwartz and Böhm in the tradition of rationalists like Berlage.

Liturgical Reform

The cathedral was consecrated in 1962, the tercentenary of the Book of Common Prayer, enshrined as the legal standard for liturgy in the worship conducted by the Church of England, and still in regular use for the offices in Coventry today. In 1964, H. C. N. Williams, Provost of Coventry, *published 20th Century Cathedral: An Examination of the Role of Cathedrals in the Strategy of the Church in the Changing Pattern of a Twentieth Century Community*. In that book, the provost outlined his approach to a modern liturgy. That approach was very Cranmerian, in that, just as Cranmer had done in the compilation of the Prayer Book, 'he refused to abandon the ancient liturgical forms as urged by the extreme reformers, and tried to put the old offices into a shape that would express the new teaching and make it popular with the laity'.[48]

   Williams contended that the balance between word and sacrament had been 'overweighted in favour of the latter by the Oxford Movement',[49] and he describes the current services in the cathedral as informally presented and involving the laity in readings, responses, offertory, intercessions, and even the baking of the bread for the altar. All those involved in the liturgy would process together into the sanctuary and surround the altar at the beginning of the Ministry of the Sacrament. This is another possibility for 'placing the eucharist at the heart of the community', which Williams maintained: 'By making use of the flexible possibilities of the building, the absolute validity of the Form of the Holy Communion devised in 1662, requiring no changes in words, has been convincingly demonstrated.'[50] For Williams, both the flexible style of the presentation of the liturgy and the flexible possibilities of the architecture played their part in this modern celebration in the twentieth-century cathedral, while demonstrating the 'absolute validity' of 1662. This was clearly Williams fighting a rearguard action against criticism of the likes of Peter Hammond in Liturgy and Architecture, who argued that Coventry failed to establish a theological and liturgical programme as the function that would give rise to the necessary architectural form. He wrote in connection with Coventry:

> What really matters is whether or not the building embodies a modern understanding of the Christian mystery; whether or not it is informed by a theological programme which takes account of the new insights of biblical theology and patristic and liturgical scholarship. If it is not so informed, then no amount of contemporary detail, no glass or sculpture or painting, however fine in itself, can make that building a modern church.[51]

The next year, and this is where the Phoenix may have risen too soon, on 4 December 1963, the Second Vatican Council published the Constitution on the Sacred Liturgy. 'In the restoration and promotion of the sacred liturgy the full and active participation by all the people is the aim to be considered before all else, for it is the primary and indispensable source from which the faithful are to derive a true Christian spirit.'[52] That full participation had the further consequence that the language of the Mass was to change from Latin to the vernacular; though it was intended that Latin would remain the language of the liturgy in some churches, many national hierarchies made that very difficult. The main modernizing thrust of the constitution tended to be pretty comprehensively applied.

There were architectural consequences to these Roman Catholic reforms, with the altar brought forward and the priest facing the people rather than the altarpiece on the east wall. There were places where that had always been the case, as at the ancient church of San Clemente in Rome, where it is physically impossible to celebrate at the altar facing east because of the floor levels. But that does not mean that this literal *volte face* by a highly centralized and hierarchical organization was not a sudden shock, even though the reforms took about a decade to achieve. The building that, despite its scale, most fully embodies the principles of Vatican II is the Roman Catholic Cathedral in Liverpool. Its designer, Frederick Gibberd, echoed Hammond in explaining: 'You only get architecture by a strict discipline. This discipline begins with an analysis of the purpose of the building, its function. You do not start by striving after visual effect. If you pursue beauty, charm, the picturesque, or monumentality the result is likely to be decorative, not architectural.'[53] Gibberd, like Spence, had won the competition to build the cathedral, but, unlike the confused instructions at Coventry, in the competition for this Liverpool Cathedral the bishop wrote to the competitors:

> The high altar is the central feature of every Catholic church. It must be the focus of the new building. The trend of the liturgy is to associate the congregation ever more closely with the celebrant of the Mass. The ministers at the altar must not be remote figures. They must be in sight of the people with whom they offer the sacrifice.
>
> Holy Mass is the great mystery of faith. The high altar is not an ornament to embellish the cathedral building; the cathedral, on the contrary is built to enshrine the altar of sacrifice.[54]

Church, theology, liturgical thinking, and architect were all aligned, and the building was met with considerable excitement. Curiously, it was Hammond who 'rather acidly said . . . "Long thin churches are out and round churches with central altars are now the fashion"'. Gibberd ruefully quoted this as he tried to justify his radical design. There have been technical problems with the finished building, and in 2015, millions were spent resetting the glass in the huge lantern and the tiles on the massive ribs. There have been problems for the liturgy too, and Pope Benedict XVI began to argue that the Second Vatican Council has been misinterpreted as issuing a counsel of discontinuity and should be interpreted in terms of continuity with the tradition. That means that the emphasis on intimacy and the full participation of all has been achieved at the expense of the majesty and awe of the sacrifice of the Mass *ad orientem*, eastward facing, and in Latin.

The Phoenix

Was Coventry a 'Phoenix Too Soon' in liturgical terms? To be fair on Spence, he had long discussions with Bishop Gorton about the position of the choir and the relationship of the congregation with the sanctuary, altar, and clergy. They wanted the choir, the clergy, and the bishop behind the altar, which would have been brought right forward to the front of the sanctuary, but this, he reported, 'caused a near riot' on the Reconstruction Committee, and Spence was told to revert to his previous plan.[55]

Spence's book *Phoenix at Coventry* revealed a Romantic side, and Hammond complained that Coventry 'contributes nothing to the solution of the real problems of church design and perpetuates a conception of a church which owes far more to the romantic movement than to the New Testament or authentic Christian tradition'.[56] Kitty Hauser described the cathedral as 'Neo-Romantic archaeological imagination in architectural form' and connected neo-romanticism generally to nationalism, saying: 'Well suited, as we have seen, to the conditions of war, Neo-Romanticism also found a place in the immediate post-war years, when its nationalist orientation could be applied to a broad concern with the survival of the national spirit.'[57]

Britain had met the architectural and national crisis square on with a compromise. The reconstruction of Coventry Cathedral with the participation of so many interest groups, both secular and lay, national and local, was the symbol of national reconstruction—the brief for the competition was a compromise among a whole range of differing positions; the panel of judges was carefully balanced to represent that compromise. 'Cometh the hour, cometh the man', they say, and Basil Spence produced the perfect compromise scheme, precisely embodying 'the spirit of the age', bright, optimistic, just a little naive, all rather fixed in the Festival of Britain, and sadly difficult to use—even now at Coventry, form frustrates function.

But that is also to draw the function narrowly in terms of the Eucharistic Service, while for a cathedral there is much more besides, and Coventry continues to inspire, impress, and recall that moment in history at which, and for which, it was built. It recalls strength of faith in adversity, and all the foibles that have gone into this tale—and yes, it is a great (functional) multifaceted project to the honour and glory of God in Christ and that peace that the world cannot give. That is the theological rather than the Romantic side, and, measured against that, the cathedral is a success in its direct and bold communication of the lessons of history.

This modern 'Battle of the Styles' was occasioned by confusion as to whether the cathedral was to be a monument to a historic moment of costly victory, or a place to celebrate a changed world and to participate in that change. Style involves deliberate aesthetic choices and does not spring fully formed from function. The choices made speak loudly and polemically, rhetorically even, of the architect's, client's, and patron's conception of their place in history—and these are the 'flames' that give such life as may be to whatever 'phoenix' arises.

Notes

INTRODUCTION

1. Eusebius, *Life of Constantine*, trans. and ed. Averil Cameron and Stuart G. Hall (Oxford: Oxford University Press, 1999), III.28, p. 133.

CHAPTER I

1. For an extended discussion of the Status Quo, see Raymond Cohen, *Saving the Holy Sepulchre: How Rival Christians Came Together to Rescue their Holiest Shrine* (Oxford: Oxford University Press, 2008), 612; the relevant information is on pp. 8–9.
2. Kathleen M. Kenyon, *Jerusalem: Excavating 3000 Years of History* (London: Thames and Hudson, 1967), 154 'can be authentic'; Shimon Gibson, *The Final Days of Jesus: The Archaeological Evidence* (Oxford: Lion Hudson, 2009), ch. 8, 'Who Moved the Stone?', 149–65, is cautiously positive, like Kenyon; see also Martin Biddle, *The Tomb of Christ* (Stroud: Sutton Publishing, 1999), 69–70; but there is also Jerome Murphy-O'Connor, *The Holy Land: An Oxford Archaeological Guide*, 5th edn (Oxford: Oxford University Press, 2008), 49, who ventures: 'Yes, very probably.' He has expanded this very positive response with a very strong extended argument in an article 'The Argument for the Holy Sepulchre', *Revue biblique*, 117/1 (January 2010), 55–91.
3. Gibson, *The Final Days of Jesus*, 7, accepts the date as 30; as does Martin Goodman, *Rome and Jerusalem: The Clash of Ancient Civilizations* (London: Penguin, 2008), 579; Simon Sebag Montefiore, *Jerusalem: The Biography* (London: Weidenfeld and Nicolson, 2011), prefers 33, but lays out the arguments 'most likely between 29 and 33' (p. 99 and n.); Géza Vermes, *The Resurrection: History and Myth* (London: Doubleday Books, 2008), is willing to be very specific: 'with the help of known astronomical data, the most likely date for the event—Friday, 7 April AD 30—corresponding to the eve of the Passover full moon' (p. 1); Montefiore, *Jerusalem*, 106, eventually goes for '14th of Nisan or Friday 3 April 33'.

4. For a map of the sites in the biblical narrative, see Meir Ben-Dov, *Historical Atlas of Jerusalem*, trans. David Louvish (New York and London: Continuum, 2002), 129; for Josephus, see *Josephus*, 10 vols; i–viii and x, trans. H. St J. Thackeray; ix, trans. Louis H. Feldman (Cambridge, MA: Harvard University Press; London: Heinemann, 1931); on the public works, see *Jewish Antiquities*, bk XVIII, sect. 59.2, in *Josephus*, trans. Feldman, ix. 47; not all of these public works were popular: the aqueduct was built with money from the temple treasury, which caused an uprising; on Herod the Great and Herod Antipas, see Gibson, *The Final Days of Jesus*, 38; on their prosperity, see Goodman, *Rome and Jerusalem*, *passim*, but see especially 7, 579.

5. Josephus, *The Jewish War*, bks IV–VII, in *Josephus*, trans. Thackeray, iii. 649, from the 'Slavonic 'Additions'. This and other additions may be Christian interpolations, but they are contained in a version that may 'have preserved, at least in part, the author's original draft of the *Jewish War*' (iii. 648–9).

6. The importance of the saying about the stone that the builders rejected is underlined by its appearance in Matt. 21:42, Mark 12:10–11, Luke 20:17, and the Acts 4:11, when Peter uses it in his defence following his arrest in the temple after the first healing by the apostles; the allusion is to Psalm 118:22.

7. On the date of the quarry, see Shimon Gibson and Joan E. Taylor, *Beneath the Holy Sepulchre, Jerusalem: The Archaeology and Early History of Traditional Golgotha* (London: Committee of the Palestine Exploration Fund, 1994), 16–17; also Murphy-O'Connor, 'The Argument for the Holy Sepulchre', 73; Gibson, *The Final Days of Jesus*, 117–22; and Charles Coüasnon, *The Church of the Holy Sepulchre in Jerusalem*, trans. J -P. and Claude Ross, The Schweich Lectures of the British Academy (London: Oxford University Press for the British Academy, 1972); for the authenticity of the site, see pp. 8–11; for Calvary itself, p. 39; and Kenyon, *Jerusalem*, 152–3.

8. Josephus, *Jewish Antiquities*, bk XVIII, sect. 63.3, in *Josephus*, trans. Feldman, ix. 49–51.

9. See Murphy-O'Connor, 'The Argument for the Holy Sepulchre', 63, and Murphy-O'Connor, *The Holy Land*, 50.

10. Magen Broshi, 'Excavations in the Holy Sepulchre in the Chapel of St Vartan and the Armenian Martyrs', in Yorem Tsafrir (ed.), *Ancient Churches Revealed* (Jerusalem: Israel Exploration Society, 1993), 118–22, at 121. But see Gibson and Taylor, *Beneath the Holy Sepulchre, Jerusalem*, 37–8, who think the mast was 'unstepped intentionally' and give a long discussion of the inscription; they note that Broshi ('Excavations', 352) believes

'that the drawing was executed by a Christian pilgrim at the time of the construction of the Constantinian building, circa 330', which they dispute, saying that 'the ship drawing was made during the 2nd century AD and that it is not the work of a Christian pilgrim of the fourth century…The precise meaning of the inscription and the identity of the artist remains a mystery' (p. 48); see also Colin Morris, in *The Sepulchre of Christ in the Medieval West: From the Beginning to 1600* (Oxford: Oxford University Press, 2005), 11, who considers it to be a pre-Constantinian pagan offering.

11. Kenyon, *Jerusalem*, 153; Montefiore, *Jerusalem* (caption to the illustration between pp. 94 and 95), considers that it possibly dates from around 33 AD.

12. See also Luke 4–31.

13. See also Luke 4.38–9.

14. Trans. in Mary Beard, John North, and Simon Price, *Religions of Rome*, i. *A History*; ii. *A Sourcebook* (Cambridge: Cambridge University Press, 1998), ii. 337; for the meal in the Jerusalem church and the possible use of the courtyards for the congregation, see Dennis E. Smith, *From Symposium to Eucharist: The Banquet in the Early Christian World* (Minneapolis: Fortress Press, 2003), especially 179 ff.; James F. Strange and Hershel Shanks, 'Has the House where Jesus Stayed in Capernaum Been Found?', *Biblical Archaeology Review*, 8/6 (November–December 1982), 26–37, question whether it was a house church; Sean Freyne, in 'A Galilean Messiah?', *Studia Theologica*, 55 (2001), 198–218, interprets the 'room' as just another courtyard.

15. Tertullian, *Apology*, trans. S. Thelwall, in Alexander Roberts and James Donaldson (eds), *The Ante-Nicene Fathers: Translations of the Writings of the Fathers down to AD 325* (1884), rev. A. Cleveland Cox (Grand Rapids, MI: Eerdmans, 1973), iii. 46–7.

16. See Stanislao Loffreda, *Recovering Capharnaum*, 2nd edn (Jerusalem: Franciscan Printing Press, 1993), 32–64; quotation from the text preserved in 'Peter the Deacon's Book on the Holy Places', trans. in *Egeria's Travels*, ed. and trans. John Wilkinson, 3rd edn (Warminster: Aris and Phillips, 2002), 97; but caution has to be exercised in ascribing sections of Peter the Deacon's book to Egeria; see Anne McGowan and Paul F. Bradshaw, *The Pilgrimage of Egeria: A New Translation of the* Itinerarium Egeriae *with Introduction and Commentary* (Collegeville, MN: Liturgical Press Academic, 2018), 17.

17. There has been a long-standing controversy whether Peter ever came to Rome. The current debate in its various dimensions represented by a range of authors is to be found in S. Heid (ed.), *Petrus und Paulus in*

Rom: eine interdisziplinäre Debatte (Freiburg: Herder, 2011), well summarized by Markus Bockmuehl in a detailed review where he concludes: 'The overwhelming opposition to Otto Zwierlein's unnecessarily sceptical construal of the sources nevertheless allows a clear if slightly lopsided consensus to emerge on certain points: even though the presence and martyrdom of Peter and Paul cannot straightforwardly be derived from any one early document, it nevertheless follows reasonably from the cumulative weight of complex literary, archaeological, liturgical and traditional sources.' *A Journal of Biblical Textual Criticism*, vol. 17 (2012), open access electronic journal accessed on 20 August 2019. See also Otto Zweirlein, *Petrus in Rom: die Literarischen Zeugnisse*, 2nd edition (Berlin and New York: De Gruyter, 2016), and Brent D. Shaw, 'The Myth of the Neronian Persecution', in *The Journal of Roman Studies*, no 105 (2015), 73–100, arguing that it was propaganda by Tacitus. There is a rejoinder by Christopher Jones, in 'The Historicity of the Neronian Persecution: A Response to Brent Shaw', in *New Testament Studies*, vol. 63, issue 1 (January 2017), 146–52.

18. See Goodman, *Rome and Jerusalem*, 580–1.
19. Josephus, *The Jewish War*, VII.3.1, in *Josephus*, trans. Thackeray, iii. 307.
20. Josephus, *The Jewish War*, VII.v.5, in *Josephus*, trans. Thackeray, iii. 351–5.
21. See Montefiore, *Jerusalem*, 129–30.
22. Quoted in *Egeria's Travels*, ed. and trans. Wilkinson, 10.
23. Eusebius, *The History of the Church from Christ to Constantine*, ed. Andrew Louth, trans. G. A. Williamson (London: Penguin, 1989), sect. 8.6, p. 111.
24. Eusebius, *History of the Church*, sect. 4.6, p. 108.
25. Eusebius, *History of the Church*, sect. 6.11, p. 189.
26. Origen, *Commentary on Matthew 27*, 32–3, and Fred Norris, 'Origen', in Philip Esler (ed.), *The Early Christian World* (London and New York: Routledge, 2000), 1005–26; Jerome, *Commentary on Ephesians*, 5.18, on the verse 'Awake, O sleeper, and arise from the dead and Christ shall give you light'; see Dennis Brown, 'Jerome', in Esler (ed.), *The Early Christian World*, ii. 1151–74, at 1168.
27. The earlier account is in Lactantius, *De Mortibus Persecutorum*, 44.5, trans. J. L. Creed (Oxford: Oxford University Press, 1984), 63; the other is in Eusebius, *Life of Constantine*, trans. and ed. Averil Cameron and Stuart G. Hall (Oxford: Oxford University Press, 1999), I.28–9, pp. 80–1. For a fuller discussion of the issues surrounding Constantine's conversion, see Allan Doig, 'Constantine, Continuity and Change', in Doig, *Liturgy and Architecture: From the Early Church to the Middle Ages* (Aldershot: Ashgate, 2008), 21–52, at 21–4, and Bill Leadbetter, 'Constantine', in Esler (ed.), *The Early Christian World*, ii. 1069–87, at 1071–5.

28. G. W. Bowersock has raised an interesting question about the dating of St Peter's to the time of Constantine in 'Peter and Constantine', in William Tronzo (ed.), *St Peter's in the Vatican* (Cambridge: Cambridge University Press, 2005), 5–15; he is sceptical about the Constantinian connection and believes 'it was very probably Constans', Constantine's son, who built St Peter's (see p. 13).

29. Eusebius, *Life of Constantine*, II.65.1, p. 116.

30. Eusebius, *Life of Constantine*, III.15.2, p. 127.

31. Eusebius, *Life of Constantine*, II.46.3, p. 111 I.28–9. For a fuller discussion of the issues surrounding Constantine's conversion, see Doig, 'Constantine, Continuity and Change', 21–52, at 21–4; and Bill Leadbetter, 'Constantine', in Esler (ed.), *The Early Christian World*, ii. 1069–87, at 1071–5; the letter to Eusebius is in *Life of Constantine*, II.46.1–3.

32. Eusebius, *Life of Constantine*, III.31, p. 135.

33. Eusebius, *Life of Constantine*, III.26.2, p. 132.

34. Murphy-O'Connor, 'The Argument for the Holy Sepulchre', 58; see also Morris, *The Sepulchre of Christ in the Medieval West*, 22–4, on the discovery of the cross.

35. See Murphy-O'Connor, *The Holy Land*, 59–62, and 'The Argument for the Holy Sepulchre', 59; on the reuse of materials, see also Gibson and Taylor, *Beneath the Church of the Holy Sepulchre, Jerusalem*; for other Hadrianic work, see 'Hadrianic Walls', 17–19; for the bisected column, see Coüasnon, *The Church of the Holy Sepulchre in Jerusalem*, 30–2 and plate XIX; Denys Pringle, *The Churches of the Crusader Kingdom of Jerusalem: A Corpus*, iii. *The City of Jerusalem* (Cambridge: Cambridge University Press, 2007), 7, identifies them as first to third century; Murphy-O'Connor, *The Holy Land*, 56, says it 'graced either the Capitoline Temple of Hadrian or the C4 Holy Sepulchre', and it is difficult to see where it would have come from in the fourth-century Holy Sepulchre.

36. Eusebius, *Life of Constantine*, III.28, p. 133.

37. See the caption to the illustration of the ship graffiti in Montefiori, *Jerusalem*, between pp. 94 and 95.

38. Eusebius, *Life of Constantine*, III.30.4, p. 134.

39. Murphy-O'Connor ('The Argument for the Holy Sepulchre', 59) believes this to be a reference to the True Cross, as did Edward Yarnold before him in *Cyril of Jerusalem* (London and New York: Routledge, 2000), 14, while Cameron and Hall (in Eusebius, *Life of Constantine*, 279–81, 282–3) present an extended argument to establish that it refers to the tomb, presenting a discussion of the work of other scholars.

40. Eusebius, *Life of Constantine*, III.31.3–32.2, p. 135.

41. See Yarnold, *Cyril of Jerusalem*, 18–19; Yarnold sees the dome in the apse mosaic as the east end of the Martyrium but thinks it was a complete dome, as do Gibson and Taylor, *Beneath the Holy Sepulchre, Jerusalem*; the various interpretations in the end remain informed conjecture; but see also Wilkinson in *Egeria's Travels*, 20, n. 4; also Richard Krautheimer, *Early Christian and Byzantine Architecture*, 4th edn (London: Penguin, 1986), 60–3; concerning the Rotunda, see Coüasnon, *The Church of the Holy Sepulchre in Jerusalem*, 15–16.

42. Eusebius, *Life of Constantine*, III.33.3 and III.34, p. 135.

43. Eusebius, *Life of Constantine*, III.33.1–2, p. 135.

44. See Murphy-O'Connor, *The Holy Land*, 75–7.

45. Trans. Wilkinson, in *Egeria's Travels*, 31–4.

46. Pringle, *The Churches of the Crusader Kingdom of Jerusalem*, iii. 7.

47. Eusebius, *Life of Constantine*, I.32.2, p. 82.

48. See Biddle, *The Tomb of Christ*, 65.

49. Eusebius, *Life of Constantine*, III.31.3, p. 135.

CHAPTER 2

1. For an outline of the current debate whether Peter ever reached Rome and whether there was a Neronian persecution, see chapter 1 footnote 17.

2. See Richard A. Etlin, 'St Peter's in the Modern Era', in William Tronzo (ed.), *St Peter's in the Vatican* (Cambridge: Cambridge University Press, 2005), 270–304, at 294.

3. Josephus, *The Life*, I.3–4, in *Josephus*, 10 vols; i–viii and x, trans. H. St J. Thackeray; ix, trans. Louis H. Feldman (Cambridge, MA: Harvard University Press; London: Heinemann, 1931), i. 9.

4. Irenaeus of Lyons, *Against Heresies*, III.3.2, trans. Robert M. Grant, *Irenaeus of Lyons* (London and New York: Routledge, 1997), 57–186, at 124–5.

5. Richard Krautheimer, *Corpus Basilicarum Christianarum Romae: The Early Christian Basilicas of Rome (IV–IX Century)*, v. (Vatican City: Pontificio Instituto di Archeologia Cristiana, 1977), 182; this gives a detailed summary of the archaeology of the site.

6. Quoted by Eusebius, *The History of the Church from Christ to Constantine*, ed. Andrew Louth, trans. G. A. Williamson (London: Penguin, 1989), II.25, p. 63.

7. Cyprian, 'On the Unity of the Catholic Church', 4–6, Corpus Scriptorum Ecclesiasticorum Latinorum, III.i.212–15, trans. in *A New Eusebius: Documents Illustrative of the History of the Church to AD 337*, ed. J. Stephenson (London: SPCK, 1968), 243–4.

8. 'Letter of Firmilian, Bishop of Caesarea in Cappadocia, to Cyprian on the Rebaptism of Heretics' (Cyprian, *Ep.* LXXV. 17, trans. Stephenson, in *A New Eusebius*, 255.

9. Clark Hopkins, *The Discovery of Dura Europos* (New Haven: Yale University Press, 1984), 95.

10. For more on Dura Europos, see Allan Doig, *Liturgy and Architecture: From the Early Church to the Middle Ages* (Aldershot: Ashgate, 2008), 10–18.

11. For greater detail concerning the excavations under St Peter's, see Paulo Liverani, 'L'area vaticana e la necropoli prima della Basilica', in Maria Grazia Mattioni and Serenella Sancese (eds), Cristina Carlo-Stella (executive ed.), *Petros Eni; Pietro è Qui: Catalogo della Mostra, Città del Vaticano, Braccio di Carlo Magno, 11 ottobre 2006–8 marzo 2007* (Vatican: Fabbrica di San Pietro, 2006), 173–81 and the related catalogue entries that follow on pp. 174–95.

12. See Carlo-Stella (ed.), *Petros Eni*, 188–90, catalogue entry IV.6 on the 'Volta con figura del Cristo-Sol', and John Beckwith, *Early Christian and Byzantine Art* (New Haven and London: Yale University Press 1979), 19.

13. *Biblical Archaeologist*, 2/3 (September 1939), 34.

14. *Biblical Archaeologist*, 2/3 (September 1939), 35.

15. Pope Pius XII, *Summi Pontificatus*, sect. 104.

16. Engelbert Kirschbaum and Antonio Ferrua, advised by Bruno Apollonj-Ghetti and Enrico Josi.

17. The bones were identified by Margherita Guarducci; Ferrua's obituary in *The Times*, 13 June 2003, emphasized his scepticism; Father Antonio Ferrua, SJ, Jesuit priest and archaeologist, was born on 31 March 1901; he died on 25 May 2003, aged 102.

18. G. W. Bowersock ('Peter and Constantine', in Tronzo (ed.), *St Peter's in the Vatican*, 5–15) has raised an interesting question about the dating of St Peter's to the time of Constantine; he is sceptical about the Constantinian connection and believes 'it was very probably Constans', Constantine's son (p. 13).

19. See R. Ross Holloway, 'The Tomb of St Peter', in Holloway, *Constantine and Rome* (New Haven and London: Yale University Press, 2004), 120–55.

20. The *ex voto* is detailed in Carlo-Stella (ed.), *Petros Eni*, 182; for details of the offerings, see Holloway, 'The Tomb of St Peter', 139.

21. Quoted in Holloway, 'The Tomb of St Peter', 151.

22. Holloway ('The Tomb of St Peter') believes that the bodies of Peter and Paul were buried in San Sebastiano (as quoted (p. 154)). Holloway discusses the varying hypotheses on pp. 150–3. Bowersock ('Peter and Constantine') considers this 'extravagant speculation' (p. 6) and that it is pointless to speculate 'whether bones were translated' (p. 7). See

also the discussion of the documentary evidence in Henry Chadwick, *The Church in Ancient Society: From Galilee to Gregory the Great* (Oxford: Oxford University Press, 2001), 321–5.

23. Catalogue entry by Danilo Mazzolini (IV.9) for the plaster fragment with graffiti from the *triclia* in San Sebastiano in Carlo-Stella (ed.), *Petros Eni*, 193–4; the second option is maintained by Holloway ('The Tomb of St Peter'); Paulo Liverani is a powerful advocate along with Mazzolini of the former.

24. Krautheimer, *Corpus Basilicarum Christianarum Romae*, v. 173; and p. 84 for the refrigeria.

25. Krautheimer, *Corpus Basilicarum Christianarum Romae*, v. 172; but Bowerstock ('Peter and Constantine', 11) reads the brickstamps to be from the reign of Constantine's son Constans.

26. See Doig, *Liturgy and Architecture*, 24–5.

27. Richard Krautheimer, *Early Christian and Byzantine Architecture*, 4th edn (London: Penguin, 1986), 56.

28. Krautheimer, *Corpus Basilicarum Christianarum Romae*, v. 97.

29. Eusebius, *Life of Constantine*, trans. and ed. Averil Cameron and Stuart G. Hall (Oxford: Oxford University Press, 1999), I.28–9, p. 81.

30. J. H. Jongkees, *Studies in Old St Peter's*, Archaeologica Traiectina series, Edita AB, Academiae Rheno-Traiectinae Instituto Archaeologico, VIII (Groningen: J. B. Wolters, 1966), 37–40.

31. See the discussion in Doig, *Liturgy and Architecture*, 25–6.

32. See Chadwick, *The Church in Ancient Society*, 315–21, at 21.

33. See Diarmaid MacCulloch, *A History of Christianity: The First Three Thousand Years* (London: Penguin, Allen Lane, 2009), 296.

CHAPTER 3

1. See Henri Grégoire, 'The Byzantine Church', in N. H. Baynes and H. St B. Moss (eds), *Byzantium: An Introduction to East Roman Civilization* (Oxford: Oxford University Press, 1962), 99–101.

2. Procopius, *History of the Wars*, I.xxiv.37–43, trans. H. B. Dewing, Loeb Classical Library, 6 vols (London: Heinemann; Cambridge, MA: Harvard University Press, 1961), i. 231–3; ch. xxiv provides the narrative of the Nika insurrection.

3. *Chronicon Paschale*, 1.544, trans. in Cyril Mango (ed.), *The Art of the Byzantine Empire, 312–1453: Sources and Documents* (Toronto: University of Toronto Press, 1986); first published in the series Sources and Documents in the History of Art, ed. H. W. Jansen (New York: Prentice Hall, 1972), 26.

4. Jonathan Shepard, review of Constantine Porphyrogenitus, *The Book of Ceremonies and Pseudo-Kodinos and the Constantinopolitan Court: Offices and Ceremonies*, in *English Historical Review*, 130/545 (August 2015), 949–52, at 949.

5. See Averil Cameron, *Procopius and the Sixth Century* (London: Duckworth, 1985), 7–8.

6. Procopius, *Buildings*, I.i.5–15, trans. Dewing, vii. 7.

7. Procopius, *Buildings*, I.ii.5–12, trans. Dewing, vii. 35.

8. Procopius, *Buildings*, I.x.10, trans. Dewing, vii. 85.

9. Procopius, *Buildings*, I.x.16–21, trans. Dewing, vii. 87.

10. Procopius, *Buildings*, I.i.16, trans. Dewing, vii. 9.

11. Procopius, *Buildings*, I.i.20–3, trans. Dewing, vii. 9–11.

12. Procopius, *Buildings*, I.i.69–78, trans. Dewing, vii. 29–31.

13. For a fuller version of the prayer, see Alexander van Millingen, *Byzantine Constantinople: The Walls of the City and Adjoining Historical Sites* (1899; Cambridge: Cambridge University Press, 2010, online 2011), 332.

14. *Patria Constant.*, 145, trans. in Mango (ed.), *The Art of the Byzantine Empire*, 29–30; two head-reliquaries of John the Baptist containing parts of his cranium and his arm-reliquary are still to be found in the Topkapi Palace.

15. Paul the Silentiary, *Desc. S. Sophiae*, trans. in Mango (ed.), *The Art of the Byzantine Empire*, 80–91, at 85. The precise location of the *metatorion* has long been a subject of debate, and Rowland J. Mainstone, *Hagia Sophia: Architecture, Structure and Liturgy of Justinian's Great Church* (London: Thames and Hudson, 1997), 65–6, weighs up the arguments between Thomas Mathews, (*The Early Churches of Constantinople: Architecture and Liturgy* (University Park, PA; London: University of Pennsylvania Press, 1971), 134), who thinks the throne was 'in the corner of the central bay that is nearest to the ambo and sanctuary', and C. Strube (review of Mathews, *The Early Churches of Constantinople*, in *Byzantinische Zeitschrift*, 67 (1974), 412), who 'argued that the spacing of the sockets is too irregular to have served as fixings for a throne'. Mainstone favours the area on the south side of the eastern bay of the south aisle as more likely. On the other hand, there is a group of sockets in the former area that are regularly spaced if others are considered to be for a different use at another date. The regularly spaced sockets would provide for a double screen towards the nave and a group of four on a square plan providing a base for a throne. To the west of that group of four, marks on the pavement may indicate steps to an elevated throne. There are further lines of sockets that would have provided for the area to be completely enclosed by screens.

16. Gilbert Dagron, *Emperor and Priest: The Imperial Office in Byzantium*, trans. Jean Birrell (Cambridge: Cambridge University Press, 2003), 61–3.

17. Procopius, *Buildings*, I.i.21, trans. Dewing, vii. 11.

18. Procopius, *Buildings*, I.i.60–2, trans. Dewing, vii. 27.

19. See Agathias, *Hist.* V.9.2–5, and Theophanes, A.M. 6051, pp. 232–3, in Mango (ed.), *The Art of the Byzantine Empire*, 78–9.

20. Paul the Silentiary, *Desc. S. Sophiae*, trans. in Mango (ed.), *The Art of the Byzantine Empire*, 80–91, at 87.

21. The ekphrastic text is translated in Cyril Mango and John Parker, 'A Twelfth-Century Description of St Sophia', in Cyril Mango, *Studies on Constantinople*, Variorum Series (Aldershot: Ashgate, 1993), ch. xvii; first published in *Dumbarton Oaks Papers*, xi (Washington: Dumbarton Oaks, 1960), 233–45.

22. Michael, Rector of the Patriarchal Academy, trans. in Mango and Parker, 'A Twelfth-Century Description', in Mango, *Studies on Constantinople*, 239

23. Michael, trans. in Mango and Parker, 'A Twelfth-Century Description', in Mango, *Studies on Constantinople*, 239.

24. Michael, trans. in Mango and Parker, 'A Twelfth-Century Description', in Mango, *Studies on Constantinople*, 240.

25. Paul the Silentiary, *Descr. Ambones*, V.224, trans. in Mango, *The Art of the Byzantine Empire*, 91–6, at 95.

26. Eusebius, *Oration on the Tricennalia of Constantine*, trans. in *A New Eusebius: Documents Illustrative of the History of the Church to AD 337*, ed. J. Stephenson (London: SPCK, 1968), 391–92, at 391.

27. Eusebius, *Oration*, in *A New Eusebius*, ed. Stephenson, 392.

28. Trans. in John Meyendorff, *Imperial Unity and Christian Divisions: The Church 450–680 AD* (Crestwood, NY: St Vladimir's Seminary Press, 1989), 209, where there is valuable discussion.

29. See *The History of the Church from Christ to Constantine*, ed. Andrew Louth, trans. G. A. Williamson (London: Penguin, 1989), IX.9.20.821, p. 293; *Life of Constantine*, trans. and ed. Averil Cameron and Stuart G. Hall (Oxford: Oxford University Press, 1999), I.38.2, p. 84; Dagron, *Emperor and Priest*, 98.

30. Dagron, *Emperor and Priest*, 105–9.

31. See Charlotte Roueché, 'The Factions and Entertainment', in Brigitte Pitarkis (ed.), *Hippodrome: A Stage for Istanbul's History*, i (Istanbul: Pera Museum Publication 39, 2010), 50–64, at 56–7, especially fig. 4.7

32. Cyril Mango, 'A History of the Hippodrome of Constantinople', in Pitarkis (ed.), *Hippodrome: A Stage for Istanbul's History*, i. 36–43, at 41; and J. M. Featherstone, 'The Great Palace as Reflected in the *De Ceremoniis*', in *Visualisierungen von Herrschaft: Frühmittelalterliche Residenzen Gestalt*

und Zeremoniell, in *Byzas*, 5 (Istanbul: Ege Yayinlari/German Institute of Archaeology, 2006), 47–60, at 58.

CHAPTER 4

1. *The Russian Primary Chronicle*, trans. and ed. S. H. Cross and O. P. Sherbowitz-Wetzor (Cambridge, MA: Mediaeval Academy of America, 1953), 10.
2. See Dimitry Obolensky, 'Medieval Russian Culture in the Writings of D. S. Likhachev', in Obolensky, *The Byzantine Inheritance of Eastern Europe* (London: Variorum Reprints, 1982), ix. 1–16, at 3; first published in *Oxford Slavonic Papers*, 9 (1976), 1–16.
3. *Russian Primary Chronicle*, 3.
4. *Russian Primary Chronicle*, 7–8.
5. Dimitry Obolensky, 'The Byzantine Sources on the Scandinavians in Eastern Europe', in *Varangian Problems. Scando-Slavica*, suppl. 1 (Athens: Athenai, 1980), repr. in Oblensky, *The Byzantine Inheritance of Eastern Europe*, vi. 149–64, at 151, where he makes it clear that he believed the attacks were by Scandinavians, or Northmen.
6. Jonathan Shepard, 'Rus'', in Nora Berend (ed.), *Christianization and the Rise of Christian Monarchy: Scandinavia, Central Europe and Rus', c.900–1200* (Cambridge: Cambridge University Press, 2007), 369–416, at 379–80.
7. Trans. in W. R. Lethaby and Harold Swainson, *The Church of Sancta Sophia Constantinople: A Study of Byzantine Building* (London and New York: Macmillan, 1894), 101.
8. A. P. Vlasto, *The Entry of the Slavs into Christendom: An Introduction to the Medieval History of the Slavs* (Cambridge: Cambridge University Press, 1970), 250.
9. Shepard, 'Rus'', 381.
10. Shepard, 'Rus'', 374–5.
11. *Russian Primary Chronicle*, 10; see also Diarmaid MacCulloch, *A History of Christianity: The First Three Thousand Years* (London: Penguin, 2009), 506; and Vlasto, *The Entry of the Slavs into Christendom*, 255–6.
12. Hubert Faensen and Vladimir Ivanov, *Early Russian Architecture*, trans. Mary Whittall (London: Paul Elek, 1972), 13.
13. Analysis and comment on Rus' polity are from Shepard, 'Rus'', 384.
14. *Primary Chronicle*, quoted in Shepard, 'Rus'', 384.
15. Vlasto, *The Entry of the Slavs into Christendom*, 262.
16. Shepard, 'Rus'', 386.

17. William Craft Brumfield, *A History of Russian Architecture* (Cambridge: Cambridge University Press, 1993), 11.

18. See M. Karger, *Novgorod the Great*, trans. K. M. Cook (Moscow: Progress Publishers, 1973), 30.

19. Quoted in Shepard, 'Rus", 402.

20. See A. Chiniakov, with M. Fehner, V. Ivanov, M. Rudko, and S. Zemtzov (eds), *Preservation and Restoration of Monuments of Architecture in the USSR* (Moscow: Soiuz arkhitektorov, 1964), 11–12, where the research and conservation of the interior by I. Morgilevsky and the architects Y. Aseyev and P. Yurchenko are described.

21. Dimitry Obolensky, 'The Byzantine Impact on Eastern Europe' (Athens: Athenai, 1980), repr. in Obolensky, *The Byzantine Inheritance of Eastern Europe*, iii. 148–68, at 167; iv. 3–20, at 5; and xv. 1–16, at 14.

22. Brumfield, *A History of Russian Architecture*, 26.

23. David Roden Buxton, *Russian Mediaeval Architecture: With an Account of the Transcaucasian Styles and their Influence in the West* (Cambridge: Cambridge University Press, 1934), 18; also Faensen and Ivanov, *Early Russian Architecture*, 360.

24. Brumfield, *A History of Russian Architecture*, 28.

25. Karger, *Novgorod the Great*, 14.

26. Karger, *Novgorod the Great*, 40–1.

27. Chiniakov et al. (eds), *Preservation and Restoration of Monuments of Architecture in the USSR*, 8.

28. Buxton, *Russian Mediaeval Architecture*, 28, and Faensen and Ivanov, *Early Russian Architecture*, 399.

29. Brumfield, *A History of Russian Architecture*, 95.

30. Brumfield, *A History of Russian Architecture*, 84.

31. Shepard, 'Rus", 394.

32. Nikolai Voronin and Stanislav Maslenitsyn, *Vladimir: Architectural Landmarks* (Leningrad: Aurora, 1988), 19–27, 34.

33. Faensen and Ivanov, *Early Russian Architecture*, 399.

34. The dating is in Michael S. Flier, 'The Throne of Monomakh: Ivan the Terrible and the Architectonics of Destiny', in James Cracraft and Daniel Rowland (eds), *Architectures of Russian Identity: 1500 to the Present* (Ithaca, NY, and London: Cornell University Press, 2003), 21–33, at 27.

35. On Constantine and the problem of imperial presence at a liturgy, see Allan Doig, *Liturgy and Architecture: From the Early Church to the Middle Ages* (Aldershot: Ashgate, 2008), 52. See also Flier, 'The Throne of Monomakh', 21; also pp. 23–4 on the position of the throne and the cooperation of Tsar and Patriarch; and p. 30 on the small Zion.

36. Faensen and Ivanov, *Early Russian Architecture*, 401.

37. See Chiniakov et al. (eds), *Preservation and Restoration of Monuments of Architecture in the USSR*, 7; also Faensen and Ivanov, *Early Russian Architecture*, 402.

38. Faensen and Ivanov, *Early Russian Architecture*, 403.

39. Kathleen Berton, *Moscow: An Architectural History* (London: Studio Vista, 1977), 199.

40. Chiniakov et al. (eds), *Preservation and Restoration of Monuments of Architecture in the USSR*, 5–6.

41. Berton, *Moscow*, 27.

42. Details are in Alec Luhn, 'Moscow's Tonic for the Troops is a New Army of Battlefield Priests', *Daily Telegraph*, Saturday, 29 December 2019, 18–19, at 19.

43. Roman Olearchyk, 'Church Split Marks Victory for Ukraine', *Financial Times*, Monday, 7 January 2019, front page.

CHAPTER 5

1. Thanks to Isabel Blumenroth of the Department of History, RWTH, Aachen, for pointing this out. I am also indebted to Professor Max Kerner of the department, and most especially to Dombaumeister Helmut Mainz for sharing his intimate knowledge of the building.

2. Einhard, *Life of Charlemagne*, ch. XVIII, in Einhard and Notker the Stammerer, *Two Lives of Charlemagne*, trans. and intro. David Ganz (London: Penguin, 2008), 30.

3. See Allan Doig, *Liturgy and Architecture: From the Early Church to the Middle Ages* (Aldershot: Ashgate, 2008), 114–17, and see the panel of the 'Women at the Tomb', *c*.420, in the British Museum, illustrated in Colin Morris, *The Sepulchre of Christ and the Medieval West: From the Beginning to 1600* (Oxford: Oxford University Press, 2005), 74, and noted in Peter Lasko, *Ars Sacra, 800–1200*, 2nd edn (New Haven and London: Yale University Press, 1994), 11; the knockers from the Hospital of the Knights of St John were excavated on the site of the original hospital in Jerusalem and are in the Museum of the Order of St John of Jerusalem in London, items LDO SJ 5616 & 5617.

4. See the catalogue of the Aachener Domschätze by Herta Lepie and Georg Minkenberg, trans. Manjula Dias Hargarter, as *The Cathedral Treasury of Aachen* (Regensberg: Schnell and Steiner, 2010), 12; Lepie maintains that 'whether Charlemagne had the bronze brought to his castle in Aachen in order to establish it as a sign of the "Roma Secunda" is questionable and cannot be proven' (p. 12).

5. See Helmut Mainz, 'Dendrochronologische Datierung Holzringanker Oktogonkuppel und Fundamentholz Oktogonpfeiler Nr. 7', in Helmut Mainz, Ute Mainz, and Christine Kaiser (eds), *Dombaumeistertagung 2009: Europäische Vereinigung der Dombaumeister, Munsterbaumeister und Hüttenmeister* (Dombauleitung, Aachen, 2009), 145–50, at 148–9; also K. Reicherter, A. Schaub, T. M. Fernàndez-Steeger, T. Kohlberger-Schaub, and C. Grützner, 'Historische Erdbebenschäden im Dom zu Aachen: Aquisgrani terrae motus factus est', in Mainz, Mainz, and Kaiser (eds), *Dombaumeistertagung 2009*, 159–76, at 168, 73; for the dating of the consecration, see Rosamond McKitterick, *Charlemagne: The Formation of a European Identity* (Cambridge: Cambridge University Press, 2008), 339.

6. McKitterick, *Charlemagne*, 49–54, 155, 159; for the envoys hailing Charlemagne as *imperator* and *basileus*, see p. 281.

7. See Notker's description, in Einhard and Notker the Stammerer, *Two Lives of Charlemagne*, 92–7.

8. The background is admirably described in David Levering Lewis, *God's Crucible: Islam and the Making of Europe, 570–1215* (New York and London: Norton, 2008), 156–73; see also Jerrilyn D. Dodds, María Rosa Menocal, and Abigail Krasner Balbale, *The Arts of Intimacy: Christians, Jews, and Muslims in the Making of Castilian Culture* (New Haven and London: Yale University Press, 2008), 14.

9. McKitterick, *Charlemagne*, 70–1, gives detail; Charlemagne's age is calculated on pp. 72–3.

10. Gilbert Dagron, *Emperor and Priest: The Imperial Office in Byzantium*, trans. Jean Birrell (Cambridge: Cambridge University Press, 2003), 305.

11. Purse reliquary of St Stephen, in 2000 dated to 800 in Sven Schütte, 'Forschungen zum Aachener Thron', in Mainz, Mainz, and Kaiser (eds), *Dombaumeistertagung 2009*, 177–90, 188; Kunsthistorisches Museum, Vienna, Schatzkammer (SK XIII 26); illustrated in Martina Bagnoli, 'The Stuff of Heaven: Materials and Craftsmanship in Medieval Reliquaries', in Martina Bagnoli, Holger A. Klein, C. Griffith Mann, and James Robinson (eds), *Treasures of Heaven: Saints Relics and Devotion in Medieval Europe* (London: British Museum, 23 June–9 October 2011), 137–47, illustrated on p. 129.

12. For further discussion of the throne, see Allan Doig, 'Building, Enacting and Embodying *Romanitas*: The Throne of Charlemagne', in Ekaterina Staniukovich-Denisova and Anna Zakharova (eds), *Actual Problems of Theory and History of Art*, v (St Petersburg: Hirov, 2015), 376–82.

13. The research and conclusions are to be found in Schütte, 'Forschungen zum Aachener Thron', 177–90.

14. See Walter Ullmann, 'Ecclesiology and Carolingian Rulership', in Ullmann, *Carolingian Renaissance and the Idea of Kingship*, the Birkbeck Lectures, 1968–9 (London: Methuen, 1969), 43–70, at 50, for reference to the *Fürstenspiegel* by Maragdus; for the throne and its placing, see Schütte, 'Forschungen zum Aachener Thron', 189.

15. I am grateful to Richard Etlin for bringing this example to my attention.

16. See Henry Mayr-Harting, 'Charlemagne as a Patron of Art', in Diana Wood (ed.), *The Church and the Arts* (Oxford: Blackwell, 1992), 43–77, at 48–50.

17. See Notker's description in Einhard and Notker the Stammerer, *Two Lives of Charlemagne*, 36; for the pope's permission to remove marble, see McKitterick, *Charlemagne*, 339.

18. Ermold, *In honorem Hlodowici christianissimi Caesaris Augusti*, ed. E. Faral, in *Ermold le Noir: Poèm sur Louis le Pieux et épîtres au roi Pépin* (Paris: Les Classiques de l'histoire de France, 1932), ll. 2068–165, at ll. 2150–1, p. 164, quoted in McKitterick, *Charlemagne*, 164.

19. See D. P. S. Peacock, 'Charlemagne's Black Stones: The Re-Use of Roman Columns in Early Medieval Europe', *Antiquity*, 71 (1997), 709–15, at 712.

20. This has been convincingly argued in Morris, *The Sepulchre of Christ*, 153.

21. There has been a recent debate whether the use of *spolia* by Charlemagne was polemical or purely aesthetic; see Dale Kinney, 'The Discourse of Columns', in Claudia Bolga, Rosamond McKitterick, and John Osborne (eds), *Rome across Time and Space: Cultural Transmission and the Exchange of Ideas, c.500–1400* (Cambridge: Cambridge University Press, 2011), 182–99, at 197–8; the understanding of history and the role of liturgy, relics, and annals to religious and political ends is argued in Rosamond McKitterick, *Perceptions of the Past in the Early Middle Ages* (Notre Dame, IN: Notre Dame University Press, 2006); see the summary pp. 91–4.

22. The elders and their thrones are found in Rev. 4:2–7, the measurements are to be found in 21:17, and the gems in 21:19; Roger Stalley points out the relationship of the measurements in *Early Medieval Architecture* (Oxford: Oxford University Press, 1999), 73.

23. See especially Ullmann, 'Ecclesiology and Carolingian Rulership'; see p. 48 for the exaltation of the monarch and p. 43 for the *populus Dei*.

24. Bryan Ward-Perkins, *The Fall of Rome and the End of Civilization* (Oxford: Oxford University Press, 2005), 68–9; Cassiodorus, *Variae* III.17, in *The Letters of Cassiodorus, Being a Condensed Translation of the Variae Epistolae of Magnus Aurelius Cassiodorus, Senator*, intro. Thomas Hodgkin (London: Henry Frowde, 1886; Oxford: Horace Hart, 1886).

25. Cassiodorus, *Variae* III. 9; on *spolia*, see also Beat Brenk, 'Spolia from Constantine to Charlemagne: Aesthetics versus Ideology', *Dumbarton Oaks Papers*, 41 (1987), 103–9, especially 107–8, where he discusses 'Theodoric and the "Nova Gloria Vetustatis"' through Cassiodorus' *Variae*.

26. *Carolingian Chronicles: Royal Frankish Annals and Nithard's Histories*, trans. Bernhard Walter Scholz with Barbara Rogers (Ann Arbor: University of Michigan Press, 1970), 46.

27. Roger Collins, *Early Medieval Europe 300–1000*, 2nd edn (Basingstoke and New York: Palgrave, 1999), 280.

28. Walter Pohl, 'Invasions and Ethnic Identity', in Cristina La Rocca (ed.), *Italy in the Early Middle Ages 476–1000* (Oxford: Oxford University Press, 2002), 11–33, 28; Lewis, *God's Crucible*, 238–40.

29. The rulers are variously identified: as 'Saragossa's governor, Sulayman ibn Yaqzan' alone by Dodds, Menocal, and Balbale, *The Arts of Intimacy*, 18; as 'independent Arab rulers of Barcelona and Zaragoza' by Collins, *Early Medieval Europe*, 283; and as 'Sulayman ibn al-A'rabi, Abbasid *amir* of Barcelona and Girona, along with his co-conspirators, al-Hussayn ibn Sa'd ibn Ubada, *wali* of Zaragoza, and the unidentified *wali* of Huesca' by Lewis, *God's Crucible*, 244.

30. Lewis, *God's Crucible*, 244.

31. Einhard, *Life of Charlemagne*, ch. XVII, in Einhard and Notker the Stammerer, *Two Lives of Charlemagne*, 29–30; there is mention also by Notker on p. 94.

32. Janet L. Nelson, 'The Lord's Anointed and the People's Choice: Carolingian Royal Ritual', in David Cannadine and Simon Price (ed.), *Rituals of Royalty: Power and Ceremonial in Traditional Societies* (Cambridge: Cambridge University Press, 1987), 137–80, at 142–3, on Carolingian Royal ritual.

33. *Catalogue des abbés de Fleurie*, trans. Xavier Barral I Altet, *The Early Middle Ages: From Late Antiquity to AD 1000* (Cologne, London, and Madrid: Taschen, 2002), 137–8.

34. The inscription is translated in Paul Edward Dutton (ed.), *Carolingian Civilization: A Reader*, 2nd edn (Peterborough, Ontario: Broadview Press, 2004), 100. Copies of the palatine chapel in Aachen are discussed in Stalley, *Early Medieval Architecture*, 73–4, who notes the presence of the Virgin's shroud and the ability of the forms to convey a variety of meanings; and by Eva-Maria Wagner, in Louis Groedecki, *Pre-Romanesque Art*, ed. Harald Busch and Bernd Lohse (London: Batsford, 1966), pp. xxiii–xxiv.

35. See James L. Boone, 'The Parable of the Horseshoe Arch', in Boone, *Lost Civilization: The Contested Islamic Past in Spain and Portugal* (London: Duckworth, 2009), 128–34, especially 130–2.

36. Morris, *The Sepulchre of Christ*, 93–4; McKitterick, *Charlemagne*, 51.

37. Einhard, *Life of Charlemagne* II.16, trans. P. E. Dutton, in *Einhard: Vita Karoli Magni*, 6th edn, ed. G. Waitz, in *Monumenta germaniae Historica: Scriptores rerum Germanicarum in usum scholarum* (Hanover: Impensis Bibliopolii Aulici Hahniani, 1911; repr. 1965), repr. in Dutton (ed.), *Carolingian Civilization*, 26–49, at 37.

38. Morris, *The Sepulchre of Christ*, 96–7; Denys Pringle, *The Churches of the Crusader Kingdom of Jerusalem: A Corpus*, iii. *The City of Jerusalem* (Cambridge: Cambridge University Press, 2007), 10; on the keys, see McKitterick, *Charlemagne*, 371.

39. Kenneth John Conant, *Carolingian and Romanesque Architecture 800 to 1200* (New Haven and London: Yale University Press, 1978), 48.

40. On the question of Romanization, see also Yitzhak Hen, *Culture and Religion in Merovingian Gaul, AD 481–751* (New York: Brill, 1995), and also *The Royal Patronage of Liturgy in Frankish Gaul to the Death of Charles the Bald* (London: Boydell and Brewer, 2001).

41. Einhard, *Life of Charlemagne*, ch. XXXVII, in Einhard and Notker the Stammerer, *Two Lives of Charlemagne*, 36–7.

42. Notker, *The Deeds of Charlemagne*, sect. 7, in Einhard and Notker the Stammerer, *Two Lives of Charlemagne*, p. 60.

43. For Charles's grants of position or lands, see Notker, *The Deeds of Charlemagne*, sect. 13, in Einhard and Notker the Stammerer, *Two Lives of Charlemagne*, 64.

44. The extent of this patronage is noted by Chris Wickham, *The Inheritance of Rome: A History of Europe from 400 to 1000* (London: Penguin, 2010), 380–1.

45. See Denis Nineham, *Christianity, Medieval and Modern: A Study in Religious Change* (London: SCM Press, 1993), 28; the quotation from Theodulf is translated by G. E. McCracken and A. Cabaniss, in *Early Mediaeval Theology*, Early Christian Classics, 9 (Philadelphia: Westminster Press, 1957), 382–99; repr. in Dutton (ed.), *Carolingian Civilization*, 106–20, at 107; for obedience to the king's laws, see Ullmann, 'Ecclesiology and Carolingian Rulership', 49–53.

46. Rosamond McKitterick, *The Frankish Church and the Carolingian Reforms, 789–895* (London: Royal Historical Society, 1977), 2–3.

47. This is from a description in 1617 by the papal librarian J. Grimaldi, trans. in Dutton (ed.), *Carolingian Civilization*, 60.

48. Einhard, *Life of Charlemagne*, ch. XXXIII, in Einhard and Notker the Stammerer, *Two Lives of Charlemagne*, 40.

49. Einhard, *Life of Charlemagne*, ch. XXXIV, in Einhard and Notker the Stammerer, *Two Lives of Charlemagne*, 41.

50. A version of this chapter was presented as a paper at a symposium at the Lincoln Cathedral Centre in January 2012 and subsequently published as 'Charlemagne's Palace Chapel at Aachen: Apocalyptic and Apotheosis', in Nicholas Temple, John Shannon Hendrix, and Christian Frost (eds), *Bishop Robert Grosseteste and Lincoln Cathedral: Tracing Relationships between Medieval Concepts of Order and Built Form* (Farnham: Ashgate, 2014), 179–200.

CHAPTER 6

1. In 249 CE, Decius had become emperor, and the following year issued an edict requiring all to sacrifice to the Roman gods. For the dating of St Denis's martyrdom to the reign of the emperor Decius, see Gregory of Tours, *The History of the Franks*, I.30, trans. Lewis Thorpe (London: Penguin, 1974), 86–7. For the dating to Domitian, see Jacobus de Voragine, *The Golden Legend: Readings on the Saints*, trans. William Granger Ryan, intro. Eamon Duffy (Princeton and Oxford: Princeton University Press, 2012), 620–7, at 625–6. For the writings of Pseudo-Dionysius, see Jean Leclercq, 'Influence and Noninfluence of Dionysius in the Western Middle Ages', in *Pseudo-Dionysius: The Complete Works*, ed. Juroslav Pelikan et al., trans. Colm Luibheid (New York: Paulist Press, 1987), 25–32, at 27–8.

2. Abbot Suger, *De Administratione* XXIII, trans. in Erwin Panofsky (ed. and trans.), *Abbot Suger on the Abbey Church of St-Denis and its Art Treasures* (Princeton: Princeton University Press, 1946), 65.

3. Suger, *De Consecratione* II, in Panofsky (ed. and trans.), *Abbot Suger*, 89.

4. Suger, *De Consecratione* II, in Panofsky (ed. and trans.), *Abbot Suger*, 87–9. A fragment of the Crown of Thorns, known as the 'Crown of the Lord', was kept at Saint-Denis; there are references to it in Suger's *De Consecratione*, and Erik Inglis in 'Expertise, Artefacts and Time in the 1534 Inventory of the St-Denis Treasury' (*The Art Bulletin*, vol. 98, no 1 (March 2016), 14–42 at 15) notes that it appears in 'The Mass of St Giles' (National Gallery, London), see Plate 13. The Crown of the Lord appears in the 1634 Inventory of the treasury of Saint-Denis, see Blaise de Montesquiou-Fezensac with Danielle Gaborit-Chopin, *Le Trésor de Saint-Denis*, vol. 1, *Inventaire de 1634*, vol. 2, *Documents divers*, vol. 3, *Planches et notices* (Paris: Éditions A et J Picard, 1973–77), vol. 1 at 233–5.

5. On the seven bishops, see Gregory of Tours, *The History of the Franks*, I.30, trans. Thorpe, 87; on royal burial, see V.34, trans. Thorpe, 296–8. See also Anne-Marie Romero, *Saint-Denis: Emerging Powers*, trans. Azizeh Azodi (Paris: Caisse Nationale des Monuments), 15; May Vieillard-Troiekouroff, *Les Monuments religieux de la Gaule d'après les oeuvres de Grégoire de Tours* (Paris: Honoré Champion, 1976), 262–5.

6. Suger, *De Consecratione* II, in Panofsky (ed. and trans.), *Abbot Suger*, 87.

7. Suger, *De Administratione* XXV, XXIX, in Panofsky (ed. and trans.), *Abbot Suger*, 45, 51.

8. Suger, *De Consecratione* II, in Panofsky (ed. and trans.), *Abbot Suger*, 91.

9. Suger, *De Consecratione* II, III, in Panofsky (ed. and trans.), *Abbot Suger*, 91–7.

10. Suger, *De Administratione* XXXII, in Panofsky (ed. and trans.), *Abbot Suger*, 59.

11. Suger, *De Administratione* XXV, in Panofsky (ed.and trans.), *Abbot Suger*, 45.

12. For detail relating to the Kingdom of the Franks, see Allan Doig, *Liturgy and Architecture: From the Early Church to the Middle Ages* (Aldershot: Ashgate, 2008), 109 ff.

13. Suger, *De Administratione* XXV, in Panofsky (ed. and trans.), *Abbot Suger*, 45.

14. Kenneth John Conant, *Carolingian and Romanesque Architecture, 800–1200* (New Haven and London: Yale University Press, 1978), p. 43 notes: 'Pepin was buried at the entrance. To augment the dignity of this part of the church an apse was projected, which would have made the building a 'double-ender' like many notable later Carolingian churches, but two small towers and a porch were ultimately built.'

15. See Sumner McKnight Crosby, *The Abbey of St-Denis, 474–1122* (New Haven and London: Yale University Press and Oxford University Press, 1942), i. 97.

16. Trans. in Eleanor Shipley Duckett, *Alcuin, Friend of Charlemagne: His World and his Work* (New York: Macmillan, 1951), 87.

17. Sumner McKnight Crosby et al., *The Royal Abbey of Saint-Denis in the Time of Abbot Suger (1122–1151)*, exhibition catalogue (New York: Metropolitan Museum of Art, 1981), 13–15.

18. Marilyn Dunn, *The Emergence of Monasticism: From the Desert Fathers to the Early Middle Ages* (Oxford: Blackwell, 2000), 92.

19. See Gregory of Tours, *The History of the Franks*, II.14, I.48, trans. Thorpe, 130, 97.

20. The crowning and subsequent move to Paris is in Gregory of Tours, *The History of the Franks*, II.38, trans. Thorpe, 154.

21. Suger, *De Consecratione* I, in Panofsky (ed. and trans.), *Abbot Suger*, 85.

22. Gregory of Tours, *The History of the Franks*, II.14, trans. Thorpe, 130.

23. Gregory of Tours, *The History of the Franks*, II.15, trans. Thorpe, 131.

24. Gregory of Tours, *The History of the Franks*, II.20, trans. Thorpe, 133.

25. St Bernard of Clairvaux, 'Apologia to William, Abbot of St-Thierry', trans. in Elizabeth Gilmore Holt, *A Documentary History of Art: The*

Middle Ages and the Renaissance (Princeton: Princeton University Press, 1947), 20.

26. Dunn, *The Emergence of Monasticism*, 92.

27. Suger, *De Administratione* XXIII, in Panofsky (ed. and trans.), *Abbot Suger*, 65.

28. Suger, *De Administratione* XXII, in Panofsky (ed. and trans.), *Abbot Suger*, 59.

29. Suger, *De Administratione* XXIII, in Panofsky (ed. and trans.), *Abbot Suger*, 65.

30. See Pamela Z. Blum, *Early Gothic Saint-Denis: Restorations and Survivals* (Berkeley and Los Angeles: University of California Press, 1992), and Crosby et al., *The Royal Abbey of Saint-Denis*; the Eleanor Vase is in the Musée du Louvre, Paris; Suger's chalice is in the National Gallery of Art, Washington DC, Widener Collection C-1; the Eagle Vase is in the Musée du Louvre, Paris.

31. Suger, *De Administratione* XXXIV A, in Panofsky (ed. and trans.), *Abbot Suger*, 79.

32. MS Grec 437 fol., in Jean-Michel Leniaud and Philippe Plagnieux, *La Basilique Saint-Denis* (Paris: Editions du Patrimoine, 2012), 17.

33. Eusebius, *The History of the Church from Christ to Constantine*, ed. Andrew Louth, trans. G. A. Williamson (London: Penguin, 1989), sect. 4.23, p. 130.

34. *Pseudo-Dionysius: The Complete Works*, ed. Pelikan et al., trans. Luibheid, 22.

35. Jacobus de Voragine, *The Golden Legend*, 627.

36. See Panofsky (ed. and trans.), *Abbot Suger*, 17–18.

37. Pseudo-Dionysius, 'The Divine Names', 697D, 700C, trans. in *Pseudo-Dionysius: The Complete Works*, ed. Pelikan et al., trans. Luibheid, 74–5; the quotation is from St Paul's Epistle to the Romans, 1:20.

38. Suger, *De Administratione* XXVII, in Panofsky (ed. and trans.), *Abbot Suger*, 47–9.

39. See Erwin Panofsky, 'Introduction', in Panofsky (ed. and trans.), *Abbot Suger*, 3, 7–8.

40. Panofsky, 'Introduction', in Panofsky (ed. and trans.), *Abbot Suger*, 10.

41. *De Consecratione* VII, in Panofsky (ed. and trans.), *Abbot Suger*, 117.

42. *De Consecratione* V, in Panofsky (ed. and trans.), *Abbot Suger*, 107.

43. Simon Lloyd, 'The Crusading Movement, 1096–1274', in Jonathan Riley-Smith (ed.), *The Oxford History of the Crusades* (Oxford: Oxford University Press, 2002), 35–67, at 37.

44. Jonathan Riley-Smith, *The First Crusaders, 1095–1131* (Cambridge: Cambridge University Press, 1997), 82; also in Jonathan Riley-Smith, 'The State of Mind of Crusaders to the East, 1095–1300', in Riley-Smith (ed.), *The Oxford History of the Crusades*, 68–89, at 69–70.

45. Leniaud and Plagnieux, *La Basilique Saint-Denis*, 40.

46. Panofsky, 'Introduction', in Panofsky (ed. and trans.), *Abbot Suger*, 10.

47. In Panofsky (ed. and trans.), *Abbot Suger*, 5–6.

48. For the dating, see Panofsky (ed. and trans.), *Abbot Suger*, 144.

49. Jacobus de Voragine, *The Golden Legend*, 626.

50. For this alternative view to the argument for innovation, see Eric Fernie, 'Suger's "Completion" of Saint-Denis', in Virginia Chieffo Raguin, Kathryn Brush, and Peter Draper (eds), *Artistic Integration in Gothic Buildings* (Toronto: University of Toronto Press, 1995), 84–91, and William W. Clark, '"The Recollection of the Past is the Promise of the Future": Continuity and Contextuality: Saint-Denis, Merovingians, Capetians and Paris', in Raguin, Brush, and Draper (eds), *Artistic Integration*, 92–113.

51. See Otto von Simson, *The Gothic Cathedral: Origins of Gothic Architecture and the Medieval Concept of Order*, 3rd edn (Princeton: Princeton University Press, 1988), 61–2.

52. Suger, *De Administratione* XXIX, in Panofsky (ed. and trans.), *Abbot Suger*, 53.

CHAPTER 7

1. J. Catto and R. Evans (eds), *The History of the University of Oxford*, ii. *Late Medieval Oxford* (Oxford: Oxford University Press, 1992), 719; cited in John A. A. Goodall, *God's House at Ewelme: Life, Devotion and Architecture in a Fifteenth-Century Almshouse* (Aldershot: Ashgate, 2001), 12, which is the principal publication on the subject and an indispensable resource.

2. R. L. Storey, 'University and Government', in Catto and Evans (eds), *The History of the University of Oxford*, ii. 709–46, at 719, and M. B. Parkes, 'The Provision of Books', in Catto and Evans (eds), *The History of the University of Oxford*, ii. 407–83, at 474.

3. See Goodall, 'The Statutes of God's House, Ewelme', in *God's House at Ewelme*, appendix 1; there is an introduction on pp. 213–22; the Statues can be found on pp. 223–55.

4. Goodall, *God's House at Ewelme*, 225.

5. G. H. Cook, *Mediaeval Chantries and Chantry Chapels* (London: Phoenix House, 1947), 165.

6. John Saltmarsh, *King's College: A Short History* (Cambridge: privately printed, 1958), 1; the volume was prepared as a contribution to the Victoria County History, vol. III, *Cambridge and the Isle of Ely*, and privately printed for the college. Some of the footnotes in this volume are fuller than in the Victoria County History volume, and some points of clarification have been added.

7. Saltmarsh, *King's College*, 3.

8. Cook, *Mediaeval Chantries*, 166–7.

9. Henry Malden, *An Account of King's College Chapel in Cambridge, Including a Character of Henry VI, and a Short History of the Foundation of his Two Colleges King's and Eton* (Cambridge: privately printed, 1769), 21–2.

10. Goodall, *God's House at Ewelme*, 29–34.

11. See Arthur Preston, *Christ's Hospital, Abingdon: The Almshouses, the Hall and the Portraits* (Oxford: Oxford University Press, 1929), 12–15, 21.

12. Preston, *Christ's Hospital*, 15, and Goodall, *God's House at Ewelme*, 33, 98.

13. Preston, *Christ's Hospital*, 26–7.

14. Michael Prestwich, *Plantagenet England, 1225–1360* (Oxford: Oxford University Press, 2005), 272, and M. H. Keen, *England in the Later Middle Ages: A Political History* (London and New York: Routledge, 1973), 162; a summary of the family's rise in status is found in John A. F. Thomson, *The Transformation of Medieval England, 1370–1529* (London and New York: Longman, 1983), 128–9.

15. See Goodall, *God's House at Ewelme*, 67–9.

16. *Concise DNB* (Oxford: Oxford University Press, 1993).

17. The heraldic descriptions are: for Roet, '*Gules, three wheels gold*'; for Berghersh of Ewelme, *Argent*, '*Silver a chief gules with a double-tailed lion gold over all*', given by E. A. Greening Lamborn, 'The Arms of the Chaucer Tomb at Ewelme', *Oxoniensia*, 5 (1940), 78–93, at 81, 83; and for Roet '*Gules, three roets or*', and for Berghersh '*Argent, a chief gules with a lion rampant queue-forché or over all*' in Goodall, *God's House at Ewelme*, 193.

18. Goodall, *God's House at Ewelme*, 9; on Maine, see Thomson, *The Transformation of Medieval England*, 195–6.

19. Michael Jones and Malcolm Underwood, *The King's Mother: Lady Margaret Beaufort, Countess of Richmond and Derby* (Cambridge: Cambridge University Press, 1992), 35–9.

20. T. A. R. Evans, 'The Number, Origins and Careers of Scholars', in Catto and Evans (eds), *The History of the University of Oxford*, ii. 485–538, at 512.

21. Goodall, *God's House at Ewelme*, 11–12; Stanley Gillam, *The Divinity School and Duke Humphrey's Library at Oxford* (Oxford: Oxford University Press, 1988), 13 and n., attributes this donation to Elizabeth de la Pole as Duchess of Suffolk, but John was not restored to the Dukedom by Henry VI until 1465 (*DNB*).

22. *Victoria County History: A History of Oxfordshire*, vol. III, ed. H. E. Salter and Mary D. Lobel (Oxford: Oxford University Press, 1954), 44.

23. Here there does not appear to be a chief, as displayed in the chantry, but on Philippa Roet's tomb in Westminster Abbey 'the Burghersh arms are there correctly drawn without the chief'; the arms were sometimes used interchangeably; see Greening Lamborn, 'The Arms of the Chaucer Tomb at Ewelme', 85, 88.

24. See the Royal Commission on Historical Monuments England, *An Inventory of the Historical Monuments in the City of Oxford* (London: Her Majesty's Stationery Office, 1939), 68, for a full list.

25. Gillam, *The Divinity School*, 33.

26. Storey, 'University and Government, 1430–1500', ii. 732.

27. Gillam, *The Divinity School*, 36, quoting A. Wood, *The History and Antiquities of the University of Oxford*, i. *1792–6*, ed. J. Gutch (Oxford: printed for the editor, 1792–6), 638.

28. Storey, 'University and Government, 1430–1500', ii. 393–4, 434.

29. 'John de la Pole, Earl of Lincoln', in *Concise DNB*.

30. The family connection with Iffley is that, as lords of the manor of Donnington, Berkshire, they were also patrons of the hospital founded there as God's Poor House in 1393 by their predecessor Sir Richard Abberbury, after whom the road in Iffley is named, and the hospital was endowed with the manor of Iffley; noted in Greening Lamborn, 'The Arms of the Chaucer Tomb at Ewelme', 93.

31. See Thomson, *The Transformation of Medieval England*, 35.

32. Letter from William Lomnor to John Paston, 5 May 1450, in *The Paston Letters: A Selection in Modern Spelling*, ed. Norman Davis (Oxford: Oxford University Press, 1983), 26–9, at 27–8.

33. See Goodall, *God's House at Ewelme*, 235.

34. Just how widespread this was in the fifteenth and even the early sixteenth centuries is discussed in Christopher Haigh, *English Reformations: Religion, Politics and Society under the Tudors* (Oxford: Oxford University Press, 1993), 36–9.

35. Lines 12–15 in the preamble to the Statutes, in Goodall, *God's House at Ewelme*, 234.

36. For a broader discussion of this, see Eamon Duffy, 'Provision against Purgatory: Wingfield College, Suffolk', in Duffy, *Royal Books and Holy Bones: Essays in Medieval Christianity* (London: Bloomsbury, 2018), 239–53.

37. There is also a special sequence for the Mass of the Five Wounds of Christ found only in Bodleian MS Barlow 1 and an Irish Augustinian Missal, MS BL Add. 24198; see Richard W. Pfaff, *The Liturgy in Medieval England: A History* (Cambridge: Cambridge University Press, 2009), 519–20.

38. Eamon Duffy, *The Stripping of the Altars: Traditional Religion in England, 1400–1580* (New Haven: Yale University Press, 1992), 369.

39. Duffy, *The Stripping of the Altars*, 369–73, gives a detailed and fascinating account of the tariff; see also Duffy, 'Provision against Purgatory', 245–7.

40. See Jones and Underwood, *The King's Mother*, 208–18.

41. Eamon Duffy, *Saints, Sacrilege and Sedition: Religion and Conflict in the Tudor Reformations* (London: Bloomsbury, 2012), 137.

42. Duffy, *Saints, Sacrilege and Sedition*, 147–9.

43. Haigh, *English Reformations*, 163.

44. See Simon Roffey, *The Medieval Chantry Chapel: An Archaeology* (Woodbridge: Boydell Press, 2007), 127.

45. Haigh, *English Reformations*, 167, 172.

46. For the sequence of events, see S. B. Chrimes, *Henry VII* (New Haven and London: Yale University Press, 1999), 92–3.

47. J. J. Scarisbrick, *Henry VIII*, 2nd edn (New Haven and London: Yale University Press, 1997), 32.

48. Jennifer Sherwood and Nikolaus Pevsner, *The Buildings of England: Oxfordshire* (London: Penguin, 1974), 597.

49. Goodall, *God's House at Ewelme*, 202.

50. See David Knowles, *Bare Ruined Choirs: The Dissolution of the English Monasteries* (Cambridge: Cambridge University Press, 1976), 55.

CHAPTER 8

1. See Anne McGowan and Paul F. Bradshaw, *The Pilgrimage of Egeria: A New Translation of the* Itinerarium Egeriae *with Introduction and Commentary* (Collegeville, MN: Liturgical Press Academic, 2018), 20–2.

2. Chris Wickham, *The Inheritance of Rome: A History of Europe from 400 to 1000* (London: Penguin, 2010), 48; also Brian Ward-Perkins, *The Fall of Rome and the End of Civilization* (Oxford: Oxford University Press, 2005), *passim*.

3. Wickham, *The Inheritance of Rome*, 78–9.

4. See Rose Walker, Art in Spain and Portugal from the Romans to the Early Middle Ages: Routes and Myths (Amsterdam: Amsterdam University Press, 2016), 109.

5. Pedro Marfil Ruiz, 'Córdoba de Teodosio a Abd Al-Rahmán III', in *Visigodos y Omeyas: Un debate entre la Antigüedad tardía y la alta Edad Media* (Mérida, abril de 1999), ed. L. Caballero Zoreda and P. Mateos Cruz (Madrid: Consejo Superior de Investigaciones Científicas, Instituto de Historia & Consorcio de la Ciudad Monumental de Mérida, 2000), 117–41, at 123–30.

6. On non-dynastic kingship, see Marianne Barrucand and Achim Bednorz, *Moorish Architecture in Andalusia* (Cologne: Taschen, 2007), 21; and Wickham, *The Inheritance of Rome*, 133–4, continues the history with Reccared's conversion and Suinthila's victory over the Byzantines.

7. Walker, *Art in Spain and Portugal*, 133–4; Walker argues that this church is of reused stone and possibly even on reused Roman foundations,

redating the building to the tenth century, but the weight of consensus is that the building is earlier, displaying Byzantine influence.

8. Wickham, *The Inheritance of Rome*, 134–5.

9. Henri Stierlin, *Islam: Early Architecture from Bagdad to Cordoba* (Cologne: Taschen, 2002), 34.

10. See Shahid Suhrawardy, *The Art of the Mussulmans in Spain* (Oxford: Oxford University Press, 2005), 3.

11. Barrucand and Bednorz, *Moorish Architecture in Andalusia*, 21, present the 'crisis' thesis to explain the quick defeat of the kingdom in 711, while Wickham, *The Inheritance of Rome*, 138–9, emphasizes their strength and the contingencies of their defeat in a single battle, like the Anglo-Saxons at Hastings.

12. Markus Hattstein, 'Spanish Umayyads: History', in Markus Hattstein and Peter Delius (eds), *Islam: Art and Architecture* (Cologne: Könemann, 2000), 208–19, at 208.

13. Quoted in Jerrilyn D. Dodds, María Rosa Menocal, and Abigail Krasner Balbale, *The Arts of Intimacy: Christians, Jews, and Muslims in the Making of Castilian Culture* (New Haven and London: Yale University Press, 2008), 16.

14. Mahmoud Makki, 'The Political History of al-Andalus (92/711–897/1492)', in Salma Khadra Jayyusi (ed.), *The Legacy of Muslim Spain* (New York: Brill, 1992), 3–87, at 15.

15. Einhard, *Life of Charlemagne*, ch. XVII, in Einhard and Notker the Stammerer, *Two Lives of Charlemagne*, trans. and intro. David Ganz (London: Penguin, 2008), 29–30.

16. Rosamond McKitterick, *Charlemagne: The Formation of a European Identity* (Cambridge: Cambridge University Press, 2008), 134.

17. Barrucand and Bednorz, *Moorish Architecture in Andalusia*, 39; also Suhrawardy, *The Art of the Mussulmans in Spain*, 7.

18. Barrucand and Bednorz, *Moorish Architecture in Andalusia*, 39; and Hattstein and Delius (eds), *Islam*, 218; the price is given in Bernard Bevan, *History of Spanish Architecture* (London: Batsford, 1938), 27, and in Suhrawardy, *The Art of the Mussulmans in Spain*, 33.

19. Suhrawardy, *The Art of the Mussulmans in Spain*, 9, 34; as compared with Barrucand and Bednorz, *Moorish Architecture in Andalusia*, 40.

20. See Barrucand and Bednorz, *Moorish Architecture in Andalusia*, 39–40.

21. See John D. Hoag, *Islamic Architecture* (New York: Abrams, 1975), 92.

22. Stierlin, *Islam*, 30.

23. Wickham, *The Inheritance of Rome*, 342.

24. See Suhrawardy, *The Art of the Mussulmans in Spain*, 13–14.

25. Dodds, Menocal and Balbale, *The Arts of Intimacy*, 23–4 and the genealogy on p. 282.

26. Henri Stern, *Les Mosaïques de la Grande Mosquée de Cordoué* (Berlin: Walter Gruyter, 1976), 36–8, 46.

27. See Allan Doig, *Liturgy and Architecture: From the Early Church to the Middle Ages* (Aldershot: Ashgate, 2008), 143, and Kenneth John Conant, *Carolingian and Romanesque Architecture 800 to 1200* (New Haven and London: Yale University Press, 1978), 177–8.

28. Suhrawardy, *The Art of the Mussulmans in Spain*, 16–17, 33.

29. Dodds, Menocal and Balbale, *The Arts of Intimacy*, 26; also Suhrawardy, *The Art of the Mussulmans in Spain*, 16.

30. Hattstein and Delius (eds), *Islam*, 216.

31. Quoted in Hattstein and Delius (eds), *Islam*, 222.

32. See Louis Grodecki, *Gothic Architecture* (London: Faber and Faber, 1986), 191–2.

33. See Diarmaid MacCulloch, *Reformation: Europe's House Divided, 1490–1700* (London: Penguin, 2003), 62–3, 330–1.

34. Malcolm Billings, 'Muslims' Ancient Mosque Appeal', in *From Our Own Correspondent*, broadcast on Saturday, 1 May 2004, at 11.30 BST on BBC Radio 4; see also Elizabeth Nash, 'Madrid Bombers "Were Inspired by Bin Laden Address"', *Independent*, 7 November 2006.

35. Giles Tremlett, 'Vatican Rebuff to Spanish Muslims', *Guardian*, 3 May 2004.

36. Ben Sills, 'Cathedral May See Return of Muslims', *Guardian*, 19 April 2004.

37. Giles Tremlett, 'Two Arrested after Fight in Former Mosque', *Guardian*, 1 April 2010; also Rachel Donadio, 'Name Debate Echoes an Old Clash of Faiths', *New York Times*, 4 November 2010.

CHAPTER 9

1. See Dale Kinney, 'Spolia', in William Tronzo (ed.), *St Peter's in the Vatican* (Cambridge: Cambridge University Press, 2005), 16–47, at 18.

2. Jerome, *In Ezekiel*, in Jaques-Paul Migne, 'Praef., Migne, *Patrologia Latina* (Paris, 1845), XXV, coll. 15–16, 75D, trans. in Bryan Ward-Perkins, *The Fall of Rome and the End of Civilization* (Oxford: Oxford University Press, 2005), 28.

3. See Averil Cameron, *The Mediterranean World in Late Antiquity AD 395–600* (London and New York: Routledge, 1993), 38, and Ward-Perkins, *The Fall of Rome*, 21–22; St Augustine, *The City of God against the Pagans*, trans. George McCracken (London: Heineman, 1957; Cambridge, MA: Harvard University Press, 1957), 13.

4. See Ward-Perkins, *The Fall of Rome*, 172–5; see also 40–1.

5. See Roger Collins, *Early Medieval Europe 300–1000*, 2nd edn (Basingstoke and New York: Palgrave, 1999), 71–3.

6. See Antonio Iacobini, 'EST HAEC SACRA PRINCIPIS AEDES: The Vatican Basilica from Innocent III to Gregory IX (1198–1241)', in Tronzo (ed.), *St Peter's in the Vatican*, 48–63, at 48.

7. Collins, *Early Medieval Europe*, 231–2.

8. Quoted in Chris Wickham, *The Inheritance of Rome: A History of Europe from 400 to 1000* (London: Allen Lane, 2009), 376; see also Allan Doig, *Liturgy and Architecture: From the Early Church to the Middle Ages* (Aldershot: Ashgate, 2008), 110–11.

9. See the *Clausule de unctione Pippini*, trans. in Paul Dutton (ed.), *Carolingian Civilization: A Reader*, 2nd edn (Peterborough, Ontario: Broadview Press, 2004), 13–14.

10. See Diarmaid MacCulloch, *A History of Christianity: The First Three Thousand Years* (London: Penguin, 2009), 349.

11. See Julia M. H. Smith, *Europe after Rome: A New Cultural History 500–1000* (Oxford: Oxford University Press, 2005), 286–8.

12. The occasion and its political meaning are described in Smith, *Europe after Rome*, 277–82.

13. Letter of Cnut to the English, in William of Malmesbury, *Gesta Regum Anglorum*, ii. 183, trans. R. A. B. Mynors, ed. R. M. Thomson and M. Winterbottom, 2 vols (Oxford: Oxford University Press, 1998–9), 326–7, quoted in Smith, *Europe after Rome*, 283.

14. See Iacobini, 'EST HAEC SACRA PRINCIPIS AEDES', 51–61, where further aspects of the iconography of papal authority are also discussed.

15. Christof Thoenes, 'Renaissance St Peter's', in Tronzo (ed.), *St Peter's in the Vatican*, 64–92, at 65.

16. Thoenes, 'Renaissance St Peter's', 74.

17. Details of this episode are given in Diarmaid MacCulloch, *Reformation: Europe's House Divided, 1490–1700* (London: Penguin, 2003), 120–1; also in Hartmann Grisar, *Luther*, ed. Arthur Preuss (Westminster, MD: Newman Press, 1960), 90–1.

18. *Reformation Writings of Martin Luther: Translated with Introduction and Notes from the Definitive Weimar Edition*, trans. and ed. Bertram Lee Woolf, 2 vols, vol. i. *The Basis of the Reformation* (London: Lutterworth Press, 1952), 37–8, 42; see also Hans Hillebrand, 'The Age of the Reformation', in Geoffrey Barraclough (ed.), *The Christian World: A Social and Cultural History of Christianity* (London: Thames and Hudson, 1981), 185–200, at 188–9.

19. See G. R. Elton, *Reformation Europe, 1517–1559* (London and Glasgow: Collins, 1963), 15–22; Robert Kolb, 'Martin Luther and the German Nation', in R. Po-chia Hsia (ed.), *A Companion to the Reformation World* (Oxford: Blackwell, 2004), 39–55, at 41–3.

20. See Christopher Haigh, 'The Reformation in England to 1603', in Po-chia Hsia (ed.), *A Companion to the Reformation World*, 135–49, at 136–7.

21. Thoenes, 'Renaissance St Peter's', 83.

22. A splendid discussion of the development of the project during the Renaissance can be found in Thoenes, 'Renaissance St Peter's'; Bramante's piers are discussed on p. 82.

23. *The Book of Common Prayer: The Texts of 1549, 1559, and 1662*, ed. Brian Cummings (Oxford: Oxford University Press, 2011), 27.

24. Joseph Leo Koerner, *The Reformation of the Image* (London: Reaktion, 2004), 403.

25. A detail is illustrated in C. A. van Swigchem, T. Brouwer, and W. van Os, *Een Huis voor het Woord: Het protestantse kerkinterieur in Nederland tot 1900* (The Hague: Staatsuitgeverij, 1984), 78–9, attributed to C. van Dalem, *c.*1530–*c.*1575, and J. van Wechelen, *c.*1530–70 (Rijksmuseum, Amsterdam).

26. The example of Torgau is discussed in Koerner, *The Reformation of the Image*, 205–10.

27. Illustrated and documented by Johannes Schilling, 'Die Reformation in Lübeck', in Jan Friedrich Richter (ed.), *Lübeck 1500: Kunstmetropole im Ostseeraum* (Petersberg: Michael Imhof, 2015), 45–53.

28. See the entries by Christoph L Frommel in Maria Grazia Mattioni and Serenella Sancese (eds), Cristina Carlo-Stella (executive ed.), *Petros eni; Pietro è qui: Catologo della Mostra; Città del Vaticano, Braccio di Carlo Magno, 11 ottobre 2006–8 marzo 2007* (Vatican: Fabbrica di San Pietro, 2006), 76–7, 42–3.

29. Mattioni and Sancese (eds), *Petros eni*, 74–5.

30. Thoenes, 'Renaissance St Peter's', 87.

31. *Reformation Writings of Martin Luther*, trans. and ed. Bertram Lee Woolf, i. 215.

32. See Doig, *Liturgy and Architecture*, 187, for the ceremonial at Wells; Allan Doig with Michael Sadgrove, 'Sacred Space and its Use', in David Brown (ed.), *Durham Cathedral: History, Fabric and Culture* (New Haven: Yale University Press, 2015), 350–65, at 354, for the Easter sepulchre at Durham; and Allan Doig, 'Sacred Journeys/Sacred Spaces: The Cult of St Cuthbert', in Margaret Coombe, Anne Mouron, and Christiania Whitehead (eds), *Saints of North-East England, 600–1500* (Turnhout, Belgium: Brepols, 2017), 305–25, at 321, for Corpus Christi.

33. John Calvin, *Institutes of the Christian Religion*, iv. 14, 1–26 (1559), trans. Ford Lewis Battles (Philadelphia: Westminster Press, 1960; London: SCM Press, 1960), xxi. 1277, abridged in James F. White (ed.), *Documents of Christian Worship: Descriptive and Interpretive Sources* (London: T&T Clark, 1992), 133.

34. 'The Canons and Decrees of the Council of Trent' (1551, 1562), trans. Philip Schaff, in *The Creeds of Christendom* (Grand Rapids, MI: Baker Book House, 1877), abridged in White (ed.), *Documents of Christian Worship*, 207.

35. Stefano Borsi, 'The Sixteenth Century: The Golden Age', in Marco Bussagli (ed.), *Rome: Art and Architecture* (Königswinter: Tandem, 2007), 402–93, at 412.

36. Henry A. Millon, 'Michelangelo to Marchionni, 1546–1784', in Tronzo (ed.), *St Peter's in the Vatican*, 93–110, at 93–4.

37. Mattioni and Sancese (eds), *Petros eni*, 41–3.

38. See John F. Moffitt, 'Bernini's "Cathedra Petri" and the "Constitutum Constantini"', *Notes in the History of Art*, vol. 26, no 2, (Winter 2007), 23–31; see also Irving Lavin, 'Bernini at St Peter's; Singularis in Singulis, in Omnibus Unicus', in Tronzo (ed.), *St Peter's in the Vatican*, 111–243, at 157.

39. See Irving Lavin, 'Bernini at St Peter's: Singularis in Singulis, in Omnibus Unicus', in Tronzo (ed.), *St Peter's in the Vatican*, 111–243, at 156–8.

CHAPTER 10

1. See Philip Endean, 'The Spiritual Exercises', in Thomas Worcester (ed.), *The Cambridge Companion to the Jesuits* (Cambridge: Cambridge University Press, 2008), 52–67, at 54.

2. Quoted in Endean, 'The Spiritual Exercises', 54; emphasis added.

3. Andrea Pozzo, *Perspectiva pictorum et architectorum*, 2 vols (1693, 1698; English edn, London: printed for J. Senex and R. Gosling, W. Innys, J. Osborn, and T. Longman, 1707).

4. See Robert Bireley, *The Refashioning of Catholicism, 1450–1700* (Basingstoke: Macmillan, 1999), 96–120, at 98–9.

5. See Bireley, *The Refashioning of Catholicism, 1450–1700*, 96–9.

6. See Rodney Palmer, 'The Bizarre', in Michael Snodin and Nigel Llewellyn (eds), *Baroque, 1620–1899: Style in the Age of Magnificence* (London: V&A Publishing, 2009), 80–95, at 80.

7. See Gauvin Alexander Bailey, 'Jesuit Architecture in Colonial Latin America', in Worcester (ed.), *The Cambridge Companion to the Jesuits*, 217–42, at 224–8, citing Germain Bazin, *L'Architecture religieuse baroque au Brésil*, 2 vols (Paris: Librairie Plon, 1956), i. 58–66.

8. Andrew Laird, 'Nahuas and Caesars: Classical Learning and Bilingualism in Post-Conquest Mexico: An Inventory of Latin Writings by Authors of the Native Nobility', *Classical Philology*, 119/2 (April 2014), 150–69, at 152–3.

9. Bireley, *The Refashioning of Catholicism, 1450–1700*, 152.

10. Diarmaid MacCulloch, *A History of Christianity: The First Three Thousand Years* (London: Penguin, 2009), 697, and Bireley, *The Refashioning of Catholicism, 1450–1700*, 158.

11. From Bartolomé de las Casas, 'The Only Method of Attracting All People to the True Faith' (1530s), in *Witness: Writings of Bartolomé de las Casas*, ed. and trans. George Sanderlin (Maryknoll, NY: Orbis, 1992), 137–42, and in Norman Thomas (ed.), *Readings in World Mission* (London: SPCK, 1995), 28.

12. From Pope Paul III, *Siblimis Deus* (1537), in John Tracy Ellis (ed.), *Documents of American Catholic History*, 3 vols (Wilmington, DE: Glazier, 1987), i. 8, and Thomas (ed.), *Readings in World Mission*, 29.

13. See MacCulloch, *A History of Christianity*, 692

14. MacCulloch, *A History of Christianity*, 710, and Bireley, *The Refashioning of Catholicism, 1450–1700*, 163.

15. See MacCulloch, *A History of Christianity*, 711–12.

16. R. Po-chia Hsia, *A Jesuit in the Forbidden City: Matteo Ricci, 1552–1610* (Oxford: Oxford University Press, 2010), 41.

17. For a fuller discussion of architectural style, religion, and politics, see David M. Kowal, 'Innovation and Assimilation: The Jesuit Contribution to Architectural Development in Portuguese India', in John W. O'Malley, Gauvin Alexander Bailey, Steven J. Harris, and T. Frank Kennedy (eds), *The Jesuits: Cultures, Sciences and the Arts, 1540–1773* (Toronto: University of Toronto Press, 1999), 480–504, especially 488; also Mallica Kumbera Landrus, 'Goa: The "Rome of the Orient"', in Snodin and Llewellin (eds), *Baroque: Style and Magnificence*, 42–51, at 42–3.

18. Quoted in Po-chia Hsia, *A Jesuit in the Forbidden City*, 41–3.

19. M. Antoni J. Üçerler, 'The Jesuit Enterprise in Sixteenth- and Seventeenth-Century Japan', in Worcester (ed.), *The Cambridge Companion to the Jesuits*, 153–68, at 164.

20. Andrew C. Ross, 'Alessandro Valignano: The Jesuits and Culture in the East', in O'Malley et al. (eds), *The Jesuits*, 336–51, at 338–9.

21. Engravings from Marc-Antonio Ciappi, *Compendio delle heroiche et gloriose attioni et santa vita di Papa Gregorio XIII* (Rome: Stamperia degli Accolti, 1596), 39–40, reproduced in Üçerler, 'The Jesuit Enterprise in Sixteenth- and Seventeenth-Century Japan', 154.

22. See Liam Matthew Brockley, *Journey to the East: The Jesuit Mission to China, 1579–1724* (Cambridge, MA: Harvard University Press, 2007), 41–2.

23. Bireley, *The Refashioning of Catholicism, 1450–1700*, 170.
24. Po-chia Hsia, *A Jesuit in the Forbidden City*, 211–12.

CHAPTER 11

1. For an extended discussion of the Status Quo, see Raymond Cohen, *Saving the Holy Sepulchre: How Rival Christians Came Together to Rescue their Holiest Shrine* (Oxford: Oxford University Press, 2008), 6–12, at 8–9.
2. Cohen, *Saving the Holy Sepulchre*, 8.
3. Bodleian Library, Oxford, USPG Archive, C/Crimea/3/f3.
4. Bodleian Library, Oxford, USPG Archive, C/Crimea/3/f3.
5. Bodleian Library, Oxford, USPG Archive, C/Crimea/3/f3.
6. Bodleian Library, Oxford, USPG Archive, C/Crimea/3/f3.
7. Bodleian Library, Oxford, USPG Archive, C/Crimea/3/f3.
8. Details are from the announcement of the architectural competition published in the *Ecclesiologist*, 17 (August 1856), 294–6, and the *Builder*, 14 June 1856, to be found in the Paul Joyce Archive, Paul Mellon Centre, London; see also Geoffrey Tyack, 'The Crimean Church, Istanbul: A Monument to Victorian Gothic', *Cornucopia*, 5/25 (2002), 78–93, at 80.
9. *The Times*, 24 May 1856.
10. Letter from Charles Curtis, chaplain, 6 August 1856, in Bodleian Library, Oxford, USPG Archive, C/Crimea/3/f3.
11. Bodleian Library, Oxford, USPG Archive, C/Crimea/3/f1.
12. Letters of 23 July 1856 and of 7 August 1856, in Bodleian Library, Oxford, USPG Archive, C/Crimea/3/f3.
13. *Ecclesiologist*, 17 (August 1856), 294, in the Paul Joyce Archive, Paul Mellon Centre, London.
14. *Ecclesiologist*, 17 (August 1856), 295.
15. Even those, like Newman, who were not involved in the polemical arguments concerning architecture could still have considerable involvement in church architecture, as so clearly demonstrated by William Whyte in *Unlocking the Church: The Lost Secrets of Victorian Sacred Space* (Oxford: Oxford University Press, 2017). Some of the material here and in what follows on the two architectural societies was previously published in Allan Doig, 'The Nineteenth-Century "Church Catholic": Liturgy, Theology and Architecture', in Joseph Sterrett and Peter Thomas (eds), *Sacred Text— Sacred Space: Architectural, Spiritual and Literary Convergences in England and Wales* (Leiden and Boston: Brill, 2011), 227–45. For the general background, see Nikolaus Pevsner, 'The Cambridge Camden Society and the Ecclesiologists', in Pevsner, *Some Architectural Writers of the Nineteenth Century* (Oxford: Oxford University Press, 1972), 123–38.

16. Bodleian Library, Oxford, USPG Archive, C/Crimea?3/f3.
17. Mr Freeman, 'The Development of Roman and Gothick Architecture, and their Moral and Symbolical Teaching', minutes for 12 November 1845, in *The Rules and Proceedings of the Oxford Society for Promoting the Study of Gothic Architecture, 1839–1847* (Oxford: printed by I. Shrimpton, 1850), 23–45.
18. See discussions in Pevsner, 'The Cambridge Camden Society and the Ecclesiologists'; Anthony Symondson, 'Theology and Worship in the late Victorian Church', in Chris Brooks and Andrew Saint (eds), *The Victorian Church: Architecture and Society* (Manchester: Manchester University Press, 1995), 192–222; and Nigel Yates, 'The Liturgical Impact of the Oxford Movement', in Yates, *Buildings, Faith and Worship: The Liturgical Arrangement of Anglican Churches 1600–1900* (Oxford: Oxford University Press, 1991), 127–49.
19. Quoted in Pevsner, 'The Cambridge Camden Society and the Ecclesiologists', 124.
20. For the numbers, see Chris Brooks, 'Introduction', in Brooks and Saint (eds), *The Victorian Church*, 1–29, at 9–10.
21. Examples are given in Frances Knight, *The Church in the Nineteenth Century* (London and New York: I. B. Taurus, 2008), 18-19.
22. Bodleian Library, Oxford, USPG Archive, C/NZ/NZ/1 1, 4, 17 (SPG resolution), and 32a (Selwyn's preparations).
23. 'Parish Churches in New Zealand', *Ecclesiologist*, 1/1 (November 1840).
24. G. A. Bremner, *Imperial Gothic: Religious Architecture and High Anglican Culture in the British Empire, c.1840–1870* (New Haven and London: Yale University Press, 2013), 26–7.
25. Bremner, *Imperial Gothic*, 169–70.
26. Bodleian Library, Oxford, USPG Archive, C/CAN/NFL 4, add. f279/98.
27. Bodleian Library, Oxford, USPG Archive, C/CAN/NFL 4, add. f279 & 154 (laying of foundation stone and valedictory addresses).
28. Peter Richardson and Douglas Richardson, *Canadian Churches: An Architectural History* (Richmond Hill, Ontario: Firefly Books, 2007), 84.
29. *Ecclesiologist*, 13, NS 10 (1852), 276, quoted in J. Mordaunt Crook, *The Dilemma of Style: Architectural Ideas from the Picturesque to the Post Modern* (London: John Murray, 1987), 63.
30. Letter of T. Chamberlain, *Ecclesiologist*, 16 (June 1855), 197.
31. Lord Stratford de Redcliffe to the Earl of Clarendon, 2 March 1857, Bodleian Library, Oxford, USPG Archive, C/CRIMEA/3/f3, which contains extensive correspondence regarding the site.
32. *Builder*, 21 March 1857, p. 162, accompanied by an illustration of the plan and a perspective, in the Paul Joyce Archive, Paul Mellon Centre, London.

33. *Ecclesiologist*, 18 (April 1857), 98–116, Report of the Judges, and disagreement.
34. *Building News*, 3 (1857), 345.
35. Bodleian Library, Oxford, USPG Archive, C/CRIMEA/3/f3.
36. Bodleian Library, Oxford, USPG Archive, C/CRIMEA/3/f3.
37. Bodleian Library, Oxford, USPG Archive, C/CRIMEA/3/f3.
38. Bodleian Library, Oxford, USPG Archive, C/CRIMEA/3/f3.
39. Bodleian Library, Oxford, USPG Archive, C/CRIMEA/3/f3.
40. Bodleian Library, Oxford, USPG Archive, C/CRIMEA/3/f3.
41. Letters recorded in 'Correspondence', in the Paul Joyce Archive, Paul Mellon Centre, London.
42. Wilfrid Castle to Paul Joyce, letter, 3 March 1964, in 'Correspondence', in the Paul Joyce Archive, Paul Mellon Centre, London.
43. 'Correspondence', in the Paul Joyce Archive, Paul Mellon Centre, London.

CHAPTER 12

1. Bede, *Ecclesiastical History of the English Nation*, trans. L. Gidley (Oxford and London: James Parker, 1870), bk iii, ch. xxv, p. 255.
2. Quoted in Giovanni Fanelli, Jan de Heer, and Vincent van Rossem, *Hendrick Petrus Berlage: Het Complete Werk* (Alphen aan den Rijn: Atrium, 1988), 20.
3. Peter Kidson, Peter Murray, and Paul Thompson, *A History of English Architecture* (London: Penguin, 1978), 317.
4. Gregory Dix, *The Shape of the Liturgy*, 2nd edn (London: A&C Black, 1945), ch. XVII, 'Throughout all Ages, World without End', 735-52, at 735.
5. William Lockett, 'A Lesson from Anglican History', in William Lockett (ed.), *The Modern Architectural Setting of the Liturgy: Papers Read at a Conference held at Liverpool, September 1962* (London: SPCK, 1964), 42–54, at 45.
6. Lockett, 'A Lesson from Anglican History', 45.
7. Doreen Yarwood, *The Architecture of Britain* (London: Batsford, 1976), 238.
8. Joe Riley, *Today's Cathedral: The Cathedral Church of Christ, Liverpool* (London: SPCK, 1978), 6.
9. Printed in *RIBA Journal*, 11 November 1933, pp. 5–14, quoted in Gavin Stamp, 'Giles Gilbert Scott: The Problem of Modernism', *Architectural Design*, 49/10–11 (1979), 72–83, at 76.
10. Incorporated Church Building Society, 'Complete List of Consecrated Anglican Churches Erected in England during the Years 1930–1945', in R. J. McNally (ed.), *Fifty Modern Churches* (London: Incorporated Church Building Society, 1947), 8–14, at 3.

11. Peter Hammond, *Liturgy and Architecture* (London: Barrie & Rockliff, 1960), 1.

12. Louise Campbell, *Coventry Cathedral: Art and Architecture in Post-War Britain* (Oxford: Oxford University Press, 1996), 1.

13. Ernest Short, 'Foreword', in Ernest Short (ed.), *Post-War Church Building* (London: Hollis and Carter, 1947), p. xiv.

14. Eric Gill, *Sacred and Secular* (London: J. M. Dent and Sons, 1940), 140 ff.

15. Eric Gill to Father O'Connor, quoted in Hammond, *Liturgy and Architecture*, 148; there is a detailed discussion of the design and its circumstances at pp. 147–8.

16. Incorporated Church Building Society, *Fifty Modern Churches*, 95.

17. Interference by the bishop is noted by Hammond, *Liturgy and Architecture*, 73–4, but Clare Price has been unable to find any mention of this in the diocesan archives.

18. Incorporated Church Building Society, *Fifty Modern Churches*; see Camelford St Thomas of Canterbury on pp. 32–3, and Airedale, the Holy Cross, on pp. 90–1, 'built of old stone from a late Georgian house (Fryston Hall)' reusing Ionic columns as the centrepiece of what is otherwise a stone shed.

19. Sir Charles Nicholson, 'Building the Church: Styles and Requirements', in Short (ed.), *Post-War Church Building*, 60–77, at 72–3.

20. Texts cited in Campbell, *Coventry Cathedral*, 29; a fuller discussion of the complexities of the situation will be found on pp. 22–5, and also in Louise Campbell, 'Towards a New Cathedral: The Competition for Coventry Cathedral 1950–51', *Architectural History*, 35 (1992), 208–34, especially 208–12.

21. Nicholas Bullock, *Building the Post-War World: Modern Architecture and Reconstruction in Britain* (London: Routledge, 2002), quoting J. M. Richards, 'Royal Festival Hall: Criticism', *Architectural Review* (June 1951), 357.

22. Quoted in Bevis Hillier, 'Introduction', in Mary Banham and Bevis Hillier (eds), *A Tonic to the Nation: The Festival of Britain* (London: Thames and Hudson, 1976), 10–19, at 10.

23. Gerald Barry, 'Recollections of the Festival', in Hillier (ed.), *A Tonic to the Nation*, 20–5, at 22–3.

24. Basil Spence, *Phoenix at Coventry* (London: Geoffrey Bles, 1962), app. B, 'Schedule of Requirements and Accommodation', 109–16, at 113.

25. 'Coventry Cathedral Competition', *Architectural Design* (September 1951), 258, quoted in Bullock, *Building the Post-War World*, 79.

26. See Spence, *Phoenix at Coventry*, app. D: 'Report by Assessors to the Chairman and Members of the Coventry Cathedral Reconstruction Committee', 131–3 at 131; John Thomas, *Coventry Cathedral* (London and Sydney: Harper Collins, 1987), 93–4; and Campbell, *Coventry Cathedral*, 45.

27. Spence, *Phoenix at Coventry*, app. D, 133.

28. Spence, *Phoenix at Coventry*, app. D, 132.

29. Stephen Kite and Sarah Menin, 'Towards a New Cathedral: Mechanolatry and Metaphysics in the Milieu of Colin St John Wilson', *arq*, 9/1 (2005), 81–90, at 86.

30. See the obituary in *arq*, 11/2 (2007), 103–8 at 103; the obituary ascribes a deep Christian faith to him.

31. C. St J. Wilson, 'Architecture: Public Good and Private Necessity', *RIBA Journal*, 86/3 (March 1979), 107–15.

32. Quoted in Kite and Menin, 'Towards a New Cathedral', 88.

33. Robert Maquire, Keith Murray, and John Catt, 'The Editors', *church-building*, 8 (January 1963), 3; compare the brief treatment in Hammond, *Liturgy and Architecture*, 135–6.

34. Alison Smithson and Peter Smithson, 'Architects' Report', *churchbuilding*, 8 (January 1963), 5–12, at 9.

35. See Arthur Schopenhauer, *The World as Will and Representation*, trans. E. F. J. Payne, 2 vols (New York: Dover, 1966), 2 at 417–18; thanks to Richard Etlin for pointing this out in his book *Frank Lloyd Wright and Le Corbusier: The Romantic Legacy* (Manchester: Manchester University Press, 1994), at 5–6.

36. Smithson and Smithson, 'Architects' Report', 8.

37. Smithson and Smithson, 'Architects' Report', 8.

38. Smithson and Smithson, 'Architects' Report', 5.

39. Smithson and Smithson, 'Architects' Report', 12.

40. Spence, *Phoenix at Coventry*, 9.

41. Spence, *Phoenix at Coventry*, 10.

42. Basil Spence, 'Contemporary Expressions of Cathedral Traditions', in John Knox Shear (ed.), *Religious Buildings for Today: An Architectural Record Book* (New York: F. W. Dodge, Corp., 1957), 126–33, at 128; Spence (*Phoenix at Coventry*, 6) tells the same story, but with less emotive pressure placed on the historic cost: 'I got one of those pictures that architects sometimes get. This one, however, was unusually clear—a great nave and an altar that was an invitation to Communion, and a huge picture behind it. But as always with mind's pictures, it was ever changing. I could not see the altar clearly but through the bodies of the Saints. In these few moments the idea of the design was planted. In essence it has never changed.'

43. Basil Mitchell, 'A Phoenix Too Soon?', *churchbuilding*, 8 (January 1963), 25–6.

44. See Spence, *Phoenix at Coventry*, 82.

45. Cuthbert Bardsley, 'Resurrection at Coventry', *Anglican World*, Whitsun number (1962), 10–17, at 11–13; and Spence interviewed in Dewi

Morgan, 'Man of the Moment: Basil Spence', *Anglican World*, Whitsun number (1962), 15–16 and 61, at 16.

46. Bardsley, 'Resurrection at Coventry', 13–14.

47. Hammond, *Liturgy and Architecture*, 6.

48. Bishop J. W. C. Wand, *Anglicanism in History and Today*, quoted in H. C. N. Williams, *20th Century Cathedral: An Examination of the Role of Cathedrals in the Strategy of the Church in the Changing Pattern of a Twentieth Century Community* (Guildford and London: Hodder and Stoughton, 1964), 62.

49. Wand, *Anglicanism in History and Today*, 63.

50. Wand, *Anglicanism in History and Today*, 67.

51. Hammond, *Liturgy and Architecture*, 7.

52. *Vatican Council II: The Conciliar and Post Conciliar Documents*, gen. ed. Austin Flannery, *The Constitution on the Sacred Liturgy*, Ii.14 (Leominster: Fowler Wright Books, 1975), 8.

53. Frederick Gibberd, 'The Liverpool Metropolitan Cathedral', in William Lockett (ed.), *The Modern Architectural Setting of the Liturgy: Papers Read at a Conference Held at Liverpool, September 1962*, with a foreword by F.W. Dillistone (London: SPCK, 1964), 55–69, at 58.

54. Gibberd, 'The Liverpool Metropolitan Cathedral', 58.

55. Spence, *Phoenix at Coventry*, 43–4.

56. Hammond, *Liturgy and Architecture*, 6–7.

57. Kitty Hauser, *Shadow Sites, Photography Archaeology, & the British Landscape, 1927–1955* (Oxford: Oxford University Press, 2007), 9, 249.

Bibliography

Bagnoli, Martina, 'The Stuff of Heaven: Materials and Craftsmanship in Medieval Reliquaries', in Martina Bagnoli, Holger A. Klein, C. Griffith Mann, and James Robinson (eds), *Treasures of Heaven: Saints Relics and Devotion in Medieval Europe* (London: British Museum, 23 June–9 October 2011), 137–47.

Bailey, Gauvin Alexander, 'Jesuit Architecture in Colonial Latin America', in Thomas Worcester (ed.), *The Cambridge Companion to the Jesuits* (Cambridge: Cambridge University Press, 2008), 217–42.

Banham, Mary, and Hillier, Bevis (eds), *A Tonic to the Nation: The Festival of Britain* (London: Thames and Hudson, 1976).

Bardsley, Cuthbert, 'Resurrection at Coventry', *Anglican World*, Whitsun number (1962), 10–17.

Barral I Altet, Xavier, *The Early Middle Ages: From Late Antiquity to AD 1000* (Cologne, London, and Madrid: Taschen, 2002).

Barrucand, Marianne, and Bednorz, Achim, *Moorish Architecture in Andalusia* (Cologne: Taschen, 2007).

Barry, Gerald, 'Recollections of the Festival', in Mary Banham and Bevis Hillier (eds), *A Tonic to the Nation: The Festival of Britain* (London: Thames and Hudson, 1976), 20–5.

Bazin, Germain, *L'Architecture religieuse baroque au Brésil*, 2 vols (Paris: Librairie Plon, 1956).

Beard, Mary, North, John, and Price, Simon, *Religions of Rome*, i. *A History*; ii. *A Sourcebook* (Cambridge: Cambridge University Press, 1998).

Beckwith, John, *Early Christian and Byzantine Art* (New Haven and London: Yale University Press, 1979).

Bede, *Ecclesiastical History of the English Nation*, trans. L. Gidley (Oxford and London: James Parker, 1870).

Ben-Dov, Meir, *Historical Atlas of Jerusalem*, trans. David Louvish (New York and London: Continuum, 2002).

Berton, Kathleen, *Moscow: An Architectural History* (London: Studio Vista, 1977).

Bevan, Bernard, *History of Spanish Architecture* (London: Batsford, 1938).

Biblical Archaeologist, 2/3 (September 1939), 34 and 35.

Biddle, Martin, *The Tomb of Christ* (Stroud: Sutton Publishing, 1999).

Billings, Malcolm, 'Muslims' Ancient Mosque Appeal', in *From Our Own Correspondent*, broadcast on Saturday, 1 May 2004, at 11.30 BST on BBC Radio 4.

Bireley, Robert, *The Refashioning of Catholicism, 1450–1700* (Basingstoke: Macmillan, 1999).

Blum, Pamela Z., *Early Gothic Saint-Denis: Restorations and Survivals* (Berkeley and Los Angeles: University of California Press, 1992).

Bockmuehl, Markus, 'Review of S. Heid, *Petrus und Paulus in Rom: eine interdisziplinäre Debatte'*, in *A Journal of Biblical Textual Criticism*, vol. 17 (2012), open access electronic journal, accessed on 20 August 2019.

Bodleian Library, Oxford, USPG Archive, C/Crimea/3/f1.

Bodleian Library, Oxford, USPG Archive, C/Crimea/3/f3.

Boone, James L., 'The Parable of the Horseshoe Arch', in Boone, *Lost Civilization: The Contested Islamic Past in Spain and Portugal* (London: Duckworth, 2009), 128–34.

Borsi, Stefano, 'The Sixteenth Century: The Golden Age', in Marco Bussagli (ed.), *Rome: Art and Architecture* (Königswinter: Tandem, 2007), 402–93.

The Book of Common Prayer: The Texts of 1549, 1559, and 1662, ed. Brian Cummings (Oxford: Oxford University Press, 2011).

Bowersock, G. W., 'Peter and Constantine', in William Tronzo (ed.), *St Peter's in the Vatican* (Cambridge: Cambridge University Press, 2005), 5–15.

Bremner, G. A., *Imperial Gothic: Religious Architecture and High Anglican Culture in the British Empire, c.1840–1870* (New Haven and London: Yale University Press, 2013).

Brenk, Beat, 'Spolia from Constantine to Charlemagne: Aesthetics versus Ideology', *Dumbarton Oaks Papers*, 41 (1987), 103–9.

Brockley, Liam Matthew, *Journey to the East: The Jesuit Mission to China, 1579–1724* (Cambridge, MA: Harvard University Press, 2007).

Brooks, Chris, 'Introduction', in Chris Brooks and Andres Saint (eds), *The Victorian Church: Architecture and Society* (Manchester: Manchester University Press, 1995), 1–29.

Brooks, Chris, and Saint, Andrew (eds), *The Victorian Church: Architecture and Society* (Manchester: Manchester University Press, 1995).

Brown, Dennis, 'Jerome', in Philip Esler (ed.), *The Early Christian World* (London and New York: Routledge, 2000), ii. 1151–74.

Broshi, Magen, 'Excavations in the Holy Sepulchre in the Chapel of St Vartan and the Armenian Martyrs', in Yorem Tsafrir (ed.), *Ancient Churches Revealed* (Jerusalem: Israel Exploration Society, 1993), 118–22.

Brumfield, William Craft, *A History of Russian Architecture* (Cambridge: Cambridge University Press, 1993).

Bullock, Nicholas, *Building the Post-War World: Modern Architecture and Reconstruction in Britain* (London: Routledge, 2002).

Buxton, David Roden, *Russian Mediaeval Architecture: With an Account of the Transcaucasian Styles and their Influence in the West* (Cambridge: Cambridge University Press, 1934).

Calvin, John, *Institutes of the Christian Religion*, trans. Ford Lewis Battles (Philadelphia: Westminster Press, and London: SCM Press, 1960).

Cameron, Averil, *Procopius and the Sixth Century* (London: Duckworth, 1985).

Cameron, Averil, *The Mediterranean World in Late Antiquity AD 395–600* (London and New York: Routledge, 1993).

Campbell, Louise, 'Towards a New Cathedral: The Competition for Coventry Cathedral 1950–51', *Architectural History*, 35 (1992), 208–34.

Campbell, Louise, *Coventry Cathedral: Art and Architecture in Post-War Britain* (Oxford: Oxford University Press, 1996).

Carolingian Chronicles: Royal Frankish Annals and Nithard's Histories, trans. Bernhard Walter Scholz with Barbara Rogers (Ann Arbor: University of Michigan Press, 1970).

Cassiodorus, *Variae*, in *The Letters of Cassiodorus, Being a Condensed Translation of the Variae Epistolae of Magnus Aurelius Cassiodorus, Senator*, intro. Thomas Hodgkin (London: Henry Frowde, 1886; Oxford: Horace Hart, 1886).

Catto, J., and Evans, R. (eds), *The History of the University of Oxford*, ii. *Late Medieval Oxford* (Oxford: Oxford University Press, 1992).

Chadwick, Henry, *The Church in Ancient Society: From Galilee to Gregory the Great* (Oxford: Oxford University Press, 2001).

Chiniakov, A., with Fehner, M., Ivanov, V., Rudko, M., and Zemtzov, S. (eds), *Preservation and Restoration of Monuments of Architecture in the USSR* (Moscow: Soiuz arkhitektorov 1964).

Chrimes, S. B., *Henry VII* (New Haven and London: Yale University Press, 1999).

Ciappi, Marc-Antonio, *Compendio delle heroiche et gloriose attioni et santa vita di Papa Gregorio XIII* (Rome: Stamperia degli Accolti, 1596).

Clark, William W., '"The Recollection of the Past is the Promise of the Future": Continuity and Contextuality: Saint-Denis, Merovingians, Capetians and Paris', in Virginia Chieffo Raguin, Kathryn Brush, and Peter Draper (eds), *Artistic Integration in Gothic Buildings* (Toronto: University of Toronto Press, 1995), 92–113.

Cohen, Raymond, *Saving the Holy Sepulchre: How Rival Christians Came Together to Rescue their Holiest Shrine* (Oxford: Oxford University Press, 2008).

Collins, Roger, *Early Medieval Europe 300–1000*, 2nd edn (Basingstoke and New York: Palgrave, 1999).

Conant, Kenneth John, *Carolingian and Romanesque Architecture 800 to 1200* (New Haven and London: Yale University Press, 1978).

Concise DNB (Oxford: Oxford University Press, 1993).

Cook, G. H., *Mediaeval Chantries and Chantry Chapels* (London: Phoenix House, 1947).

Coüasnon, Charles, *The Church of the Holy Sepulchre in Jerusalem*, trans. J.-P. and Claude Ross, The Schweich Lectures of the British Academy (London: Oxford University Press for the British Academy, 1972).

Crook, J. Mordaunt, *The Dilemma of Style: Architectural Ideas from the Picturesque to the Post Modern* (London: John Murray, 1987).

Crosby, Sumner McKnight, *The Abbey of St-Denis, 474–1122* (New Haven and London: Yale University Press and Oxford University Press, 1942).

Crosby, Sumner McKnight, et al., *The Royal Abbey of Saint-Denis in the Time of Abbot Suger (1122–1151)*, exhibition catalogue (New York: Metropolitan Museum of Art, 1981).

Dagron, Gilbert, *Emperor and Priest: The Imperial Office in Byzantium*, trans. Jean Birrell (Cambridge: Cambridge University Press, 2003).

Dix, Gregory, *The Shape of the Liturgy*, 2nd edn (London: A&C Black, 1945).

Dodds, Jerrilyn D., Menocal, María Rosa, and Balbale, Abigail Krasner, *The Arts of Intimacy: Christians, Jews, and Muslims in the Making of Castilian Culture* (New Haven and London: Yale University Press, 2008).

Doig, Allan, 'Constantine, Continuity and Change', in Allan Doig, *Liturgy and Architecture: From the Early Church to the Middle Ages* (Aldershot: Ashgate, 2008), 21–52.

Doig, Allan, *Liturgy and Architecture: From the Early Church to the Middle Ages* (Aldershot: Ashgate, 2008).

Doig, Allan, 'The Nineteenth-Century "Church Catholic": Liturgy, Theology and Architecture', in Joseph Sterrett and Peter Thomas (eds), *Sacred Text—Sacred Space: Architectural, Spiritual and Literary Convergences in England and Wales* (Leiden and Boston: Brill, 2011), 227–45.

Doig, Allan, 'Charlemagne's Palace Chapel at Aachen: Apocalyptic and Apotheosis', in Nicholas Temple, John Shannon Hendrix, and Christian Frost (eds), *Bishop Robert Grosseteste and Lincoln Cathedral: Tracing Relationships between Medieval Concepts of Order and Built Form* (Farnham: Ashgate, 2014), 179–200.

Doig, Allan, 'Building, Enacting and Embodying *Romanitas*: The Throne of Charlemagne', in Ekaterina Staniukovich-Denisova and Anna Zakharova (eds), *Actual Problems of Theory and History of Art*, v (St Petersburg: Hirov, 2015), 376–82.

Doig, Allan, 'Sacred Journeys/Sacred Spaces: The Cult of St Cuthbert', in Margaret Coombe, Anne Mouron, and Christiania Whitehead (eds), *Saints of North-East England, 600–1500* (Turnhout, Belgium: Brepols, 2017), 305–25.

Doig, Allan, with Sadgrove, Michael, 'Sacred Space and its Use', in David Brown (ed.), *Durham Cathedral: History, Fabric and Culture* (New Haven: Yale University Press, 2015), 350–65.

Donadio, Rachel, 'Name Debate Echoes an Old Clash of Faiths', *New York Times*, 4 November 2010.

Duckett, Eleanor Shipley, *Alcuin, Friend of Charlemagne: His World and his Work* (New York: Macmillan, 1951).

Duffy, Eamon, *The Stripping of the Altars: Traditional Religion in England, 1400–1580* (New Haven: Yale University Press, 1992).

Duffy, Eamon, *Saints, Sacrilege and Sedition: Religion and Conflict in the Tudor Reformations* (London: Bloomsbury, 2012).

Duffy, Eamon, 'Provision against Purgatory: Wingfield College, Suffolk', in Eamon Duffy, *Royal Books and Holy Bones: Essays in Medieval Christianity* (London: Bloomsbury, 2018), 239–53.

Dunn, Marilyn, *The Emergence of Monasticism: From the Desert Fathers to the Early Middle Ages* (Oxford: Blackwell, 2000).

Dutton, Paul Edward (ed.), *Carolingian Civilization: A Reader*, 2nd edn (Peterborough, Ontario: Broadview Press, 2004).

Egeria's Travels, ed. and trans. John Wilkinson, 3rd edn (Warminster: Aris and Phillips, 2002).

Einhard and Notker the Stammerer, *Two Lives of Charlemagne*, trans. and intro. David Ganz (London: Penguin, 2008).

Ellis, John Tracy (ed.), *Documents of American Catholic History*, 3 vols (Wilmington, DE: Glazier, 1987).

Elton, G. R., *Reformation Europe, 1517–1559* (London and Glasgow: Collins, 1963).

Endean, Philip, 'The Spiritual Exercises', in Thomas Worcester (ed.), *The Cambridge Companion to the Jesuits* (Cambridge: Cambridge University Press, 2008), 52–67.

Ermold, *In honorem Hlodowici christianissimi Caesaris Augusti*, ed. E. Faral, in *Ermold le Noir: Poèm sur Louis le Pieux et épîtres au roi Pépin* (Paris: Les Classiques de l'histoire de France, 1932).

Esler, Philip (ed.), *The Early Christian World* (London and New York: Routledge, 2000).

Etlin, Richard A., *Frank Lloyd Wright and Le Corbusier: The Romantic Legacy* (Manchester: Manchester University Press, 1994).

Etlin, Richard A., 'St Peter's in the Modern Era', in William Tronzo (ed.),
    St Peter's in the Vatican (Cambridge: Cambridge University Press, 2005),
    270–304.

Eusebius, *Oration on the Tricennalia of Constantine*, trans. in *A New Eusebius:
    Documents Illustrative of the History of the Church to AD 337*, ed. J. Stephenson
    (London: SPCK, 1968), 391–2.

Eusebius, *A New Eusebius: Documents Illustrative of the History of the Church to
    AD 337*, ed. J. Stephenson (London: SPCK, 1968).

Eusebius, *The History of the Church from Christ to Constantine*, ed. Andrew
    Louth, trans. G. A. Williamson (London: Penguin, 1989).

Eusebius, *Life of Constantine*, trans. and ed. Averil Cameron and Stuart G. Hall
    (Oxford: Oxford University Press, 1999).

Evans, T. A. R., 'The Number, Origins and Careers of Scholars', in J. Catto
    and R. Evans (eds), *The History of the University of Oxford*, ii. *Late Medieval
    Oxford* (Oxford: Oxford University Press, 1992), 485–538.

Faensen, Hubert, and Ivanov, Vladimir, *Early Russian Architecture*, trans. Mary
    Whittall (London: Paul Elek, 1972).

Fanelli, Giovanni, Heer, Jan de, and Rossem, Vincent van, *Hendrick Petrus
    Berlage: Het Complete Werk* (Alphen aan den Rijn: Atrium, 1988).

Featherstone, J. M., 'The Great Palace as Reflected in the *De Ceremoniis*',
    in *Visualisierungen von Herrschaft: Frühmittelalterliche Residenzen Gestalt
    und Zeremoniell*, in *Byzas*, 5 (Istanbul: Ege Yayinlari/German Institute of
    Archaeology, 2006), 47–60.

Fernie, Eric, 'Suger's "Completion" of Saint-Denis', in Virginia Chieffo
    Raguin, Kathryn Brush, and Peter Draper (eds), *Artistic Integration in Gothic
    Buildings* (Toronto: University of Toronto Press, 1995), 84–91.

Flier, Michael S., 'The Throne of Monomakh: Ivan the Terrible and the
    Architectonics of Destiny', in James Cracraft and Daniel Rowland (eds),
    Architectures of Russian Identity: 1500 to the Present (Ithaca, NY, and London:
    Cornell University Press, 2003), 21–33.

Freyne, Sean, 'A Galilean Messiah?', *Studia Theologica*, 55 (2001), 198–218.

Freeman, Mr, 'The Development of Roman and Gothick Architecture, and
    their Moral and Symbolical Teaching', minutes for 12 November 1845,
    in *The Rules and Proceedings of the Oxford Society for Promoting the Study
    of Gothic Architecture, 1839–1847* (Oxford: printed by I. Shrimpton, 1850),
    23–45.

Gibberd, Frederick, 'The Liverpool Metropolitan Cathedral', in William
    Lockett (ed.), *The Modern Architectural Setting of the Liturgy: Papers Read
    at a Conference Held at Liverpool, September 1962*, with a foreword by
    F. W. Dillistone (London: SPCK, 1964), 55–69.

Gibson, Shimon, *The Final Days of Jesus: The Archaeological Evidence* (Oxford: Lion Hudson, 2009).

Gibson, Shimon, and Taylor, Joan E*., Beneath the Holy Sepulchre, Jerusalem: The Archaeology and Early History of Traditional Golgotha* (London: Committee of the Palestine Exploration Fund, 1994).

Gill, Eric, *Sacred and Secular* (London: J. M. Dent and Sons, 1940).

Gillam, Stanley, *The Divinity School and Duke Humphrey's Library at Oxford* (Oxford: Oxford University Press, 1988).

Goodall, John A. A., *God's House at Ewelme: Life, Devotion and Architecture in a Fifteenth-Century Almshouse* (Aldershot: Ashgate, 2001).

Goodman, Martin, *Rome and Jerusalem: The Clash of Ancient Civilizations* (London: Penguin, 2008).

Greening Lamborn, E. A., 'The Arms of the Chaucer Tomb at Ewelme', *Oxoniensia*, 5 (1940), 78–93.

Grégoire, Henri, 'The Byzantine Church', in N. H. Baynes and H. St B. Moss (eds), *Byzantium: An Introduction to East Roman Civilization* (Oxford: Oxford University Press, 1962).

Gregory of Tours, *The History of the Franks*, trans. Lewis Thorpe (London: Penguin, 1974).

Grisar, Hartmann, *Luther*, ed. Arthur Preuss (Westminster, MD: Newman Press, 1960).

Grodecki, Louis, *Pre-Romanesque Art*, ed. Harald Busch and Bernd Lohse (London: Batsford, 1966).

Grodecki, Louis, *Gothic Architecture* (London: Faber and Faber, 1979).

Haigh, Christopher, *English Reformations: Religion, Politics and Society under the Tudors* (Oxford: Oxford University Press, 1993).

Haigh, Christopher, 'The Reformation in England to 1603', in R. Po-chia Hsia (ed.), *A Companion to the Reformation World* (Oxford: Blackwell, 2004), 135–49.

Hammond, Peter, *Liturgy and Architecture* (London: Barrie & Rockliff, 1960).

Hattstein, Markus, 'Spanish Umayyads: History', in Markus Hattstein and Peter Delius (eds), *Islam: Art and Architecture* (Cologne: Könemann, 2000), 208–19.

Hattstein, Markus, and Delius, Peter (eds), *Islam: Art and Architecture* (Cologne: Könemann, 2000).

Heid, S., (ed.), *Petrus und Paulus in Rom: eine interdisziplinäre Debatte* (Freiburg: Herder, 2011).

Hen, Yitzhak, *Culture and Religion in Merovingian Gaul*, A.D. 481–751 (New York: Brill, 1995).

Hen, Yitzhak, *The Royal Patronage of Liturgy in Frankish Gaul to the Death of Charles the Bald* (London: Boydell and Brewer, 2001).

Hauser, Kitty, *Shadow Sites, Photography, Archaeology, & the British Landscape, 1927–1955* (Oxford: Oxford University Press, 2007).

Hillebrand, Hans, 'The Age of the Reformation', in Geoffrey Barraclough (ed.), *The Christian World: A Social and Cultural History of Christianity* (London: Thames and Hudson, 1981), 185–200.

Hillier, Bevis, 'Introduction', in Mary Banham and Bevis Hillier (eds), *A Tonic to the Nation: The Festival of Britain* (London: Thames and Hudson, 1976), 10–19.

Hoag, John D., *Islamic Architecture* (New York: Abrams, 1975).

Holloway, R. Ross, 'The Tomb of St Peter', in R. Ross Holloway, *Constantine and Rome* (New Haven and London: Yale University Press, 2004), 120–55.

Holt, Elizabeth Gilmore, *A Documentary History of Art: The Middle Ages and the Renaissance* (Princeton: Princeton University Press, 1947).

Hopkins, Clark, *The Discovery of Dura Europos* (New Haven: Yale University Press, 1984).

Iacobini, Antonio, 'EST HAEC SACRA PRINCIPIS AEDES: The Vatican Basilica from Innocent III to Gregory IX (1198–1241)', in William Tronzo (ed.), *St Peter's in the Vatican* (Cambridge: Cambridge University Press, 2005), 48–63.

Incorporated Church Building Society, 'Complete List of Consecrated Anglican Churches Erected in England during the Years 1930–1945', in R. J. McNally (ed.), *Fifty Modern Churches* (London: Incorporated Church Building Society, 1947), 8–14.

Inglis, Erik, 'Expertise, Artefacts and Time in the 1534 Inventory of the St-Denis Treasury', *The Art Bulletin*, vol. 98, no 1 (March 2016), 14–42.

Irenaeus of Lyons, *Against Heresies*, trans. Robert M. Grant, *Irenaeus of Lyons* (London and New York: Routledge, 1997), 57–186.

Jacobus de Voragine, *The Golden Legend: Readings on the Saints*, trans. William Granger Ryan, intro. Eamon Duffy (Princeton and Oxford: Princeton University Press, 2012).

Jones, Christopher, 'The Historicity of the Neronian Persecution: A Response to Brent Shaw', *New Testament Studies*, vol. 63, issue 1 (January 2017), 146–52.

Jones, Michael, and Underwood, Malcolm, *The King's Mother: Lady Margaret Beaufort, Countess of Richmond and Derby* (Cambridge: Cambridge University Press, 1992).

Jongkees, J. H., *Studies in Old St Peter's*, Archaeologica Traiectina series, Edita AB, Academiae Rheno-Traiectinae Instituto Archaeologico, VIII (Groningen: J. B. Wolters, 1966).

Josephus, 10 vols; i–viii and x, trans. H. St J. Thackeray; ix, trans. Louis H. Feldman (Cambridge, MA: Harvard University Press; London: Heinemann, 1931).

Karger, M., *Novgorod the Great*, trans. K. M. Cook (Moscow: Progress Publishers, 1973).

Keen, M. H., *England in the Later Middle Ages: A Political History* (London and New York: Routledge, 1973).

Kenyon, Kathleen M., *Jerusalem: Excavating 3000 Years of History* (London: Thames and Hudson, 1967).

Kidson, Peter, Murray, Peter, and Thompson, Paul, *A History of English Architecture* (London: Penguin, 1978).

Kinney, Dale, 'Spolia', in William Tronzo (ed.), *St Peter's in the Vatican* (Cambridge: Cambridge University Press, 2005), 16–47.

Kinney, Dale, 'The Discourse of Columns', in Claudia Bolga, Rosamond McKitterick, and John Osborne (eds), *Rome across Time and Space: Cultural Transmission and the Exchange of Ideas, c.500–1400* (Cambridge: Cambridge University Press, 2011), 182–99.

Kite, Stephen, and Menin, Sarah, 'Towards a New Cathedral: Mechanolatry and Metaphysics in the Milieu of Colin St John Wilson', *arq*, 9/1 (2005), 81–90.

Knight, Frances, *The Church in the Nineteenth Century* (London and New York: I. B. Taurus, 2008).

Knowles, David, *Bare Ruined Choirs: The Dissolution of the English Monasteries* (Cambridge: Cambridge University Press, 1976).

Koerner, Joseph Leo, *The Reformation of the Image* (London: Reaktion, 2004).

Kolb, Robert, 'Martin Luther and the German Nation', in R. Po-chia Hsia (ed.), *A Companion to the Reformation World* (Oxford: Blackwell, 2004), 39–55.

Kowal, David M., 'Innovation and Assimilation: The Jesuit Contribution to Architectural Development in Portuguese India', in John W. O'Malley, Gauvin Alexander Bailey, Steven J. Harris, and T. Frank Kennedy (eds), *The Jesuits: Cultures, Sciences and the Arts, 1540–1773* (Toronto: University of Toronto Press, 1999), 480–504.

Krautheimer, Richard, *Corpus Basilicarum Christianarum Romae: The Early Christian Basilicas of Rome (IV–IX Century)*, v. (Vatican City: Pontificio Instituto di Archeologia Cristiana, 1977).

Krautheimer, Richard, *Early Christian and Byzantine Architecture*, 4th edn (London: Penguin, 1986).

Lactantius, *De Mortibus Persecutorum*, 44.5, trans. J. L. Creed (Oxford: Oxford University Press, 1984).

Laird, Andrew, 'Nahuas and Caesars: Classical Learning and Bilingualism in Post-Conquest Mexico: An Inventory of Latin Writings by Authors of the Native Nobility', *Classical Philology*, 119/2 (April 2014), 150–69.

Landrus, Mallica Kumbera, 'Goa: The "Rome of the Orient"', in Michael Snodin and Nigel Llewellyn (eds), *Baroque, 1620–1899: Style in the Age of Magnificence* (London: V&A Publishing, 2009), 42–51.

Las Casas, Bartolomé de, 'The Only Method of Attracting All People to the True Faith' (1530s), in *Witness: Writings of Bartolomé de las Casas*, ed. and trans. George Sanderlin (Maryknoll, NY: Orbis, 1992), 137–42.

Lasko, Peter, *Ars Sacra, 800–1200*, 2nd edn (New Haven and London: Yale University Press, 1994).

Lavin, Irving, 'Bernini at St Peter's: Singularis in Singulis, in Omnibus Unicus', in William Tronzo (ed.), *St Peter's in the Vatican* (Cambridge: Cambridge University Press, 2005), 111–243.

Leadbetter, Bill, 'Constantine', in Philip Esler (ed.), *The Early Christian World* (London and New York: Routledge, 2000), ii. 1069–87.

Leclercq, Jean, 'Influence and Noninfluence of Dionysius in the Western Middle Ages', in *Pseudo-Dionysius: The Complete Works*, ed. Juroslav Pelikan et al., trans. Colm Luibheid (New York: Paulist Press, 1987), 25–32.

Leniaud, Jean-Michel, and Plagnieux, Philippe, *La Basilique Saint-Denis* (Paris: Editions du Patrimoine, 2012).

Lepie, Herta, and Minkenberg, Georg, trans. Hargarter, Manjula Dias, *The Cathedral Treasury of Aachen* (Regensberg: Schnell and Steiner, 2010).

Lethaby, W. R., and Swainson, Harold, *The Church of Sancta Sophia Constantinople: A Study of Byzantine Building* (London and New York: Macmillan, 1894).

Lewis, David Levering, *God's Crucible: Islam and the Making of Europe, 570–1215* (New York and London: Norton, 2008).

Liverani, Paolo, 'L'area vaticana e la necropoli prima della Basilica', in Maria Grazia Mattioni and Serenella Sancese (eds), Cristina Carlo-Stella (executive ed.), *Petros Eni; Pietro è Qui: Catalogo della Mostra, Città del Vaticano, Braccio di Carlo Magno, 11 ottobre 2006–8 marzo 2007* (Vatican: Fabbrica di San Pietro, 2006), 173–81.

Lloyd, Simon, 'The Crusading Movement, 1096–1274', in Jonathan Riley-Smith (ed.), *The Oxford History of the Crusades* (Oxford: Oxford University Press, 2002), 35–67.

Lockett, William, 'A Lesson from Anglican History', in William Lockett (ed.), *The Modern Architectural Setting of the Liturgy: Papers Read at a Conference held at Liverpool, September 1962* (London: SPCK, 1964).

Loffreda, Stanislao, *Recovering Capharnaum*, 2nd edn (Jerusalem: Franciscan Printing Press, 1993).

Luhn, Alec, 'Moscow's Tonic for the Troops is a New Army of Battlefield Priests', *Daily Telegraph*, Saturday, 29 December 2019, 18–19.

Luther, Martin, *Reformation Writings of Martin Luther: Translated with Introduction and Notes from the Definitive Weimar Edition*, trans. and ed. Bertram Lee Woolf, 2 vols (London: Lutterworth Press, 1952).

Luther, Martin, *Luther's Works*, trans. A. T. W. Steinhäuser, Frederick C. Ahrens, and Abdel Ross Wentz (Philadelphia: Fortress Press, 1960).

Luther, Martin, 'On the Power and Efficacy of Indulgences' (1517), in *The Works of Martin Luther*, i, trans. Adolph Spaeth, L. D. Reed, Henry Eyster Jacobs, et al. (Philadelphia: A. J. Holman Company, 1915), 29–38.

McCracken, G. E., and Cabaniss, A., *Early Mediaeval Theology*, Early Christian Classics, 9 (Philadelphia: Westminster Press, 1957).

MacCulloch, Diarmaid, *Reformation: Europe's House Divided, 1490–1700* (London: Penguin, 2003).

MacCulloch, Diarmaid, *A History of Christianity: The First Three Thousand Years* (London: Penguin, Allen Lane, 2009).

McGowan, Anne, and Bradshaw, Paul F., *The Pilgrimage of Egeria: A New Translation of the* Itinerarium Egeriae *with Introduction and Commentary* (Collegeville, MN: Liturgical Press Academic, 2018).

McKitterick, Rosamond, *The Frankish Church and the Carolingian Reforms, 789–895* (London: Royal Historical Society, 1977).

McKitterick, Rosamond, *Perceptions of the Past in the Early Middle Ages* (Notre Dame, IN: Notre Dame University Press, 2006).

McKitterick, Rosamond, *Charlemagne: The Formation of a European Identity* (Cambridge: Cambridge University Press, 2008).

McKnight, Scott, *Reading Romans Backwards* (London: SCM, 2017).

Mainstone, Rowland J., *Hagia Sophia: Architecture, Structure and Liturgy of Justinian's Great Church* (London: Thames and Hudson, 1997).

Mainz, Helmut, 'Dendrochronologische Datierung Holzringanker Oktogon-kuppel und Fundamentholz Oktogonpfeiler Nr. 7', in Helmut Mainz, Ute Mainz, and Christine Kaiser (eds), *Dombaumeistertagung 2009: Europäische Vereinigung der Dombaumeister, Munsterbaumeister und Hüttenmeister* (Dombauleitung, Aachen, 2009), 145–50.

Makki, Mahmoud, 'The Political History of al-Andalus (92/711–897/1492)', in Salma Khadra Jayyusi (ed.), *The Legacy of Muslim Spain* (New York: Brill, 1992), 3–87.

Malden, Henry, *An Account of King's College Chapel in Cambridge, Including a Character of Henry VI, and a Short History of the Foundation of his Two Colleges King's and Eton* (Cambridge: privately printed, 1769).

Mango, Cyril (ed.), *The Art of the Byzantine Empire, 312–1453: Sources and Documents* (Toronto: University of Toronto Press, 1986).

Mango, Cyril, 'A History of the Hippodrome of Constantinople', in Brigitte Pitarakis (ed.), *Hippodrome: A Stage for Istanbul's History* (Istanbul: Pera Museum Publication 39, 2010), i. 36–43.

Mango, Cyril, and Parker, John, 'A Twelfth-Century Description of St Sophia', in Cyril Mango, *Studies on Constantinople*, Variorum Series (Aldershot: Ashgate, 1993), ch. xvii; first published in *Dumbarton Oaks Papers*, xi (Washington: Dumbarton Oaks, 1960), 233–45.

Maquire, Robert, Murray, Keith, and Catt, John, 'The Editors', *churchbuilding*, 8 (January 1963), 3.

Mathews, Thomas, *The Early Churches of Constantinople: Architecture and Liturgy* (University Park, PA; London: University of Pennsylvania Press, 1971).

Mattioni, Maria Grazia, and Sancese, Serenella (eds), Carlo-Stella, Cristina (executive ed.), *Petros eni; Pietro è qui: Catologo della Mostra; Città del Vaticano, Braccio di Carlo Magno, 11 ottobre 2006–8 marzo 2007* (Vatican: Fabbrica di San Pietro, 2006).

Mayr-Harting, Henry, 'Charlemagne as a Patron of Art', in Diana Wood (ed.), *The Church and the Arts* (Oxford: Blackwell, 1992), 43–77.

Meyendorff, John, *Imperial Unity and Christian Divisions: The Church 450–680 AD* (Crestwood, NY: St Vladimir's Seminary Press, 1989).

Millingen, Alexander van, *Byzantine Constantinople: The Walls of the City and Adjoining Historical Sites* (1899; Cambridge: Cambridge University Press, 2010, online 2011).

Millon, Henry A., 'Michelangelo to Marchionni, 1546–1784', in William Tronzo (ed.), *St Peter's in the Vatican* (Cambridge: Cambridge University Press, 2005), 93–110.

Mitchell, Basil, 'A Phoenix Too Soon?', *churchbuilding*, 8 (January 1963), 25–6.

Moffitt, John F., 'Bernini's "Cathedra Petri" and the "Constitutum Constantini"', *Notes in the History of Art*, vol. 26, no 2 (Winter 2007), 23–31.

Montefiore, Simon Sebag, *Jerusalem: The Biography* (London: Weidenfeld and Nicolson, 2011).

Montesquiou-Fezensac, Blaise de, with Danielle Gaborit-Chopin, *Le Trésor de Saint-Denis*, vol. 1, *Inventaire de 1634*, vol. 2, *Documents divers*, vol. 3, *Planches et notices* (Paris: Éditions A et J Picard, 1973–77).

Morgan, Dewi, 'Man of the Moment: Basil Spence', *Anglican World*, Whitsun number (1962), 15–16 and 61.

Morris, Colin, *The Sepulchre of Christ and the Medieval West: From the Beginning to 1600* (Oxford: Oxford University Press, 2005).

Murphy-O'Connor, Jerome, *The Holy Land: An Oxford Archaeological Guide*, 5th edn (Oxford: Oxford University Press, 2008).

Murphy-O'Connor, Jerome, 'The Argument for the Holy Sepulchre', *Revue biblique* (January 2010), 55–91.

Nash, Elizabeth, 'Madrid Bombers "Were Inspired by Bin Laden Address"', *Independent*, 7 November 2006.

Nelson, Janet L., 'The Lord's Anointed and the People's Choice: Carolingian Royal Ritual', in David Cannadine and Simon Price (ed.), *Rituals of Royalty: Power and Ceremonial in Traditional Societies* (Cambridge: Cambridge University Press, 1987), 137–80.

Nicholson, Sir Charles, 'Building the Church: Styles and Requirements', in Ernest Short (ed.), *Post-War Church Building* (London: Hollis and Carter, 1947), 60–77.

Nineham, Denis, *Christianity, Medieval and Modern: A Study in Religious Change* (London: SCM Press, 1993).

Norris, Fred, 'Origen', in Philip Esler (ed.), *The Early Christian World* (London and New York: Routledge, 2000), 1005–26.

Obolensky, Dimitry, 'The Byzantine Sources on the Scandinavians in Eastern Europe', in *Varangian Problems. Scando-Slavica*, suppl. 1 (Athens: Athenai, 1980), repr. in Dimitry Obolensky, *The Byzantine Inheritance of Eastern Europe* (London: Variorum Reprints, 1982), vi. 149–64.

Obolensky, Dimitry, 'The Byzantine Impact on Eastern Europe' (Athens: Athenai, 1980), repr. in Dimitry Obolensky, *The Byzantine Inheritance of Eastern Europe* (London: Variorum Reprints, 1982), iii. 148–68; iv. 3–20; xv. 1–16.

Obolensky, Dimitry, 'Medieval Russian Culture in the Writings of D. S. Likhachev', in *Oxford Slavonic Papers*, 9 (1976), 1–16; repr. in Dimitry Obolensky, *The Byzantine Inheritance of Eastern Europe* (London: Variorum Reprints, 1982), ix. 1–16.

Olearchyk, Roman, 'Church Split Marks Victory for Ukraine', *Financial Times*, Monday, 7 January 2019, front page.

O'Malley, John W., Bailey, Gauvin Alexander, Harris, Steven J., and Kennedy, T. Frank (eds), *The Jesuits: Cultures, Sciences and the Arts, 1540–1773* (Toronto: University of Toronto Press, 1999).

Ousterhout, Robert, *Eastern Medieval Architecture: The Building Traditions of Byzantium and Neighboring Lands* (Oxford: Oxford University Press, 2019).

Palmer, Rodney, 'The Bizarre', in Michael Snodin and Nigel Llewellyn (eds), *Baroque, 1620–1899: Style in the Age of Magnificence* (London: V&A Publishing, 2009), 80–95.

Panofsky, Erwin (ed. and trans.), *Abbot Suger on the Abbey Church of St-Denis and its Art Treasures* (Princeton: Princeton University Press, 1946).

Parkes, M. B., 'The Provision of Books', in J. Catto and R. Evans (eds), *The History of the University of Oxford*, ii. *Late Medieval Oxford* (Oxford: Oxford University Press, 1992), 407–83.

The Paston Letters: A Selection in Modern Spelling, ed. Norman Davis (Oxford: Oxford University Press, 1983).

Paul Joyce Archive, Paul Mellon Centre, London.

Paul the Silentiary, *Desc. Ambones*, trans. in Cyril Mango (ed.), *The Art of the Byzantine Empire, 312–1453: Sources and Documents* (Toronto: University of Toronto Press, 1986).

Paul the Silentiary, *Desc. S. Sophiae*, trans. in Cyril Mango (ed.), *The Art of the Byzantine Empire, 312–1453: Sources and Documents* (Toronto: University of Toronto Press, 1986).

Peacock, D. P. S., 'Charlemagne's Black Stones: The Re-Use of Roman Columns in Early Medieval Europe', *Antiquity*, 71 (1997), 709–15.

Pevsner, Nikolaus, 'The Cambridge Camden Society and the Ecclesiologists', in Nikolaus Pevsner, *Some Architectural Writers of the Nineteenth Century* (Oxford: Oxford University Press, 1972), 123–38.

Pevsner, Nikolaus, *Some Architectural Writers of the Nineteenth Century* (Oxford: Oxford University Press, 1972).

Pfaff, Richard W., *The Liturgy in Medieval England: A History* (Cambridge: Cambridge University Press, 2009).

Pius XII, *Summi Pontificatus*, sect. 104.

Po-chia Hsia, R. (ed.), *A Companion to the Reformation World* (Oxford: Blackwell, 2004).

Po-chia Hsia, R., *A Jesuit in the Forbidden City: Matteo Ricci, 1552–1610* (Oxford: Oxford University Press, 2010).

Pohl, Walter, 'Invasions and Ethnic Identity', in Cristina La Rocca (ed.), *Italy in the Early Middle Ages 476–1000* (Oxford: Oxford University Press, 2002), 11–33.

Pozzo, Andrea, *Perspectiva pictorum et architectorum*, 2 vols (1693, 1698; English edn, London: printed for J. Senex, R. Gosling, W. Innys, J. Osborn and T. Longman, 1707).

Preston, Arthur, *Christ's Hospital, Abingdon: The Almshouses, the Hall and the Portraits* (Oxford: Oxford University Press, 1929).

Prestwich, Michael, *Plantagenet England, 1225–1360* (Oxford: Oxford University Press, 2005).

Pringle, Denys, *The Churches of the Crusader Kingdom of Jerusalem: A Corpus*, iii. *The City of Jerusalem* (Cambridge: Cambridge University Press, 2007).

Procopius, *Buildings*, trans. H. B. Dewing, Loeb Classical Library, vol 7 (London: Heinemann; Cambridge, MA.: Harvard University Press, 1961).

Procopius, *History of the Wars*, trans. H. B. Dewing, Loeb Classical Library, 6 vols (London: Heinemann; Cambridge, MA.: Harvard University Press, 1961).

Pseudo-Dionysius, *Pseudo-Dionysius: The Complete Works*, ed. Juroslav Pelikan et al., trans. Colm Luibheid (New York: Paulist Press, 1987).

Reicherter, K., Schaub, A., Fernàndez-Steeger, T. M., Kohlberger-Schaub, T., and Grützner, C., 'Historische Erdbebenschäden im Dom zu Aachen: Aquisgrani terrae motus factus est', in Helmut Mainz, Ute Mainz, and Christine Kaiser (eds), *Dombaumeistertagung 2009: Europäische Vereinigung der Dombaumeister, Munsterbaumeister und Hüttenmeister* (Dombauleitung, Aachen, 2009), 159–76.

Richards, J. M., 'Royal Festival Hall: Criticism', *Architectural Review* (June 1951), 357.

Richardson, Peter, and Richardson, Douglas, *Canadian Churches: An Architectural History* (Richmond Hill, Ontario: Firefly Books, 2007).

Riley, Joe, *Today's Cathedral: The Cathedral Church of Christ, Liverpool* (London: SPCK, 1978).

Riley-Smith, Jonathan, *The First Crusaders, 1095–1131* (Cambridge: Cambridge University Press, 1997).

Riley-Smith, Jonathan, 'The State of Mind of Crusaders to the East, 1095–1300', in Jonathan Riley-Smith (ed.), *The Oxford History of the Crusades* (Oxford: Oxford University Press, 2002), 68–89.

Riley-Smith, Jonathan (ed.), *The Oxford History of the Crusades* (Oxford: Oxford University Press, 2002).

Roffey, Simon, *The Medieval Chantry Chapel: An Archaeology* (Woodbridge: Boydell Press, 2007).

Romero, Anne-Marie, *Saint-Denis: Emerging Powers*, trans. Azizeh Azodi (Paris: Caisse Nationale des Monuments).

Ross, Andrew C., 'Alessandro Valignano: The Jesuits and Culture in the East', in John W. O'Malley, Gauvin Alexander Bailey, Steven J. Harris, and T. Frank Kennedy (eds), *The Jesuits: Cultures, Sciences and the Arts, 1540–1773* (Toronto: University of Toronto Press, 1999), 336–51.

Roueché, Charlotte, 'The Factions and Entertainment', in Brigitte Pitarakis (ed.), *Hippodrome: A Stage for Istanbul's History* (Istanbul: Pera Museum Publication 39, 2010), i. 50–64.

Royal Commission on Historical Monuments England, *An Inventory of the Historical Monuments in the City of Oxford* (London: Her Majesty's Stationery Office, 1939).

Ruiz, Pedro Marfil, 'Córdoba de Teodosio a Abd Al-Rahmán III', in *Visigodos y Omeyas: Un debate entre la Antigüedad tardía y la alta Edad Media* (Mérida, abril de 1999), ed. L. Caballero Zoreda and P. Mateos Cruz (Madrid:

Consejo Superior de Investigaciones Científicas, Instituto de Historia & Consorcio de la Ciudad Monumental de Mérida, 2000), 117–41.

The Russian Primary Chronicle, trans. and ed. S. H. Cross and O. P. Sherbowitz-Wetzor (Cambridge, MA: Mediaeval Academy of America, 1953).

St Augustine, *The City of God against the Pagans*, trans. George McCracken (London: Heineman, 1957; Cambridge, MA: Harvard University Press, 1957).

St Bernard of Clairvaux, 'Apologia to William, Abbot of St-Thierry', trans. in Elizabeth Gilmore Holt, *A Documentary History of Art: The Middle Ages and the Renaissance* (Princeton: Princeton University Press, 1947).

Saltmarsh, John, *King's College: A Short History* (Cambridge: privately printed, 1958).

Scarisbrick, J. J., *Henry VIII*, 2nd edn (New Haven and London: Yale University Press, 1997).

Schaff, Philip, *The Creeds of Christendom* (Grand Rapids, MI: Baker Book House, 1877).

Schilling, Johannes, 'Die Reformation in Lübeck', in Jan Friedrich Richter (ed.), *Lübeck 1500: Kunstmetropole im Ostseeraum* (Petersberg: Michael Imhof, 2015), 45–53.

Schopenhauer, Arthur, *The World as Will and Representation*, trans. E. F. J. Payne, 2 vols (New York: Dover, 1966).

Schütte, Sven, 'Forschungen zum Aachener Thron', in Helmut Mainz, Ute Mainz, and Christine Kaiser (eds), *Dombaumeistertagung 2009: Europäische Vereinigung der Dombaumeister, Munsterbaumeister und Hüttenmeister* (Dombauleitung, Aachen, 2009), 177–90.

Shaw, Brent D., 'The Myth of the Neronian Persecution', *The Journal of Roman Studies*, 105 (2015), 73–100.

Shepard, Jonathan, review of Constantine Porphyrogenitus, *The Book of Ceremonies and Pseudo-Kodinos and the Constantinopolitan Court: Offices and Ceremonies*, in *English Historical Review*, 130/545 (August 2015), 949–52.

Shepard, Jonathan, 'Rus'', in Nora Berend (ed.), *Christianization and the Rise of Christian Monarchy: Scandinavia, Central Europe and Rus'*, c.900–1200 (Cambridge: Cambridge University Press, 2007), 369–416.

Sherwood, Jennifer, and Pevsner, Nikolaus, *The Buildings of England: Oxfordshire* (London: Penguin, 1974).

Short, Ernest, 'Foreword', in Ernest Short (ed.), *Post-War Church Building* (London: Hollis and Carter, 1947), p. xiv.

Short, Ernest (ed.), *Post-War Church Building* (London: Hollis and Carter, 1947).

Sills, Ben, 'Cathedral May See Return of Muslims', *Guardian*, 19 April 2004.

Simson, Otto von, *The Gothic Cathedral: Origins of Gothic Architecture and the Medieval Concept of Order*, 3rd edn (Princeton: Princeton University Press, 1988).

Smith, Dennis E., *From Symposium to Eucharist: The Banquet in the Early Christian World* (Minneapolis: Fortress Press, 2003).

Smith, Julia M. H., *Europe after Rome: A New Cultural History 500–1000* (Oxford: Oxford University Press, 2005).

Smithson, Alison, and Smithson, Peter, 'Architects' Report', *churchbuilding*, 8 (January 1963), 5–12.

Snodin, Michael, and Llewellyn, Nigel (eds), *Baroque, 1620–1899: Style in the Age of Magnificence* (London: V&A Publishing, 2009).

Spence, Basil, 'Contemporary Expressions of Cathedral Traditions', in John Knox Shear (ed.), *Religious Buildings for Today: An Architectural Record Book* (New York: F. W. Dodge Corp., 1957), 126–33.

Spence, Basil, *Phoenix at Coventry* (London: Geoffrey Bles, 1962).

Stalley, Roger, *Early Medieval Architecture* (Oxford: Oxford University Press, 1999).

Stamp, Gavin, 'Giles Gilbert Scott: The Problem of Modernism', *Architectural Design*, 49/10–11 (1979), 72–83.

Stern, Henri, *Les Mosaïques de la Grande Mosquée de Cordoué* (Berlin: Walter Gruyter, 1976).

Stierlin, Henri, *Islam: Early Architecture from Bagdad to Cordoba* (Cologne: Taschen, 2002).

Storey, R. L., 'University and Government', in J. Catto and R. Evans (eds), *The History of the University of Oxford*, ii. *Late Medieval Oxford* (Oxford: Oxford University Press, 1992), 709–46.

Strange, James F., and Shanks, Hershel, 'Has the House where Jesus Stayed in Capernaum Been Found?', *Biblical Archaeology Review*, 8/6 (November–December 1982), 26–37.

Strube, C., review of Thomas Mathews, *The Early Churches of Constantinople: Architecture and Liturgy* (University Park, PA; London: University of Pennsylvania Press, 1971), in *Byzantinische Zeitschrift*, 67 (1974), 412.

Suhrawardy, Shahid, *The Art of the Mussulmans in Spain* (Oxford: Oxford University Press, 2005).

Swigchem, C. A. van, Brouwer, T., and Os, W. van, *Een Huis voor het Woord: Het protestantse kerkinterieur in Nederland tot 1900* (The Hague: Staatsuitgeverij, 1984).

Symondson, Anthony, 'Theology and Worship in the late Victorian Church', in Chris Brooks and Andrew Saint (eds), *The Victorian Church:*

Architecture and Society (Manchester: Manchester University Press, 1995), 192–222.

Tertullian, *Apology*, trans. S. Thelwall, in Alexander Roberts and James Donaldson (eds), *The Ante-Nicene Fathers: Translations of the Writings of the Fathers down to AD 325* (1884), rev. A. Cleveland Cox (Grand Rapids, MI: Eerdmans, 1973).

Thoenes, Christof, 'Renaissance St Peter's', in William Tronzo (ed.), *St Peter's in the Vatican* (Cambridge: Cambridge University Press, 2005), 64–92.

Thomas, John, *Coventry Cathedral* (London and Sydney: Harper Collins, 1987), 93–4.

Thomas, Norman (ed.), *Readings in World Mission* (London: SPCK, 1995).

Thomson, John A. F., *The Transformation of Medieval England, 1370–1529* (London and New York: Longman, 1983).

Tremlett, Giles, 'Vatican Rebuff to Spanish Muslims', *Guardian*, 3 May 2004.

Tremlett, Giles, 'Two Arrested after Fight in Former Mosque', *Guardian*, 1 April 2010.

Tronzo, William (ed.), *St Peter's in the Vatican* (Cambridge: Cambridge University Press, 2005).

Tyack, Geoffrey, 'The Crimean Church, Istanbul: A Monument to Victorian Gothic', *Cornucopia*, 5/25 (2002), 78–93.

Üçerler, M. Antoni J., 'The Jesuit Enterprise in Sixteenth- and Seventeenth-Century Japan', in Thomas Worcester (ed.), *The Cambridge Companion to the Jesuits* (Cambridge: Cambridge University Press, 2008), 153–68.

Ullmann, Walter, 'Ecclesiology and Carolingian Rulership', in Ullmann, *Carolingian Renaissance and the Idea of Kingship*, the Birkbeck Lectures, 1968–9 (London: Methuen, 1969).

Vatican Council II: The Conciliar and Post Conciliar Documents, gen. ed. Austin Flannery, *The Constitution on the Sacred Liturgy*, Ii.14 (Leominster: Fowler Wright Books, 1975).

Vermes, Géza, *The Resurrection: History and Myth* (London: Doubleday Books, 2008).

Victoria County History: A History of Oxfordshire, vol. III, ed. H. E. Salter and Mary D. Lobel (Oxford: Oxford University Press, 1954).

Vieillard-Troiekouroff, May, *Les Monuments religieux de la Gaule d'après les oeuvres de Grégoire de Tours* (Paris: Honoré Champion, 1976).

Vlasto, A. P., *The Entry of the Slavs into Christendom: An Introduction to the Medieval History of the Slavs* (Cambridge: Cambridge University Press, 1970).

Voronin, Nikolai, and Maslenitsyn, Stanislav, *Vladimir: Architectural Landmarks* (Leningrad: Aurora, 1988).

Ward–Perkins, Bryan, *The Fall of Rome and the End of Civilization* (Oxford: Oxford University Press, 2005).

Walker, Rose, *Art in Spain and Portugal from the Romans to the Early Middle Ages: Routes and Myths* (Amsterdam: Amsterdam University Press, 2016).

White, James F. (ed.), *Documents of Christian Worship: Descriptive and Interpretive Sources* (London: T&T Clark, 1992).

Whyte, William, *Unlocking the Church: The Lost Secrets of Victorian Sacred Space* (Oxford: Oxford University Press, 2017).

Wickham, Chris, *The Inheritance of Rome: A History of Europe from 400 to 1000* (London: Penguin, 2010).

William of Malmesbury, *Gesta Regum Anglorum*, trans. R. A. B. Mynors, ed. R. M. Thomson and M. Winterbottom, 2 vols (Oxford: Oxford University Press, 1998–9).

Williams, H. C. N., *20th Century Cathedral: An Examination of the Role of Cathedrals in the Strategy of the Church in the Changing Pattern of a Twentieth Century Community* (Guildford and London: Hodder and Stoughton, 1964).

Wilson, C. St J., 'Architecture: Public Good and Private Necessity', *RIBA Journal*, 86/3 (March 1979), 107–15.

Wood, A., *The History and Antiquities of the University of Oxford*, i. *1792–6*, ed. J. Gutch (Oxford: printed for the editor, 1792–6).

Worcester, Thomas (ed.), *The Cambridge Companion to the Jesuits* (Cambridge: Cambridge University Press, 2008).

Yarnold, Edward, *Cyril of Jerusalem* (London and New York: Routledge, 2000).

Yarwood, Doreen, *The Architecture of Britain* (London: Batsford, 1976).

Yates, Nigel, 'The Liturgical Impact of the Oxford Movement', in Nigel Yates, *Buildings, Faith and Worship: The Liturgical Arrangement of Anglican Churches 1600–1900* (Oxford: Oxford University Press, 1991), 127–49.

Zwierlein, Otto, *Petrus in Rom: Die literarischen Zeugnisse*, 2nd edn (Berlin and New York: De Gruyter, 2016).

Figure and Plate Acknowledgements

Figures

Plates

Index